VOLUME II

Writer's
BANE
Write, Revise, Publish, & Repeat

Formatting 101

VOLUME II

Writer's BANE

Write, Revise, Publish, & Repeat

Formatting 101

VALERIE WILLIS

4 Horsemen
Publications, Inc.

4 Horsemen
Publications, Inc.

4 Horsemen Publications, Inc.
1497 Main St. Suite 169
Dunedin, FL 34698
4horsemenpublications.com
info@4horsemenpublications.com

Cover & Typesetting by Valerie Willis
Editor Shelley Sands

Library of Congress Control Number: 2021941355

Hardcover ISBN-13: 978-1-64450-623-3
Paperback ISBN-13: 978-1-64450-168-9
eBook ISBN-13: 978-1-64450-548-9

DISCLAIMER

This book is for a wide range of writers and authors. There will be information from all levels of writing within to help everyone from aspiring to veteran authors. You will find insight on a variety of aspects that may provide support where needed. Other chapters may not be relevant to the choices you make, such as choosing a publishing path which will split between the many paths, so the writer can see the differences, evaluate the expectations, and make an informed decision. Unfortunately, the world of writers and publishing, especially self-publishing or independent publishing, changes every three to six months. At the release of this book, I aimed to be as relevant as possible to the current trends, statistics, and information available during the production of this all-inclusive guide on writing, editing, revising, formatting, publishing, and more.

In short, it is important you realize not all the content may be agreeable, set in stone, or the preferred standard. This is a based on the viewpoint from me, a fellow author, writer, and creative, who aims to do what she can to provide a variety of examples from all genres, but you should know my forte is in fantasy, paranormal, romance, and mythology remakes. Regardless, there should be enough information and content to meet a writer's needs, and you are encouraged to use this as a toolbox. Pick out the tools that best fit you and your journey and use them to write, polish, and publish your book.

Much of the examples inside are using Adobe InDesign as the main software but much of the information, guidelines, measurements, and similar are concrete no matter what software you are making your book from that rarely changes outside of trends and genre demands. In the latter half of the book, there may be duplicated sections tweaked to align with the associated book type. The reason for this is to make it convenient and limit the amount of time needed to flip back to other sections when actively designing a type of book.

WHAT IS THE WRITER'S BANE?

bane /bān/ *noun*

a cause of great distress or annoyance.
"The bane of the decorator is the long, narrow hall."

Similar: scourge, ruin, death, plague, ruination, destruction, torment, torture, menace, suffering, pain, distress, hardship, cross to bear, burden, thorn in one's flesh/side, bitter pill, affliction, calamity, despair, trouble, misery, woe, tribulation, misfortune, nuisance, pest, headache, trial, blight, curse, nightmare

ARCHAIC: *something, typically poison, that causes death.*

Definition from Oxford Languages

A bane or curse: to have a story, a desire to share it, and the task of polishing it for public consumption, facing the highs and lows of agents and publishers, traversing editors and feedback, and creating a book as the end result. It's a curse—a wonderful one—that haunts every waking and slumbering minute of a writer's life. A desire to see a story from start to finish is needed to quell it, even if it's for a mere breath of one's time on this earth.

The Writer's Bane will test your resolve, time and time again.

Search Google and you find the definition of *bane*:

―――――――――――――

*A cause of great distress
or annoyance*

―――――――――――――

Well, the Writer's Bane is exactly that. We often find ourselves in distress or annoyed with some part of the process. Whether we are fighting writer's block to trying to figure out how to Track Changes in Word, we all have our lists of issues during our start to finish process on a book. It doesn't matter if you are publishing your first novel or the thirty-millionth novel, each book or story tends to create its own batch of issues. Just look at this sentence:

―――――――――――――

*"The bane of the [writer] is
the long, narrow hall."*

―――――――――――――

This is true on so many levels. You will find yourself in narrow halls where restrictions will force you to move in one or a limited choice of direction. Whether it is writing within the expectations of a genre, romance versus horror, or following the industry standards in writing, editing, and publishing, this cursed hallway gets longer and narrower. In fact, it can be a creative killer if you're not prepared. Be sure to arm yourself properly.

The Writer's Bane is a toolbox. *Your toolbox.* A suitcase to hold onto as you traverse one hall and turn down the next one of your choosing. Down these halls, you find the doors labelled with warnings, *bane's* many synonyms:

Scourge. Ruin. Death.
Plague. Ruination.
Destruction.

You will counter each of these on some level. Worst, you may feel these about your work, the process, or yourself. We call this *imposter syndrome* when we doubt the idea that we can be the writer and author we already have become. Just remember and know that only you can tell and write your story. There will be a good amount of blood, sweat, and tears shed in each hall you travel down. Some of these parts will *plague* you, others will feel like a slow *death*, and other times you will feel as if you've brought the whole project to *ruin*.

It's okay. We live through this.

Remember you're cursed but still fighting and have a lucky charm (this book). Use the tools to destroy the *scourge* with your confidence and resilience. The only person who can make this story idea turn itself into a book is YOU. No one else. It's an age-old fact and has been this way since the days of Charles Dickens selling the *Christmas Carol.* He resisted! How? By performing live readings because he had to "self-publish" after being turned down by publishers. Only the writer can overcome and cure the curse, no matter what form it takes.

This book is designed to be a lucky charm to combat your curse, this curse, and more importantly, *our* curse as writers. This covers front to back, start to finish, the process, thoughts, knowledge, and experiences collected by author Valerie Willis. A lot of it isn't just for the publishing industry or writers but branches into the realm of game development and graphic design. It may not have a cure for every part of your curse, but it aims to provide some relief and keep you moving forward.

ARCHAIC: something,
typically poison, that
causes death.

The Writer's Bane is poison. Our curse is something to build immunity to, much like a real poison. Royalty in the past such as young princes and princesses often died trying to build immunity to poisons. As a warning, your bane may kill your desire to be a writer or author. You will need to develop a thick skin, be stubborn and fight hard, and every time you fall, wipe the mud from your face and hop back on that bucking bull or bronco. There will be bumps, bruises, scrapes, and even times where you feel beyond broken. I can promise that you aren't the first to feel this way or walk these halls.

This is the Writer's Bane.

You must know this going in: find a support group of fellow writers. We all have this curse, this desire to create and tell a story, to see it made into something tangible and let it fly out into the open skies like so many creations before it. Fellow writers will be able to give you a hand through those tighter hallways where the walls squeeze you until you no longer can move. Combined with this tome of advice, other writers can pull you through, taking down some walls, unlocking some doors, and widening some halls that seemed impassable.

"Welcome to the writing tribe."

WORDS OF ENCOURAGEMENT

Moral of the story, if you read who I am, is NEVER GIVE UP. No matter how ugly life gets for you, your health, your family, and your world – IT'S UP TO YOU TO NEVER GIVE UP! Life can be unpleasant more times than not, but there are a few lessons I have learned firsthand. My favorite echo is from my great grandmother:

Life never takes you where you want to go. It only takes you where you need to go.

Wants and needs are always fighting for the spotlight in our lives. When she told me this, and repeated it often, I didn't understand the weight of her words. She was a preacher for an old church at the end of the old orange clay road in the middle of orange groves. Full of light and hope, she was a blessing in my life, and I am thankful for the time I was able to spend with her.

She was right.

My life has given me some unexpected terrifying moments. Once the dust settled, I was calm enough to reflect on the events; I realized there was hidden need for those moments to push me down a path more fitting to bring happier times. I didn't plan to be an author, but when I became a cancer survivor, a new mom, holding a foreclosure notice to my dream home and on the verge of a layoff, it forced me to take my writing career seriously. This was a life changer—the soul food I didn't know I needed. Moving forward, I developed my own mantra:

Don't be my own obstacle.

It was a promise to me. Life throws some curveballs, things we can't control, and all we can do at times is simply wait out the storm and pick up the pieces afterwards. That's okay. It happens. What you can do is make a promise to yourself. Remember not to self-sabotage or let yourself mourn or stay stagnant for too long. If you want something, and the only thing stopping you is hesitation, then act. Break your own mold, find a way to break free of self-doubt in small ways, and eventually, you'll find the only obstacles left are the ones you can't control.

THIRTEEN YEARS OF TRIBULATIONS

Life is unpredictable. Despite some wild high and low moments, I'm still writing, publishing, and sharing what I learn every chance I have. You may or may not know me. No, I'm not a best-selling author (yet). Yes, I'm an award-winning author when I enter into the contests that exist out there, but the question really is: what qualifies me of all the authors in the sea, worthy of writing a book such as this? If I had the money and a calmer chain of events in my life, I would be a best-selling writer. Let's be ambitious and honest. There's nothing more inspiring than seeing the light in another writer's eyes as you help them overcome writer's block or provide some tools they didn't realize they had in their arsenal.

Whether you want to call it "paying it forward" or "giving back to the writing community," it comes down to one fact: I love to share what I discover about writing and publishing. I'm also not one to rush into anything without research or, at best, experimenting to see things firsthand. There's a ton of advice out there, and sometimes I can't help but wonder if what echoes down that narrow hallway is truly beneficial for the all or for the one. This book is one way I get to share what I've learned, experienced, and even shared from all manner of people in the publishing and writing industries.

Ah, but who am I? What do I write? Where did I come from?

I'm a sixth-generation Floridian (on the same road!) who, through a series of unfortunate events, discovered her calling to write and create books. It wasn't obvious or a straight and narrow answer. In fact, the amount of tribulation I have faced in my life, and even now as I begin *The Writer's Bane,* makes me painfully aware that I have a fortitude like no other. Or simply put, I'm too stubborn to quit.

My heart is a lush for mixed genres that carry a lot of the values from genres like paranormal romance, dark fantasy, dark romance, epic fantasy, mythology, historical fiction, and even memoir. Like many of my fellow writers, I did a lot of writing and doodling in my younger years. The most profound was a filled composition book in fifth grade. Though my mother didn't approve and pushed for me to be a doctor or a lawyer, I never stopped. Not everyone has the endurance to watch their journals and creations tossed in a trashcan while they are ordered to stop writing—and still keep going. If only I knew being an historian was a legitimate occupation, the world might have missed out on this bookworm completely.

One of my favorite genres to read growing up was fantasy, more specifically, fantasy that is dark in tone and filled with paranormal and mythology elements. Add in a sprinkle of historical references and I am SOLD. It has always amazed me how authors create such wonderful worlds and stories with such depth. I'm glad to share my own worlds and characters with readers in hopes of inspiring future writers. At times, I feel like I'm giving back what those authors gave to me: an adventure and escape when life seemed dreadful, a lesson I didn't know I needed told through a life not my own.

My early reads circled between three authors: C.S. Lewis, R.L. Stine, and Lewis Carroll. Later, this evolved to include Robin McKinley, Cat Adams, James Clavell, Anne Rice, and Neil Gaiman. Before I stumbled on these wonderful authors, I had only read non-fiction books about drawing or animals (outside of the mandatory readings assigned by my elementary school teachers). Needless to say, I read every Zoo Book the library had, sometimes twice. From there, like many of my generation, I dove into R.L. Stine's famous Goosebumps series, but I have never enjoyed horror books beyond this scope. That doesn't mean I didn't read the genre, trying out Stephen King, Michael Crichton, and others. I even found there was a specific type of horror that leaned into the dark fantasy realm. And yet, I still continued the search for *my* genre.

It didn't take long to find C. S. Lewis and Lewis Carroll who showed me fantastical worlds that were just beyond the wardrobe or rabbit hole. These were wonderful, delightful reads, but something was still missing. Soon, I discovered another genre through James Clavell, historical fiction, where I realized that amazing fictional stories could stay true to the events and settings around them. This discovery spiraled into a search for something that blended the two genres. It was like a scavenger hunt, and I aimed to satisfy all my wants in a good book.

Discovering Elizabeth Kostova's *The Historian* opened up the door and added something new. The enjoyment I received from reading a paranormal story heavily involving the history of Vlad the Impaler was off the scales. This idea, this dark flavor that smeared the lines of fantasy, horror, and history was the flavor I had been searching for and aspired to write. It was okay to show the dark workings of characters. They didn't have to be perfect. It was the flaws in Edmund and the characters in the previous books that made them feel so real, even when devoured by dinosaurs or described as talking beavers.

Through my interactions with these wonderful authors and their stories, I started to decide what I wanted my own readers to experience. This concept seemed to help build a foundation for my storytelling early on, looking to my own favorite books for insight on what experience did I take from that and how I could mimic that in my own way within my own stories. Some of the key elements were flawed characters, writing to cater all audiences, showing love is more

than the act or the kiss, and the raw moments people exchange when no one is watching. I wanted all these in my stories!

Tattooed Angels Trilogy has been a labor of love project. It's responsible for my drive to become an author and the desire to share my work with others. There are profound moments in a writer's life, and this trilogy had a large part in my own. Throughout elementary and middle school, I was a tenacious reader with a love for fantasy books. I wrote my first novel in fifth grade. I still have the composition book I filled front to back, covered in assorted stickers from the 1990's (with the map I drew glued into the back cover).

One fateful night during my high school days, Tattooed Angels was born. I recall the clock pushing past midnight as I tried to lull myself to sleep listening to some rock music. The DJ came on, talking about this new release from a band called TOOL. In the black abyss of night, I took in the heartbeat intro of the song *Laterlus*. The first few lyrics played out, the idea of black and white, then colors started a chain reaction in my imagination. It was here, lost to the music, I started asking myself a series of questions.

*What kind of character
would be like that?
Someone who normally
sees in black and white,
but on occasion might
see something in color...
Oh! What if he was color
blind, but it was actually
secret powers he gained
from reincarnation?
Wait... I got it. What if he's
a failed reincarnation?
Hmm, what kind of
powers would...*

It went on and on and before I knew it, I was jotting the brainstorm down, doodling some sketches, and the morning alarm was blasting. It all started with the creation of Hotan, then asking what kind of character he was, what his story was, and what I wanted him to share with readers.

Thirteen Years of Tribulations

During high school, I faced a lot of complicated situations. My parents were getting divorced, my father was lost to alcoholism (He's now sober, and we've made amends), my mother's verbal abuse started becoming physical (we don't talk and attempts for counseling have failed), and I felt broken. While my friends fretted over boyfriends, parties, and popularity, I felt all alone in my own goals. I needed a job, I kept good grades, and I aimed for independence as soon as possible.

I needed a dependable place to call home or at least a place where I could feel safe.

In a lot of ways, Hotan reflected me. An adult in a teen's body, I earned the name "mother hen" because I took care of my friends, keeping them out of trouble or helping them with their schoolwork. Because everything at home was so unstable behind closed doors, I focused on being my own pillar and a cornerstone for my friends. I didn't discuss what was happening, though many of my teachers had an inkling. It was probably hard to miss the quiet kid coming early to school and crying in a dark corner.

Anyhow, Hotan was my vehicle to deliver a message to my friends and other teens while letting others learn from my mistakes. The name Hotan was originally inspired by a Japanese language website claiming it meant "origin, starting point," but that isn't accurate at all. In fact, it's more fitting to acknowledge Hotan is Biblical Greek for "when, inasmuch," which is ironic and fits even more.

Aiming to deliver a message, I started a cautionary tale, one which encouraged asking for help, especially for the hard stuff, and refusing to hide. My story showed how to speak up, accepted the idea that life is unpredictable, and reassured readers that even though it may feel as if the world is against them, the fight is normal. Life is a struggle—and that's okay.

By the time high school ended, I had twenty-five thousand hard-earned words. Many times, I lost my creation and had to start over. One time, the computer died; another time, the floppy disk was destroyed. Still worse was the time my mother trashed my work, ripping it up, and even setting a sketchbook on fire. I didn't give up. I started hiding parts of the story in the back of my math and animal science notebooks. I even printed the current copy out, put it in a binder, and asked a friend to keep it at her house. This was one thing no one could take from me: my desire to tell a story.

Life became a wild rollercoaster after I graduated. I was working several jobs and launched into college full time. The story collected dust in a box I carried, but I was hellbent on never going back home. I even lived out of my truck for a while. Years passed, and the story was forgotten until I ran into some friends I hadn't seen since high school.

"Did you ever finish that story about Hotan?"

The question rattled me. I had forgotten about the story, but somehow, it had made an impression on them. They wanted to know if it was done, if there was an end to Hotan's tale. So, I blew off the dust, figured out where I left off, and finished the story. With no fear of someone destroying it, I finished the story in a little over fifty-thousand words.

I gave it to a few friends to read and enjoy, but life hit me again, and the story found itself shelved. At least I had managed to pull together how book two and three would flow. Ah, but a book can't write itself! I went to school for Graphic Design (I was part of the ITT debacle and was one class shy of my degree), then Game Programming, but health issues interfered, and I resigned.

Things settled for a little while, but I found myself in the most insane six months of my life. The economy

popped. Our new house of barely two years, bought with equity, was now far below. The construction industry left me and my husband laid off. On top of that, I fell horribly ill, unable to keep water or food down, so the mother-in-law took me to the hospital.

"Good news! You're about a month along in your pregnancy!"

I paled. We had been trying for three years, but we had only lost our jobs two weeks before. Of course, this would stick at the worst moment ever. Within the same month, a freckle on the back of my left calf became a monstrous mole. I cried and pleaded with the doctors to biopsy. My great grandmother had one in the same spot. I knew what it meant by the look and the speed with which it grew. It took another month before a doctor heard me out.

"I'm so sorry. You were right. This is an atypical melanoma, and we need to remove it immediately."

Here I was staring at the results while pushing into four months pregnant with my first child. I couldn't believe how hard my life fell apart: twenty-four hour "morning" sickness, both of us laid off through 2009-2010 winter, mortgage company speeding up our foreclosure because we let them know "no job and stage three cancer diagnosis." I cried. Then I cried some more. Doctors called and told me where to be, sometimes the night before for a morning appointment. So many tears were shed. It all seemed unfair. This was too much—just one of these events would be enough to break a person.

In the end, they removed the back of my left calf while I was awake, a scary experience since I'd never even had a stitch or broken a bone before. I managed to shut down the foreclosure, very aware of the medical clause in my contract, sending them the football stitching down my leg and the intimate reports from the surgery with "stage 3" and "pregnant" highlighted. It was hell recovering, puking, and moving.

I sat there as our new hovel rattled. The house we thought we would never leave sold in a quick sale. Recovering with a newborn, I was alone while my husband landed a job working long hours for half the pay. Looking around, I saw my books, the boxes I could never let go—that had lived in a truck with me—these were part of my soul.

"Maybe I should do something with that novel from high school... leave something behind for our kid."

That one thought drove me to learn how to write at a professional level and publish my work. I had a memorable story, but I needed to know what it would take to make it an actual book. The answer left me crying once more: to fix it, to bring it to industry standard, required one more rewrite. A flood of sour memories followed, but this was the best decision ever.

"It's part of life to struggle. Just makes those good days that much sweeter..."

And thus, my career as an author and the start of Tattooed Angels Trilogy was born!

With these tools and inspiration, my desire for writing was renewed. I still needed helping hands from family and friends to make sure I didn't give up on my writing goals, but I finally made it. My next story, *Cedric: The Demonic Knight,* took its background from both history books and long forgotten lore and bestiaries. It took some heavy searching to dig out information on all things werewolf, vampire, and more importantly, mythology. My single wish was to expose my readers to intriguing concepts, opening the door to a time period and lore that has been skewed from the original telling. I want my readers to experience the lore firsthand, and when the conversation came up in class or at the café among friends, they had the facts etched into their hearts. I wanted to hear them say, "I know it because I lived it through Cedric/Romasanta/Lillith," and smile.

Currently, I have completed my young adult dark urban fantasy trilogy, Tattooed Angels. The first book in this series is *Rebirth*, a story I put to paper back in high school (circa 2001-2003). When I started writing this piece, I wanted it to be able to go into my high school's library and share some hard lessons about

Thirteen Years of Tribulations

selfhood and those harder moments in our lives. I made it to Chapter Six before life swept me away from it. It collected dust until it somehow came up in a conversation at work in 2005. At that time, a friend named Kelly inspired and encouraged me to continue writing. The next year, I added to it, pushing to Chapter 12 before I let life wipe it from my thoughts again.

In 2010, I found myself part of an online gaming group called *The Shadow Legion*. Somehow someone (Ruth and Ruth, along with Susannah) reminded me I had *Rebirth* waiting on me to complete. Thanks to the encouragements of my Gaming Crew, I finished my first rough draft of a complete novel. Looking back, I had no idea how significant it was for any writer to finish the story. Unfortunately, that wasn't the end of my frustration. I realized as I researched more about the professional writing field that *Rebirth* needed a mountain of work—a rewrite of my high school portions. I can't tell you how many times I sat in front of my computer staring at a screen of text, no idea how to even begin a rewrite or how to break myself away from the original writing to make a better version.

At this point, I entertained the idea of sketching out a graphic novel. There were obstacles to that piece as well. I found myself throwing out storyboard after storyboard on how to capture everything I wanted to tell the audience in this epic idea. Looking at both of these stories, *Rebirth* and *Cedric*, I had to make some hard decisions.

Rebirth deserved quality writing and attention...

...but I wasn't skilled enough, not yet. *Cedric*, on the other hand, still wasn't giving enough for the reader to see. I knew I would come to points that needed large paragraphs to explain. It hit me: take what I now knew about writing and write *Cedric* instead.

At this point, *Cedric* had three years of random research, sketches, and roughed out storyline plots. It took a year to get the whole story down in the rough and another year to refine, but *Cedric* finally made it to print, and I gained a mountain of experience in this new world where I'm called author.

Am I ready to fix Rebirth?

Holding my breath, I opened that old Word .doc file and loaded the other half of the screen with a fresh .doc file. I started to rewrite the story with tears streaming down my face. Glancing over the first chapter, I grimaced, seeing the mistakes; I could see where I didn't think of my readers' needs. There were clear moments where my fear of revealing too much derailed the content. I have since learned that if it's a good story and beautifully written, I can tell readers everything and still pull them in. That first night I pumped out over 5,000 words, expanding the first chapter so much it had to be split in two!

Progress had been made.

A full-time author was born. I haven't stopped or looked back since, and I hope to write many more stories, novels, and series. If life didn't seem wild so far, 2018 tested me on so many levels. Once more, the tribulations stacked up: my dad's double lung transplant, my mother-in-law's broken arm, my father-in-law's knee surgery and kidney problems, my littlest one's autism and need for tubes, my diagnosis of Alpha-1 (which killed dad's lungs), and so much more.

I felt drained.

Despite it all, I wrote the final book of the Tattooed Angels Trilogy, finished another book concept to query to agents, remade a few public domain reference books, hosted workshops and webinars, and spoke on panels as a guest author for MegaCon Tampa Bay & Orlando. Part of the reason for my success is that I both gave and accepted help from many others in the community. This included the Alliance of Worldbuilders founded on Authonomy before it fell, and later, in my local area, Writer's Atelier and its founder Racquel Henry. Without their guidance and encouragement, I wouldn't be writing this book or any of the books I have published, completed, and brainstormed.

I had my moments of self-doubt, even after being gushed over for the work I had achieved after only a book or two. No, self-publishing wasn't my initial aim. I wanted to be traditional, but some amazing literary agents gave me some great advice about my work and what it would take to make it into a book and get it into reader's hands. In the end, I don't fit in a box. My work is often hard to market since I don't cater a hundred percent to fantasy or romance... or paranormal or historical or mythology. My books are a mixed bag, but in a good way.

Never stop moving forward.

I never stopped. As my mantra implies, I am in control of my writing and what happens to it. Today, I find myself with contracts, sitting at tables at my favorite conventions and inspiring writers every chance I have. Keep going. It will be hard and ugly, but I promise, there's light at the end of this, and that curse will become a blessing.

"We got this! Let's go write a story!"

TABLE OF CONTENTS

Formatting 101

Design can be art.
Design can be aesthetics.
Design is so simple, that's why it is so complicated.

Albert Szent-Gyorgyi

INTRODUCTION

Formatting, or typesetting, has evolved with the evolution of technology. Typesetters once had to keep drawers and chests full of font-face metal tiles, so they could slide the content in one page at a time. This practice gave birth to the publishing industry. Though we still haven't lost some of those formatting expectations and practices, advances in computer software make digital typesetting and on-demand printing a possibility.

Welcome to the New Age of Typesetting

The rise of self-publishing and a new wave of hybrid publishers are rapidly changing the expectations in both print and eBook styles. Both versions have their own pros and cons depending on the book's target audience, distribution plan, and industry expectations. Yes, a lot goes into deciding how your book should be developed, designed, and delivered. Each variant will have more weight on one aspect over the others as we cover the options.

Again, the Writer's Bane can be frustrating, confusing, and vague. Some may even want to give up, walking away in defeat. Have no fear. This guide will shed some light on the matter, though it too will eventually be outdated. The onset of a pandemic is rapidly changing the industry, pushing the urgency of eBooks and digital access while accepting the limitations of printing physical copies. The Top 5 have become the Top 4, and imprints that have been around and considered eternal are closing doors. It's all changing.

The Publishing Industry is ever-changing, but book formatting is another matter!

Luckily for you, typesetting has been a steady art and practice over the centuries, even when comparing a Gutenberg Bible to 1800's publications to today's best sellers! We've gone digital; although, there are some older practices that still hold weight. The aim of this book is to give you the most up-to-date aspects while referring back to older practices that are still widely accepted. As you began your own journey in formatting, be sure to explore, experiment, and exhaust all of your options. What you have access to, or who you have access to, can make a huge difference in your overall experience and final product.

Worksheets and checklists are designed to help

If there is any topic I know well, it's definitely typesetting. I have been doing this for almost two decades, taught many others, pushed books via multiple software options, created every genre imaginable, and led entire teams of formatters. Like the topic of research, this is a topic I am happy to discuss. Many of the worksheets and checklists are designed to prep and organize the process, not only for the author, but for the formatters involved. As always, use this book like a toolbox and take what you need from it. Some of this may be biased according to my preferences, but in the end, I am aiming to help fellow writers struggling with this topic. Let's begin!

How to Use this Book

It took me a while to settle on how I would break this book out. At first, looking at my own resources in the past and how-to videos, I thought to follow a similar style of explaining all the things for all the types for all the readers before moving onto the next phase, but...

NOPE. No. No.
Not doing it.

It's been done before, and I always have to go searching elsewhere for more specific information... which brings me to the concept I have for the Writer's Bane books. In short, this is...

Your Toolbox

And folks, we all maintain said toolbox and its tools in different ways. One of us might keep wrenches in the top drawer, the other in the middle drawer, and others might not know what a wrench is. In the spirit of this thought, I decided this book would work based on the styles of books and their associated audiences as a means to give you a chance to go to the "drawer and its tools" that you are looking for directly. In the long run, you may find these sections overlap in places with similar or even identical content.

It's intentional. Trust me!

This way you won't have to go jumping around the book as much! Instead, start with the section you need and go through the entire process for that specific book type. Each of these sections include unique information for that type, but it also includes the information that applies to all books. I hope this layout proves more beneficial than redundant. Just be mindful that much of these practices stem from the history and foundation that the industry standards depend on. To offset this seeming repetition, the book begins with "The Basics" covering the anatomy of a book, so it's all in one place. Good luck and happy book formatting to you all!

THE BASICS

Let's start with some major terminology and review the elements of a book. There are a ton of terms involved in labelling the anatomy of any book. Using the wrong term or not realizing the vagueness of language you may be using between you and your formatter can end in disaster and frustration. For the sake of brevity, I will cover interior only, nothing about the cover or options involving the outside other than trim size. (Oh, trim size is the term for what height and width your finished book will be.)

The back of this book contains a large glossary of terms. Please don't hesitate to take a peek and look over the list as you move through this process. I have tried to include the most useful terms, building a resource that anyone could use to expand their knowledge regardless of skill level.

In this chapter, you will discover the universal elements of any book (picture book, fiction book, textbook, etc.) from the anatomy to the format parameters. These are terms you should use when communicating with your typesetter and perhaps while asking for feedback.

I suggest highlighting in different colors to help see the information you want to learn!

Before we dive into it, know that a lot of this styling has been there since the very first publication, the Gutenberg Bible. Drop caps and fanciful chapter header art has been an art form since monks and scribes used gold-leaf and colored inks; although, they have shrunk in size and aren't as dominating on the page as they once intended. Over time, when foundries (forges who made the metal tiles of individual letters and first developer of fonts) were mass producing books in the 1800's, they developed new fonts and cleaner ways to bind books. Now, APA, MLA, CMS, and a bunch of these initials oversee how we write our college essays and publish our academic books. But how do these apply to fictional works and publishing outside of the academic circle?

Which style is right for publishing?

CMS or Chicago Manual Style is the most referenced in the publishing industry—though it only serves as a guide. Consider the variety of creative layouts seen in workbooks, devotionals, and artistic chapter headers or pages. As for the content or body text, CMS serves as a consistent formatting guide to how bulleted lists, tables, citations, indent/ no indent, and other items should look. For centuries, not years or decades, books have been formatted so readers can digest information. Readers are conditioned to connect certain font sizes to specific concepts.

For example, readers know contracts are often done in smaller font like size 10 versus the traditional 14-point font. In the other direction, readers expect large print books to be over 16-point font per library definition. Copyright pages and footnotes will push their sizes as tiny as 8- or 9-point font in some cases. Average romance novels expect 12-point font, and an epic fantasy novel can be as low as 10-font. Why? SPACE.   PAGE COUNT. A physical book can only bind so many pages and signatures together and can only fit so much content on a page based on its trim size. Most manuscripts are double spaced, on 8.5 in by 11 inch pages, using 12-point font. The page count can be highly unpredictable when a layout and design is applied with single space and half that size (5 in by 8 in trim size). Meanwhile, the eBook has tossed out the need to fret over font size and page count.

A physical book can only bind so many pages!

Granted, this leaves the question of which format you design for. Well, in my own experience, you design for print that exports a strong eBook. My preferred software may be InDesign, but I'll do my best to reference other ways to do this via various software, resources, and services. This isn't the only book on the market for you to use in order to learn all the nitty gritty details. I am being selective and leaning into mostly digital typesetting throughout this book. For a greater level of detail, I highly recommend *The Book Blueprint: Expert Advice for Creating Industry-Standard Print Books* by Joel Friedlander. This book might be a little dated, but the information is very relevant, and he does a wonderful job going into deeper details than I will in my own workbook. In short, I have every typesetter I know buy or have a copy of Friedlander on hand if they want to learn more about typesetting, and I often pick it up myself to double check certain aspects.

ANATOMY OF THE BOOK

Anatomy. It seems like a weird term to relate to books, but it's exactly what I'm about to do for you. We are going to walk through a book, point at the parts, and give you the label. Think of this as that old game and song: Head, Shoulders, Knees, & Toes. We look at books all the time, but never have we ever felt the need to know all the fancy terms for what is happening on the page of the latest Heather Graham or Dean Koontz novel. Feel free to open up your books at home and see how designers before you have been creative with these parts of the book.

The head bone's connected to the...?

Looking at a book, you can break it down into three core sections: front matter, content, and back matter. Readers expect each of these to contain certain information, and each has a formatting expectation or even an order the items can follow. This doesn't mean your book needs all of these sections either. Below is a list of what you might find while the asterisk implies mandatory elements. Don't fret over seeing some in more than one column. The description for each of these explains the duplication. I listed the summaries in the way I feel is the best order, but you should definitely note why and when to flip front and back matter placement.

Front Matter
- Half Title Page
- Title Page*
- Copyright Page*
- Dedication
- Endorsements
- Table of Contents
- Foreword
- Words from the Author
- About the Author
- Acknowledgments
- Preface
- Prologue
- Introduction

Content
- Chapter Page
- Body Pages*

Back Matter
- Epilogue
- About the Author
- Acknowledgments
- Book Listing
- Preview/Sneak Peek
- Bibliography
- References
- Sources
- Endnotes
- Index
- Appendix
- Book Club Questions

The Parts...

Half Title Page

The book's title and lots of space. Why? Well, this is adopted from CMS, but in the end, it provides a great page for authors to sign and write personal messages. This should always be a right page. Sometimes this may be left out completely depending on the nature of the book.

Title Page

Title, subtitle, series name, volume number, author name, and imprint logo should all be here. In short, this should mimic the text from the front cover. This is always a right page.

Artemis
Eye of Gaea

The Cedric Series

Artemis
Eye of Gaea

Valerie Willis

4 Horsemen
Publications, Inc.

Copyright Page

This page should say who the rights of the book belongs to, whether that's the author, publisher, or company. It should include ISBN, LCCN, Publisher information, permissions for content used, editor, designer, legality information, and similar aspects that may apply. The base copyright page should be as such and located on a left page or the backside of the title page:

> BOOK TITLE
> Copyright © 2021 AUTHOR NAME. All rights reserved.
>
> PUBLISHER NAME
> STREET ADDRESS
> CITY, STATE ZIP CODE
> WEBSITE
> EMAIL
>
> COVER BY DESIGNER NAME
> TYPESETTING BY COMPANY OR DESIGNER NAME
> EDITED BY EDITOR'S NAME
>
> Permission from NAME HERE for quotes from TITLE OF THING.
>
> All rights to the work within are reserved to the author and publisher. No part of this publication may be reproduced, stored in a retrieval system, or transmitted in any form or by any means, electronic, mechanical, photocopying, recording, scanning, or otherwise, except as permitted under Section 107 or 108 of the 1976 International Copyright Act, without prior written permission except in brief quotations embodied in critical articles and reviews. Please contact either the Publisher or Author to gain permission.
>
> This is book is meant as a reference guide. All characters, organizations, and events portrayed in this novel are either products of the author's imagination or are used fictitiously. All brands, quotes, and cited work respectfully belongs to the original rights holders and bear no affiliation to the authors or publisher.
>
> Library of Congress Control Number 1234567890
>
> Paperback ISBN-13: 978-1-12345-678-9
> Audiobook ISBN-13: 978-1-12345-678-9
> EBook ISBN-13: 978-1-12345-678-9

Dedication

In most cases, the dedication is a completely optional aspect and starts on a right page right after the title page. It's usually center alignment on the page with center justification. In picture books, this is often placed above the copyrights instead of its own page as to save on cost and page count since color print has a high production cost.

DEDICATION

ENDORSEMENTS

This can be in a few places. Some books will have this as a page before the half title while others place it before or after the dedication. It definitely should be on its own page, and I find it's more impactful if kept to a single page, front and back at most. Always starts on right page.

TABLE OF CONTENTS

Thanks to today's technology, this process is painless. How? The programs are designed to pull from the Chapter Header, Headlines, and Subheads to generate these. If you have a specific look you are wanting, definitely provide a sample of this for the typesetter or at least like them know you want all the subheads included. The software even auto-updates the page numbers as content shifts! It's amazing and has been a vital tool in my own ventures. Can be done as a spread or start on right page.

FOREWORD

This has to be the most misspelled word I come across. I often see author's use Forward, but this isn't a motion. The word literally means, *the words that come before,* hence the "Fore-" and "-word" spelling versus toward, or forward meaning *to move in set direction or before where you are standing.* This section is often written by someone else as a means to introduce a reader to the book and its purpose. Sometimes the author will write these, but this is a great chance to get someone within the same scope to back or endorse your book in a more intimate way. Never be afraid to email authors, experts, keynote speakers, and public figures for this! Nothing looks more exciting than "Foreword written by YOUR FAVORITE AUTHOR" on a cover! Always starts on right page.

PREFACE OR WORDS FROM THE AUTHOR

It's this spot that can be the author variant of a foreword. It's a chance to inform readers about the content they will see and provide some insight they should have in mind as they read your work. This can also be a chance for you to have a small discussion between author and reader to best warm them up for the experience you have set before them. Always starts on right page.

PROLOGUE

Fictional work sometimes comes with a prologue. There is a great debate on the uses of this snippet and has been the huge element in many arguments. Despite that, know that in short, if you use one it should add to your first chapters in some manner. It's information that shows something that may have set the world, plot, or character in motion, but it has no direct connection to main story. As expected within your story, you should be concise and engaging here even if this is the only time we may be in the setting or with the characters involved. Always starts on right page.

TABLE OF CONTENTS

PREFACE

It was brought to my attention that I should take a moment to talk to the readers and fans of *The Cedric Series.*

In this particular book, I discovered even I had misconceptions about Oracles and Sibyls. They were not a myth, but historical entities who practiced their rituals beyond the mythologies they became part of through the people they inspired and even humbled at times. My dive went so deep that I wrote an article for SciFiFantasy Network and was floored at the number of readers who dove in to see what I had uncovered.

Overall, I wish to share my inspirations for writing this story. This will explain a lot on how I came about creating these amazing ideas, characters, creatures, and events as a fictional work with heavy fantasy and romance elements in the mix. If one really wanted to drag out all its genres, I could label this a historical fiction, mythology, or even occult and paranormal. So far, Fantasy Romance has done this work the most justice for my readers' expectations.

Historical fiction can be applied to several parts throughout the series, whether it's a scene, event, or even a reflection of a character and their on-goings. What do I mean by this? Well a lot of you might get the Vladimir Tepes, or Vlad the Impaler references, but it dove deeper than that. King Frederic was the First King of Germans, the lepers in those times did indeed have to ring bells and seek refuge in colonies, Cerdanya was a real trade town, and so on. There are a ton of subtle hints here and there because I wanted to bring the unseen, untold side of the history during Medieval Times to a tangible state.

CHAPTER 1

Egos

CEDRIC

Cedric welcomed the bright, warm sunlight as they left the cave's security behind. Wylleam led them down a path through thick woods while Fenrir kept close behind Cedric in the back of the assemble. The singing of birds filled the air like an orchestra. Flowers and fruit filled every tree they walked pass, the air engulfed in their sweet and bitter scents. They had passed through into the realm of Gaea but were shocked to see not much had changed beside the oddness of the trees and the overwhelming enthusiasm of the birds. The sun in the sky, dirt at their feet, and even the need to breathe.

The path winded through the thick forest. Cedric's shoulders and wings would brush against the trunks of trees, making him groan in annoyance. It was as if his body absorbed the thicker magic in the air, engorging on its power. Fenrir chuckled, watching as Cedric tried unsuccessfully to get used to this new, larger version of himself. Wylleam took a hard turn to the right. Anxious to keep pace, Cedric turned too soon, and a horn slammed into a nearby tree, gouging a deep groove into the bark. Cursing under his breath as birds scattered in alarm. Flowers floated on the wind and fruit plopped to the ground all around him, one bouncing off his shoulder.

Everyone stopped and stared at him. Gritting his fangs, it was all he could do to not lose his temper. His mind focused on Angeline and wondering where Artemis had taken her.

At least this time she's with someone who will protect her.

1

Artemis: Eye of Gaea

"Are you all right?" Wylleam's voice expressed concern, recognizing the signs of Cedric's frustration. Cedric shot him a knowing glare that said, *this isn't the time to discuss it.* "My cabin's not much further. There's an opening in the trees. It will lead you there."

Sighing, Cedric nodded. "I look forward to no more trees."

Fenrir, Romasanta, and Nyctimus chuckled until an angry green glare hit them. As promised, they walked about five hundred yards further in the dense underbrush before a meadow housing a small cabin blossomed before them. Fenrir circled in a thick grassy spot before flopping down on his belly, watching Wylleam lead Romasanta and Nyctimus through the door. Cedric moved to follow, but Wylleam held up a hand, signaling he was to wait. The door clicked close and Cedric began pacing. After a few rounds, he could no longer ignore the massive white wolf's golden heated stare.

Halting his steps, Cedric stood tall, crossing his arms. "What is it, wolf?"

"You're in a rush, considering you haven't stopped to assess this new environment." Fenrir snorted. "You're quite the fool."

Cedric narrowed his eyes. "What's there to know?" he retorted. "There's ground and trees, a sky and sun. Everything smells the same."

"True." Fenrir wagged his tail, back and forth. "But you still haven't adjusted."

"I don't have the luxury of playing with my dick all day," scoffed Cedric, continuing to pace.

"I too once found myself in your state over a female." Rising to his feet, Fenrir shook his fur free of grass. "But, if you don't learn to trust in her strength and abilities, she'll never discover them at all."

He stopped, his back towards the wolf.

"Struck a nerve with you, didn't I, pup?" Fenrir's voice fell deeper with his next words. "Don't make the same mistake I did, believing she's incapable of protecting herself, incapable of being by your side, let alone, by herself."

Formatting 101

INTRODUCTION

Non-fiction often will have an introduction. This is an informative section that gives an overview of the topic or topics within the book. It, at times, might supply recommendations on how to use the book or what they intended the book to do for the topic it spans. It's often a great tool for covering the basics of a topic so the reader doesn't get lost in the more in-depth areas of the book. Always starts on right page.

CHAPTER PAGE OR CHAPTER START

This should at the very least be spaced and laid out via type and header art. It signals the start of a chapter. The first chapter always starts on a right page and this begins your normal numeral page numbers of 1, 2, 3... until the end of the book. Most software will not even allow page 1 to start on a left page, and CMS inspires this particular practice. After chapter 1, it's usually up to the designer and/or author whether they all start on a right page or are laid out in a continuous style (left and right pages).

BODY PAGES

These are the pages that fill the entire page with content. They often feature a header reflecting the book title, author, current chapter, or subhead. They fill right and left pages until the next chapter page or back matter section.

EPILOGUE

Much like the prologue, this should reveal something about the story. Some use this as a chance to fast forward to show how the romance really ended or lasted. Others will use this to rewind to a moment and reveal a sleight of hand or another character's point of view. At times, within series, it can set the next book in the series to start and hint where the story is going or who your next story might be about. Always starts on right page.

ABOUT THE AUTHOR

Here's a chance to get to know the mastermind of the story. In non-fiction work, this is included in the front matter to express what makes the author qualified to write a book on the given topic. In memoirs, it may not be included at all since the book is normally about them until their current stance. It should at the least have a biography but may include a picture and website links to social media and official pages. *Check out my article on the 4HorsemenPublications.com on writing a strong author bio!* Always starts on right page.

BOOK LISTING OR RECOMMENDED READING

Sometimes this can be featured in the front of a book for a best-selling author or long-running series. I highly recommend listing current books or books that will eventually be out within a year or so. This provides titles for readers to seek out and purchase if they want more content from you. Don't have a list? Recommend a reading list of fellow writers within the same genre and ask for a return shout out! Always starts on right page.

Preview or Sneak Peek

I see this mostly in romance novels. They often include chapter 1 and chapter 2 of the next book in the series to entice a reader to keep going. It's a great way to showcase where you might be going and leave the reader on a bigger cliff-hanger that might drive them to buy or preorder. Always starts on right page.

Acknowledgments

Again, this is a section often placed in both the front or back matter sections. Many support-driven books with a larger version or long list of names are placed in the back as to shrink the front matter and allow readers to enjoy the story first. If this is more like an extended dedication that's a page long, feel free to add it right behind or in place of your dedication! Always starts on right page.

Appendix

Some non-fiction work refers to materials or provides side materials. Appendix are a great way to provide a resource in whole in lieu of a citation, footnote, or endnote. They can reference it as needed. Sometimes these can be a detailed example of a topic that wasn't needed in the area referenced or would disrupt the content for those who don't need the resource. Other times it's to provide additional materials that had no place in the content but are very relevant to the book's materials and could aid further research. Always starts on right page.

Bibliography or References or Sources

A great alternative for footnotes and endnotes. I often default to these methods in my own articles due to the fact I have spent two decades absorbing books, articles, and even discussions with experts on various topics in mythology, legend, and book design. It's a great way to provide your own go-to resources and materials for readers. This also serves as a means to provide sources to support what you covered within your book and strengthen the concepts and information you are passing to the reader throughout your content. Citations should follow CMS styling guidelines. Always starts on right page.

About the Author

Valerie Willis is a Fantasy Paranormal Romance author based out of Central Florida. She loves crafting novels with elements inspired by mythology, superstitions, legends, folklore, fairy tales and history. She received the Reader's Favorite Bronze medal in 'Fiction – Mythology' and FAPA's President's Silver medal in 'Fantasy/Sci-fi.' You can find her hosting workshops or a guest speaker at many events sharing her expertise in self-publishing, novel writing, research in fiction, world-building, character development, book design, reader immersion and more.

Her Award-Winning Dark Fantasy Paranormal Romance, 'The Cedric Series,' is a wonderful blend of genres that appeal to a wide-range of readers described as "dramatic, lustful, and fantasy fulfilling." The motto here is: "No immortal is beyond the ailments of man" and that includes powerful creatures, demons, witches, and Gods. Many of the monsters present in the content is derived from Medieval Bestiaries and adds a fun flavor of new yet deeply rooted assortment of creatures such as Coin Iotair, Shag Foal, Cynocephali, and many more.

For Young Adult readers look for her Dark Urban Fantasy filled with coming-of-age and beyond life lessons, the 'Tattooed Angels Trilogy.' Hotan is a failed reincarnation and is becoming immortal against his will. Life is complicated and often we withdraw within ourselves and shut others out when life becomes hard.

234

4 Horsemen Publications
Fantasy/Paranormal Romance
J.M. Paquette
Klauden's Ring
Solyn's Body
The Inbetween
Hannah's Heart

Horror & Suspense
Erika Lance
Jimmy
Illusions of Happiness
No Place for Happiness
I Hunt You

Young Adult Fantasy
C.R. Rice
Denial
Anger
Bargaining
Depression
Acceptance

J.B. Moonstar
Russ and The Hidden Voice
Taylor and the Red Wolf Rescue
Jenna and the Legend of the White Wolf
Jenna and the Return of the White Wolf
Jan and the Chinese Crested Tern Rescue

4HorsemenPublications.com

INDEX

These are rare with the new age of PDF, and digital formats have the ability to search for words. An index of key topics and words is often saved for cookbooks and textbooks. This is best as a list to give to a typesetter, and after formatting is completed, do a full audit of which pages should be referenced based on the final product. Always starts on right page.

ENDNOTES

If the author used endnotes, they show up in the back. These should be hyperlinked together through the endnote systems within the software. You may have to convert them into footnotes for eBook format per vendor needs as policies and requirements change in regards to these.

BOOK CLUB QUESTIONS

A new growing trend is book club questions in the back of the book. There's no need to provide an answer key in most cases. Think of open-ended questions about the plot, character, and world. This could be a call to action to send them to research or look further into something you used for inspirations

BOOK CLUB DISCUSSION QUESTIONS

1. What enemy do you think proved the most challenging?

2. What is the significance in separating Cedric and Angeline?

3. What changes internally were unfolding with Cedric?

4. A lot was revealed in this book, which one stood out to you? Why?

5. At last we see Gaea! How did she differ from your initial impression of her?

6. What do you suspect has happened to Tony?

7. Do you think Lillith came personally as a powerplay or a show of honesty?

8. The Otherworld takes its Tir system from Celtic Mythology. What other mythology and legends were revealed?

9. Aether was mentioned many times and in reference to Cedric. What do you think is being implied?

10. This quest was intended for Romasanta, but Cedric did all the heavy lifting. Do you think this was planned out or luck?

11. There is a significant amount of heavy duty weapon gathering happening. Do you think this is foreshadowing for what will be happening in later books?

237

READY FOR BOOK FIVE? KING INCUBUS: A NEW REIGN

Is waiting for you here on Amazon:
http://mybook.to/CedricSeries

REVIEWS ARE MY TIP JAR!

If you enjoyed the book, or something really nagged you about the story, I encourage you to speak your mind about my book in the form of a review. Both authors and readers depend on them to know if they will like the story and characters within the pages.

Where can we leave the reviews? There are a lot of places! Amazon and GoodReads are great places to leave them, but feel free to visit your favorite online venues and leave them there. Whether it's a one-liner that sums up how you feel, a in-depth review of breaking down the book and characters, or a spoiler warning of the rant to follow – ALL ARE ENCOURAGED.

You may leave reviews here:

Amazon

GoodReads
https://www.goodreads.com/author/show/7822183.

or more of a debate topic to spark the group to decide whether they agreed with what unfolded or a character's actions. These can be useful tools for selling to teachers and schools for a classroom book or for running a tabled event to showcase how your series has questions for those seeking books for their clubs and wine parties.

CALL TO ACTION

Don't forget to include some means of doing a "call to action" for the reader. This is often leaders to your work or to ask the reader to act or click. One way to do this is to encourage reviews, join your newsletter, or perhaps even offer an exclusive sneak peek of the next book's chapters. These are vital for growing an author's platform via their books and can serve as convenient clicking for readers to go where they want via your eBook, increasing the chances of more buys and gathering your following.

THE GUTS

Well, you've learned the basics of head, shoulders, and knees... but there's still the guts and the anatomy found here. That's right! The actual elements within this monster list has their own terms and purpose. Granted, there's a smaller learning curve here since most of the pages use the same elements throughout the entire book. It's vital that a book is designed with a level of consistency and limited options for fonts. Sure, it seems fun that all twenty-seven characters should have their own font when they talk! In the end, the reader has a hard time reading the materials, and it can create physical headaches, blurry eyesight, which at the end of the day means they stop reading!

It's not just faces! Font size and color can cause certain readers and even age groups to be excluded. As you continue to explore this book, you will discover how all these elements impact each audience and book type. Children's books often have to consider which font face to use per the age group, and they shouldn't be using footnotes in bedtime stories! The purpose and function of a book should never be broken unless you do it within a reasonable understanding of the audience you are building the book for. This is usually seen more often in planners and workbooks that are constantly re-inventing how to present information in new ways. Wait, that's what I've done here! DOH!

Let's walk through the guts of the typography and elements found within the content and matter. This should give you the labels needed to communicate stronger with your typesetter or designer no matter what book you are making. These terms are universal and have been in use within the industry for a long time in some cases. Again, I will take this moment to plug my personal go-to resource for examples and detailed information, *The Book Blueprint: Expert Advice for Creating Industry-Standard Print Books* by Joel Friedlander, who has a wider variety of advice that I didn't dive into as deeply as he covers in his own book. This book is meant to get you off the ground and encourage you to find other resources to dive deeper and expand from here.

1. CHAPTER HEADER

This is the verbiage usually signified by numbers of "Chapter 1" or "Chapter One" depending on the book. It's usually styled as Heading 1 in eBooks and word documents. Chapter headers always start on a fresh page and signal the reader that a new chapter is starting. It is sometimes accompanied with artwork or a design to visually signal or add an artistic flair.

2. HEADLINE

The next line, if applicable, is the title that goes with the chapter. This is sometimes lumped with the chapter header in a manuscript and broken out during formatting. It's sometimes referred to as the chapter title or heading 2.

3. GLYPH

In most typesets, a glyph is added to add ornamental or artistic flair on a typography level. Glyphs are often a font-face graphic referred to as a dingbat, glyph, or ornament font face. These are usually converted to outlines or actual images, so they can carry over into an eBook and don't simply leave a floating letter or keystroke.

01 **CHAPTER 1**

02 EGOS

03 CEI

Cedric welcomed the brigh
cave's security behind. W
through thick woods while
in the back of the assemble. The
an orchestra. Flowers and fruit f
the air engulfed in their sweet a
through into the realm of Gaea b
had changed beside the odd ess

4. DROP CAP

The large letter or letters that are placed at the beginning of body text in the first paragraph. Often this is bypassed if the opening paragraph is a subhead, quote, or similar. There are a variety of styles and drop cap-based font faces (face refers to the look of a font family or set such as Times, Times New Roman, Helvetica, etc.) for this purpose. It's not unusual to see these span 2-3 lines and often is seen on the chapter header page or a fresh page of front/back matter.

5. FIRST LINE

In lieu of a drop cap, some formatters may choose to do an artful first line. This is more common in non-fiction books, or certain genres like politics or self-help will feature a special font for the entire first line of the first paragraph.

6. BODY TEXT

This is what makes up the majority of most books. The reader spends more time reading and taking in the words in these areas as they digest the content within the book you've written or formatted. It is vital to keep the font face consistent and know when to apply character styles, drop caps, line breaks, and similar visual signals that inform the reader of what the content is doing or even where one section ends and the next begins. This is where the reader will also encounter words emphasized in italics, **bold**, or underlined.

7. SUBHEAD

A subhead is the headings within a chapter. These don't always match the style of the headline but stand out visually to separate sections. These are often labelled heading 3, 4, 5... and sometimes are included in the table of contents.

8. HEADER AND FOOTER

The header is typically where you will see the title, author name, or current chapter or its subhead. Traditionally you will see the author name or book title on the left page, and on the right page, book title or chapter header or even the current headline. As for the footer, it is more common to simply see the page number. Take a moment and look at books you will be competing against. Depending on the book type and genre, many use these areas in unique ways and include a wide variety of information. A prime example is how running headers work for a dictionary or encyclopedia.

CHAPTER 1

EGOS

CEDRIC

Cedric welcomed the bright, warm cave's security behind. Wylleam through thick woods while Fenrir in the back of the assemble. The singing an orchestra. Flowers and fruit filled ev the air engulfed in their sweet and bitte through into the realm of Gaea but were had changed beside the oddness of the tr enthusiasm of the birds. The sun in the even the need to breathe.

The path winded through the thick and wings would brush against the tru groan in annoyance. It was as if his bc magic in the air, engorging on its power. as Cedric tried unsuccessfully to get us sion of himself. Wylleam took a hard t

ARTEMIS: EYE OF GAEA

right?" Wylleam's voice expre nizing the signs of Cedric's frustration. Cedric glare that said, *this isn't the time to discuss it.* " further. There's an opening in the trees. It will Sighing, Cedric nodded. "I look forward Fenrir, Romasanta, and Nyctimus chuc green glare hit them. As promised, they walke yards further in the dense underbrush before a small cabin blossomed before them. Fenr grassy spot before flopping down on his belly lead Romasanta and Nyctimus through the do follow, but Wylleam held up a hand, signalin door clicked close and Cedric began pacing. A could no longer ignore the massive white wolf

Halting his steps, Cedric stood tall, cross is it, wolf?"

"You're in a rush, considering you haven't s new environment." Fenrir snorted. "You're qu

Cedric narrowed his eyes. "What's there to "There's ground and trees, a sky and sun. Everyt

"True." Fenrir wagged his tail, back and for en't adjusted."

"I don't have the luxury of playing with my Cedric, continuing to pace.

"I too once found myself in your state ove his feet, Fenrir shook his fur free of grass. "But trust in her strength and abilities, she'll never

He stopped, his back towards the wolf.

"Struck a nerve with you, didn't I, pup?" Fe with his next words. "Don't make the same mi she's incapable of protecting herself, incapable let alone, by herself."

2

9. QUOTE OR CITATION

Quotes and citations are usually marked in italics with paragraph indents of 0.25" to 0.5" from the margin. Paragraphing spacing before and after help make these sections standout and signal to readers this is a quote or citation, and even include a source at times. On occasion a border is included, but it should be used sparingly and reserved for a pull quote instead.

"Life's like a box of chocolates; you never know what you're gonna get"–Forrest Gump

"Life's like a box of chocolates; you never know what you're gonna get"

10. PULL QUOTE

Pull quotes highlight a line, a quote, or citation that you want to make a visual impact. You see these used a lot in magazines, textbooks, self-help, and devotionals. They feature artistic elements and borders, and the body text flows around these as if they were images or illustrations on the page.

11. SECTION OR SCENE BREAK

A secction or scene break is added space to signal a hard change in content. In fictional work, it's not uncommon to use one for time jumps, scene change, or character point-of-view change, and it is visually marked as asterisks (***), line art, or a double return. As a formatter, double returns are frowned upon and often replaced with a paragraph style that adds space after to mimic the same look. The reason for this is to have more control on this aspect and to secure the space in eBook format. It's not uncommon double returns aren't registered at all in eBooks or on certain devices. Not every book will need an ornament for these sections so be sure to consult the author!

12. PAGE BREAK

Page breaks can be manually added in places and often are inserted to push content to the next page. They can even be programmed in certain software to only show up on odd (right page) or even (left page) pages. These aren't visible unless you have hidden characters showing. When you make a page break, don't forget to double check that you don't need to change page alignment to top align!

13. BULLET LIST OR NUMBERED LIST

These can be simple or complex depending on the type of book you are formatting. These often feature a paragraph left indent of some kind that increases with each level of the list. CMS defines various types but not every manuscript follows these recommendations. In most cases, a formatter will mimic what the author has used as to not misconstrue the intended content.

- Main Bullet Point
  - Secondary Point
    - Third Point
    - Third Point

1. Main Number Bullet Points
   a. Secondary Point
      i. Third Point
      ii. Third Point

- My Goofy Bullet Points
  - Secondary Point
    - Third Point
    - Third Point

14. IMAGE OR ILLUSTRATION

Some books feature images, photos, or illustrations of some kind. These should always be saved at 300 to 600 DPI to accommodate the printers needs and limit the risk of blurry or pixelated images. Depending on the type of book, images may be the main aspect of storytelling as seen in picture books versus textbooks and memoirs that often have textual content flowing around them or feature pages with images. These often also have a caption to add additional information or give credit to the work.

15. WATERMARK

These come in many forms whether a light ghosted image in the background or a stamp of sorts to address who the content belongs to. In legal forms, you often see "COPY" ghosted on images or the company name and "DO NOT COPY" on occasion. Sometimes this is nothing more than an image. Be mindful that watermarks and other layered content will not show in an eBook unless you turn that page into an image which could make it difficult or impossible for reader to read the content. For example, the ghosted lettering on this page reading "Writer's Bane: Formatting 101" is a type of watermark.

16. CROPMARKS

When sending and prepping files for certain offset printers, you may be asked to add cropmarks or send the PDF or files in a certain way. The good news: this is a feature you can add last and usually via a feature for saving out to PDF, a common file type for final production. This will often have a color grid for calibrating CMYK (When printing, they use ink coloration divided into Cyan, Magenta, Yellow, and Black that each take turns being dropped on the page unlike a screen that uses RGB, or Red, Green, and Blue coloration.), black bars for black and white balance, and lines to show where pages should be cut. These marks are often in the bleed zone or further out depending on the type of parameters required by the press or printer.

17. END LEAVES OR END PAGES

If you want end leaves or end pages, you will have to go the offset printing. These are the fancy cardstock pages glued to the back of the cover and often makeup the first page or connect with the first page. They usually have custom artwork, solid colors, or patterned in relation to the book. This is not a feature Print-on-Demand books will have access to. You usually have to provide a color code or pattern via the files. Each printer has templates as to how they want a formatter or graphic designer to provide this information, so be sure to check with them.

18. PRINT-ON-DEMAND BLANK PAGE OR BARCODE

If you are choosing to use Print-on-Demand to print your book, know that its mandatory to leave a blank, left page. This page serves as an area for the printer to leave a barcode that retains information about that printed version of your book.

SOFTWARE, PROGRAMS, AND APPS - OH MY!

Here comes the technical aspect of all of this. As a disclosure, my programs of choice have asterisks, and on a lot of my instructions, I tried very hard to make them generic enough to be followed in a wide range of programs. I have used everything and experimented with many. So much so, that I often can list out the weird bugs and point out the potential problems that can occur in certain cases. Part of mastering a program, in my opinion, is being aware of its shortcomings and how you want to work around those issues. Despite that, my writing preference falls into the notorious Microsoft Word bin, and I can't express how amazing InDesign can be when you utilize all the features and build templates. So, let's showcase some of the options I know or have worked with personally.

THE WORD PROCESSORS!

A word processor is simply that. It's a place where you put all the words and it processes them how you tell it to do so. This is an older term, or one not referenced as commonly as it had been back in the 1990's. Let's review some of the different ones commonly used today.

GOOGLE DOC OR GDOC

Those who don't have access to Word or want to share their document often default to GDOC or Google Document. Don't fret! You can save this file out or "Download As" a Word document or RTF format. This is super helpful for importing into layout software or uploading your file to an aggregator.

MICROSOFT WORD*

This is the most common one and universally accessible via internet, work, and school. I love the improvements happening with this software including the recent advancements for the Spelling and Grammar aspect. This program also has plenty of helpful plugins for the editing process including one for ProWritingAid. The best part is if you use the standard tools in this software, they often import into a layout software without any issues. This includes linked footnotes or endnotes, character styles, and the in-built or custom-made styles import into paragraph styles even in InDesign. These can be adjusted or reassigned to make formatting easier across the board.

Word Processor

NOTEPAD

This only works if you have no character styles (bold, italics, underline, etc.). It is simply made for programming and the baseline variant of a word processor. It can type all the characters on your keyboard, and not much else beyond that. I discourage creating a manuscript or book with this program unless you plan on programming your eBook from scratch with XML or simplified HTML5/CSS3 file package.

SCRIVENER

When Word isn't doing it for you, or for authors who need something that has a stronger means of organizing content, Scrivener is a great alternative. For writers who brainstorm, use scene notes, or don't necessarily write chronologically, they will find the features only this software provides a fresh of breath air. Again, you should at the very least be able to export a copy of your book in RTF format.

WORDPAD

Old. Yes, it's still there in the start menu of your Windows 10 system. When you don't have internet or don't own a trendy software, this still gets the job done! You can save as RTF and this will work no differently than the others. It's a nice, basic word processor, and it's solid because it's not trying to do anything fancy beyond the means of creating a Rich Text Format file.

THE LAYOUT SOFTWARE!

This refers to any program designed to help you layer images and text within a layout or design of your choosing. Some are more focused on book design such as InDesign and QuarkXpress while others are better suited for visual-based application that can be useful for journals and picture books.

CALIBRE

OpenSource software has its pros and cons. I have to admit: Calibre is an amazing collaboration and rather reliable for the most part. It gives you the opportunity to even add DOCX and convert that into a EPUB or eBook format of your choice. If that wasn't awesome news, you can edit metadata and make sure your cover, title, ISBN, author, and more are digitally attached to the file and correct. Be warned though, it can break an eBook design. but, in most cases, it gives you tools to solve any flagged issues via iTunes and the likes thanks to the epic "Edit Book" feature.

Canva

A lot of us discovered this app for epic level social media post making. Did you know it's designed to handle print design? Canva is a powerful and very accessible app and makes for a great means of creating picture-based books or even workbooks within. Granted, you may want to do this via the web browser interface, but it's doable. At the end of the day, vendor sites are wanting to see PDF to print from and you can get that from this. As for an eBook, maybe not the best option unless doing a picture book that uses a PDF to make an image-based eBook or a workbook/journal that won't have an eBook edition.

InDesign*

This is hands-down my all-time favorite. As a professional typesetter, this software provides me the ability to build templates and tools that fit a wide range of book types and clients. It also has means to help track an image's DPI and if used wisely, it can be used to design print books that export into great eBooks without any extra work needed. I am pro-efficiency and with the current templates I've built, I can design in-depth books with high word counts in a matter of an hour or two if necessary. It's one of the most recommended programs and with recent changes to how Adobe provides software access to users, one can easily pay for just this program for $20.99 a month.

Microsoft Word

I know, this seems crazy, but yes you can make a book from this. It's a pain. It has its quirks like when you start doing more advance section breaking and header/footer design work. In the end, if you are very strong in this word processor, you should be able to export or save as a PDF to upload to the vendor or into a program like Calibre for eBook creation.

QuarkXpress

It's gone. Well, not entirely? A lot of folks still have their old QuarkXpress programs and are using it. This has been replaced by InDesign, and honestly, it's the only comparable software I ever came across between the two. Just be wary that if not used with caution, you can inadvertently make more work for yourself. It often had flow issues, which InDesign excels at.

Vellum

An amazing software to simplify book formatting and eBook creation! Only one issue: *it's only available for Mac and Apple!* If you so happen to be a Mac user, this is definitely a great solution for print and eBook formatting. It's definitely at a great price point with premade templates and styles to drop your book into. Though, this software is hyper focused on text-only books and particularly for fiction books.

PRINT-ON-DEMAND

The current mainstream means for self-publishers, small presses, and even the top publishers to catch when they run out of limited print runs is using a Print-on Demand supplier. Below I cover some well-known entities, who make-up a majority for the current market in regards to uploading files for books printed for self-publishers to large publishers. These are listed in order of popularity, and for this portion, we are more focused on printed books though I will cover what other options each of these can provide. For these, they do not make the book for you unless you purchase additional services through them or combine efforts with other options. Be sure to take advantage of templates and file guides in order to typeset your book in a way that it can be accepted by the distributor of your choice.

INGRAMSPARK, LIGHTNING SOURCE, AND CORESOURCE+

Ingram is one of the biggest distributors for Print-on-Demand and digital options. CoreSource+ has over a 450+ channel reach that includes academia, libraries, big retailers (Amazon, Barnes & Noble, Walmart, and more), and 20+ audiobook venues (Audible, Apple, Storytel, Hoopla, and more). Self-publishers and small publishers often start with IngramSparks (simply sign up and you're good to go!), for more print options you must apply to gain access to Lightning Source. A step above that and you gain a paid contract to gain a digital reach on par with top publishers including large imprints and new publishers such as Avon, Harlequin, Macmillan, Simon and Schuster, HarperCollins, 4 Horsemen Publications, and Kensington.

Print options include paperbacks of varying sizes, laminate case hardcover, and even dust jacket options. As for their digital reach, they take in EPUB format and MP3 or WAV Audiobook formats and can distribute to many of the other distributors and retailers listed below with access to hard-to-reach channels. For example, to publish work through OverDrive, you must provide a minimum of 100+ titles per month. Many starting out or only publishing their own work can't meet this demand in order to get their books into libraries, so using Ingram or a similar distributor can help you achieve this. Another advantage is the level of control you have with a book's metadata, pricing, and even wholesale discounts. This is the means in which I recommend for those reasons.

Amazon, KDP, and ACX

A pro-consumer market, Amazon makes up 50-60% of the digital market for eBook sales for almost a decade now. With growing trends and accessibility, they are losing their ground, but it's not uncommon for publishers and authors to only publish here (and in some cases, prefer not to publish here at all!). The KDP dashboard and account for publishing books on Kindle or Paperback has made several changes in the last few years since they absorbed CreateSpace. Now authors and small publishers can do both within the same location with worldwide access. Because many of the metadata and wholesale options are pulled away or simplified, launching a book via KDP can be less daunting than other areas though you give much control of pricing and other aspects over to Amazon to do with it as they see fit. You can get worldwide reach via Amazon and a limited number of third-party associations. What these are is not exactly clear, but with Amazon giving KDP user exclusive access to control series landing pages, promotions, and similar exclusive deals, it can be tempting for most to use this platform alongside many others.

Barnes & Noble and NookPress

Publishing through Barnes & Noble requires you to use Nook Press. Again, this only is published via their store's chains and the few partners connected to them. With direct nook and paperback sales, you do get a slightly bigger cut in royalties going direct. Unlike Amazon, they don't offer much in the ways of exclusive and also don't give the author and publisher access to fully control wholesale and similar aspects. They have their own category system that can prove hard to navigate for some; however, it opens the door for some niche markets while completely missing more common ones.

Lulu.com

Back in the early years of self-publishing Print-on-Demand books, Lulu and CreateSpace were leading go-to distributors. After CreateSpace was swallowed up by Amazon, Lulu found itself still standing and reaching to provide better services to compete with the growing number of aggregators that made eBooks easier over print books. Now authors and publishers can print not only paperbacks and hardcovers, but they can also find options for photobooks, comics, magazines, yearbooks, and calendars. You will find much of the selection here a simplified selection compared to Ingram's options.

They also provide optional binding such as coil bound (similar to spiral bound notebooks), perfect bound (paperback and hardcover), and saddle stitch. Cost per book is competitive with Ingram and Amazon, and like Ingram, provide templates to aid in prepping files and covers for final product. You can sell your book directly via Lulu, bulk order, and/or open it up to the few channels they have with retailers, including Amazon, Apple, Kobo, and similar. They are user friendly and provide a lot of resources that can help first-time publishers.

WHAT'S AN AGGREGATOR?

An aggregator is a service that does a few things for the author. First, it's capable of converting your book into other formats as long as you provide the core file type they request. Secondly, they will then broadcast your book to vendor sites. These sometimes require money to gain wider access or more services.

BookBaby

This is more in the realm of author services, but much like Draft2Digital, BookBaby provides a large selection of print and eBook packages. Some of these are more in line with offset printing, and others are for Print-on-Demand setups. They can do formatting, conversions, and more. I can't say I've used their service directly, but I love the blog and newsletters. They often have up-to-date industry practices and ready information, and that alone makes them a resource worthy of mentioning or making authors aware of.

Draft2Digital

I have met many of their team in person at conferences and conventions. They are amazing and provide great customer service and support to their authors. If formatting proves a challenge, this company also provides services to format your book for you as well! Just like with SmashWords, they take a DOC or RTF of your manuscript and convert it into an eBook. From there, they will broadcast your book to vendors including Amazon, Barnes & Noble, Kobo, and more. Authors that I know personally who have used them have been very happy with their experience.

SmashWords

A free eBook-based aggregator but be mindful on what is needed to get your book cleared for the Premium Catalog. This is the side of SmashWords that will allow your book to gain access to the bigger vendors including Kobo and Barnes & Noble. They often host sales, and you have wider control on book pricing than you will find anywhere else. They do take a cut, so be sure to read the fine print and make sure you're ok with the terms of using them as a means to broadcast the digital version of your books.

OFF-SET PRINTING

Bigger publishers and those with access, contracts, or funding tend to favor off-set printing. These printers and presses can produce books with a broader spectrum of materials and options. Some of the options only found here is Smyth-sewn bound hardcovers, board books, higher paperweights and brightness, slipcovers for books and book sets, leather options, faux leather, embossing, gold-leaf elements, and lower overall production cost. However, the amount needed upfront to bulk print, or do a limited-print run, can be costly. After that, a means for warehousing and shipping the books will need to be arranged or established. There are places that provide this type of distribution, but it's not uncommon for small publishers to handle this in-house. Certain retailers, such as Amazon, have a warehouse and shipped based foundation, and there are ways to provide product to them to house and sell on their sites in the manner. It's completely up to you to provide product placement with retailers at this point or use a distributor with established contracts to act on your behalf to do so. Many offset print houses with the best pricing are located out of the Asian markets, including China, India, and Korea. That doesn't mean printers out of the United States, Canada, and United Kingdom that can't provide similar services with competitive pricing. A lot of these printers provide other products and packaging, such as Tarot cards and specialty products. Always research and review their previously produced products as a point of reference.

WHAT OTHER OPTIONS DO I HAVE?

You have gotten this far and might be feeling overwhelmed looking at the software and aggregators thinking, "What other options are out there?" And you're right! There are other options out there that you might have tried for or can't decide on. Even if you choose one of these paths, remember this book is meant not only to guide someone aiming to make their book themselves, but to also help the communicate with someone else that might be making the book for you. So, who would that be?

TRADITIONAL PUBLISHERS

Querying a publisher is one way to get a book out there. You might have already tried this option or previously decided not to go down this path. With this option, you don't get much of a say-so in the final results, but if you need to point out issues, this book should provide the vocabulary you need to get those corrections and adjustments done more accurately.

AUTHOR SERVICES & VANITY PRESSES

These are publishers you pay to make and publish your book. Traditional track or vanity presses not only need payment for the services to make your manuscript into a book, but you have to buy a certain number of copies before they will go any further. On the other end of this type is author services or digital printing services. Many aggregators also straddle this realm with package pricing for different facets of making a book with cover design, typeset or formatting, uploading fees, and even annual renewal costs to keep the book published.

Depending on the company and process, you might have a lot of input on the design and focus while others may be no different from a regular publisher and you don't have any input on the final result. I always advise caution when choosing a publisher in this realm since they aren't as accommodating as an aggregator or other options. There are far more predatory companies in this scope than any other part of the industry. Consumer beware!

SUBCONTRACTORS OR FREELANCERS

If typesetting your own book is overwhelming or too hard of a learning curve to meet the deadline you have set, then consider finding a professional formatter, typesetter, and/or graphic designer. Much like any other field, I recommend exploring their credentials as well as scope out their previous work. Consider your book a house being built, and you just put on your general contractor's hat. You will coordinate with all the other hats or roles from there, including editorial, cover design, typesetting, illustrator, marketer, and more.

This too can be an overwhelming undertaking and using this book to help create a more concrete communication between you and typesetter can make a world of difference in the final outcome. Make sure the professional you choose can show similar genre work and styles for what you are hoping to have within the pages of your book. Have they designed a picture book before? Do they know how to create and adjust an eBook? Are they familiar with upload file requirements and how to troubleshoot them? How much do they charge for revisions or corrections?

Asking questions and choosing someone who can double as a guide into the next stages can help tremendously for first time self-publishers. It is perfectly ok and even recommended to schedule a meeting and review what it is you are hoping the end result to look like as well as what they need from you to make that happen. Be sure to know to who and where you will be uploading your book, so you can get the files in the correct size and format from the start. Better yet, if you are making a picture book, be sure to have a three-way meeting to make sure everyone involved can communicate needs and address concerns, and you can make decisions sooner and not find yourself in a standstill and paying extra for changes that could have been avoided.

You can find freelancers and subcontractors in a variety of places. Some professionals have websites that list their services and you can reach out via email or contact forms. Others use websites like Fiverr and Upwork too.

Before You Start Prepping the Manuscript

*Don't tell me the moon is shining;
show me the glint of light on broken glass.*

Anton Chekhov

Introduction

Before we dive straight into formatting all the different books, there is one last topic to discuss that overlaps and has a huge influence on how easy or difficult typesetting can become: *the manuscript.* I can't express the importance of having an editor go through the manuscript, and in most cases, they will alert you of major formatting issues from time to time. Regardless, failing to make sure you have a polished, complete and ready to publish manuscript can increase the number of mistakes that can unfold. Don't forget that how your book looks written in "letter" size with "1-inch margins" is going to drastically shift depending on the trim size and options you create the final version for.

If your book needs content to land on a fresh page, do so by adding a page break or chapter title to signal to the typesetter. This also ensures it doesn't get lost when imported into the content or if changes move text that holds that break in place. In most cases, I always recommend, if editing a book after it's been formatted, to simply fix the manuscript and have it retyped or typeset again. Asking a formatter to make a list of changes leaves too much margin for mistakes or miscommunication of what needs to happen with your book. Always be mindful, a typesetter or formatter isn't actively reading your book and material. That's left for you, an editor, a proofreader, or a reader to do. We simply organize and layout the content on a visual level for ease of reading to support the content.

That doesn't mean we don't do our best to compliment the topic and essence of the book. It's perfectly ok to give the typesetter the book blurb, comparable titles and designs you like, genre or target audience, and other information for best results. Many typesetters when first learning to master this art will try to mimic a book style and keep repeating that same book to build familiarity with the software and how to best, and most efficiently, create a style. Time and time again, you will see we do our best to prepare you for typesetting or having a discussion with a typesetter in hopes of making the overall learned curve more of hill than a mountainous task. Let's start with some ways to prepare your manuscript to aid in the process!

What is Formatting?

Formatting is the art of organizing and arranging content (text, images, tables, and layout) on a page or pages that best suits the reader and median's needs. When it comes to typesetting or formatting books, it is important to be aware that this needs to be pleasing to the eye yet legible. It should always be consistent in styling, it should be clean and compliment the paper or digital median it is being read on. This

and

may already have your head spinning, but it is important that you are aware of what formatting involves. Font choices, spacing, returns, page or section breaks, alignment, logos or branding, headers, footers, page numbers, artwork, illustrations, and more are just some of the elements that make up formatting. These elements also need your attention when formatting. The first step is sending a manuscript that best supports the process and conveys information.

THE MANUSCRIPT

W hether you are traditionally or self-publishing, or somewhere in-between, the manuscript is expected to be formatted in a very particular way across the board. Always follow the guidelines the typesetter gives you if you are working with someone, but below are some things to take into consideration before submitting or moving to the next step of creating your book. Why? It's a means to make the file as clean as possible so that the editor, typesetter, and anyone else who is reviewing or using your file can do their job efficiently with little to no mistakes. If done properly, it can import into any software and snap in place how you intended or at the very least, take the guess work out for the book designers. Literary agents, publishers, editors, typesetters, and even author services will have similar, if not identical, parameters but may not go into the detail as to *who, what, when, where, or why*. Let's discuss some of those in greater detail!

FILE TYPES

The most common submission file types are DOC, DOCX, and RTF. When you save a file in Microsoft Word, older versions have DOC, and the up-to-date variant is DOCX. Word document file type is the most requested and imports beautifully as long as the author did not use custom macros or citations made from third-party plugins. I've processed a lot of manuscripts in my career from a variety of authors, and I have come across this on rare occasion, which has made it impossible to import and typeset the file in InDesign. Using the in-built Reference tools, such as Insert Endnotes/Footnotes, they carry over into the layout software as long as no additional programming is applied. The reason behind this is Microsoft Word uses XML coding to assign styles and information, which is also used in software and eBooks to maintain the look of your content.

Another common and more accessible file type is RTF or Rich Text Format. EVERY software old and new has the ability to SAVE AS for this format. (Even Windows 95 software has this! It's a staple file format and timeless.) Some typesetters prefer first saving all manuscripts in this format and import the RTF versions into a layout software such as InDesign and QuarkXpress. As software evolves, the aspects between Word Processors (Word, Scrivener, etc.) and Layout Software (InDesign, QuarkXpress) grow more sufficient for both the author and typesetter's needs. If you are experiencing issues, I highly recommend using this simple solution to see if your problems clear out. Another trick formatters will do is convert a DOC to a DOCX since the more up-to-date the file type is, the more support it has in current software to address issues or prevent problems and distortions. Also, stripping formatting completely in a document can serve as a last-ditch effort to clear out buggy XML coding.

With the rise of browser programs, access to programs for writing has increased. Know that all of these programs have a Download As or Save As option and allow you to save in the RTF or DOCX (Word) format. Be warned, saving in TXT or text format will result in losing all your bold, italics, and similar character styling. Google Docs even allows you to Download As a Word Document and can serve as a great alternative on a budget.

As for saving in Acrobat PDF format, it's not recommended until you are ready to send the final product to vendors and readers. Unless it's the images for your book, this format prevents a formatter from being able to typeset your manuscript and does not translate into reflowable EPUB format (reflowable refers to the eBooks ability to be adjusted on the device and "reflow" or rearrange according to the users setting for font, size, spacing, and more). Yes, Acrobat does have a means of converting a PDF into a DOC, but be warned this isn't a perfect conversion. Often this drops headers, footers, and page numbers into the content that needs to be removed. It also has a tendency of adding rogue hard returns in midsentence wherever a drop cap or page change occur. If you have no other means of recovering your manuscript and use this method, make sure you thoroughly edit and fix your manuscript before moving onto formatting. Be sure to show hidden paragraph marks to see where issues are as well as thoroughly edit the work. If it converted from a flat image to DOC, it's not uncommon for words and numbers to be used interchangeably such as "15" where "is" should be. Using advance feature in Find/Replace in Word can help untangle things faster, but always thoroughly edit and review a document created with this feature.

Page Size aka Trim Size

Page size default for most manuscript is letter sized or 8.5 by 11 or A4 depending on what you are using to write your work with. The book's trim size is often smaller, which means the way your pages look in your manuscript will be changing. A manuscript is often in portrait orientation, but you may be designing a picture book or non-fiction piece that's intended for landscape. The average book trim size is 6 in by 9 in or smaller for memoirs and fiction, 7 x 10 and large for textbook or workbooks, and landscape 11 x 8.5 or square trim for children's books. If you wish to layout the pages in a certain way, I highly recommend changing your manuscript's page size to the desired trim size and mimic the same margins as needed for final print version (but please remember that Word does not lay text and flow it from page-to-page the same way InDesign and other software might have). I see this issue mainly with poetry, devotionals, and certain textbooks and workbooks, where space and placement and readers' needs weren't accounted for and often require a hands-on meetings with the author to move forward with designing live or with them over my shoulder.

CMS, APA, MLA - Formatting Styles

CMS, or Chicago Manual Style, is the basis for a majority of the books in the publishing industry in terms of formatting guidelines. As you venture into non-fiction, certain academic or non-fiction publishers may prefer APA (American Psychological Association) or MLA (Modern Language Association) based on the schools and industries they are adjacent to or partnered with. For the most part, the basics of the manuscript are the same until you start doing more advance formatting for citations, footnotes, in-depth bullets, or number listings, and so forth. Opening pages or cover pages, as well as header and footer expectations, vary and may even be requested different from the recommendations these styles offer. I highly recommend searching or grabbing reference books to aid in this. A complete guide to CMS can be costly, but books on covering format at a glance can be vital savers for all these styles. See books like Simon and Schuster's *Handbook for Writers* as well as Prentice Hall's *Handbook for Writers.* Even older editions are useful for a majority of an author's woes and needs on formatting, or consult a teacher or editor for guidance. These books cover style, grammar, and a range of how-to's in writing.

PARAGRAPH JUSTIFICATION

It's best to use justified aligned left when writing the textual content or normal body text. I know that may sound like some mysterious unicorn, doesn't it? Alignment and justifications all refer to how the page is handling the distribution of your paragraph and words. Page justification is how you want the text box or frame to handle the content. Align to top is normal default in word processors, but in a book layout with pages full of text you may want to consider justified page settings to lay lines out evenly while a copyright page may align to bottom. As for paragraph justification, you want justified alignment in your final format and is often the default choice for book designers, so you have straight clean edges on the right and left of the frame or columns. The ragged lines created for a left aligned body text is expected in a manuscript, but you want to make sure everything looks clean. This doesn't mean you can't center align or right align content intended to fall differently on the page. Other times you may want to simply add or change indentations, more about this use in moment. Below is a snapshot of what the standard alignment choices are.

ALIGN RIGHT

Ut venis quae. Andisti orumquae con explitias neseque dusdand erferum exersperferi blab in remporisqui omnihiciis peribust elloribus, undis est, sollab ipsa aut volesto taeribeaquis aut as volorepe mos molum volorem qui ditisquia corro cuscid maionse molor remporesto occum ditem dollorem ut et hillecto inis nos ulpa doloreium dolorita consecab inveles is autet la quia verumquia verum fugit idicipit laborate vellaceatet vel in reptat.

Que cuscia coreptaspis at volor mint maiosto officid uciendae consequate rem quistibus.. dollorem ut et hillecto inis nos ulpa doloreium dolorita consecab inveles is autet la quia verumquia verum fugit idicipit laborate vellaceatet vel in reptat.

ALIGN JUSTIFY

Ut venis quae. Andisti orumquae con explitias neseque dusdand erferum exersperferi blab in remporisqui omnihiciis peribust elloribus, undis est, sollab ipsa aut volesto taeribeaquis aut as volorepe mos molum volorem qui ditisquia corro cuscid maionse molor remporesto occum ditem dollorem ut et hillecto inis nos ulpa doloreium dolorita consecab inveles is autet la quia verumquia verum fugit idicipit laborate vellaceatet vel in reptat.

Que cuscia coreptaspis at volor mint maiosto officid uciendae consequate rem quistibus.. dollorem ut et hillecto inis nos ulpa doloreium dolorita consecab inveles is autet la quia verumit idicil in reptat.

ALIGN LEFT

Ut venis quae. Andisti orumquae con explitias neseque dusdand erferum exersperferi blab in remporisqui omnihiciis peribust elloribus, undis est, sollab ipsa aut volesto taeribeaquis aut as volorepe mos molum volorem qui ditisquia corro cuscid maionse molor remporesto occum ditem dollorem ut et hillecto inis nos ulpa doloreium dolorita consecab inveles is autet la quia verumquia verum fugit idicipit laborate vellaceatet vel in reptat.

Que cuscia coreptaspis at volor mint maiosto officid uciendae consequate rem quistibus.. dollorem ut et hillecto inis nos ulpa doloreium dolorita consecab inveles is autet la quia verumquia verum fugit idicipit laborate vellaceatet vel in reptat.

ALIGN JUSTIFY LEFT (RECOMMENDED)

Ut venis quae. Andisti orumquae con explitias neseque dusdand erferum exersperferi blab in remporisqui omnihiciis peribust elloribus, undis est, sollab ipsa aut volesto taeribeaquis aut as volorepe mos molum volorem qui ditisquia corro cuscid maionse molor remporesto occum ditem dollorem ut et hillecto inis nos ulpa doloreium dolorita consecab inveles is autet la quia verumquia verum fugit idicipit laborate vellaceatet vel in reptat.

Que cuscia coreptaspis at volor mint maiosto officid uciendae consequate rem quistibus.. dollorem ut et hillecto inis nos ulpa doloreium dolorita consecab inveles is autet la quia verumit idicil in reptat.

LEADING OR LINE SPACING

Manuscripts are often requested to be in double space or 2.0-line spacing. This doesn't mean your book should be this way! This is mainly for editing and fast reading on the editor, agent, or publisher's end and never intended for the final product or typeset. Know that your final book's line spacing is most like going to fall closer to single spacing, but no more than 1.25-line spacing to use the space more efficiently and increase ease of reading for readers who aren't planning to edit or leave comments. Page count is impacted a lot by this, and that can save on printing costs. Also, the font chosen sometimes has more or less space above or below the lettering that may aid in this area. For example, Calibri often can fall back to single spacing since it has great gapping naturally whereas Garamond will need 1.15 to 1.25 for a cleaner line spacing.

MARGINS, INDENTS, & PARAGRAPH SPACING

Often these terms are used interchangeable when they mean very different things to a typesetter! Much of the confusion between author and formatter happen where one of these terms is added to the instructions, and it's vital both sides are aware of what these refer to in terms of formatting on a page. This is where you are adjusting for the appropriate blank space or white space in the over layout and design, and often it can be miscommunicated from both sides. When all else fails, printing a page and marking it up with arrows and direction is one way to make sure it's understood. Regarding your manuscript, it will change a lot based on the design of the book, but most documents are set to have a 0.5" to 1" margin all around with no indent or only the first line indented with no paragraph spacing. Let's dive into each of these and what they look like and are intended to communicate in reference to formatting.

MARGINS

Margins refer to the spacing between the content and the paper's edge. Beyond the edge and outward is referred to as the bleed over—what is overprinted for the trimming process. From this edge to the text is the margin, and those fall from the top, bottom, inner, and outer margins. Inner margins can fluctuate according to the number of pages the book will have. The higher the page count the larger this margin will need to be in order to keep content from *falling into the crack or spine* of the book. As for the top and bottom margins, these tend to need to accommodate the space a footer and header may need before the body text or core content. As for outer margin, this is often where a reader's thumb will be to hold open a page and should fall between 0.5" to 0.7" to achieve this.

If images are meant to bleed off or to the page edge, they should do so here. The trim edge can shift depending on the printer, machine, and other unforeseeable factors. Many Print-on-Demand printers and vendors will not accept files and proofs that have any textual content in a 0.5" margin from the page edge and often need a 0.125" bleed edge.

INDENTS

As for indents, these impact first line, last line, or an entire paragraph on pushing the textual content further left and/or right making it narrow or offset. You commonly see this being used for tiered bulleted lists or quoted material between two paragraphs. Sometimes we are taught to "tab the first line" when we should be adding a first line indent of 0.25" to 0.5" to keep paragraph formatting consistent. Tabs should be reserved for table making or programming and you can reference that section further in this chapter. A common style for an indented paragraph often has a left and right indent of 0.5" to express quoted material or excerpt of significance.

Paragraph Spacing

Paragraph spacing refers to the gap created after or before a paragraph. This is done for various reasons, but mainly seen being applied for stylistic appeal and to signal a change of topics in nonfiction or a passing of time and swapping of character point-of-view in fiction work. Sometimes authors prefer to have paragraph with no first line indents, in which case a typesetter should add a space after paragraph, so readers know where one ends, and the next paragraph begins.

Choosing Font

For the manuscript, I recommend keeping it all the same font face. It's best to use a cornerstone font that handles even foreign characters and is highly compatible with a wide range of software and devices such as Times New Roman, Arial, Calibri, Helvetica, or Garamond. In order to yield the best results from a typesetter or book formatter, focus on character styles (bold, italics, underline, etc.), font size (i.e. larger for chapters, section headings, and subheads), and using Word or GDOC styles to save time. I do not recommend adding a DropCap or mimicking a manually made DropCap since this often creates unforeseen issues. Simply inform the typesetter or aim to add this visual option for the final version.

Personal Use, Free for Commercial Use, and Others

There is a huge difference in personal use and free for commercial use fonts. We are fortunate enough to be in an age where access to artful fonts is just a click away, but for publishing and selling products with font aspects, you have to make sure you are using one with the rights for that purpose. Do not use personal use fonts unless you have bought the commercial use rights. Free for commercial use or public domain fonts are safe to utilize. As far as freeware and shareware, you may want to read their fine print to understand what limitations they have or what to add to your copyright page.

Font Face and Size

Most agents, publishers, and editors request your manuscript to be in Times, Times New Roman, Arial, or even Helvetica font faces. These are accessible on every system and are easy on the eyes. This is usually 12-point font size teamed with double line spacing. If you have designed your book to have a variety of fonts, you should be aware of a few complications regarding this. First, unless the person has that particular font on their computer too, the software will default to replace the font with something "similar" or Times New Roman. You would have to also supply a PDF version of the book to showcase the font choices and provide a list of fonts used. Second, the more fonts you have, the bigger your eBook file becomes. It can also cause your content to be difficult to read smoothly, even creating headaches or blurry eyes. Most eBook devices can't read beyond a small list of fonts or will not unpack embedded fonts in a EPUB file. In short, don't be shocked when a formatter or even editor takes away your font choices. Stay away from hard to read fonts for your body text such as Courier, Curlz, Comic Sans, and similar artsy fonts. These are reserved for chapter headers, titles, headlines, and subheads. The only scenario where it's encouraged to do multiple font faces is with picture books and children's book where they are trying to visually express important words or hint their meanings. If you want your book to be considered for large-tint qualification and placement in the library, start with 16-point font for your body text. This chart should help give a snapshot of how these sizes look

This is what to expect for something at 10-point font. It's made for contracts and tables.

This is what to expect for something at 11-point font. It's made for contracts, tables, and high word count novels like epic fantasy and science fiction.

This is what to expect for something at 12-point font. Super common! Most often the default for many programs and body text options.

This is what to expect for something at 14-point font. It's common as a larger option for smaller word count books or chapter books for kids.

This is what to expect for something at 16-point font. Books at this size fall into the easy reader or large print category in the library.

This is what to expect for something at 18-point font. Often reserved for chapter headers, headlines, and subheads.

This is what to expect for something at 20-point font. Picture books start to use this size or larger.

This is what to expect for something at 22-point font. A common size in picture books.

This is what to expect for something at 24-point font. A great size for younger readers or first-words books.

This is what to expect for something at 26-point font. A great size for younger readers or first-words books.

SERIF VERSUS SANS-SERIF

Serif fonts are often older font styles and more common such as Times, Garamond, Georgia, and Caslon. These fonts often feature foots, or serifs, at the end of the lines or off of certain connections. Naturally, a sans-serif font wouldn't have this feature as seen in Helvetica, Arial, Gills sans, and Calibri. Often textbooks, small font sized documents, and fiction works feature a serif font. On the other hand, children's books, self-help, digital-only, and science-fiction books are more likely to be designed with a sans-serif font or at least chapter headers, headlines, and subheads in this style. It's important to be mindful when and how you are blending and how you are doing so. It's not uncommon to have all the body text elements one style and all the chapter headers, headlines, and subheads another way.

SERIF FONTS
Times
Garamond
Caslon

SANS-SERIF FONTS
Alegreya Sans
Calibri
Arial

TEXT BOXES

Please try to avoid using textboxes inside a manuscript meant to be formatted. It's more practical to label or leave instructions for the typesetter to put something into a textbox or pull a quote of sorts. You can highlight these spots in various colors or add bracketed notes. Even then, an indented paragraph style can also help break content apart and later be formatted to have border or special style applied that would translate better for print and digital formats. Just make sure the notes or manner in which you do this stays consistent, so they are easier to search or see for whoever might be trying to format your book. Text boxes can cause random paragraphs to disappear on import or stop the import midway through the process altogether. Until software updates address the buggy variety of complications that unfold with this feature, it's best to remove them and leave notes or format in a way that mimics a custom citation or quote.

TABLES

If the manuscript has tables, you have to decide how you want to tackle this. In the formatting stage, you can place them in line with the text or import them and place them like an image. My recommendation is base it off how the table was made and how complex it is. Often tables made in the manuscript are for 8.5 in x 11 paper and don't account for actual book trim size and margins. This complicates how they translate into the design. In a scenario like this, consider rebuilding it in the layout software and be ready to break it over multiple pages or create a two-page spread style table. Remember this is one of the few areas that smaller font sizes are acceptable, but try not to push any lower than 9-point font unless desperate. By 7-point font, the text may be illegible to majority of readers! Sometimes the tables provided or used are simply an image of one or created in another software and saved as an image file. In a case like this, you should treat it no differently than an image and place it accordingly. Note that Word tables often import into InDesign rather well and just need some reformatting, but it can save some steps in the process of making the table fit and look clean for the trim size. As a side note, be aware there is a maximum word or character count per table box and maximum rows and columns an eBook can read!

COLUMN 1	COLUMN 2

PUBLIC DOMAIN AND COPYRIGHT NEEDS

Let's take a moment to talk about this. Don't be shocked if I bring this up in a few places, but it's one of the things that some writers may not realize has a lot of parameters. Public domain is dependent on author's death date or publication dates. In order to know which an image or piece of writing falls under, you'll have to review your country's copyright parameters and rules. Most countries require the piece to be over 100 years past one or the other of these dates. In the US, it is only 70 years. This doesn't mean someone hasn't come through and renewed rights or bought the rights for the image or work, so you will be doing some research in some cases.

Majority of classic literature and religious books do fall in public domain. When creating works using images and artwork falling under public domain, you need to be aware of requirements that may prevent you from being able to file for a copyright on a book you designed. If you are simply remaking a public domain piece with some minor updates, you can't file a copyright on it. You need 20% original content added to the piece to file for a copyright and own it. Same goes for devotionals or pieces that are taking citations from multiple resources. You need 20% original written content, or you simply can't copyright it.

IMAGES

If the manuscript has images throughout it, you may want to create a text only version of your manuscript for importing reasons or even for your editor. These images can import janky and many word processors lower the DPI on an image. For example, depending on the version and type of computer you have, Microsoft Word defaults to saving images as 120 or 220 DPI. There are ways to change this setting to 300 or high fidelity but remember that the content is being autoflowed into the layout software and placement will need to change accordingly. A majority of books have a trim size far below letter-sized paper, the default size, for most word processors. It also speeds up importing and prevents any broken XML coding that may be created unintentionally. If you do need to make a text only format, it's perfectly fine to leave image placement notes, but be consistent with how it's done and add any needed notes if you wish. I recommend putting them into brackets or adding a keyword that can be searched, so you can find these areas easily.

EXAMPLES

[Image04 – Align left within text]

{Image90}

(Figure 2.6 – This is a diagram of your brain on scrambled eggs. *Place this here between the two paragraphs.*)

HYPERLINKS & URLS

Be careful with these. With the changes in eBook formatting, certain URLs or broken links can prevent your book from being able to go live online with digital vendors including Amazon, Apple, and Barnes & Noble. Stay away from links that are no longer functional or at the very least deactivate these. Don't use links to website searches or searches in general. These will not show the same results on other computers and often are flagged and cause the eBook to be blocked. The same goes for social media posts that may be inactive or set to a privacy level that blocks the content for anyone not directly connected. You can, however, share links to Facebook pages (not posts and private profiles), public profiles, and similar landing pages. Links to exact news articles or blog post are also still viable along with base URLs and official website links. Who you use to publish your eBook will decide if links to vendors and product pages are acceptable. For example, SmashWords forbids this, and they have to be removed.

FOOTNOTES AND ENDNOTES

Many word processors and layout software have footnote and endnote systems. It's best to utilize these in-built systems to avoid complications when importing a manuscript into a program. Custom macros and plugins don't have the means to communicate with the software conversion or import features and will often drop content, be left out, or even cause the layout software to crash.

Footnotes[1] is the best one to use for a few reasons. With eBook industry changes, there has been a huge wave preferring and requiring eBooks to use this method from vendors like Amazon and Apple. Interestingly enough, in print these will show up on the bottom of the page, but eBooks will push them to the end of the section or chapter.

As for endnotes, these are found in the back of the book. Software doesn't renumber these for each chapter or section, but footnotes will. There is a means to do this, though it may make it difficult to revisit the book to make large format or content changes. In the end, I always encourage my clients to consider footnotes since the eBook industry, as well as layout software abilities, favor them the most. Fortunately, most programs, Word and InDesign for sure, have a convert feature, so no major work has to be done to change from one type to the other.

MACROS & PLUGINS

Word and other word processors use prebuilt macros to do certain tasks, and these rarely interfere with XML coding and importing within layout software. As you start to custom code or add-in new macros, the more coding they involve, the higher chances they will bug out and cause issues in the import process. Some issues aren't as clearly noticeable until you start formatting and realize random sections of work is missing or odd citations or characters were dumped in areas of the work. Third-party plugins that use JavaScript to make citations, indexing, and similar changes to the manuscript can also cause the system to break. A way to utilize these is to save two versions of your manuscript. One for formatting that doesn't have these applied and another where you use them to create other documents for index listing. Remember the page numbers for the content will shift as the final book never match the manuscript due to variety of variables as previously discussed.

---

[1] Hi, I'm a footnote! You will always find me in small font at the bottom of print books or end of chapters in an eBook.

Do's and Don'ts in Your Manuscript

When sending to an agent or publisher, they simply want the story which may involve prologue, chapters, and epilogue. As for prepping a manuscript for a formatter or to be formatted, you want to take the time to put as much in there in the order you want it to fall. Start with mimicking the anatomy as discussed in the *Anatomy of the Book* section. Give them the title page, the dedication, put a line in to "INSERT TOC HERE" for table of contents to be generated within the software. Remember that a typesetter will be following your lead and relies on your consistency in how you wrote and initially formatted your manuscript for clues as to how to organize the visual aspects of your text on the page. Inconsistency or breaking the normal expectations of when to apply certain spacing can drastically confuse and slow a typesetter down and you want to avoid this as best as you can!

Authors come from a variety of backgrounds and experience levels. Some are writing to leave their family a legacy book while others aim to compete within the market. A majority fall in the realm between. Not all of these authors have gone through editors and querying to traditional publisher loops. Regardless, please take care that you prep your manuscript in the above description to limit your frustrations whether you aim to format yourself or hire someone to format. Keep these do's and don'ts in mind:

Do this...

- Stay Consistent
- Limit the variety of fonts
- Hard returns for new paragraph (Enter)
- Manual line breaks to force to new line (Shift+Enter)
- Set your paragraph settings
- Create Styles and Assign
- Accept All Changes
- Stop Tracking Changes
- Delete Comments

Don't do this...

- Use tabs to Indent
- Hold Space or Tabs for new line
- Hard return for each line (Not a typewriter!)
- Add text boxes
- Custom Macros
- Third-party plugin
- Switch body text styling
- Manually leave editing marks
- Save in RTF, DOC, or DOCX format

DO'S AND DON'TS

EXAMPLES OF MANUSCRIPTS

Below is a list of different ways you may receive or set a manuscript up. The most common in the industry are the first two options: Textual Only and Text with Image Placement. From chapter books to textbooks, these are the typical format you will receive the textual content for typesetting. As you venture into workbooks, picture books, comic books, and graphic novels, you will want to use story bounce (an outline of key points), detailed format (a detailed outline), storyboarding (rough sketches with notes), or script (all text or final draft of a manuscript) styles to capture all the parts. Unlike text-based or heavy books, these require guidance and cues as to where images or text should be placed on a page to accurately tell the story intended. Each book type will lean more so on one kind of manuscript, and it's important to be aware of this as you prep your manuscript for typesetting. This can be a huge influence on how well key elements are designed, whether you intend to format your own book or hand your book to someone else.

TEXTUAL ONLY

This is the most common manuscript for mass market fiction work. No images are tied into it, and it's simply importing the manuscript into the software and applying the indicated styling where deemed appropriate. A typesetter's aim is to streamline the text to the best of their abilities as to not break a reader's immersion with weird visual discrepancies, such as a slight tweak in line spacing (common in manuscripts where portions where dictated via speech-to-text and other written on a computer). You have to remember that we've been reading books with the same patterns and margins for centuries and keeping those expectations, while being creative, can be a hardline to walk for anyone designing a book.

For a textual-based manuscript, follow the Do's and Don'ts to prevent any unseen issues in the content. As for trim and font choices, it will fall back to the audience, genre, and type of book you are working on. You should be able to copy-paste content into a clean Word document or use InDesign's "File > Place" feature to import text and its associated styles. In the case of the latter, be sure to run Scripts to lock in these styles and save time from having to do manual changes by using the PrepText and other tools often found in open source (websites, forums, and individuals who provide tools or resources they've created for free to others for use) or pre-programmed into InDesign for use. Most manuscripts imported this way come as double-spaced in Times or similar font at 12 pt. If the manuscript has a variety of font faces, I recommend streamlining it to a single font face to prevent issues when formatting the book. Also, be aware many of these come with double spacing, which is intended for editorial purposes. Never keep this line spacing!

Chapter 2: The Old Farmer

Deafened by my thoughts, I sat there on the wet boulder for hours. The ancient mountain

forest encased me, tall and dark, the embodiment of solitude. Flurries started to fall, and I lost sight

of the glow from the city braziers. I traveled far beyond the territory of *The House*, well into the

sacred grounds of the Old Farmer, a forbidden place. Rumors about the old man say he would kill

a daemon for trespassing. Much to my amusement, one record written in the royal ledger states he

is the only man to have ever faced Viceroy Falco and survive. In fact, they claim my father had

rewarded the man this property to persuade him to lay down his sword and leave the war.

nobility looking for an excuse to dress in lavish attire outside of the usual ball. The crowd coming through the door started to thin, and I rolled my shoulders, growing bored of the honeyed words each person offered John at the pulpit. In the past, it had been me shaking those same hands and receiving empty words of praise.

The banter came to a hair-raising silence as Viceroy Falco walked through the open doors. A woman shaking John's hand hurried away to sit, making the air grow cold around us. The sunlight pouring in did nothing to break the dark aura Falco carried into the church and down the aisle. Eyes avoided looking his way, afraid to draw his attention. He started with a wide grin, but with each step, each glance, his grin fell further into a scowl. We had managed to do more work, with more materials than he had given us money for, and he was losing his first round of the game he set in motion. John was beaming to see Falco falter.

[[IMAGE23.jpg: *Father John glares at Viceroy Falco.*]]

"I'm so happy to see you made it, Viceroy Falco." John bowed his head, his blue stare unafraid of the disdain dripping from Falco's glare. "Is King Traibon still attending?"

"Where did you find the extra coin for this?" Falco wasted no time as he waved an arm around the church. He was aiming to crucify John publicly in front of his potential flock. "This pattern is pricey, the new pews, the runners, all of this and the horse are more than what I gave you. Are you stealing from my people or swindling folks for charitable donations already, Father John?"

John stood tall, back straight with a sheepish expression. "My dear Viceroy, you must know

---

MY TITLE HERE BY AUTHOR NAME

INTERIOR OF INTERNET CAFE. JAMIE IS SITTING AT A TABLE WITH NOT COMPUTER, MINI-CAFETERIA AREA.

Beverly walks in and sits down. Jamie slides the hot tea he ordered for her closer to her.

            BEVERLY
      Why are we meeting here again?

            JAMIE
      Give me a minute.

Jamie's eyes start to glow steel green.

            BEVERLY
      (whispering) Are you kidding me?
      That's illegal to do-

He raises a hand to silence her, casually drinking his coffee. She puffs her cheeks in frustration.

            JAMIE
      What if I told you this is the second
      time I caught someone trying to hack
      YOUR system from here?

            BEVERLY
      Wh-what?

            JAMIE
      So, what is project *Greenbacks* anyhow?

            BEVERLY
      And here I thought this was going to
      be a legitimate date...

TEXT WITH IMAGE PLACEMENT

For this book type, this is going to be the more common type encountered with textbooks, workbooks, or image heavy content. Throughout the text, there should be indications for image placement and should be clearly marked, much like a subhead or citation. For visual aid, I always encourage highlighting these yellow and treat them as their own paragraph. It's also helpful to use a keyword like "IMAGE" and brackets to help make the image placement stand up, for example:

[[IMAGE01: This picture shows the difference between nightshade and chili pepper flowers]]

These one-liners should be placed between the paragraphs they should be near or on the same page as the text. The importance of this is so when creating an eBook, the typesetter can make sure it falls inline at the right point of the content. It can also make it easier to play with the page layout as they apply the design and text begins to autoflow from page to page with the changes.

SCRIPT

Script writing is nothing like any other manuscript format you will encounter. This is mostly for video adaptation, plays, animation, comics, and graphic novels. In terms of typesetting, the most common scenario of receiving a manuscript written in this style will be for comics and graphic novels. This should tell you where images fall, and the textual content expected. Unlike the narrative and transitional paragraphs seen in normal textual content, this simplifies and divides the content into key elements. Settings, characters, scenes, camera angles, and dialogue are all broken out to be loud on the pages with special caps and indentations.

Be sure to meet or design side-by-side with your artist, author, and typesetter. Communication and storyboards can help pull the script together best so that the pages and visuals are in the right order per the author's intended visions. You can find free software to aid in script writing such as *Celtx.com* or books that can aid such as *Save the Cat! The Last Book on Screenwriting You'll Ever Need* by Blake Snyder. For comic books and graphic novels in specific, I recommend *The Art of Comic Book Writing* by Mark Kneece and *The Complete Idiot's Guide to Creating a Graphic Novel* by Nat Gertler and Steve Lieber.

Story Bounce

This simply is stating what goes where in the manuscript as it bounces through the story beats or pages. Be mindful of how much textual content you are providing on pages and identify which image to be used concisely. For example, a manuscript using this format might appear like this:

I.   Title page (right)
II. Copyright (left) with Dedication
    A.   Image01 at the top, small
    B.   Dedicated to all the kids who seek an adventure of their own
    C.   Copyright 1999 Author J. Smith etc.
III. Page 1 (right) Image02
    A.   "Wow, the world sure is big when I'm all alone," marveled John.
IV. Page 2 & 3 (spread) Image03
    A.   John lost his dog when they moved. His mommy decided it was time little John Wick got a new puppy. Today, they would visit the animal shelter!
V.   Page 4 (left) Image04 & Image05
    A.   Image04: John couldn't believe the amount of doggies who needed homes.
    B.   Image05: Barking and bouncing, each one was excited to see him.
VI. Page 5 (right) Image06
    A.   They came in so many shapes, sizes, and colors. None of them reminded him of his old doggy Daisy.

Note how there is no mistake where in the book these images and their text go as you 'flip through' the book. It's important to leave nothing out while keeping your instructions consistent and cohesive with same naming methods and delivery. This gives the typesetter a little room for choosing where content falls and to adjust content if needed based on images and text needed on each spread. You can even leave it up to the typesetter to decide which keywords they emphasize or encourage them to do so.

Detailed Format

This is for authors who have something more specific in mind for placement, including giving instructions as to where the textual content falls and may give a variety of more in-depth directions. For comparison, this would be the above example with additional bullets where a greater level of instructions addresses text locations, specialty font changes, and even image placement for a variety of page layout styles. In this example, words in bold are assumed to need font or artistic touch to emphasize the word's meaning and provide visual clues for early readers.

- Font Face: Palatin Kids
- Size 24 where possible
- Emphasize highlighted words artfully
- Title page (right)
- Copyright (left) with Dedication
  - Image01 at the top, small
  - Text in larger font, italics:
    - Dedicated to all the kids who seek an adventure of their own
  - Copyright 1999 Author J. Smith etc.
- Page 1 (right) Image02
  - Text on the bottom of page
    - "Wow, the **world** sure is **big** when I'm all **alone**," marveled John.
- Page 2 & 3 (spread) Image03
  - Text on top left
    - John lost his dog when they moved. His mommy decided it was time little **John Wick got a new puppy**.
    - Text on bottom right
    - Today, they would visit the **animal shelter**!

- Page 4 (left) Image04 & Image05
  - Top left Image04: John couldn't believe the amount of **doggies** who needed **homes**.
  - Bottom right Image05: **Barking** and **bouncing**, each one was excited to see him.
- Page 5 (right) Image06
  - Text at top of page:
    - They came in so many **shapes, sizes**, and **colors**.
    - Text on bottom of page:
    - None of them reminded him of his old doggy **Daisy**.

STORYBOARDING

When it comes to picture books, I highly recommend this method or combining one of the above with this as a visual guide or blueprint. You can print, cut, and paste the elements to rough out the entire book's look and feel. This is a fantastic way to build a mockup of the book you intend to make and format for print and give concise expectations to a typesetter or experiment with what you had in mind for the final product. Before starting digitally, this allows you to troubleshoot issues that may need you to adjust text and illustrations prior to formatting the book. Most issues found this way are still relatively easy to fix by simply changing methods, book options, or changing fonts and images. Storyboarding can also be a great means to discover how many images you will need the illustrator to make as well as to where they need to be mindful of page edges and space for text to overlay. The following types of issues can be revealed at a glance by using this method:

- Illustrations not allowing enough space for text to overlay
- Images that have the characters too close to the edge and will be cut when stretched to the bleed edge and cross the trim
- Images that have text as part of the image in need of adjusting to fit trim
- Trim size and orientation versus illustration size and orientation
- Amount of text for the page (too much is the common issue)
- Number of illustrations needed
- Amount of pages the story needs
- Story page flip and how that impacts the reader and story

CREATING A STORYBOARD

One of the best ways to help you plan out your picture book is to outline it in the form of a storyboard as seen in comics and animated films. Print images and clip out text and move things around, or take a sketchbook out and doodle a rough version. Stick figures and shapes work are just fine! You will need to account for the layout and limitations of the printed version from the beginning, even if you are still revising the text. Everything in a picture book impacts how the final look of a page turns out, for better or worse.

GET CRAFTY!

Sometimes it helps to roll up your sleeves and do more than write it or click and drag on the computer. One of my favorite things to see is where a picture-book author has printed, cut, and pasted content in a mock-up book. Something about this can be eye-opening to an author, and content awareness and available space become alarmingly tangible. I recommend using a manila folder and cardstock pages to piece this impromptu scrapbook together. Whether you have a portrait or landscape layout, you should be able to mimic the look enough to be able to understand how images, trim size, margins, and text interact within the design. Using a square trim size? No biggie! Just cut the folder down to size!

Others simple staple pages together and cut and paste printed elements onto the page. This can serve as an excellent guide as you format the book or for your typesetter to rely on. Being able to see the real-world demo of the end-product may simply be stick fingers and glue stick cut outs, but it provides a kinetic means of design that you only see in workbooks. Well, if crafts aren't your thing, here's some worksheets to aid you in designing your storyboard for your book! Don't think this is only good for children's books. This can make a world of difference in creating and formatting comics, graphic novels, workbooks, and image layouts in textbooks.

STORYBOARD

PICTURE [_____]

ACTION [_____]

_____
_____
_____
_____
_____
_____
_____

PICTURE [_____]

ACTION [_____]

_____
_____
_____
_____
_____
_____
_____
_____

PICTURE [_____]

ACTION [_____]

_____
_____
_____
_____
_____
_____
_____

PICTURE [_____]

ACTION [_____]

_____
_____
_____
_____
_____
_____
_____
_____

STORYBOARD – PORTRAIT

PROJECT TITLE: _____ GENRE: _____

STORYBOARD - LANDSCAPE

STORYBOARD - SQUARE

COMIC STORYBOARD

COMIC STORYBOARD

ILLUSTRATIONS, ILLUSTRATORS, & GRAPHIC DESIGNERS

If you know your trim size and orientation, then you're now ready to decide on how you want to create your illustrations. Some authors illustrate their books themselves, but that's not an option for others. You have a few options in this matter, and it's highly dependent on the type of book you're making such as a picture book, middle grade book, or textbook. If you are planning to hire someone to help you create and format your book, consider seeking out a graphic designer or illustrator who is knowledgeable in typesetting or at least picture book layouts. They will be able to incorporate and go through more steps with you as your guide. If you do this yourself, be sure to take your time to read the content in the Picture Book section for information specifically for making one and how to best prepare before starting.

Every book type has its own tweaks to the system or may have areas that are a must for one and not the others. If you intend to gather illustrations to give to a typesetter or format yourself, seek out an illustrator who draws in a style you enjoy and within the price range you need. They will not only need to be aware of the trim size and orientation for a picture book, but they need to include room for a 0.25" to 0.5" cutaway bleed so your core image doesn't get chopped when printed. For illustrations added to a section of a single page, you just simply need an image slightly bigger than intended use for best quality when it prints.

If your illustrator is using a physical median (watercolor, markers, acrylics, etc.) over digital painting, make sure you pass on information for file type, resolution (DPI), color mode, and so on. The more information you provide, the easier it is for them to give you the correct variant of scans. If they aren't able to provide you with scans, I recommend hiring an art photographer. If your median is light colored or watercolors, you should consider digitally enhancing the coloration, performing a black/white balance, and checking the levels of said image. In the end, do not expect those colors to match or look the same as the original as there is a loss of detail, texture, and shift in colors that is impossible to recreate by the time it prints in the book.

No matter the book, there is a standard need for file type and settings here when you aim to use images in your book.

- These files should be in CMYK color mode
- Saved at 300-600 DPI (resolution)
- Be in these file types: JPEG, PNG, or TIFF

You can also utilize PDF and export out to image or place as PDF but be mindful most software will be converting all these into a more manageable JPEG format. Sticking with JPEG and saving editable originals can be very effective in keeping overall file size for the PDF and eBook formats down to acceptable levels. This often comes into play with vendors with files size maximums, such as Barnes & Noble requiring eBooks to be 20 MB or below.

What if you can't find an illustrator or have funding restrictions? There's another possibility! Prepare to go on a deep search and rethink your initial book design. Stock photo sites are a wonderful resource for those who can't afford the illustrators or struggling to find one. This includes ShutterStock, DepositPhoto, iStockPhoto, Adobe Stock, and many more sites have a variety of artists who submit sheets and multiple images of characters for all audiences. A fitting example of this is the character you see throughout Writer's Bane! The more active an artist is on these sites, the better chance for the collection to grow and pull from. Some give you a means to reach out to them as well! You can always reach out to them and see if they will also commission pieces.

Basics of Digitally Enhancing Illustrations

Thanks to the digital age, many artists or illustrators have taken to producing art via software. This has made it a better means to reproduce images in a higher brilliance and sharper hues. That doesn't mean hand drawn artwork and watercolors can't join this high-tech advantage. Traditional art can be scanned or photographed to be pulled into the digital realm and in some cases, adjusted. This doesn't come without its share of pros and cons. One being the most common is the lack of capturing texture, hues, or even soft pencil strokes that all-too-often get washed out by the scanner or camera's light. If your art is too big to scan, an art photographer should be able to use a black/white balance card and even adjust and check it.

Once an image has been placed in digitally, you or a design have the freedom to adjust the image as needed. This can be moving elements, changing hues, brightening the overall saturation, and even resetting black and white tones to make richer levels so the image prints sharper. If you can apply a lot of these easy tricks to an image and balance the CMYK spectrum to a richer level, it will make a huge difference when printed. Not every image or color will be able to translate well; for example, blues and purples are often a struggle to lock in without shifting when ink is laid to paper.

Warning About Watercolors

Out of all the medians your illustrations can be made from, this one comes with a loss of detail and color just from scanning or photographing it. From there, it sways again depending on the options you choose. If you are ok with digitizing and drastically shifting your watercolors for print and not looking to match the original artwork, you will feel this impact the least. As for those looking to match it and capture the watercolor pieces as they are, you won't get this result. First, the act of scanning or taking a photo removes the texturing that watercolors often have, as well removing some of the sharpness and overlapping details. From there, I recommend offset printing with gloss or semi-gloss paper at about 100+lb. paper with alcohol-based printing for closest match to original work. If you decide to move forward with Print-on-Demand, be warned that you will continue to lose vibrancy and details due to the fact only matte paper is available and most are water-based ink printing and may cause saturation issues. This becomes most noticeable with a picture-book printer in Print-on-Demand.

Black and White Balance

If you are using Photoshop, Fire Alpaca, or some other photo editing software, you should be able to do this. Many of the photography editing software may be able to assist with this technique as well as the others to follow. Whichever software you use, there should be tutorials out there to assist you best as far as this book goes, the aim is to explain what it's meant to do and hint as to why you might want to apply this to your own formatting and images. As for this one, it helps establish true black and true white on the image and adjusts the image color range accordingly. Often when we scan an image, the black has a shine to it and might come off as a dark gray or even brown. This gives you a chance to "reset" the expectations and identify where these are on the image if you have both visible.

Levels in Spectrum

Images come with levels that spread a variety of hues and channels. Often black and white being on opposite ends, they come with slight dips beyond the peak of these colors that can take away from the overall sharpness of the image spectrum. Cutting out or knocking them to the peaks or using auto levels features can bring an image to pop more visually.

Hue & Saturation

Hue and saturations levels or using filters that shift these can do a wide range for an image. If the colors seem to have washed out, you might be able to recover faded colors using this feature. Also scanned or photographed images may have washed out and either you can darken the hue values or even adjust contrast and brightness settings to recover the look of the original artwork. Sometimes this setting allows

a moment for you to change the hue or coloration of the art and make decisions you normally would have missed out on. Using a masked layer stacked with this can even allow you to change a color on a single item in the image, but that's best for a tutorial as it delves into photo editing and is beyond this book's conversation focused on typesetting.

DPI, Image Size, and Resolution Adjustments

The resolution of an image is very important! The first aspect to this is the size. You don't need your image to be 44 inches by 21 inches if your book is only 11 inches by 8.5 inches. If you are bleeding images off the edge, the image needs to only be 11.25 inches by 8.75 inches at the very least to give some room for image placement that allows bleed and trim. It's always smart to have the image slightly bigger, but too large and it may cause the program or computer to crash (especially those on personal or home systems). It also makes saving backups or throwing it on a cloud storage much more feasible.

Once the size is within a reasonable range (exact with bleed or slightly larger in the same orientation or ratio), you need to make sure the resolution is set between 300-600 DPI. Anything under 300 is at risk to pixelate or be blurry. Know that most images saved from internet are usually only 72-96 DPI, so make sure what you are saving is the full image and not a smaller web version or down-sampled variant. Images that are over 600 DPI are at risk of the printer shrinking and may result in unwanted quality or results. It's always best to avoid these sorts of situations and keep the control and final product in your hands.

CMYK versus RGB

Print and physical books are printed using CMYK colorations. This uses a set amount of cyan, magenta, yellow, and black layered on the page. Depending on the printer this can be applied with alcohol or water-based inks and vary in brightness (often influenced by the paper chosen). Water based inks are limited to 240% CMYK saturation level with paperweights at 70lbs or less as seen in Print-on-Demand applications.

Image Naming

Be sure to be consistent or concise with how you are naming your images. You can do this in a number of ways which includes consecutively (image01, image20, image03…), by location (Chapter01, Chapter02_SUBHEAD, Chapter02_Figure1.1), or

labelled by what they are (Flowers01, RosesAndBees, AuntMayAndHerPig…). You should always avoid using symbols and spaces since these may cause issues in final formats. Depending on your software and how you export for eBook format, having images with names that include open spaces, dollar signs ($), hashtags (#), and similar often will cause them not to load or fail when uploaded to a vendor. I highly recommend using only alphabet and numbers with underscore if need be. In programming we do this as well and often default to camelCase (LittleTimmysWagon, IHateThisPictureTheMost, ImageNameLikeThis…) as the safest means to prevent programming errors.

Image File Types

Images come in a variety of types and the best ones to use for publishing are JPEG and TIFF formats. You can use a PNG, which preserves the transparency unlike JPEG or even a PDF file. You should keep these between 300-600 DPI and at least a little larger than the intended size to make sure you have room to trim the image if needed. TIFF is considered the best format and has been used in the printing and graphic design world as the superior option. Most Print-on-Demand printers want the files saved in PDF2001XA format, and this converts images to JPEG. Same thing happens when exporting to EPUB; the images are often converted to JPEG or PNG depending on what you are using. Thus, it is recommended to save in JPEG for several reasons, including the fact it's a smaller size, translates into eBook without issues, and prevents any issues when converting to final PDF format changes to the images.

Permissions & Usage Rights

Images and artwork can fall under public domain rights, but if they don't, you will need to purchase usage rights or get permission. If you pulled your images from a service like ShutterStock or similar stock photo site, they usually have different levels you can purchase for usage rights. This is the safest means for images and artwork. If you intend to hire an illustrator, be sure to cover the usage and contract with them how books are sold and their images will be used from the book to creating swag, bookmarks, banners, and more. Some may clear you for using the images in the book only and not for marketing materials. Be sure to add the permissions granted in the copyright section or even an illustration rights section as a type of appendix. It's always best to give credit where it's due on your copyright page at the very least.

How Long Will This Take Me to Format?

The whole concept in prepping the manuscript is to lower the amount of the time spent troubleshooting when you should be designing and formatting. Expect to spend hours applying, placing, adjusting, and designing all the elements your book needs. It can be very intimidating when you're new to typesetting or looking at the materials and wondering how this impacts the time spent creating your final rendition of the book for publication. A seasoned formatter or typesetter can make a massive book with a selection of images in no time, but for the sake of all things, this book is designed to prepare new formatters and new-to-the-skill typesetters for the timeframe so not to discourage you.

A new typesetter can take 8-16 hours to weeks or months - depends on the book type with fiction being easiest!

Below are some mindful things, and if you are thinking it doesn't take this much time, it would be due to your own experience and talents. A seasoned typesetter should be hitting time in the 30-50% range of the below. For example, it may take a new typesetter 8-16 hours to do a typeset, and an expert typesetter can do that same book in 2 hours or less. Experience and knowledge show in this position, and a personally hands-on trained typesetter can start in that high range, and after constantly formatting, be in that 3–5-hour range in a few weeks, and 2-hour range months later. As they say, *practice makes perfect. The first two-factors that can lower time before starting is cleaning the manuscript and creating a template with The Parts and The Guts ready to apply.*

- 50,000-word count 2-3 hours, so a 130,000-word manuscript can take between 6-9 hours. It's ok to take breaks when doing larger works. These hours can be spread out, so you walk through the process at your own pace.

- Each image adds 10-15 minutes. If they are ready to go and no editing is needed, this number can drop to 5 minutes each on average. Be sure to be consistent on how they are framed, and don't forget to anchor or drop them in line with text so they pull into an eBook format.

- Tables and pull quotes add 15-30 minutes each. If the table stretches more than one page, count each page into the equation. For example, a table that spans into 5 total pages might take you between 1-3 hours. It's vital to create Table Styles, Paragraph Styles, and Object Styles you can apply or drop in to save time here!

- Designing and making decisions on fonts takes time too! 1-4 hours can be spent here picking fonts, setting up master page designs, and even after the initial formatting you always want to circle back and make sure to table of contents is updated, all the pages are where they need to be, change justified to top alignment, and other housekeeping quality control checks and adjustments.

- Overall, a new typesetter or formatter should take 6-12+ hours on their first few books until they develop a routine and build up muscle memory for key components. It gets easier and proper manuscript prepping can keep the hours spent here to a minimum as to not exhaust the typesetter.

The Checklist!

Here is a checklist that should help you make sure you finished prepping the manuscript and materials before starting the formatting. Often we don't think to ask or double check to include some of these things and it can be detrimental in the final stages leading up to printing the actual book. Whether you are formatting your own book or formatting someone else's, this checklist is to help you gather everything you need before you start.

BOOK TITLE: _____

SUBTITLE: _____

TYPESET CHECKLIST

☐ Manuscript text in a DOC, DOCX, RTF file

☐ All the images listed in Manuscript present:

☐ CMYK mode

☐ Between 300-600 DPI.

☐ Trim Size _____ width x _____ height

☐ Author Pen Name - FIRST_____LAST_____

☐ Dedication: Yes or No

☐ Author Bio: Yes or No

☐ Copyright

☐ Publisher information

☐ Additional mention such as artist, design, or typesetter? _____

☐ Scriptures cited from…. Any public domain original publication mentions? _____

☐ Permission granted from… Any materials that have permissions needing to be listed here?

☐ ISBNs for Paperback: _____ Hardcover_____

☐ Audiobook_____ eBook_____

☐ LCCN pending or listed?_____

☐ Front Matter (Acknowledgements, Foreword, Preface, etc.)

☐ Do they want a Table of Contents: Yes or No

☐ Do they have tables to import: Yes or No

☐ Do they want pull quotes: Yes or No

BOOK TITLE: _____

SUBTITLE: _____

TYPESET CHECKLIST

☐ Manuscript text in a DOC, DOCX, RTF file

☐ All the images listed in Manuscript present:

☐ CMYK mode

☐ Between 300-600 DPI.

☐ Trim Size _____ width x _____ height

☐ Author Pen Name - FIRST_____LAST_____

☐ Dedication: Yes or No

☐ Author Bio: Yes or No

☐ Copyright

☐ Publisher information

☐ Additional mention such as artist, design, or typesetter? _____

☐ Scriptures cited from…. Any public domain original publication mentions? _____

☐ Permission granted from… Any materials that have permissions needing to be listed here?

☐ ISBNs for Paperback: _____ Hardcover_____

☐ Audiobook_____ eBook_____

☐ LCCN pending or listed?_____

☐ Front Matter (Acknowledgements, Foreword, Preface, etc.)

☐ Do they want a Table of Contents: Yes or No

☐ Do they have tables to import: Yes or No

☐ Do they want pull quotes: Yes or No

Diving into Design

Design is not just what it looks like and feels like.
Design is how it works.

Steve Jobs

INTRODUCTION

Typesetting, or book formatting, serves as a function aimed to process textual content and develops it into the expected visual design considered to be what we come to call a book. We aren't just making art, but something that has to aid and strengthen communication between the author and reader. This is done by taking into consideration several factors, such as audience, industry expectations, the type of book or manuscript, limitations of the format, and even influence of the genre. This doesn't mean you can't get creative and do something new or revolutionary, but be sure to master the foundation of typesetting and build from a sturdy starting point. Understanding why you are breaking out of the norm and how to do it successfully requires a strong understanding of the limitations of the art form as a whole, as well as the history and exposure of the audience it serves.

DESIGNING FOR OFFSET VERSUS PRINT-ON-DEMAND

For the most part, it simply affects the material options and final product quality more so than anything else. With offset printing, you have a wider range of options for paper, binding, and trim sizes. It gains you access to features like end pages, embossing, and even specialty printing for pop-up books and beyond. For the sake of this workbook, we are focused on mass market style books and basic design elements that are accessible and produced by any printer. Offset printing only shifts how you typeset when a different binding is involved. These may require overlapping images or offsetting a portion of an image to accommodate how the binding will be sewn or folding into one another as seen in cross-over binding. For the sake of catering to the majority, the typesetting techniques here can shift to meet the needs of most, but seek your printer for guidance on what the file parameters require. Saddle stitch, perfect bound should have little variance, if any at all, with the techniques taught here in regard to binding types. These are three common types today:

- **PERFECT BOUND –** Cover is glued to interior pages. This is the most common and only option currently for Print-on-Demand books. It's the cheapest binding and is faster than other options. Paper choice can limit the amount of pages you are able to have, and it's recommended to be cautious when dealing with a book with over 500 pages. This comes in paperback and hardcover options.

- **SADDLE STITCH –** This is common in smaller books and especially in children's books. Often some Print-on-Demand vendors will provide this for smaller page-count books. It is noted that this is bound together with staples and has little to no gutter to offset for interior design. This is for paperback only but inexpensive to bind.

- **SMYTHE SEWN –** This is a common type for hardcover, non-Print-on-Demand books. It is most notable by the rolled threads seen on the bound edge glued to the hardcover. It is durable and requires for offset printing costs upfront and limited print runs. This is only available as a hardcover.

Keep in mind the concept behind Print-on-Demand is meant to be accessible worldwide with the limited materials and trim sizes that are available. These elements cater and support digital printing platforms. For example, you can upload a book and launch it from your home in Orlando, Florida, US. Within hours, in London, UK, your reader can purchase a print copy. Instead of printing at a certain location and shipping it across the world, the book will be printed at a press closest to the customer's address and shipped from there. The idea is in lieu of printing books in advance, incurring costs storing

and shipping them, you are taking a bigger hit when the book is produced. It's true, a Print-on-Demand book costs more to produce, but the convenience and accessibility without large sums of money in the beginning might be a more financially feasible option for some authors and publishers.

AUDIENCE

Before you start designing, you should always be aware who the audience for the book should be. Are we creating a book for small children, a textbook for college students, maybe a devotional for older people, or a mass market romance? Each audience and age group has expectations and can weigh heavily what fonts, font size, colors, and layouts will communicate best with them. For example, red fonts are often too hard for older eyes to read, larger fonts pushing over 16-point font size will work best for younger or older audiences alike, and floral decorations would be a bad choice for a book meant for an audience who reads horror. Be mindful who the readers are and the expectations they may have on the type and genre of book you are creating.

INDUSTRY EXPECTATIONS

Typesetters do their best to be aware of style changes, current trends, and be up to date on publishing practices. With the rise of Print-on-Demand, it's vital to know the difference in creating a book for Print-on-Demand versus offset printing. Even then, the type of book and genre can decide on the layout elements expected to identify a book for that genre. Often trends evolve over time, most commonly seen in covers and the number of covers bestselling books revise to keep up with industry changes (i.e. Stephen King's *The Stand*). Inside the book, we see trends change thanks to the growing number of digital typesetting practices and advances in layout software. In short, the efficiency, speed, layout, and trends all need to be competitive to keep up with the changing industry. In the end, you may want to consider the elements you use and their timelessness, or settle with having to revamp or redesign your book later on to keep up.

INFLUENCE OF GENRE

Don't overlook the importance of comparing the competition and doing marketing research on the genre your book belongs to or identifies with. Many of these can tighten the overall design of a book and often can add, delete, or modify front and back matter in a manuscript. If you are designing a fiction novel, the font choices can impact how the atmosphere of the story is perceived. You don't want scratchy, bold, drippy fonts with a horror vibe with your chapter header font in a sweet, Christian romance. This can cause mixed signals or even make a reader put the book down thinking they've "bought the wrong book," or worse, leave a negative review! If you don't think font choice has an impact, take a look at this example of chapter headers, and think about the vibe and imagery it gives you reading it in the different font faces:

Grandma's First Night Out

Grandma's First Night Out

Grandma's First Night Out

Grandma's First Night Out

Grandma's First Night Out

TYPE OF BOOK

This element is the foundation of the back half of this book where instruction and information has been cut into a few core types of books and how they should be designed. As you travel from picture books to fiction to textbook styles, you will see the information shift as well as the overall design inside a book. Images can expose the shift loudest at first glance, but as you make decisions of layout and how to display textual content to the appropriate audience. This can change how one will be creating and designing each portion of the book and what can't be abandoned in order for the audience and industry to identify your book correctly before even reading the title or text. Scary to consider, but it happens often including being able to have the title on the spine of your cover for it to be on shelves in brick-and-mortar stores! The industry is full of these gatekeeping standards.

LIMITATIONS OF FORMAT

It can't be expressed enough that as your book takes on many formats (hardcover, paperback, eBook, etc.) that each of these serve a different intent. Never expect your eBook to match your printed version. We're not talking about a PDF, but those formats made for devices that read EPUB, MOBI, and similar. These files are a single layer file format that can't recreate the artful side of a print book. You can embed fonts, but depending on the user settings and device, they may not be able to "unpack" those font files to bring that element to life. Remember that eBooks are intended for ease of reading the content based on the reader's wants and needs. They literally can break the layout to suit the visual needs of readers, which is why so many graphics and tables fall in line with text and not to the right or left as intended in the print version. Each format serves readers in different ways. Not every book will be viable for digital format either, and that's ok!

PAGE LAYOUTS

Every section of a book has a consistency despite the number of different page layouts used in the final product. For example, we all know what a copyright page looks like with tiny font and aligned at the bottom of the page. The industry has been using a lot of the same styles dating back to the time of the Gutenberg Bible, and be aware your readers have been trained to read and digest information best due to this. The most common style guide is Chicago Manual Style although it serves as a main foundation for most of the mass market books in the world. That doesn't mean another style is needed when you specialize for foreign markets or even academia publications. It's always best to ask if there are any such requirements before designing your pages.

Half Title versus Title Page

This comes from CMS style guidelines. A simpler way of thinking of the half page is that it's the page with only the title, leaving space for the author to sign and leave a message. Some textbooks and picture books forfeit this page. Every book should have full title page that reflects the textual content from the cover such as title, subtitle, author, and so on. This page is usually also the one that has a publisher logo or name at the bottom.

Copyright Page

This will always have the smallest font, sometimes pushing the limitations with 6–8-point font size. It should have the rights, permissions, publisher, ISBN, Library of Congress Control Number, and similar information. They often feature legal jargon to protect the author, the content, and/or publisher. Any means to discover a typesetter, who published the book, and similar should be contained here thought not always fully listed. It's at the discretion of the publisher what is and isn't allowed here. This is always bottom, left alignment, sometimes with a right indent and placed on the back of the title page.

Chapter Page

The most decorated page is often the chapter page. These should be consistent, and as the typesetter, it's best to know if you plan on right page only layout or continuous (new subsequent chapters will land on left and right pages). This is where you will see the most variety of fonts which can be made up of a Chapter Header, Headline or Chapter Title, Drop-Cap, and sometimes a subhead. It's ok here to mix and match fonts, but strongly advised to keep it the same chapter-to-chapter to help readers identify when a new chapter starts. Also, body text, quotes, bulleted lists, and similar should have the same base font and use indentations and character styles (italics, bold, underline, etc.) to bring emphasis to themselves.

Body Page

For text-based books and the majority of the typeset, you will spend most of your time with the body page. These pages are designed as either 1- or 2-column text boxes that make up a majority of the margined space on a single page. Above this there is commonly a header which consists of the title, author, chapter, and/or similar information. Below would be a footer containing similar information. In most books the footer holds the page numbers located either in the center or on the outer corners of the book's full spread or two-page layout. It's is set on top of a blank page with text being the focus point.

Book Layouts

There are several ways to use images and textual content within a book. The most common is an image filling the entire page or spread with text added on a layer on top, a white space for caption, or even captions on the adjacent page per the spread. You see this more common in art books, wildlife books, or books with maps and similar graphics. Other designs have elements spread all over the page interacting with the text as often seen in textbooks with multiple columns or self-help books with pull quotes. Be sure to look at books your readers like and see how they are layering these elements. Does the font use up a lot of the page space? Are things layered or separated? How often does the placement of images change? Always keep up to date with the readership and competition.

When styling the pages, you have to be consistent since this is a means of relaying information based on the textual content. It cannot be said enough regarding formatting books on how important it is to walk the readers through the information with the chapter pages serving as mile markers of how far they've traveled through the book, story, or lesson. If you are sticking to industry expectations, be aware of how often images are interacting with the content in comparison to the expected age group.

Remember as you design your book that you can mix and match all the page and spread layouts to help tell your story visually with a combination of images and text. Picture books and workbooks both require a lot of designing to be completed in the forefront for best results (In short, work adjacent to illustrators, graphic designers, and storyboarding out sections or worksheets) unlike fiction and chapter books that are text only or have images sprinkled throughout. Prior to hiring an illustrator for your book, it's vital to know how many pages and layouts are in your book along with how many images are needed and where they will go within the layout. Creating a storyboard that you share with an illustrator or even a hired formatter can prevent many headaches on both ends and speed up the process.

Picture Book Layouts

The most common picture book layout is an image filling the entire page or spread with text added on a layer above this. Sometimes in older books or self-published children's books you will have a spread split to a page with the image and a colored or white page featuring the text. Other designs have elements spread all over the page interacting with the text as often seen in Dr. Seuss books. When styling the pages of a picture book, you have to be consistent. It should walk the child and readers through the tale as if playing out a movie of sorts, the page flips timed in the right moment to make the child feel as if they are pushing the story forward. If you are sticking to industry expectations, you'll discover you have a very limited number of pages to tell the story visually. It cannot be expressed enough that prior to hiring an illustrator, you need to create a storyboard or keen sense of direction in your manuscript. Picture books can prove a challenge for both sides, and the more communication exchanged with examples the better the outcome for all involved.

Diving into Design

IMAGE + TEXT SPREAD LAYOUT

This is a dated and older layout style regarding the realm of picture books. It features the image on one page of the spread with the text of the story on the other. If you intend to compete aggressively on the market against other books, you may want to avoid using this layout. As for someone looking to tell a story to share with family and friends, this works perfectly well.

When along came Daisy, all ready to play.
She whined and she whimpered in that puppy dog way.

"Come down here, Leo, I know what to do.
We'll have an adventure, just me and you."

IMAGE WITH TEXT OVERLAY PAGE LAYOUT

The most common of the current layout choices for picture book designs is this one. In this layout, images cover all of the page (bleeding off the page), and the font is placed on top in a contrasting color, size, style, and/or faded background to pull it out of the image.

MULTIPLE IMAGE PAGE LAYOUT

These pages usually have the most whitespace in all the picture book. Either a singular image or an array of single images with text emphasize the character or certain objects or even actions. This is a wonderful opportunity to recycle an image of a character from another scene and use it differently as seen in many mass market picture books such as *Mother Bruce*.

Leo yelped and he yowled, "I want to go home! No more adventures. **Just leave me alone!**"

Leo shook his head no. His happy was here, but a cricket hopped up and looked ready to steer.

Diving into Design

FULL SPREAD LAYOUT

The image or text (not both) stretches across 2 pages, a left and right page, to show as one large landscape image or two pages of textual content. In a lot of cases the text may only be present on one page and not the other, but other layouts might have several spots all around the image to show the story unfolding in a sequence or multi-action spread.

RULE OF THIRDS SPREAD LAYOUT

Across a two-page span, an image, graph, or pull quote will cover one complete page and a portion of the adjacent page to leave room on a far left or right edge for font to place. In concept, the object is using two-thirds of the design area to draw the eye to the text or away from the text by doing so. The Rule of Thirds is often used in marketing, print design, or even in filming. It splits the viewing area into thirds from top to bottom and side to side. From this point, you break the content and subject matter up at the key sections to help draw the eye in a certain direction or pull it towards or away.

Split Design Image & Text Page Layout

Again, this is similar to the Image + Text layout seen in picture books and textbooks. On a single page, whether it's the right or left, the image and text split the space. Sometimes this is done in a 50/50 spit, or a two-thirds split, but often features a white space or colored space where the text will be. Again, this is an older means of designing a picture book, but it may be useful elsewhere.

Whitespace Page Layout

This page is often an indicator of a chapter starting or ending. Sometimes it can be a section or partition marker of some kind. It's notorious for having a lot of white space or empty, unused space on the page spread. What little content is there usually is textual to guide or inform the reader in preparation of something changing or a transition within the book. You see this a lot in textbooks and fiction books with right page only chapter starts.

2-Column Design

More commonly seen in back matter, such as index, glossaries, and listings, or in large reference and textbooks, column design mimics the above spreads with the added feature of two columns. This can pull more text onto a page, especially with a small gutter and margins teamed with single line spacing and 11- or 12-point font. If you are struggling with large page count, this could provide a means of dropping and managing it more easily. It also allows for a more formula-based means to place images and captions, or even the occasional boxed content or pull quote.

Not every page has to be in this style in a book, but it should be used consistently as to not throw the reader from the content presented on the page. Also, it's not uncommon that headings are set to span all columns or even opening paragraphs to content while the subhead information falls into two-column style. Play with the features and options, look at samples, and decide how to best apply these in a large book or workbook as needed. Recommended for large formats though, such as 7 x 10, 8 x 10, and 8.5 x 11.

Diving into Design

Comic Book and Graphic Novel Layouts

This is where things get tricky. A lot of graphic design and art should be done in advance, but in the case you need to pull together the components, let's talk about what that might look like. You will need to use a layout and layers to aid you, and in some cases, PhotoShop or similar programs might be your best option. This is so you can mask and layer the work as needed and save as an image out to import in for typeset for best results, especially if you intend on making an eBook version of the comic or graphic novel. Regardless, you will be creating custom line boxes and elements with the images provided with storyboards to assist how they should be put together. Luckily, there are plenty of premade templates, boxes, dialogue balloons and similar available-as-stock-images and highly encouraged to use them as a jumping board. There are also manga or comic focus software that can also come in handy in these scenarios.

Evenly Divided Span

This is a comic that has 4-6 even squares on a page for the comic to exist. This is the most simplistic, and it is easier to manage design-wise. Also, it is the most common seen as short one-shot scripts for web or social media originally and then later printed once enough have been produced.

Classic Comic or Static Layout

Panels and diagonal and white-spaced borders abound. These premade layouts can be grabbed up from stock photo or premade toolbox of templates to drag and drop as you see fit. These don't breakout beyond the intended margins; nothing bleeds off the page, and they always tend to have a page number at the least and sometimes headers.

Modern or Dynamic Layout

Now we are bleeding off the page in area when emphasizing aspects of the story. In most modern comic books, all the images usually do this or add characters taking up a third of a 2-page layout to break the static or monotonous vibe of the former style. These work great for action-packed stories.

ON THE WAY TO SUCCESS

POW!

Developing a Pattern for Functionality

One of the most important things to know, whether you are designing books or video games, is people are pattern-seeking apes. We love to see patterns, follow repetitive actions, and even see and find a means of creating these subconsciously when known are to be found. Pattern feeds consistency and that tends to create a sense of stability and control. When you are using workbooks and planners, it's often to provide a tool or means to establish or even change habits and patterns within a certain area of knowledge, skills, life, or similar topic. Hence, the functionality of the book becomes the primary focus when typesetting. It's going to be touch and go at times, as well as sometimes frustrating, and it will take several attempts to master a system and design that works for both the author and its intended audience. Let's break it down to some vital areas! This is vital for any book that will contain worksheets, instructional elements, and similar aspects like seen in planners.

Even in textbooks and reference books, there is a pattern established for the delivery of content. A great example of this is the formatting seen in dictionaries and encyclopedias. At a glance, you can quickly tell which you have when flipping through the pages. You also know how to find what you are seeking thanks to the order being established via the alphabet, a common knowledge element!

Producing the Order

Slowing down and considering instructional design practices can go a long way here. The order and level of details given in directions is impacted by the intended use and audience. It's always best to overprovide than underprovide and leave them confused and lost. One can't simply get in car and start driving. You have to first unlock the car, sit in the driver seat, adjust the mirrors, start the engine, and put it in reverse to back out of the driveway before you can even start heading to where you're going. The order in which you create the content should do just that! First, get them strapped in properly before starting the core content and purpose. In text heavy works and textbooks, you see this in the form of chapters and subheaders that may even use 1.1, 1.2, and other titling to step the reader through slower. There's no one way to achieve this.

Repeat Pages & Duplication

It's ok and important to repeat or provide duplicates of key worksheets or areas where needed. Many get nervous about providing these. Be mindful of how you need them to use the book. If they should be able to make copies and just enter a few entries to try out during the lesson, then 3-5 duplicates should suffice.

Some authors provide special PDFs for free that are comprised of the worksheets only, so readers can print the sheets. Repeated elements can help establish consistency and curb the need to reteach how to use areas of the book too! So keep in mind how they will be interacting with these and how signaling and directing at a glance can go a long way with how easy it is the use the materials provided. In textbooks you see this often to signal the start of examples or exercises to reflect what was taught in the lesson.

Building a Sense of Consistency

As you design these elements for use, make sure to use font choices, layout, and backgrounds to signal and establish a sense of consistency. Flipping through a workbook, a reader should be able to tell where they will be writing versus reading a lesson at a glance. Even then, in a textbook, this happens with key elements boxed and marked in the same manner over and over again throughout the book. If keywords or vocabulary need to stand out, it's often in the same bold font, whether it's chapter one or twenty. Don't be afraid to utilize practices commonly used to give your design a jumpstart of feeling familiar and stay consistent with the genre or book-type standards used most often.

FORMATTING THE BOOK

Hooray! Now that we've talked and prepped this thing to no end, you should be ready to format this book with confidence. Why? Because it is so much easier to resolve problems at the manuscript and prepping stage than when you are formatting and making the book. Although, as said before, I am an avid user of Word to InDesign, I will do my best throughout the book to provide information in an all-encompassing and design angle. If you are looking for software tutorial, this isn't the book for you. Getting detailed instructions on how to set parameters in Word, Scribd, and similar word processors isn't the aim.

Instead, we will be focusing on the typesetter-based elements and areas that will be par the course for any book you design. Dependent on the software you are using to design your book, it could present its own issues and information may be labeled slightly different or found in different areas. In tandem with a software book, this book may provide some keywords in order to gain the affects you were aiming for in order for you to gain a greater value out of using said programs. In my years of looking for instructional manuals for book design, most of what I have learned was via videos, trial and error, typography college courses, and simply diving into the industry headlong with an open mind and understanding of the roots of publishing and its history. It probably also helped I delved in some game design, development, and programming, so I could troubleshoot creative solutions.

Without further ado, it's time to make this book using these step-by-step, or page-by-page, instructions below. Feel free to adjust this to suit your own style and needs since there are various methods to achieve the results seen here. Again, the aim here is to simplify the process while being able to make quality print books, enhance eBooks, and create a PDF that falls close as possible to being ADA compliant (Americans with Disabilities Act).

INSTRUCTIONAL DESIGN

Though this book can't dive into the full spectrum of instructional design practices and methods, it is strongly recommended to seek out resources to assist when creating textbooks, workbooks, self-help, and similar books. The importance of how material is presented, the order in which it is given, and the amount of details in the directions can make a world of difference in how well someone can understand and master the content, or utilize the tools you've designed for them. Often I have felt this in programming software books where key steps or explanation of concepts are skipped and have found myself instantly lost and lacking a key step that was assumed I would know to use. It can be the difference in someone being frustrated and unable to continue versus mastering and singing the praises of a book. Remember we have to open the jars before making the sandwich and unlock the car and start the engine before taking that trip!

HOW TO USE THE BOOK

When it comes to books intended to be put to use, adding a section or discussing how to use the book can help prep a reader properly. It doesn't mean every reader will slow down and use it, but if they get stuck, they will search for guidance here. This should inform the readers what the intent of the book is, how they should be utilizing it, and how to best start using the tool you have created for them. If you are being diligent, the consistent markers and identifying aspects in the books should be shown and defined so they understand their intent and how to perceive them as they travel through the book.

EXAMPLES & SAMPLES

Giving samples and examples can make all the difference in understanding the content and lessons being taught. When providing worksheets, it's always a great idea to either review how to use them in the content or provide one filled out. In many math and English textbooks, you will find ample amounts of examples of problems and grammar being used incorrectly and correctly. The ability to see a math problem broken down into slower steps and done more than once in examples can make or break a student's ability to learn a new method or apply how to process a certain principle.

WAYS TO GUIDE READERS

Play around with instructional design on a visual level. There are plenty of ways to guide readers through the content with using graphics and clever placement of materials. One of the more obvious means is the use of arrows placed on a page to point the eyes to read the content in the right way. Other means have included a character or boxing material in a consistent way to make it stand out in some way. Even then, laying out a page and its elements in a certain pattern for key moments can also clue the reader into knowing the difference between content, examples, and exercises at a glance without ever needing to read the text!

FILE SETUP

The file or page size should match the trim size in width and height. Make sure the intended orientation matches what you intended, specifically landscape versus portrait. Depending on the program, you may have to set bleed settings to include a 0.125" bleed on all sides or for outer margins. For some Print-on-Demand vendors, they may want the inner margin to have no bleed since this is the side of the page that is glued to the spine of the book. You usually get to set up or define the overall margins as well.

Be mindful that with picture books you will be saving a flat PDF for eBook design and that you don't have to fret over threading text boxes together as seen with all other book types. It's more important to make sure images are bleeding off to the marked edges just pass the trim edge, that elements are layered and overlayed in the right order, and textual content is within the margins provided by the printer or the Print-on-Demand requirements of 0.5" from trim size edge. Here are my recommended settings for this book type:

- Industry Standard Numbers:
  - 0.125" Bleed from trim edge
  - 0.5" Margin for content inward from trim edge
  - Large page counts will require a larger 0.625" or higher inner margin or gutter
  - Special binding may change the needs for inner margins

- Inner or inside margin: 0.625" for books under 300 pages and

- 0.75" to 0.8" for books pushing far into the 500+ range since where the pages' bind needs more space to avoid words falling into the crack of the book.
  - Granted, this is a picture book, and you can sometimes get away with a 0.5" margin.

- Outer or outside margins (including top and bottom) should be 0.5" to 0.625"
  - Typically have main body pages with header and footer set, and you can increase the top and bottom margins to 0.8-0.875" to give yourself space to place and space these from your body text.

Wondering where these numbers come from? Your vendors should have File Creation Guides via a PDF or webpage. No matter if you plan on using offset printing, KDP, IngramSparks, or a similar vendor, these parameters never change. This is the basic needs of a file going to print and will give the press some wiggle room. These parameters will change if you choose more elaborate binding and use certain presses. Always make sure you get these settings from the printer and design the book with these in place from the start.

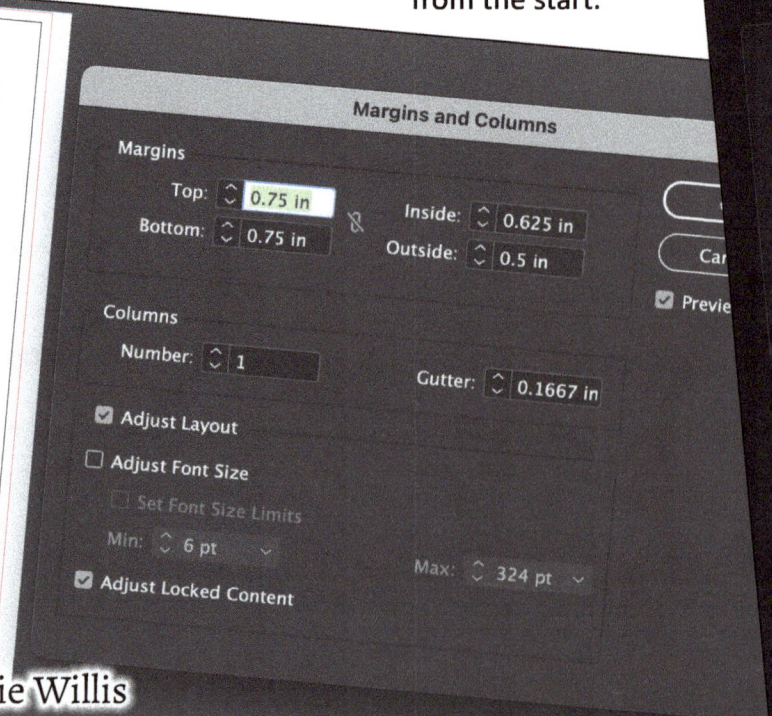

Leo perched on his sill, the best place to be.
He had sun, he had calm, and all he could see.

Margins and Columns

Margins

Top: 0.75 in   Inside: 0.625 in
Bottom: 0.75 in   Outside: 0.5 in

Columns

Number: 1   Gutter: 0.1667 in

☑ Adjust Layout
☐ Adjust Font Size
☐ Set Font Size Limits
Min: 6 pt   Max: 324 pt
☑ Adjust Locked Content

USING LAYERS

Most of the layout software allows you to create layers such as InDesign (not any of the word processors though they do have header footer options). These come in handy in keeping content stacked or arranged in the right order. This includes making sure watermarks are below the body text layer and even keeping the header and footer elements on the top and not lost behind images and such. A bonus to using this feature is the ability to lock them and make sure you don't accidently change, move, or delete them unintentionally. With picture books, you often use images that take up the entire page and risk losing these elements completely. Recommended layers include the following listed in the order they should fall and usage:

- **Header and Footer Layer** – This will have your top layer text boxes that contain the header and footer, which usually hold page numbers, title, author, and/or current chapter. You can control these with master pages. In a word processor, this is an option or specific setting that is influenced by section breaks to change how they look from section to section of the book's layout.

- **Default or Body Text Layer** – Here you will manage the primary text box in which the main content autoflows through threaded textboxes or pages.

- **Background Layer** – At the bottom of the list, there should be a background layer that is designed for images, spreads, and watermarks that need to fall under the textual content.

This doesn't mean you need to use all these layers, but it's highly recommended to give you more control when formatting. If the program you are using doesn't provide layers, check for features that define objects on the page as needing to be "Ordered" or "Arranged" with sub-options for "Bring to Front" or "Bring to Back," which mimic what layering does. This should aid you in making sure text and images overlap appropriately.

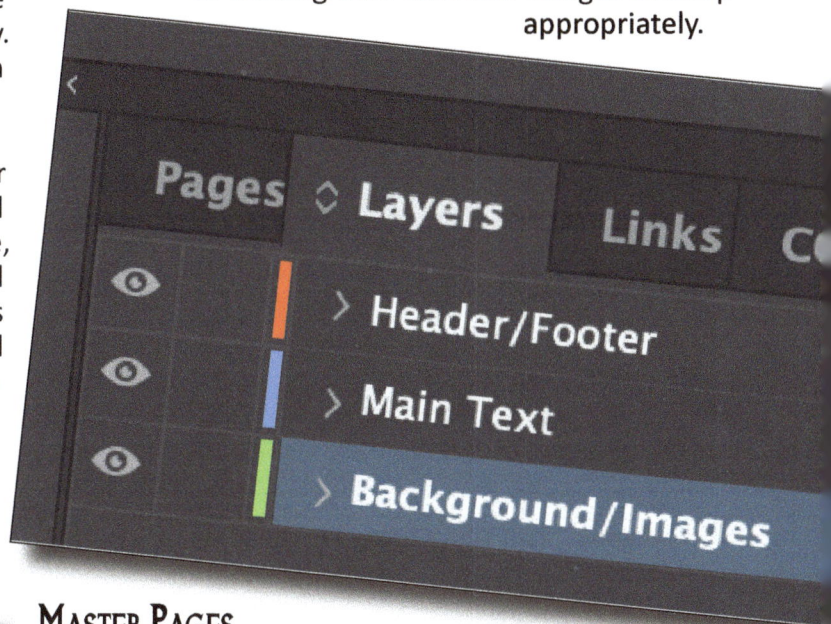

MASTER PAGES

These pages, or templates, are premade pages you can drag and drop into the layout to help speed things along and stay consistent. Know that this is more commonly found as a feature in layout software such as InDesign. Even with a freeform style book, there's a level of consistency with placement of elements such as header, footer, page numbers, watermarks, and other elements that you may not want to shift and wish to keep level throughout the book. In any book, you are going to be applying a few key layout pages. I recommend the following master pages or templates be made in advance to speed up the typeset process:

- **A blank page** with only the margin lines set. You may include a primary text box version for dedication or anchoring title page images into place. Works great for print-on-demand with that last page needing to be blank as well. These will also set your title pages and copyright page as well.

- **A body page** made of a blank page with only the header and footer with a main text box. I recommend putting the header and footer on a top layer that's locked. Predesign a left and right page, often featuring the book title on left and author name on right. You may even design a running header or chapter header that auto updates depending on the software you are using. Adding glyphs and art to page numbers and headers can add a nice creative flair.

- **A chapter start page** that can add art, designs, and spacing shifts to accommodate the style implied. I always make right and left page versions, so if I need to change from right page only chapters to continuous, it's ready to adapt accordingly.

- **A numbered blank page** can be useful for areas that may contain images, maps, tables, and similar content where you simply want page numbers only.

- **Worksheets or Special Pages** should be designed or a foundation premade or decided on before getting too far into the design. Prepping these pages in advance can help in your efforts and provide a sense of how much space they truly need in order to interact with the content as your design the book.

- **A two-column body page or variants** can provide a means to design smart and save on page count where you can. Also, two-column pages can provide easier means to place images as often seen in textbooks, reference books, and workbooks alike.

- **Section breaks** become vital for non-fiction books. Occasionally these hard pages or spreads have an image or color to help standout when certain passing of time, events, topics, and provide a sense of dividers for the reader. Prepping a page or spread for these can save time and provide consistency when applicable.

Pages | Layers | Links | CC Lib

[None]

A–BODY

B–CHAPTER

C–BLANK

D–EXTRA

Joyride
C

i

C | A

ii, 1

A | A

2–3

A | A

4–5

FONT CHOICES AND PREP

Font has the most weight in typesetting and interior book design. Your choices and attention to detail to the spacing, size, and types will have a significant impact for better or worse. There are a few things you can do to help yourself prep and streamline your design depending on if you are using styles in Microsoft Word or a combination of Paragraph and Character styles in Adobe InDesign. Prepping and setting up pre-saved files with master pages and these elements can save a lot of hunting and frustrations, especially if you want to shift or change fonts later. If you intend to do typesetting full time or work heavily with fonts, I recommend investing into Font Management programs, such as FontExplorer. This can make it easier to keep your growing library from bogging down your computer while making it easier to test out and organize fonts.

PARAGRAPH STYLES OR STYLES

These will make up most of the formatting application in textual content. They work in particular order and repeat as you start a new section or chapter. Making a style in advance can help you quickly adjust, fix, or change the entire typeset without hunting and pecking for certain content in the book. Instead, applying a style and changing the style can shift and fix the book as a whole.

- **Chapter Header** – Should be the largest font and be a font face that reflects genre. Content here is often just numbers, "Chapter" text, or some section marker text.

- **Headline** – This is often a subtitle or section title that follows behind the Chapter Header, normally directly below it. It should be the second largest text and also have a legible but creative font that captures the genre.

- **Subhead** – Should be a slight larger than the body text but clear and bolder in some way. It's common for these to be the same font as body text and simply in all-caps or small caps.

- **Drop Cap** – Whether it's a single letter, word, or line, this is the first paragraph in a chapter or section. It's a way to artfully signal to a reader where to begin reading or add more to the chapter page that makes it stand out other than whitespace.

- **Body Text** – This will be the majority of your content. It should be a legible font comfortable for readers and remain the same throughout the entire book. It builds the font foundation for Drop Caps, Citations/Quotes, Subheads, Tables and more.

- **Citations/Quote** – This paragraph style should center or have an indent of 0.25" to 0.05" on the right and left sides. It's also

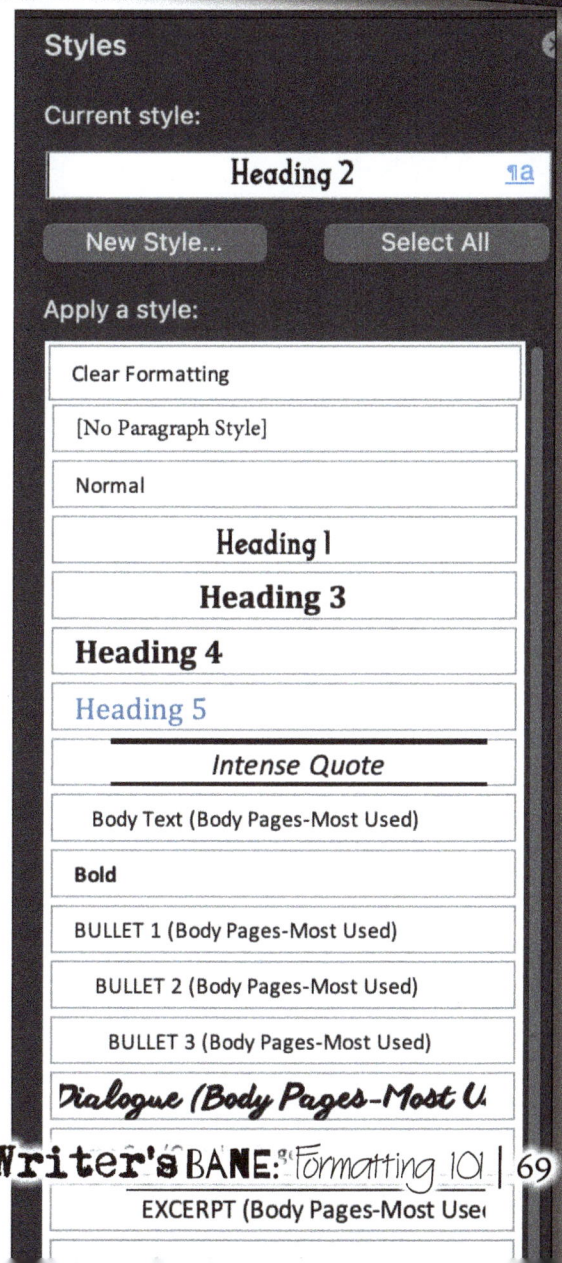

Paragraph Styles   Char   Obje   ≡

(No Styles)   [a+]   ⚡

   [Basic Paragraph]

⌄ 📁 Front Pages

   Copyright

   FRONT HEADLINE

   TOC title

   TOC body text

   TOC PAGE NUMBERS

⌄ 📁 Opening Pages

   CHAPTER   Shift+Num 1

   HEADLINE   Shift+Num 2

   Drop Cap   Shift+Num 7

   Drop Cap-2   Shift+Cmd+Num 7

⌄ 📁 Body Pages–Most Used

   Body Text   Shift+Num 0

   Space After   Shift+Num 3

   Space Before   Shift+Cmd+Num 3

   Quote   Shift+Num 4

   Quote...fore   Shift+Cmd+Num 4

   Subhead   Shift+Num 5

   Subhe... NSA   Shift+Cmd+Num 5

   Bullets/N...red lists   Shift+Num 6

   No Indent   Shift+Num 8

   No In...nt SA   Shift+Cmd+Num 8

   Centered   Shift+Cmd+Num 9

⌄ 📁 Misc

   PAGE BREAK   Shift+Num 9

   Image placer   Shift+Cmd+Num 6

   Image CAPTIONS

   Ornament

⌄ 📁 Special Formatting

   Footnotes

   Section HEADER

common to add space before and after this paragraph style so the quote or citations pops. Often there is an italics character style applied.

✐ **Bullet Points** – Lists and bullets have similar indentation and spacing. Setting the preference or making a variety of these to create multi-tier systems in the varying styles can save a typesetter grief as well as the means to remembering how APA, MLA, and CMS are different from one another.

✐ **Dialogue Text** – Any time font is in a dialogue bubble, it should be in a handwritten or architect style font. The most infamous of these is Comic Sans. This should be a paragraph style or character style depending on the way you want to typeset the comic book or graphic novel. Regardless, picking a consistent size, spacing, and similar can make it easier to read.

✐ **Boxed Text** – This is for text that is placed in a predesigned box or similar graphics that can sometimes be programmed into these. Keep it consistent if it's a sans-serif or serif font. This often should mimic similar size or spacing as the body or dialogue text depending on the type of book you are making.

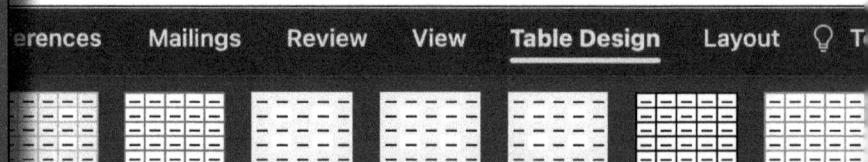

Para   **Character Styles**   Obje   ≡

(No Styles)   [a+]   ⚡

   [None]   ✎

   FUN PHRASES

   superscript

   NO BREAK

   Initial Cap

   Italic

erences   Mailings   Review   View   **Table Design**   Layout   💡 T

CHARACTER STYLES OR SUBFAMILY FONTS

Creating premade character style can help you gain more control on the style of the manuscript as a whole. It also helps build coding within certain programs for eBook creation and keeps these vital aspects from disappearing in the process.

- **Bold** – used to identify keywords, bring words to the front, and stand out louder. There is never a need to make a whole manuscript bold. Instead, choose a thicker or heavier font.

- *Italics* – this has many uses from quotes, to signaling key elements in content, and even to signal internal dialogue in stories.

- Underline – much like bold, this is used to make content stand out, signify a reference (depending on styles like APA), hyperlinks (or clickable content in text), or signal something of importance.

- Keyword - This comes in handy when wanting to stay consistent in font face and size changes in books where you need vocabulary words or key visuals to pop.

- SMALL CAPS – Common to see in reference works or to address religious names or keywords, this is easier to manage as a character style and carries over into eBook better.

- **Dialogue Text** – Any time font is in a dialogue bubble it should be in a handwritten or architect style font. The most infamous of these is Comic Sans.

OBJECT STYLES OR TABLE STYLES

These are special styles that influence objects, images, and tables. They make sure designs and placement match and can even streamline how items show up in an eBook. Not every software has the means to define these or set them up. As for InDesign, these can help guide image frames, table cells, and more so that you can save time when adding content into the layout and saving you the grief of cracking open object options to adjust every detail.

| Paragr | Charac | ◇ Object Styles |

[Basic Text Frame]

   [None]

   [Basic Graphics Frame]

   [Basic Text Frame]

   PAGE LEFT

   PAGE RIGHT

   TOP J...IFIED   Opt+Num 0

   CENTERED   Opt+Num 1

Border Styles   ½ pt   Pen Color   Borders   Border Painter

SAVING THE FILES

Now that you have completed the book, be sure you save the files appropriately. This means for both your work files and the final product for the printer. Be sure to always ask clients and printers what file format and needs are required. For the sake of all things, we will focus on the most common and most versatile versions. If you used InDesign, you can go to File > Package and the software will do its best to grab font files, images, and more into a folder. For those who are using other means, here's a breakdown of the work folder and what to save:

- ✐ FOLDER NAMED AFTER BOOK
    - ✎ Work File (InDesign, Word, etc.)
    - ✎ PDF (2001-xa format aka Press Quality with Bleed recommended)
    - ✎ EPUB (Optional, reflowable a must)
    - ✎ ORIGINAL folder
        - ✏ Holds original text file and any related materials

- ✐ FONT folder
    - ✏ Copies of font files used (truetype, openface, etc.)
- ✐ IMAGE folder
    - ✏ Any image used should be placed in here in case you need or decide to edit or replace later.

As for prepping files for upload to a vendor, the two main types will be PDF and EPUB (reflowable). No matter if you are self-publishing or using a service, these two are the current staple in the industry and have the ability to upload to a variety of distributors and vendors with very little issue.

- ✐ PDF Format
    - ✎ This is used for print design applications, paperback, Print-on-Demand, and similar.
    - ✎ For printing, PDF-X/a: 2001 Format is the most accepted.
    - ✎ For web pdf, use web preferred file setting, but remember this file loses values needed for printing for a book.
    - ✎ Make sure Bleed Settings are applied or this could cause the file to kick back or be denied.

- ✐ EPUB Format
    - ✎ Always use reflowable.
    - ✎ Write in as much File Info and Metadata information as possible.
    - ✎ If attaching a cover image, it should be at least 1600x2400 pixels, 150 dpi, RGB color mode to avoid being kicked back from online vendors.
    - ✎ Most accepted eBooks type currently with enhanced ability access.

BOOK TITLE: _____

SUBTITLE: _____

SAVING CHECKLIST

- ☐ A copy of the Manuscript or text file in a DOC, DOCX, RTF file that you used

- ☐ All the images in a LINKS or IMAGES folder

- ☐ Folder named after book to house all other files and folders

- ☐ Work files in folder (Recommend having a main one and back-up, i.e. *.indd and *idml)

- ☐ PDF version (2001-xa format for print-ready or print quality)

- ☐ EPUB (Reflowable) - optional

- ☐ Folder for fonts called FONT with copies of the files for future (they can go obsolete later)

- ☐ Did you save in the correct color profile (CMYK, RGB, 240% CMYK, etc)?

- ☐ Did you run ADA Compliance check in Adobe for ADA PDF needs? (optional)

- ☐ Do you need to convert EPUB to MOBI? (Consider using Calibre or similar converters)

- ☐ Has someone reviewed the file for issues besides you?

- ☐ Are the Header and Footers showing the correct text?

- ☐ Is your Table of Contents correct and numbered or not missing a chapter?

- ☐ Do your images bleed to the BLEED edge pass the TRIM edge?

- ☐ Double check that all your text is 0.5" from TRIM edge including Header and Footer

- ☐ Have you printed test pages on a local computer?

- ☐ Does your file meet the needs of your printer (Print-on-Demand AND Offset printers)

- ☐ Viewing for Web and Emails PDF - Did you save a "Reduced Size" PDF version?

- ☐ Has your customer signed off and reviewd the document before uploading to vendors?

BOOK TITLE: _____

SUBTITLE: _____

SAVING CHECKLIST

☐ A copy of the Manuscript or text file in a DOC, DOCX, RTF file that you used

☐ All the images in a LINKS or IMAGES folder

☐ Folder named after book to house all other files and folders

☐ Work files in folder (Recommend having a main one and back-up, i.e. *.indd and *idml)

☐ PDF version (2001-xa format for print-ready or print quality)

☐ EPUB (Reflowable) - optional

☐ Folder for fonts called FONT with copies of the files for future (they can go obsolete later)

☐ Did you save in the correct color profile (CMYK, RGB, 240% CMYK, etc)?

☐ Did you run ADA Compliance check in Adobe for ADA PDF needs? (optional)

☐ Do you need to convert EPUB to MOBI? (Consider using Calibre or similar converters)

☐ Has someone reviewed the file for issues besides you?

☐ Are the Header and Footers showing the correct text?

☐ Is your Table of Contents correct and numbered or not missing a chapter?

☐ Do your images bleed to the BLEED edge pass the TRIM edge?

☐ Double check that all your text is 0.5" from TRIM edge including Header and Footer

☐ Have you printed test pages on a local computer?

☐ Does your file meet the needs of your printer (Print-on-Demand AND Offset printers)

☐ Viewing for Web and Emails PDF - Did you save a "Reduced Size" PDF version?

☐ Has your customer signed off and reviewd the document before uploading to vendors?

Picture Books

Don't give people what they want,
give them what they need.

Joss Whedon

Preparing the Manuscript

Picture books requires the most preparation and planning before writing and typeset. These books are highly dependent on the author's understanding of what the final product is aiming for far in advance unlike those who write fiction and non-fiction. Authors developing this book type need to be very aware of the choices they are making from the start and coordinate with an illustrator or review the illustrations they wish to utilize in their book. It's not uncommon that the typesetter and illustrator are the same person, but this is something that needs to be asked of those who are hired or contracted out. The best course is work up a storyboard or mock-up, but we'll dive into detail how to go about making this for purposes to aid the typesetting process.

Picture books need the author to decide trim and orientation first!

The types of decisions that need to be made upfront include trim size, orientation, illustrator versus typesetter, age of target reader, and number of pages. It can feel like the complete opposite to typesetting any other type of book because the decisions that have to be made beforehand would typically be made last after a manuscript is completed. Here, you have to write with which page, the layout of images and font, and more in mind so that you are delivering the content in a way that matches the expectations of the audience and who may be reading the book to them.

Unlike other genres and book types, picture books have a split audience.

Unlike other genres and book types, picture books have a split audience, which can make the process a challenge at times. This among several other factors make picture books a high pressure book to write. Not only are they writing to tell a story to children from 0 to 12 years of age, but they have to convince parents, schools, and libraries why this book should be given to their audience or read to them. Let's break down some of the factors and decisions you should be making in advance, even as you write and edit your picture book content.

WHAT TYPE OF PICTURE BOOK ARE YOU CREATING?

This may be hard to believe, but you do need to decide early on what the function of your picture book will be and what age ranges you are making it for. If you are aiming to compete with the market, there are several breakdowns in the industry on the expectations expected for picture books. Straying too far from these expectations could limit your book's ability to reach its audience through the filter of the guardians and parents who decide on which books to purchase for them.

For starters, there's a number of things you shouldn't see, such as chapters, footnotes, more text than picture on a page, two-column layouts, and so on. The moment it fails visually to look like a picture book or looks like something more wordy than what is expected, it'll be abandoned. Here is a table of the current trends expectations, including page count and word count. Much of what this section will cover is a collection of information from active publishers, authors, and experts, such as author and founder of Orange Blossom Publishing, Arielle Haughee.

Name	Age	Word count	Pages	Illustration	Trim size
Board books (inc. interactive; traditional and offset only)	0–2	Up to 300	5–7 spreads	Every page	Smaller sizes, varies
Young Picture Book (inc. concept)	2–3	Up to 500	32 pages	Every page	8"–11"
Preschool Picture Book	4–6	Up to 800	32 pages	Every or most	8"–11"
Early readers	6–7	Up to 1000	32+ pages	Every or most	6 x 9
Non-Fiction Picture Book	2–18	Varies	Varies	Every or most	Varies
Graphic novels	6–18	Varies	Varies	Every page	Varies

Choosing a Trim Size

The first step for a picture book is knowing what trim size you a choosing and why. It's vital you choose now and relay this information to illustrators and be mindful throughout the process of this choice. Unlike other books that can wait for this decision until you have a manuscript ready for typeset, picture books need you to create and write the book with this in mind. The younger the audience, the larger the book tends to be or higher chances of choosing a landscape-trim size. Most books are also hardcover to increase their durability. If you are aiming to self-publish, be aware that many vendors do not provide hardcover, or even so, may not have a landscape option. Be sure to investigate this ahead of time. IngramSparks does provide both of these, but the most available landscape size option within the Print-on-Demand world is 11 in by 8.5 in.

Common Trim Sizes for Picture Books

- 11 x 8.5
- 10 x 10
- 10 x 8
- 10 x 7
- 8.5 x 11
- 8 x 10
- 8.5 x 8.5
- 8 x 8

Chapter Books to Middle Grade

- 6 x 9
- 6 x 6
- 5.25 x 8
- 5 x 8
- 4 x 7

Portrait, Landscape, or Square

This has to be the most missed aspect when a children's book comes across my desk. I will have a portrait picked trim size with images in square and landscape orientation – nothing matches the trim option! The colliding orientation can create a nightmare of issues with the author and formatter as it forces the typesetter to make hard decisions, such as how to leave or create white space and whether to chop a portion of the provided images off to force a bleed look (when the picture goes to the edge of the page).

Regardless, the decision you make can have a massive impact on how you layout your book. It's best to know the book trim size, orientation, and reader expectations as you start to plan out a picture book even though for many authors this may feel "backwards" in workflow. You should be aware and choose only ONE orientation for all of your images and page layouts. That doesn't mean you can't have a different sized image anywhere, but you do need to know how you plan on incorporating them and how you will make up for the whitespace it may create.

A square is self-evident as an image that is as wide as it is tall. As for a landscape orientation, this is a horizontal design that pans left to right like the landscape before you. Portrait is a vertical setup,

Picture Books

and you can remember this by thinking of the orientation of the Mona Lisa portrait. I highly recommend looking at similar books for the same audience or purpose as your own and see what trim sizes and orientations have been used. If you are having a tough time deciding which orientation to use for you story, here's recommendations that I see often including over on *Kindlepreneur.com*:

- **Landscape or Horizontal** – Great for books about a journey or needing panoramic scenes whether they are on a single page or two-page spread. Examples: *The Grumbler, Magic School Bus, Where the Wild Things Are*

- **Portrait or Vertical** – Character focused and sharing emotions of the characters or story as part of the lesson. Examples: *There's a Monster at the End of This Book, Green Eggs and Ham, The Giving Tree*

- **Square** – Perfect for non-fiction, educational, or instructional-based books. Also great for character focused stories where landscape scenes might be needed at some point. Examples: *Baby's First Words, Whose Habitat is That?, How to Catch a Dinosaur*

FONT EXPECTATIONS

Font becomes an art form in picture books. It's big, it's fun, and it's one of the few times you can add more than one font face! It's the only time you can, simply because a picture book is designed to help kids read and identify the meaning behind those unfamiliar words they are attempting to learn and memorize. One of the more unique aspects about picture books is the decision involving size and font face. The younger the reader, the larger the font should be. A shiver font looks like it's cold, and a slimy font looks like it is dripping down the page. A roar can scream across a two-page spread and blast a character on the other side. You can play with these but be mindful to treat these as part of the image while helping your audience identify words.

When you begin typesetting this type of book, it's always best to place your textual content and images on their own layers for changes and corrections. Again, this book type is very artful and being able to change only one aspect without recreating it goes a long way to make your job easier. Writing text onto or within the image can be risky, especially if your illustrator and typesetter are not one and the same. That doesn't mean you can't have the illustrator include a keyword that's part of the image be included (such as an artful roar or similar image provided for those keywords as seen in books like *There's a Monster at the End of This Book*). It's common for font size to be larger than 20-point size in picture books. This isn't seen often in other book types unless it's a workbook or pull quote. Be sure to take a look in the Before You Start section where there is a chart of font sizes.

One last detail involving font you should consider Is if the font face has one-story or two-story styled lettering. A terrific way to distinguish the two is when learning our letters and learning to write we are taught one-story style lettering. Two-story fonts are often prominent in the body text in chapter books and fiction work. Depending on your audience and subject matter, this may have an enormous impact on the lessons and readership for the picture book you are making. So much so, one-story font is also called primary school font for that reason. Here are some fonts to consider for these two types:

One-story
- Vitesse
- Chalet
- Futura
- FSAlbert
- Sassoon Primary

Two-story
- Times
- Helvetica
- Calibri
- Garamond
- Brocha

Maximum Word and Page Counts

As you prepare to flesh out and design your picture book, make sure the manuscript is adhering to the fact you are expected to have a certain word and page count. The younger the audience, the smaller these maximums tend to be. The older the audience, the more you should consider moving your manuscript into the next type, such as chapter books and middle grade books, or cutting content to match the market and expectations you are aiming to interact with. Refer to the chart at the start of this section for an idea of the expectations of how much textual content is the industry standard.

For example, for toddlers to pre-kindergarten aged audiences, the max pages are around 35-40 pages, including front and back matter. As you span into chapter and middle grade books, they mimic the length of short stories and novellas with images included throughout. As the word count and audience grows, they start to be designed in black and white as the story becomes larger; eventually, we venture into teen and young adult books that mimic mass market interiors with very little deviation.

Materials and Print Options

Many of these restrictions and options are based on the materials used for printing picture books. When you explore these books in a store or at a library, you will see material not found when making other book types such as chapter books, fiction, or even workbooks. Heavier paperweights, hard covers with embossing, and sometimes additional elements like pop-ups make up a picture book. A lot of these options may not be available if you plan on using Print-on-Demand to distribute your book. Unlike offset printing and traditional publishers who have specialty presses and printers, many picture book authors are limited to a small selection of publishing venues and often must stick with lighter, thinner paper, standard coloring, and mostly paperbacks made with perfect binding or glued. If you are aiming to have a book designed in landscape, know that Print-on-Demand options become super limited with 11 in by 8.5 inches being your only option. Make sure before reaching out to an illustrator, that you've decided on a trim size and how the book should be printed. There might be unexpected needs to make the book depending on your binding type and offset printer's requirement.

ILLUSTRATIONS, ILLUSTRATORS, & GRAPHIC DESIGNERS

The fun part of a picture book is the art and illustrations that make up most of the storytelling, but also the deciding factor on how you will format your book. If you know your trim size and orientation, then you're now ready to decide on how you want to create your illustrations. It is vital that you understand the parameters, requirements, and other needs of the images in regard to the trim size and layout you are intending the final product to have. Some authors illustrate their books themselves, but that's not an option for others. You have a few options in this matter, and it's highly dependent on the type of art you wish your book to have.

If you are planning to hire someone to help you create and format your book, consider seeking out a graphic designer or illustrator who is knowledgeable in typesetting or at least picture book layouts. Be sure to hand over the information on how you intend to print the book and pass along information, such as bleed parameters, binding requirements, and other layout information that could influence how the art and typeset is created. They will be able to incorporate and go through more steps with you as your guide. If you do this yourself, be sure to take your time to read the content in this section for information specifically for making one and how to best prepare before starting. Being able to see the full process step-by-step can show how the information and discussions here influence the overall difficulty and ability to make a picture book in the final stage when typesetting.

The art and illustrations that make up most of the storytelling.

If you intend to gather illustrations to give to a typesetter or format yourself, seek out an illustrator who draws in a style you enjoy and within the price range you need. They will not only need to be aware of the trim size and orientation for a picture book, but they need to include room for a 0.25" to 0.5" cutaway bleed so your core image doesn't get chopped when printed. For illustrations added to a section of a single page, you just simply need an image slightly bigger than intended use for best quality when it prints.

If your illustrator is using a physical median (watercolor, markers, acrylics, etc.) over digital painting, make sure you pass on information for file type, resolution (DPI), color mode, and so on. The more information you provide, the easier it is for them to give you the correct variant of scans. If they aren't able to provide you with scans, I recommend hiring an art photographer. If your median is light colored or watercolors, you should consider digitally enhancing the coloration, performing a black/white balance, and checking the levels of said image. In the end, do not expect those colors to match or look the same as the original as there is a loss of detail, texture, and shift in colors that is impossible to recreate by the time it prints in the book.

No matter the book, there is a standard need for file type and settings here when you aim to use images in your book.

- These files should be in CMYK color mode

- Saved at 300-600 DPI (resolution)

- Be in these file types: JPEG, PNG, or TIFF

You can also utilize PDF and export out to image or place as PDF but be mindful most software will be converting all these into a more manageable JPEG format. Sticking with JPEG and saving editable originals can be very effective in keeping overall file size for the PDF and eBook formats down to acceptable levels. This often comes into play with vendors with files size maximums, such as Barnes & Noble requiring eBooks to be 20 MB or below.

What if you can't find an illustrator or have funding restrictions? There's another possibility! Prepare to go on a deep search and rethink your initial book design. Stock photo sites are a wonderful resource for those who can't afford the illustrators or struggling to find one. This includes ShutterStock, DepositPhoto, iStockPhoto, Adobe Stock, and many more sites have a variety of artists who submit sheets and multiple images of characters for all audiences. A fitting example of this is the character you see throughout Writer's Bane! The more active an artist is on these sites, the better chance for the collection to grow and pull from. Some give you a means to reach out to them as well! You can always reach out to them and see if they will also commission pieces.

Basics of Digitally Enhancing Illustrations

Thanks to the digital age, many artists or illustrators have taken to producing art via software. This has made it a better means to reproduce images in a higher brilliance and sharper hues. That doesn't mean hand drawn artwork and watercolors can't join this high-tech advantage. Traditional art can be scanned or photographed to be pulled into the digital realm and in some cases, adjusted. This doesn't come without its share of pros and cons. One being the most common is the lack of capturing texture, hues, or even soft pencil strokes that all-too-often get washed out by the scanner or camera's light. If your art is too big to scan, an art photographer should be able to use a black/white balance card and even adjust and check it.

Once an image has been placed in digitally, you or a design have the freedom to adjust the image as needed. This can be moving elements, changing hues, brightening the overall saturation, and even resetting black and white tones to make richer levels so the image prints sharper. If you can apply a lot of these easy tricks to an image and balance the CMYK spectrum to a richer level, it will make a huge difference when printed. Not every image or color will be able to translate well; for example, blues and purples are often a struggle to lock in without shifting when ink is laid to paper.

> *Offset printing with gloss or semi-gloss paper at about 100+lb. paper with alcohol-based printing for closest match to original work.*

Warning About Watercolors

Out of all the medians your illustrations can be made from, this one comes with a loss of detail and color just from scanning or photographing it. From there, it sways again depending on the options you choose. If you are ok with digitizing and drastically shifting your watercolors for print and not looking to match the original artwork, you will feel this impact the least. As for those looking to match it and capture the watercolor pieces as they are, you won't get this result. First, the act of scanning or taking a photo removes the texturing that watercolors often have, as well removing some of the sharpness and overlapping details. From there, I recommend offset printing with gloss or semi-gloss paper at about 100+lb. paper with alcohol-based printing for closest match to original work. If you decide to move forward with Print-on-Demand, be warned that you will continue to lose vibrancy and details due to the fact only matte paper is available and most are water-based ink printing and may cause saturation issues. This becomes most noticeable with a picture-book printer in Print-on-Demand.

Black and White Balance

If you are using Photoshop, Fire Alpaca, or some other photo editing software, you should be able to do this. Many of the photography editing software may be able to assist with this technique as well as the others to follow. Whichever software you use, there should be tutorials out there to assist you best as far as this book goes, the aim is to explain what it's meant to do and hint as to why you might want to apply this to your own formatting and images. As for this one, it helps establish true black and true white on the image and adjusts the image color range accordingly. Often when we scan an image, the black has a shine to it and might come off as a dark gray or even brown. This gives you a chance to "reset" the expectations and identify where these are on the image if you have both visible.

Levels in Spectrum

Images come with levels that spread a variety of hues and channels. Often black and white being on opposite ends, they come with slight dips beyond the peak of these colors that can take away from the overall sharpness of the image spectrum. Cutting out or knocking them to the peaks or using auto levels features can bring an image to pop more visually.

Hue & Saturation

Hue and saturations levels or using filters that shift these can do a wide range for an image. If the colors seem to have washed out, you might be able to recover faded colors using this feature. Also scanned or photographed images may have washed out and either you can darken the hue values or even adjust contrast and brightness settings to recover the look of the original artwork. Sometimes this setting allows a moment for you to change the hue or coloration of the art and make decisions you normally would have missed out on. Using a masked layer stacked with this can even allow you to change a color on a single item in the image, but that's best for a tutorial as it delves into photo editing and is beyond this book's conversation focused on typesetting.

DPI, IMAGE SIZE, AND RESOLUTION ADJUSTMENTS

The resolution of an image is very important! The first aspect to this is the size. You don't need your image to be 44 inches by 21 inches if your book is only 11 inches by 8.5 inches. If you are bleeding images off the edge, the image needs to only be 11.25 inches by 8.75 inches at the very least to give some room for image placement that allows bleed and trim. It's always smart to have the image slightly bigger, but too large and it may cause the program or computer to crash (especially those on personal or home systems). It also makes saving backups or throwing it on a cloud storage much more feasible.

Once the size is within a reasonable range (exact with bleed or slightly larger in the same orientation or ratio), you need to make sure the resolution is set between 300-600 DPI. Anything under 300 is at risk to pixelate or be blurry. Know that most images saved from internet are usually only 72-96 DPI, so make sure what you are saving is the full image and not a smaller web version or down-sampled variant. Images that are over 600 DPI are at risk of the printer shrinking and may result in unwanted quality or results. It's always best to avoid these sorts of situations and keep the control and final product in your hands.

CMYK VERSUS RGB

Print and physical books are printed using CMYK colorations. This uses a set amount of cyan, magenta, yellow, and black layered on the page. Depending on the printer this can be applied with alcohol or water-based inks and vary in brightness (often influenced by the paper chosen). Water based inks are limited to 240% CMYK saturation level with paperweights at 70lbs or less as seen in print-on-demand applications.

IMAGE NAMING

Be sure to be consistent or concise with how you are naming your images. You can do this in a number of ways which includes consecutively (image01, image20, image03...), by location (Chapter01, Chapter02_SUBHEAD, Chapter02_Figure1.1), or

labelled by what they are (Flowers01, RosesAndBees, AuntMayAndHerPig...). You should always avoid using symbols and spaces since these may cause issues in final formats. Depending on your software and how you export for eBook format, having images with names that include open spaces, dollar signs ($), hashtags (#), and similar often will cause them not to load or fail when uploaded to a vendor. I highly recommend using only alphabet and numbers with underscore if need be. In programming we do this as well and often default to camelCase (LittleTimmysWagon, IHateThisPictureTheMost, ImageNameLikeThis...) as the safest means to prevent programming errors.

IMAGE FILE TYPES

Images come in a variety of types and the best ones to use for publishing are JPEG and TIFF formats. You can use a PNG, which preserves the transparency unlike JPEG or even a PDF file. You should keep these between 300-600 DPI and at least a little larger than the intended size to make sure you have room to trim the image if needed. TIFF is considered the best format and has been used in the printing and graphic design world as the superior option. Most Print-on-Demand printers want the files saved in PDF2001XA format, and this converts images to JPEG. Same thing happens when exporting to EPUB; the images are often converted to JPEG or PNG depending on what you are using. Thus, it is recommended to save in JPEG for several reasons, including the fact it's a smaller size, translates into eBook without issues, and prevents any issues when converting to final PDF format changes to the images.

PERMISSIONS & USAGE RIGHTS

Images and artwork can fall under public domain rights, but if they don't, you will need to purchase usage rights or get permission. If you pulled your images from a service like ShutterStock or similar stock photo site, they usually have different levels you can purchase for usage rights. This is the safest means for images and artwork. If you intend to hire an illustrator, be sure to cover the usage and contract with them how books are sold and their images will be used from the book to creating swag, bookmarks, banners, and more. Some may clear you for using the images in the book only and not for marketing materials. Be sure to add the permissions granted in the copyright section or even an illustration rights section as a type of appendix. It's always best to give credit where it's due on your copyright page at the very least.

Designing the Pages

It is vital that as you design your picture book that you are aware of the types of pages typically seen inside them. There are several ways to execute laying text and images, whether you aim to have multiple spreads or need to find ways to emphasize the character or an item. Here is a breakdown of the types I've seen and encountered both as a mother to kids and formatter of children's books. In my experience, knowing how you can present and give agency to mix-and-match has made a significant impact on my authors, and I hope this section does the same for you. The first decision often falls to, *is this a page or a spread layout,* and from there, it's a simple assessment of image and text being applied in the best means to the reader to drive the story.

A few things to always keep in mind as you typeset your book, or even a picture book for someone, is the fact page flips are a big deal. Each time a child turns the page, there should be a clear means of doing so and the images should flow together, or the textual content should have a clear ending or pull for the next page. A great book that really takes this concept to the next level is Sesame Street's *There's a Monster at the End of This Book.* Trends in styles within the picture book industry have shifted in a few ways that keeps some styles while completely rending other layouts to be outdated. Beware of the books you are using as a reference and whether the layouts are still relatable to the current market. For example, having a two-page spread of a singular scene with text on one or both sides is still common practice while the style of an entire image on one side and text only on the other is considered an outdated style.

Picture Book Layouts

The most common picture book layout is an image filling the entire page or spread with text added on a layer above this. Sometimes in older books or self-published children's books you will have a spread split to a page with the image and a colored or white page featuring the text. Other designs have elements spread all over the page interacting with the text as often seen in Dr. Seuss books. When styling the pages of a picture book, you have to be consistent. It should walk the child and readers through the tale as if playing out a movie of sorts, the page flips timed in the right moment to make the child feel as if they are pushing the story forward. If you are sticking to industry expectations, you'll discover you have a very limited number of pages to tell the story visually. It cannot be expressed enough that prior to hiring an illustrator, you need to create a storyboard or keen sense of direction in your manuscript. Picture books can prove a challenge for both sides, and the more communication exchanged with examples the better the outcome for all involved.

Be sure to look at books your readers like and see how they are layering these elements. Does the font take up a lot of real estate? Are things layered or separated? How often does the placement of images change? Always keep up to date with the readership and competition. When styling the pages of a picture book, you have to be consistent, not only in delivery but also with the industry, or you risk the book being overlooked. I can't say this enough regarding writing and formatting books. If you are willing to stick to industry expectations, you'll discover you have a limited number of pages to tell the story visually. Glancing at the chart at the beginning of this section can help you start to plan and storyboard your layouts.

Remember as you design your picture book that you can mix and match all the page and spread layouts to help tell your story visually. The art and textual content should be delivered in a constant style, while the layout itself can shift to accommodate the story beats, like you see in the book *Mother Bruce* or *Bad Seed*. This also requires the need to have an illustrator fully aware of what layouts they

will be making for you in advance. Picture books and workbooks both require design to be in the forefront for best results unlike fiction and chapter books that are text only or have images sprinkled throughout. It cannot be expressed enough that prior to hiring an illustrator, you have decided how many pages and layouts are in your book, how much text and which page it lands on. Creating a storyboard that you share with an illustrator or even a hired formatter can prevent many headaches on both ends and speed up and improve the experience. Picture books can prove a challenge for both sides and the more communication exchanged with examples, the better the outcome for all involved.

IMAGE + TEXT SPREAD LAYOUT

This is a dated and older layout style regarding the realm of picture books. It features the image on one page of the spread with the text of the story on the other. If you intend to compete aggressively on the market against other books, you may want to avoid using this layout. As for someone looking to tell a story to share with family and friends, this works perfectly well.

IMAGE WITH TEXT OVERLAY PAGE LAYOUT

The most common of the current layout choices for picture book designs is this one. In this layout, images cover all of the page (bleeding off the page), and the font is placed on top in a contrasting color, size, style, and/or faded background to pull it out of the image.

MULTIPLE IMAGE PAGE LAYOUT

These pages usually have the most whitespace in all the picture book. Either a singular image or an array of single images with text emphasize the character or certain objects or even actions. This is a wonderful opportunity to recycle an image of a character from another scene and use it differently as seen in many mass market picture books such as *Mother Bruce*.

FULL SPREAD LAYOUT

The image or text (not both) stretches across 2 pages, a left and right page, to show as one large landscape image or two pages of textual content. In a lot of cases the text may only be present on one page and not the other, but other layouts might have several spots all around the image to show the story unfolding in a sequence or multi-action spread.

RULE OF THIRDS SPREAD LAYOUT

Across a two-page span, an image, graph, or pull quote will cover one complete page and a portion of the adjacent page to leave room on a far left or right edge for font to place. In concept, the object is using two-thirds of the design area to draw the eye to the text or away from the text by doing so. The Rule of Thirds is often used in marketing, print design, or even in filming. It splits the viewing area into thirds from top to bottom and side to side. From this point, you break the content and subject matter up at the key sections to help draw the eye in a certain direction or pull it towards or away.

SPLIT DESIGN IMAGE & TEXT PAGE LAYOUT

Again, this is similar to the Image + Text layout seen in picture books and textbooks. On a single page, whether it's the right or left, the image and text split the space. Sometimes this is done in a 50/50 spit, or a two-thirds split, but often features a white space or colored space where the text will be.

WHITESPACE PAGE LAYOUT

This page is often an indicator of a chapter starting or ending. Sometimes it can be a section or partition marker of some kind. It's notorious for having a lot of white space or empty, unused space on the page spread. What little content is there usually is textual to guide or inform the reader in preparation of something changing or a transition within the book. You see this a lot in textbooks and fiction books with right page only chapter starts.

EXAMPLES OF MANUSCRIPTS

For the sake of formatting or for authors hiring a typesetter, this section provides some insight on formatting the manuscript for the best means of communicating how to pair the illustrations with the textual content. Remember that in picture books, it's vital to clarify and be aware what lands on a left and right page, and that not every page needs text or an image depending on the layout you've chosen. Showing or having examples of other books can prove useful for designing these books and provide clear direction on layout and final look. It's vital that you write a manuscript that gives clear definition to how this book will be read.

Taking the time to scrapbook a storyboard can troubleshoot issues far in advance and make the actually formatting in software aspects easier and faster to tackle. It also provides a blueprint that can reveal early issues, such as where the next line falls versus intended page, or even expose if you have too much textual content for the illustration. Remember that page 1 and other odd-numbered pages will always be on the right per software and CMS styling, or more plainly put, the industry standard. Another thing to be mindful of is to make sure the image names match what you are using to identify with in your manuscript. Whether you are doing your own book or providing materials to someone, this helps in moments where you feel overwhelmed and are struggling to figure out where everything lands inside the book's overall design. This will limit the chances of grabbing the incorrect image of the "boy" since we might have four or five that identify as this at a glance.

TEXT WITH IMAGE PLACEMENT

For this book type, this is going to be the more common type encountered with textbooks, workbooks, or image heavy content. Throughout the text, there should be indications for image placement and should be clearly marked, much like a subhead or citation. For visual aid, I always encourage highlighting these yellow and treat them as their own paragraph. It's also helpful to use a keyword like "IMAGE" and brackets to help make the image placement stand up, for example:

[[IMAGE01: This picture shows the difference between nightshade and chili pepper flowers]]

These one-liners should be placed between the paragraphs they should be near or on the same page as the text. The importance of this is so when creating an eBook, the typesetter can make sure it falls inline at the right point of the content. It can also make it easier to play with the page layout as they apply the design and text begins to autoflow from page to page with the changes.

STORY BOUNCE

This simply is stating what goes where in the manuscript as it bounces through the story beats or pages. Be mindful of how much textual content you are providing on pages and identify which image to be used concisely. For example, a manuscript using this format might appear like this:

- Title page (right)
- Copyright (left) with Dedication
  - Image01 at the top, small
  - Dedicated to all the kids who seek an adventure of their own
  - Copyright 1999 Author J. Smith etc.
- Page 1 (right) Image02
  - "Wow, the world sure is big when I'm all alone," marveled John.
- Page 2 & 3 (spread) Image03
  - John lost his dog when they moved. His mommy decided it was time little John Wick got a new puppy. Today, they would visit the animal shelter!
- Page 4 (left) Image04 & Image05
  - Image04: John couldn't believe the amount of doggies who needed homes.
  - Image05: Barking and bouncing, each one was excited to see him.
- Page 5 (right) Image06
  - They came in so many shapes, sizes, and colors. None of them reminded him of his old doggy Daisy.

Picture Books

Note how there is no mistake where in the book these images and their text go as you 'flip through' the book. It's important to leave nothing out while keeping your instructions consistent and cohesive with same naming methods and delivery. This gives the typesetter a little room for choosing where content falls and to adjust content if needed based on images and text needed on each spread. You can even leave it up to the typesetter to decide which keywords they emphasize or encourage them to do so.

DETAILED FORMAT

This is for authors who have something more specific in mind for placement, including giving instructions as to where the textual content falls and may give a variety of more in-depth directions. For comparison, this would be the above example with additional bullets where a greater level of instructions addresses text locations, specialty font changes, and even image placement for a variety of page layout styles. In this example, words in bold are assumed to need font or artistic touch to emphasize the word's meaning and provide visual clues for early readers.

- Font Face: Palatin Kids
- Size 24 where possible
- Emphasize highlighted words artfully
- Title page (right)
- Copyright (left) with Dedication
  - Image01 at the top, small
  - Text in larger font, italics:
    - Dedicated to all the kids who seek an adventure of their own
  - Copyright 1999 Author J. Smith etc.
- Page 1 (right) Image02
  - Text on the bottom of page
    - "Wow, the **world** sure is **big** when I'm all **alone**," marveled John.
- Page 2 & 3 (spread) Image03
  - Text on top left
    - John lost his dog when they moved. His mommy decided it was time little **John Wick got a new puppy**.
    - Text on bottom right
    - Today, they would visit the **animal shelter**!
- Page 4 (left) Image04 & Image05
  - Top left Image04: John couldn't believe the amount of **doggies** who needed **homes**.
  - Bottom right Image05: **Barking** and **bouncing**, each one was excited to see him.
- Page 5 (right) Image06
  - Text at top of page:
    - They came in so many **shapes, sizes**, and **colors**.
    - Text on bottom of page:
    - None of them reminded him of his old doggy **Daisy**.

Storyboarding

When it comes to picture books, I highly recommend this method or combining one of the above with this as a visual guide or blueprint. You can print, cut, and paste the elements to rough out the entire book's look and feel. This is a fantastic way to build a mockup of the book you intend to make and format for print and give concise expectations to a typesetter or experiment with what you had in mind for the final product. Before starting digitally, this allows you to troubleshoot issues that may need you to adjust text and illustrations prior to formatting the book. Most issues found this way are still relatively easy to fix by simply changing methods, book options, or changing fonts and images. Storyboarding can also be a great means to discover how many images you will need the illustrator to make as well as to where they need to be mindful of page edges and space for text to overlay. The following types of issues can be revealed at a glance by using this method:

- Illustrations not allowing enough space for text to overlay
- Images that have the characters too close to the edge and will be cut when stretched to the bleed edge and cross the trim
- Images that have text as part of the image in need of adjusting to fit trim
- Trim size and orientation versus illustration size and orientation
- Amount of text for the page (too much is the common issue)
- Number of illustrations needed
- Amount of pages the story needs
- Story page flip and how that impacts the reader and story

CREATING A STORYBOARD

One of the best ways to help you plan out your picture book is to outline it in the form of a storyboard as seen in comics and animated films. Print images and clip out text and move things around or take a sketchbook out and doodle a rough version. Stick figures and shapes work are just fine! You will need to account for the layout and limitations of the printed version from the beginning, even if you are still revising the text. Everything in a picture book impacts how the final look of a page turns out, for better or worse.

Get Crafty!

Sometimes it helps to roll up your sleeves and do more than write it or click and drag on the computer. One of my favorite things to see is where a picture book author has printed, cut, and pasted content in a mock-up book. Something about this can be eye-opening to an author and content awareness and available space become alarmingly tangible. I recommend using a manila folder and cardstock pages to piece this impromptu scrapbook together. Whether you have a portrait or landscape layout, you should be able to mimic the look enough to be able to understand how images, trim size, margins, and text interact within the design. Using a square trim size? Not biggie! Just cut the folder down to size!

Others simple staple pages together and cut and paste printed elements onto the page. This can serve as an excellent guide as you format the book or for your typesetter to rely on. Being able to see the real-world demo of the end-product may simply be stick fingers and glue stick cut outs, but it provides a kinetic means of design that you only see in workbooks. Well, if crafts aren't your thing, here's some worksheets to aid you in designing your storyboard for your book! Don't think this is only good for children's books. This can make a world of difference in creating and formatting comics, graphic novels, workbooks, and image layouts in textbooks.

PROJECT TITLE: _____ GENRE: _____

STORYBOARD

PICTURE [_____]

ACTION [_____]

_____
_____
_____
_____
_____
_____
_____

PICTURE [_____]

ACTION [_____]

_____
_____
_____
_____
_____
_____
_____

PICTURE [_____]

ACTION [_____]

_____
_____
_____
_____
_____
_____
_____

PICTURE [_____]

ACTION [_____]

_____
_____
_____
_____
_____
_____
_____

PROJECT TITLE: _____   GENRE: _____

STORYBOARD - PORTRAIT

STORYBOARD – LANDSCAPE

STORYBOARD - SQUARE

Formatting the Book

Hooray! Now that we've talked and prepped this thing to no end, you should be ready to format this book with confidence. Why? Because it is so much easier to resolve problems at the manuscript and prepping stage than when you are formatting and making the book. Though, as said before, I am an avid user of word to InDesign, I will do my best throughout the book to provide information in an all-encompassing and design angle. If you were looking for software tutorial, this isn't the book for you. Getting detailed instructions on how to set parameters in Word, Scribd, and similar word processors isn't the aim.

Instead, we will be focusing on the typesetter-based elements and areas that will be par the course for any book you design. Dependent on the software you are using to design your book in could present its own issues and information may be labeled slightly different or found in different areas. In tandem with a software book, this book may provide some keywords in order to gain the affects you were aiming for in order for you to gain a greater value out of using said programs. In my years of looking for instructional manuals for book design, most of what I have learned was via videos, trial and error, typography college courses, and simply diving into the industry headlong with an open mind and understanding of the roots of publishing and its history. It probably also helped I delved in some game design, development, and programming, so I could troubleshoot creative solutions.

Without further ado, it's time to make this book using these step-by-step, or page-by-page instructions below. Feel free to adjust this to suit your own style and needs since there are various methods to achieve the results seen here. Again, the aim here is to simply the process while being able to make quality print books, enhance eBooks, and create a PDF that falls close as possible to being ADA compliant (Americans with Disabilities Act).

File Setup

The file or page size should match the trim size in width and height. Make sure the intended orientation matches what you intended, specifically landscape versus portrait. Depending on the program, you may have to set bleed settings to include a 0.125" bleed on all sides or for outer margins. For some Print-on-Demand vendors, they may want the inner margin to have no bleed since this is the side of the page that is glued to the spine of the book. You usually get to set up or define the overall margins as well.

Be mindful that with picture books you will be saving a flat PDF for eBook design and that you don't have to fret over threading text boxes together as seen with all other book types. It's more important to make sure images are bleeding off to the marked edges just pass the trim edge, that elements are layered and overlayed in the right order, and textual content is within the margins provided by the printer or Print-on-Demand requirements of 0.5" from trim size edge. Here are my recommended settings for this book type:

Picture Books

- **Industry Standard Numbers:**
  - 0.125" Bleed from trim edge
  - 0.5" Margin for content inward from trim edge
  - Large page counts will require a larger 0.625" or higher inner margin or gutter
  - Special binding may change the needs for inner margins

- **Inner or inside margin:** 0.625" for books under 300 pages and

- 0.75" to 0.8" for books pushing far into the 500+ range since where the pages' bind needs more space to avoid words falling into the crack of the book.
  - Granted, this is a picture book, and you can sometimes get away with a 0.5" margin.

- **Outer or outside margins** (including top and bottom) should be 0.5" to 0.625"
  - Typically have main body pages with header and footer set, and you can increase the top and bottom margins to 0.8-0.875" to give yourself space to place and space these from your body text.

- **Picture Books:**
  - Margins only apply to page numbers, textual content, and similar.
  - Images in a majority of cases bleed off the page.
  - 0.5" margin on all sides for an 18- to 34-page book is more than enough for Perfect Bound or Saddle Stitch books.

Wondering where these numbers come from? Your vendors should have File Creation Guides via a PDF or webpage. No matter if you plan on using offset printing, KDP, IngramSparks, or a similar vendor, these parameters never change. This is the basic needs of a file going to print and will give the press some wiggle room. These parameters will change if you choose more elaborate binding and use certain presses. Always make sure you get these settings from the printer and design the book with these in place from the start.

USING LAYERS

Most of the layout software allows you to create layers such as InDesign (not any of the word processors though they do have header footer options). These come in handy in keeping content stacked or arranged in the right order. This includes making sure watermarks are below the body text layer and even keeping the header and footer elements on the top and not lost behind images and such. A bonus to using this feature is the ability to lock them and make sure you don't accidently change, move, or delete them unintentionally. With picture books, you often use images that take up the entire page and risk losing these elements completely. Recommended layers include the following listed in the order they should fall and usage:

- **Header and Footer Layer** – This will have your top layer text boxes that contain the header and footer which usually hold page numbers, title, author, and/or current chapter. You can control these with master pages. In a word processor, this is an option or specific setting that is influenced by section breaks to change how they look from section to section of the book's layout.

- **Default or Body Text Layer** – Here you will manage the primary text box in which the main content autoflows through threaded textboxes or pages.

- **Background Layer** – At the bottom of the list, there should be a background layer that is designed for images, spreads, and watermarks that need to fall under the textual content.

This doesn't mean you need to use all these layers, but it's highly recommended to give you more control when formatting. If the program you are using doesn't provide layers, check for features that define objects on the page as needing to be "Ordered" or "Arranged" with sub-options for "Bring to Front" or "Bring to Back," which mimic what layering does. This should aid you in making sure text and images overlap appropriately.

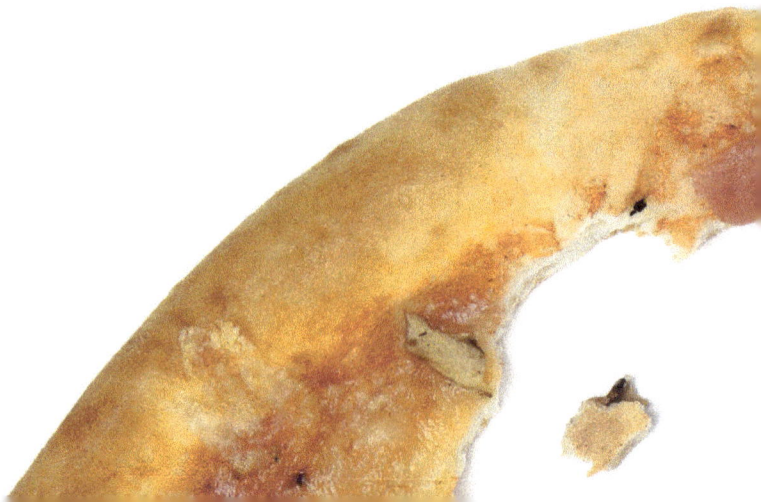

MASTER PAGES

These pages, or templates, are premade pages you can drag and drop into the layout to help speed things along and stay consistent. Know that this is more commonly found as a feature in layout software such as InDesign. Even with a freeform style book, there's a level of consistency with placement of elements such as header, footer, page numbers, watermarks, and other elements that you may not want to shift and wish to keep level throughout the book. In any book, you are going to be applying a few key layout pages. I recommend the following master pages or templates be made in advance to speed up the typeset process:

- **A blank page** with only the margin lines set. You may include a primary text box version for dedication or anchoring title page images into place. Works great for print-on-demand with that last page needing to be blank as well. These will also set your title pages and copyright page as well.

- **A body page** made of a blank page with only the header and footer with a main text box. I recommend putting the header and footer on a top layer that's locked. Predesign a left and right page, often featuring the book title on left and author name on right. You may even design a running header or chapter header that auto updates depending on the software you are using. Adding glyphs and art to page numbers and headers can add a nice creative flair.

- **A chapter page** that can add art, designs, and spacing shifts to accommodate the style implied. I always make right and left page versions, so if I need to change from right page only chapters to continuous, it's ready to adapt accordingly.

- **A numbered blank page** can be useful for areas that may contain images, maps, tables, and similar content where you simply want page numbers only.

FONT CHOICES AND PREP

Font has the most weight in typesetting and interior book design. Your choices and attention to detail to the spacing, size, and types will have a significant impact for better or worse. There are a few things you can do to help yourself prep and streamline your design depending on if you are using styles in Microsoft Word or a combination of Paragraph and Character styles in Adobe InDesign. Prepping and setting up pre-saved files with master pages and these elements can save a lot of hunting and frustrations, especially if you want to shift or change fonts later. If you intend to do typesetting full time or work heavily with fonts, I recommend investing into Font Management programs such as FontExplorer. This can make it easier to keep your growing library from bogging down your computer while making it easier to test out and organize fonts.

PARAGRAPH STYLES OR STYLES

These will make up most of the formatting application in textual content. They work in particular order and repeat as you start a new section or chapter. Making a style in advance can help you quickly adjust, fix, or change the entire typeset without hunting and pecking for certain content in the book. Instead, applying a style and changing the style can shift and fix the book as a whole.

- **Drop Cap** – Whether it's a single letter, word, or line, this is the first paragraph in a chapter or section. It's a way to artfully signal to a reader where to begin reading or add more to the chapter page that makes it stand out other than whitespace.

- **Body Text** – This will be the majority of your content. It should be a legible font comfortable for readers and remain the same throughout the entire book. It builds the font foundation for Drop Caps, Citations/Quotes, Subheads, Tables and more.

CHARACTER STYLES OR SUBFAMILY FONTS

Creating premade character style can help you gain more control on the style of the manuscript as a whole. It also helps build coding within certain programs for eBook creation and keeps these vital aspects from disappearing in the process.

- **Bold** – used to identify keywords, bring words to the front, and stand out louder. There is never a need to make a whole manuscript bold. Instead, choose a thicker or heavier font.

- *Italics* – this has many uses from quotes, to signaling key elements in content, and even to signal internal dialogue in stories.

- Underline – much like bold, this is used to make content stand out, signify a reference (depending on styles like APA), hyperlinks (or clickable content in text), or signal something of importance.

- Keyword – This comes in handy when wanting to stay consistent in font face and size changes in books where you need vocabulary words or key visuals to pop.

- SMALL CAPS – Common to see in reference works or to address religious names or keywords, this is easier to manage as a character style and carries over into eBook better.

OBJECT STYLES OR TABLE STYLES

These are special styles that influence objects, images, and tables. They make sure designs and placement match and can even streamline how items show up in an eBook. Not every software has the means to define these or set them up. As for InDesign, these can help guide image frames, table cells, and more so that you can save time when adding content into the layout and saving you the grief of cracking open object options to adjust every detail.

Page-by-Page

Let's walk through making a picture book. It's taken a lot of discussion and information to get to here, but as you take your time and refer back to key sections, you will find ways to improve and prepare. Be sure to take your time to prep your materials to avoid unwanted stress and troubleshooting for this stage. It can raise the hours this may take you to typeset, or format, exponentially no matter what your skill level may be. As an author doing your own formatting, these issues might be easier to solve on the fly, and if you intend on hiring someone or formatting for someone, this can bring production to a screeching halt until a decision or solution is made. For this I am going to showcase a book I formatted for Orange Blossom Publishing, *Joyride* by Arielle Haughee.

The Checklist!

Here is a checklist that should help you make sure you finished prepping the manuscript and materials before starting the formatting. Often we don't think to ask or double check to include some of these things and it can be detrimental in the final stages leading up to printing the actual book. Whether you are formatting your own book or formatting someone else's, this checklist is to help you gather everything you need before you start.

- Trim Size
- Book Title
- Subtitle
- Author Name (or Pen Name)
- Publisher and/or Logo
- Copyright Page
  - Author name and copyright year
  - Name illustrator, designer, editor, etc.
  - Permissions for any materials used.
  - Public domain or scripture cited.
  - ISBN numbers (Paperback, Hardcover, eBook, Audiobook, etc.)
  - LCCN (Pending or number)
  - Published information and logo
  - The usual legal jargon to protect you, your work, and the publisher.
- Front Matter
  - Foreword: Yes or No
  - Dedication: Yes or No
    - Above Copyrights or Own Page
- Images are ready, clearly named, and all accounted for
  - 300 – 600 DPI
  - Correct size for trim + bleed
  - CMYK color mode
- Manuscript – Text only edition
  - Has image directions that match image names
- Back Matter
  - Author Bio
  - Image
    - Hyperlinks
    - Illustrator Bio
    - Image
    - Hyperlinks

BOOK TITLE: _____

SUBTITLE: _____

TYPESET CHECKLIST

☐ Manuscript text in a DOC, DOCX, RTF file

☐ All the images listed in Manuscript present:

☐ CMYK mode

☐ Between 300-600 DPI.

☐ Trim Size _____ width x _____ height

☐ Author Pen Name - FIRST_____LAST_____

☐ Dedication: Yes or No

☐ Author Bio: Yes or No

☐ Copyright

☐ Publisher information

☐ Additional mention such as artist, design, or typesetter? _____

☐ Scriptures cited from.... Any public domain original publication mentions? _____

☐ Permission granted from... Any materials that have permissions needing to be listed here?

☐ ISBNs for Paperback: _____ Hardcover_____

☐ Audiobook_____ eBook_____

☐ LCCN pending or listed?_____

☐ Front Matter (Acknowledgements, Foreword, Preface, etc.)

☐ Do they want a Table of Contents: Yes or No

☐ Do they have tables to import: Yes or No

☐ Do they want pull quotes: Yes or No

THE WARM-UP!

As mentioned in the front half of this book, the preferred method for designing books is using InDesign due to the amount of control. No matter what software you are using, the parameters and keywords are all the same and much of the process can be even reflected into when you design using a word processor, such as Microsoft© Word.

- Page size needs to be set to the trim size of your book.

- Bleed settings can always be added via page setup or page layout options depending on the program.

- Make sure page margins are keeping 0.5" within the trim or page size.

- If you intend to have headers and footers, be sure margin for body text are larger (0.75" for example) on the top and bottom to give space for them to fall within that 0.5" requirement.

- Choose your fonts in advance or make a list of possibilities for:
  - Chapter
  - Headline or Chapter Title
  - Header/Footer
  - Body Text
  - Pull Quotes

- Decide on Chapter Art or Typeset design for:
  - Spacing
  - Having samples on hand
  - Write down parameters in advance
  - Choose glyph or ornamental font options
  - Prepared images in advance

- Don't forget your checklist! You'll need it for Copyright pages and specifics!

- For chapter and middle grade books:
  - A sense of direction via the manuscript or a storyboard.
  - All images and artwork needed, labeled, and saved in correct format.
  - Font choices have been decided including for keywords to emphasize.
  - Decide if header will be included or not.
  - Check for Front and Back matter needs. These should increase in this book type!

BOOK TITLE: _____

SUBTITLE: _____

WARM-UP CHECKLIST

☐ Trim size set to the page or book size

☐ Add Bleed Settings for 0.125 inches

☐ Set your margins to 0.5 inch from trim edge

☐ Top margin for header set for 0.75 inch

☐ Bottom margin for footer set for 0.75 inch

☐ Inner margin or mirrored margins set to 0.675 omch or higher for spine/glue/page count

☐ Chapter font:_____

☐ Headline font:_____

☐ Header/Footer font:_____

☐ Body Text font:_____

☐ Pull Quote font:_____

☐ Body Text Base Font Size: _____ Line Spacing: _____

☐ Chapter Art prepped and ready to go

☐ Images saved in teh right format and size in advance

☐ Manuscript prepped and image placement clearly marked or Storyboard ready

☐ Glyph and Ornaments picked out. Font: _____

☐ Printer settings and requirements handy for saving and meeting their needs

☐ Templates or Master pages set up for key pages and special pages

☐ Paragraph Styles setup in advance or styles redesigned to match selection

☐ Are you ready?

FRONT MATTER

This is the first few pages that typically consist of title pages, copyrights, and dedication pages. This is the beginning of a book and rarely changes much no matter the genre of the book. One trend to note that is different in picture books is that it's common to see the dedication and copyright on the same page.

HALF TITLE—OPTIONAL

Not necessary for picture books and completely optional, dependent on needs of book and formatting preferences. The first thing you want to prep is the front matter for the book. In this example, we are going for super basic and the most common story bounce that matches many of the mass market picture books to date. The only text here should be the title font. This page should leave room for the author to sign. It is completely optional though and can be replaced by a full title page.

FULL TITLE

Half title page versus full title page can be made simple in a picture book. Half title can feature a text title only and the full title can be the front cover of the book itself. If you decide to do a text-based version, this should have series name, title, subtitle, author name, illustrator, and publisher name and/or logo.

COPYRIGHT & DEDICATION

Increasingly popular is the dedication above the copyright page. Typically, in a picture book, page numbers start on the right page dedication or initial first page. This will always be a right page or should be per CMS style or software restrictions. See the copyright section Anatomy of a Book chapter.

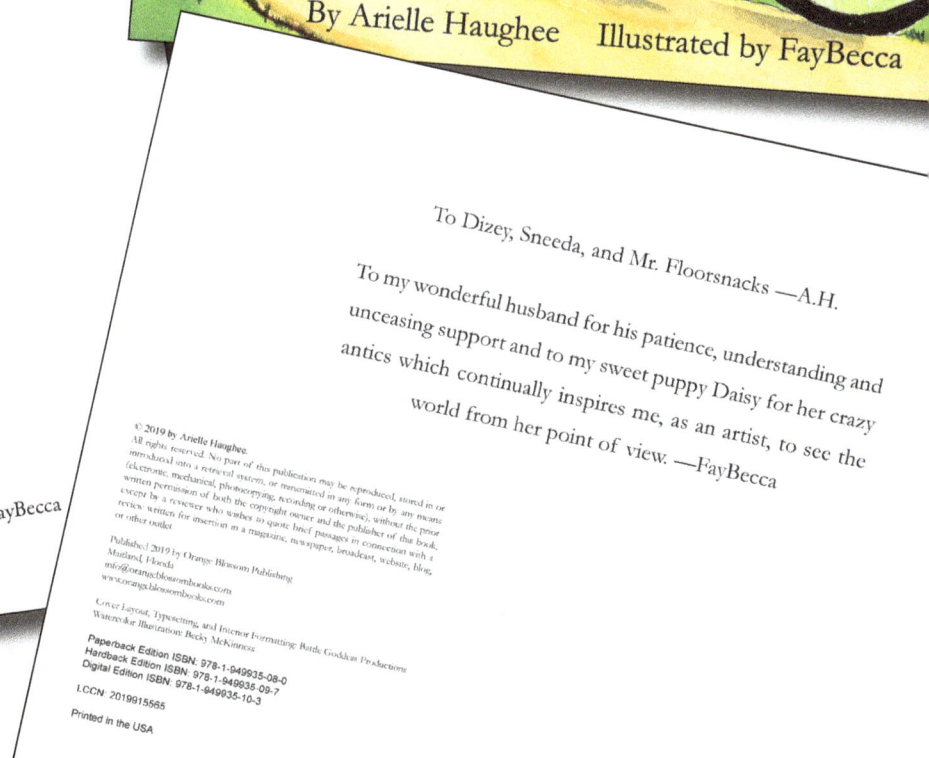

Joyride

By Arielle Haughee   Illustrated by FayBecca

Joyride

By Arielle Haughee   Illustrated by FayBecca

ORANGE BLOSSOM
PUBLISHING

To Dizey, Sneeda, and Mr. Floorsnacks —A.H.

To my wonderful husband for his patience, understanding and unceasing support and to my sweet puppy Daisy for her crazy antics which continually inspires me, as an artist, to see the world from her point of view. —FayBecca

Published 2019 by Orange Blossom Publishing
Maitland, Florida
info@orangeblossombooks.com
www.orangeblossombooks.com

Cover Layout, Typesetting, and Interior Formatting: Battle Goddess Productions
Watercolor Illustration Becky McKinness

Paperback Edition ISBN: 978-1-949935-08-0
Hardback Edition ISBN: 978-1-949935-09-7
Digital Edition ISBN: 978-1-949935-10-3

LCCN: 2019915585

Printed in the USA

CONTENT

U nlike other book types, picture books focus more on the image quality and placements. Another aspect is the fact there's no urgency or importance on threading the pages together. Instead, it comes down to making sure your images are falling on the correct pages and side of the spread, as well as making sure all your textual content is within the printer's requirements (Normally 0.5" from the trim edge). This is one of the rare occasions that you don't need to thread text boxes. You can move and put text boxes where needed, and most of the focus falls onto the images (make sure they are 300-600 dpi, CMYK!).

FIRST PAGE OR SPREAD

The book should be layered with images on bottom, story textboxes overlayed where needed, and header/footer on the top layer. Depending on the layout software, you might be able to apply drop shadow or add outer glows to help the text pop off the image or not blend into the image. Don't be afraid to change the text color as needed, change up font size, or create a variety of effects to emphasize what the word means. Slimy should have drippy lettering, fuzzy should be furry, and so on. Elements like these bring the story to life for readers who are learning what those words might mean.

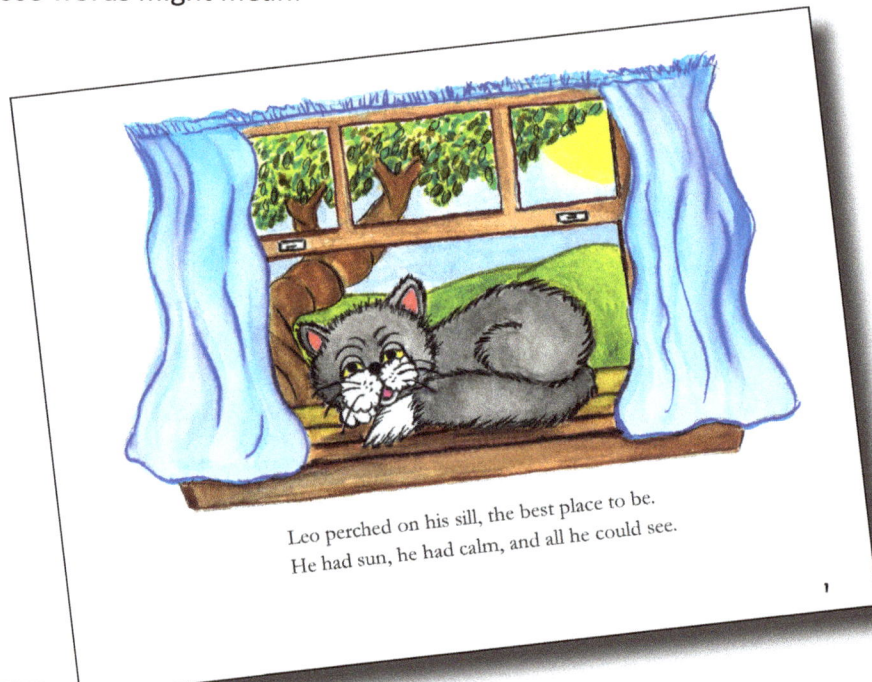

Leo perched on his sill, the best place to be.
He had sun, he had calm, and all he could see.

1

Daisy hopped on the bike and made the bell ring. "We'll **ZOOM** to the park and ride on the swing!"
The wind, how it whipped! Poor Leo clung tight.
This was **terrible, awful**—
he'd have nightmares tonight.

7

Daisy hoppe
the park and
The wind, h
This was *te*
he'd have nig

BLEED VERSUS TEXT MARGINS

Make sure the bleed goes past the trim line or paper's edge to the end of the to the bleed line. If the signature or paper shifts in print slightly, it will cause a white line on the outer edges. Many designers place a white margin or offset the inner margins on spreads. This is dependent on the page spread, number of pages, and type of binding. For beginners you may want to default to treating this as a bleed edge. In picture books, you can push images off the page and across pages in creative ways, but when it comes to text placement, you must have it within 0.5" inch from the trim edge or paper edge. This is so if the signatures or pages shift that your textual content will never be at risk of being cutoff.

STORY FLOW AND OTHER PAGES

Be sure to change up the layout on occasion of placement of font and graphics to drive the story forward and create a need to flip the page. Many formatters will adjust illustrations to white areas out or Photoshop content to allow more room for textual content. If you have the skills to do this, make sure the images blend well and appropriately. Many legacy pieces, or picture books meant for the author and family only, not to compete on a commercial level, have to fret over this less so. Always consider who the book is for and who you are aiming to compete with, if at all. Picture books that complete on a commercial level have more red-tape and parameters to meet than that of a book being put together in a simpler straight-forward layout to share with family and friends.

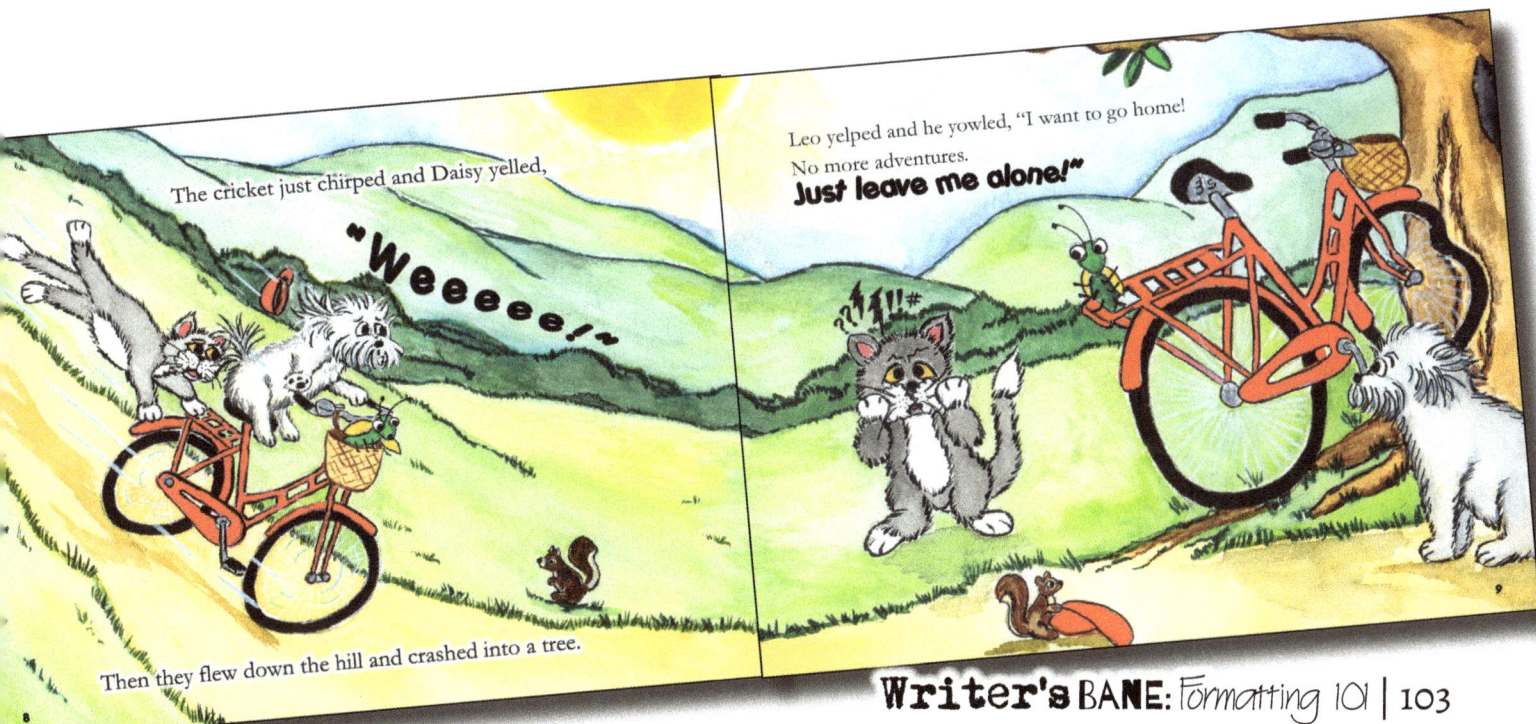

BACK MATTER

Here you will be serving a few crucial roles or bits of information that had no place in the front or core content. For starters, this section is intended to introduce the reader to last thoughts, notes, information, resources, the author and/or illustrator, how to stay in touch, and any means to continue to connect and discover books via the author or publisher, sometimes both. It's a vital resource and a marketing tool in every book as long as the genre and audience make good use of it.

STORY ENDS

In children's books, sometimes there's a special "The End" page. It differs in every book, whether this might be a spread or single page. Some even go as far as having special graphics for this page or moment while others keep it as part of that last bit of the story. There is no wrong way to do this!

BIOS FOR AUTHOR AND/OR ILLUSTRATOR

Even in picture books, it's common to see back pages that hold the biographies for the author and illustrator. This can be on the same page or on a spread across from one another. On occasion they start on their own right page, but this can jump your page count and color printing is pricey, so be mindful and flexible when including this.

RESOURCES

Some books include teacher and parent resources. This can be book club questions, fun activity pages, an information page leading to additional resources, or covering the topic in earnest. If you have a large number of resources, you may want to create a companion piece such as a coloring book or activity book that can be purchased alongside the story. Other authors will provide these as exclusive PDFs offered when you sign up to their newsletter and often make great lead magnets for marketing or exclusive swag at special events.

PRINT-ON-DEMAND – BARCODE PAGE

If you are choosing to publish using Print-on-Demand, don't forget there will be a blank last even page in the back. This is where the printer will include a barcode that contains all the information as to where the book came from and more. Offset printed books don't have this feature at all.

OFFSET PRINTING—END LEAVES

If you are planning to offset print the book, you may have to create additional files for end leaves. I highly recommend asking for templates from your specific printer since these are done slightly differently at times depending on the book binder equipment and process, they use to connect these to the cover and textual aspects of the book. If you are using Print-on-Demand, you bypassed the option to have these, or some do add solid white onto hard covers.

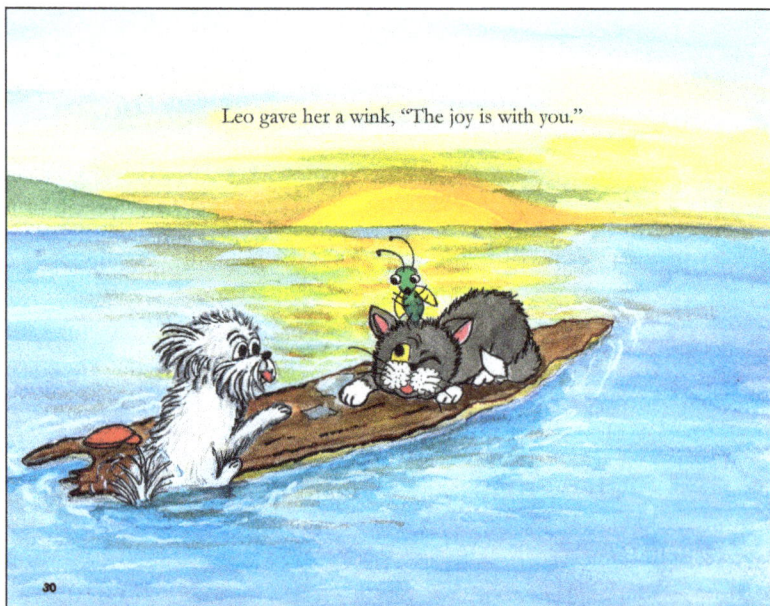

Leo gave her a wink, "The joy is with you."

The End

SAVING THE FILES

Now that you have completed the book, be sure you save the files appropriately. This means for both your work files and the final product for the printer. Be sure to always ask clients and printers what file format and needs are required. For the sake of all things, we will focus on the most common and most versatile versions. If you used InDesign, you can go to File > Package and the software will do its best to grab font files, images, and more into a folder. For those who are using other means, here's a breakdown of the work folder and what to save:

- FOLDER NAMED AFTER BOOK
    - Work File (InDesign, Word, etc.)
    - PDF (2001-xa format aka Press Quality with Bleed recommended)
    - EPUB (Optional, reflowable a must)
    - ORIGINAL folder
        - Holds original text file and any related materials

- FONT folder
    - Copies of font files used (truetype, openface, etc.)
- IMAGE folder
    - Any image used should be placed in here in case you need it or edit or replace later.

As for prepping files for upload to a vendor, the two main types will be PDF and EPUB (reflowable). No matter if you are self-publishing or using a service, these two are the current staple in the industry and have the ability to upload to a variety of distributors and vendors with very little issue.

- PDF Format
    - This is used for print design applications, paperback, Print-on-Demand, and similar.
    - For printing, PDF-X/a: 2001 Format is the most accepted.
    - For web pdf, use web preferred file setting, but remember this file loses values needed for printing for a book.
    - Make sure Bleed Settings are applied or this could cause the file to kick back or be denied.

- EPUB Format
    - Always use reflowable.
    - Write in as much File Info and Metadata information as possible.
    - If attaching a cover image, it should be at least 1600x2400 pixels, 150 dpi, RGB color mode to avoid being kicked back from online vendors.
    - Most accepted eBook type currently with enhanced ability access.

BOOK TITLE: _____

SUBTITLE: _____

SAVING CHECKLIST

- ☐ A copy of the Manuscript or text file in a DOC, DOCX, RTF file that you used

- ☐ All the images in a LINKS or IMAGES folder

- ☐ Folder named after book to house all other files and folders

- ☐ Work files in folder (Recommend having a main one and back-up, i.e. *.indd and *idml)

- ☐ PDF version (2001-xa format for print-ready or print quality)

- ☐ EPUB (Reflowable) - optional

- ☐ Folder for fonts called FONT with copies of the files for future (they can go obsolete later)

- ☐ Did you save in the correct color profile (CMYK, RGB, 240% CMYK, etc)?

- ☐ Did you run ADA Compliance check in Adobe for ADA PDF needs? (optional)

- ☐ Do you need to convert EPUB to MOBI? (Consider using Calibre or similar converters)

- ☐ Has someone reviewed the file for issues besides you?

- ☐ Are the Header and Footers showing the correct text?

- ☐ Is your Table of Contents correct and numbered or not missing a chapter?

- ☐ Do your images bleed to the BLEED edge pass the TRIM edge?

- ☐ Double check that all your text is 0.5" from TRIM edge including Header and Footer

- ☐ Have you printed test pages on a local computer?

- ☐ Does your file meet the needs of your printer (Print-on-Demand AND Offset printers)

- ☐ Viewing for Web and Emails PDF - Did you save a "Reduced Size" PDF version?

- ☐ Has your customer signed off and reviewd the document before uploading to vendors?

Chapter Books &
Middle Grade

All that I hope to say in books,
all that I ever hope to say,
is that I love the world.

E.B. White

PREPARING THE MANUSCRIPT

Chapter books and middle grade books are the bridges between picture books and teaching children to read in mass market formatted books. They mimic the interior format of a typical book while still containing images and sometimes fun elements seen more often in picture books. You will notice the trim sizes significantly smaller as well as lack of square and landscape orientation. Even more so, illustrations and images within these range from a few pages to every other chapter. Word count has jumped immensely, ranging from short story or novella sized (10,000- to 30,000-word count) to mimic a normal novel length depending on the target audience age and genre. Another shift is the lack of colored interiors in this genre as well, making the print costs significantly lower for both offset and Print-on-Demand. That doesn't mean color is off the table, and another growing trend is graphic novels and comics, but these are discussed in a different chapter and require a completely different setup from other books discussed.

WHAT TYPE OF BOOK ARE YOU CREATING?

The best way to get this answer is to decide the age group or grade level of your audience. Elementary school aged kids will be looking for chapter books heavier in graphics and no larger than a novella or 25,000 words roughly. These chapter books are designed to give them short sprints and means to work on their reading muscles for the first time. As you venture into fifth grade to middle school level, you are going to see less and less images and artful aspects within the chapters and pushing closer to a normal novel length of 50-60,000 words. Now we're giving the kids access to the whole track and get their reading strides in place. Know that as you venture into teen and young adult books, you are now designing on par with mass market books for adults (hence why these are in the same section following this book type). The bridge has been fully crossed by the time you reach the young adult group.

Name	Age	Word count	Pages	Illustration	Trim size
Early CB	Grades 1–3	3000–6000	80–120	Every few pages	Smaller than 6 x 9
Middle grade	Grades 3–8	Up to 60,000	200+ pages	Few (10) or none	Varies
Young adult	Grades 9–12	60,000–90K	200+ pages	Usually none	Varies

CHOOSING A TRIM SIZE

Going into chapter books, you will see a drastic drop in overall size of the book since the idea is to mimic the average book look and feel. This includes books being mainly in portrait size and having more textual content on the pages then graphics. *Magic Treehouse, Last Kids on Earth, Fortunately the Milk,* and other titles and series are notable examples of the layout and book size expected in this category. Below are some common sizes in this category, and I've starred the more common sizes. You'll notice they are the lower end since we are still dealing with small hands and don't want to imitate the kids from reading a normal book.

You'll see this shift again for young adult and fiction books to favor the large end of this list as the length of text increases and the readership becomes wider as well as older. It's always a great idea to check out the top sellers or bookstore section in your category or for the same age group. See what the common book sizes are and which you feel best compliments your book and its genre.

- 6 x 9
- 5.25 x 8
- 5 x 8*
- 5 X 7*
- 4 x 7*

FONT EXPECTATIONS

By this point, you no longer must fret over one-story versus two-story fonts like you do in picture book design. Most books default to a serif font for many of the book types and genres moving forward. On occasion certain tweaks to keywords to emphasize what they mean or what is happening in the story can be done artfully without disrupting the text placement. If this is mainly to be viewed online, or if it's science fiction or an educational piece, you may see the body text using a sans-serif font to reflect this. Drop caps are seen for the first time, along with the presence of a header and footer (though on a few accounts, headers may be left off as seen in Scholastic books on occasion, such as *Wings of Fire*). This is the type of book a designer is tasked with important responsibility to bridge a child's picture book with the way most adult books will be formatted. It serves as the training wheels for future readers with some pictures and some font exaggerations as needed. No pressure! With that in mind, it's perfectly normal to see larger font sizes (14- to 16-point font) with a larger line spacing (1.5-1.7 line space; never double space!) to help the kids eyes read and jump to the next line with ease.

On a few accounts, headers may be left off as seen in Scholastic books on occasion, such as Wings of Fire

---

MAXIMUM WORD AND PAGE COUNTS

Page counts are climbing, and most typesets will be shifting into a black and white interior either on white or crème paper moving forward. No longer are you bombarded with needing an image on every page; these books tend to have a few illustrations here and there depending on the print options and age group. The other significant change is you're no longer dealing with page count restrictions and have more elbow room to design with less problem solving. A great example of this is Neil Gaiman's *Fortunately, the Milk.* There's still much of the design that mimics a picture book throughout this book while other areas mimic a trade paperback. Because these are designed to be introduction to the idea of chapters and long form books, they tend to push closer to novella length piece of 25,000 words or more. Many are a collection of short stories with similar themes and tend to be portrait books ranging from 50-150 pages on average. It can be said though if your book is pushing over 60,000 words that you should take another look at the intended audience and consider moving into teen or young adult audience codes, where readers are devouring larger books comfortably.

MATERIALS AND PRINT OPTIONS

It's much easier to save on print cost with middle grade and chapter books since they can be done as black and white with line art. If you do want color illustrations, be mindful of the cost difference. In Print-on-Demand, the price can rise exponentially the larger the page count once you start hitting over 50 pages, and it may not be feasible for the author or the readers to sell a book at such a high cost. Always check pricing before locking in on a style preference regarding this type of book. As trends change, it seems more and more that colored books for this audience fall into graphic novels and comics while black and white interiors are reserved for books with high word counts. If you've created a graphic novel or comic, you should jump to the section that covers this book type since they require a completely different setup from all other book types.

ILLUSTRATIONS, ILLUSTRATORS, & GRAPHIC DESIGNERS

Specifically, for this book type, it's highly recommended to favor grayscale or for best results, black and white line art. This helps with getting kids comfortable to the monotonous black and white tone all books will carry in their future reading material. Keep this in mind no matter which path you decide on. That doesn't mean you can't find colored images to use in your eBook and have them grayscale in your printed book! There's a lot to consider and no combination is completely off limits.

If you know your trim size and orientation, then you're now ready to decide on how you want to create your illustrations. Some authors illustrate their books themselves, but that's not an option for others. You have a few options in this matter, and it's highly dependent on the type of book you're making such as a picture book, middle grade book, or textbook. If you are planning to hire someone to help you create and format your book, consider seeking out a graphic designer or illustrator who is knowledgeable in typesetting or at least picture book layouts. They will be able to incorporate and go through more steps with you as your guide. If you do this yourself, be sure to take your time to read the content in the Picture Book section for information specifically for making one and how to best prepare before starting.

Every book type has its own tweaks to the system or may have areas that are a must for one and not the others. If you intend to gather illustrations to give to a typesetter or format yourself, seek out an illustrator who draws in a style you enjoy and within the price range you need. They will not only need to be aware of the trim size and orientation for a picture book, but they need to include room for a 0.25" to 0.5" cutaway bleed so your core image doesn't get chopped when printed. For illustrations added to a section of a single page, you just simply need an image slightly bigger than intended use for best quality when it prints.

If your illustrator is using a physical median (watercolor, markers, acrylics, etc.) over digital painting, make sure you pass on information for file type, resolution (DPI), color mode, and so on. The more information you provide, the easier it is for them to give you the correct variant of scans. If they aren't able to provide you with scans, I recommend hiring an art photographer. If your median is light colored or watercolors, you should consider digitally enhancing the coloration, performing a black/white balance, and checking the levels of said image. In the end, do not

expect those colors to match or look the same as the original as there is a loss of detail, texture, and shift in colors that is impossible to recreate by the time it prints in the book.

No matter the book, there is a standard need for file type and settings here when you aim to use images in your book.

- These files should be in CMYK color mode
- Saved at 300-600 DPI (resolution)
- Be in these file types: JPEG, PNG, or TIFF

You can also utilize PDF and export out to image or place as PDF but be mindful most software will be converting all these into a more manageable JPEG format. Sticking with JPEG and saving editable originals can be very effective in keeping overall file size for the PDF and eBook formats down to acceptable levels. This often comes into play with vendors with files size maximums, such as Barnes & Noble requiring eBooks to be 20 MB or below.

> *Favor grayscale or black and white line art. This helps kids comfortably transition to the monotonous black and white tone in their future reading material.*

What if you can't find an illustrator or have funding restrictions? There's another possibility! Prepare to go on a deep search and rethink your initial book design. Stock photo sites are a wonderful resource for those who can't afford the illustrators or struggling to find one. This includes ShutterStock, DepositPhoto, iStockPhoto, Adobe Stock, and many more sites have a variety of artists who submit sheets and multiple images of characters for all audiences. A fitting example of this is the character you see throughout Writer's Bane! The more active an artist is on these sites, the better chance for the collection to grow and pull from. Some give you a means to reach out to them as well! You can always reach out to them and see if they will also commission pieces.

Basics of Digitally Enhancing Illustrations

Thanks to the digital age, many artists or illustrators have taken to producing art via software. This has made it a better means to reproduce images in a higher brilliance and sharper hues. That doesn't mean hand drawn artwork and watercolors can't join this high-tech advantage. Traditional art can be scanned or photographed to be pulled into the digital realm and in some cases, adjusted. This doesn't come without its share of pros and cons. One being the most common is the lack of capturing texture, hues, or even soft pencil strokes that all-too-often get washed out by the scanner or camera's light. If your art is too big to scan, an art photographer should be able to use a black/white balance card and even adjust and check it.

Once an image has been placed in digitally, you or a design have the freedom to adjust the image as needed. This can be moving elements, changing hues, brightening the overall saturation, and even resetting black and white tones to make richer levels so the image prints sharper. If you can apply a lot of these easy tricks to an image and balance the CMYK spectrum to a richer level, it will make a huge difference when printed. Not every image or color will be able to translate well; for example, blues and purples are often a struggle to lock in without shifting when ink is laid to paper.

Warning About Watercolors

Out of all the medians your illustrations can be made from, this one comes with a loss of detail and color just from scanning or photographing it. From there, it sways again depending on the options you choose. If you are ok with digitizing and drastically shifting your watercolors for print and not looking to match the original artwork, you will feel this impact the least. As for those looking to match it and capture the watercolor pieces as they are, you won't get this result. First, the act of scanning or taking a photo removes the texturing that watercolors often have, as well removing some of the sharpness and overlapping details. From there, I recommend offset printing with gloss or semi-gloss paper at about 100+lb. paper with alcohol-based printing for closest match to original work. If you decide to move forward with Print-on-Demand, be warned that you will continue to lose vibrancy and details due to the fact only matte paper is available and most are water-based ink printing and may cause saturation issues. This becomes most noticeable with a picture-book printer in Print-on-Demand.

Black and White Balance

If you are using Photoshop, Fire Alpaca, or some other photo editing software, you should be able to do this. Many of the photography editing software may be able to assist with this technique as well as the others to follow. Whichever software you use, there should be tutorials out there to assist you best as far as this book goes, the aim is to explain what it's meant to do and hint as to why you might want to apply this to your own formatting and images. As for this one, it helps establish true black and true white on the image and adjusts the image color range accordingly. Often when we scan an image, the black has a shine to it and might come off as a dark gray or even brown. This gives you a chance to "reset" the expectations and identify where these are on the image if you have both visible.

Levels in Spectrum

Images come with levels that spread a variety of hues and channels. Often black and white being on opposite ends, they come with slight dips beyond the peak of these colors that can take away from the overall sharpness of the image spectrum. Cutting out or knocking them to the peaks or using auto levels features can bring an image to pop more visually.

Hue & Saturation

Hue and saturations levels or using filters that shift these can do a wide range for an image. If the colors seem to have washed out, you might be able to recover faded colors using this feature. Also scanned or photographed images may have washed out and either you can darken the hue values or even adjust contrast and brightness settings to recover the look of the original artwork. Sometimes this setting allows a moment for you to change the hue or coloration of the art and make decisions you normally would have missed out on. Using a masked layer stacked with this can even allow you to change a color on a single item in the image, but that's best for a tutorial as it delves into photo editing and is beyond this book's conversation focused on typesetting.

DPI, IMAGE SIZE, AND RESOLUTION ADJUSTMENTS

The resolution of an image is very important! The first aspect to this is the size. You don't need your image to be 44 inches by 21 inches if your book is only 11 inches by 8.5 inches. If you are bleeding images off the edge, the image needs to only be 11.25 inches by 8.75 inches at the very least to give some room for image placement that allows bleed and trim. It's always smart to have the image slightly bigger, but too large and it may cause the program or computer to crash (especially those on personal or home systems). It also makes saving backups or throwing it on a cloud storage much more feasible.

Once the size is within a reasonable range (exact with bleed or slightly larger in the same orientation or ratio), you need to make sure the resolution is set between 300-600 DPI. Anything under 300 is at risk to pixelate or be blurry. Know that most images saved from internet are usually only 72-96 DPI, so make sure what you are saving is the full image and not a smaller web version or down-sampled variant. Images that are over 600 DPI are at risk of the printer shrinking and may result in unwanted quality or results. It's always best to avoid these sorts of situations and keep the control and final product in your hands.

CMYK VERSUS RGB

Print and physical books are printed using CMYK colorations. This uses a set amount of cyan, magenta, yellow, and black layered on the page. Depending on the printer this can be applied with alcohol or water-based inks and vary in brightness (often influenced by the paper chosen). Water based inks are limited to 240% CMYK saturation level with paperweights at 70lbs or less as seen in Print-on-Demand applications.

IMAGE NAMING

Be sure to be consistent or concise with how you are naming your images. You can do this in a number of ways which includes consecutively (image01, image20, image03...), by location (Chapter01, Chapter02_SUBHEAD, Chapter02_Figure1.1), or labelled by what they are (Flowers01, RosesAndBees, AuntMayAndHerPig...). You should always avoid using symbols and spaces since these may cause issues in final formats. Depending on your software and how you export for eBook format, having images with names that include open spaces, dollar signs ($), hashtags (#), and similar often will cause them not to load or fail when uploaded to a vendor. I highly recommend using only alphabet and numbers with underscore if need be. In programming we do this as well and often default to camelCase (LittleTimmysWagon, IHateThisPictureTheMost, ImageNameLikeThis...) as the safest means to prevent programming errors.

IMAGE FILE TYPES

Images come in a variety of types and the best ones to use for publishing are JPEG and TIFF formats. You can use a PNG, which preserves the transparency unlike JPEG or even a PDF file. You should keep these between 300-600 DPI and at least a little larger than the intended size to make sure you have room to trim the image if needed. TIFF is considered the best format and has been used in the printing and graphic design world as the superior option. Most Print-on-Demand printers want the files saved in PDF2001XA format, and this converts images to JPEG. Same thing happens when exporting to EPUB; the images are often converted to JPEG or PNG depending on what you are using. Thus, it is recommended to save in JPEG for several reasons, including the fact it's a smaller size, translates into eBook without issues, and prevents any issues when converting to final PDF format changes to the images.

PERMISSIONS & USAGE RIGHTS

Images and artwork can fall under public domain rights, but if they don't, you will need to purchase usage rights or get permission. If you pulled your images from a service like ShutterStock or similar stock photo site, they usually have different levels you can purchase for usage rights. This is the safest means for images and artwork. If you intend to hire an illustrator, be sure to cover the usage and contract with them how books are sold and their images will be used from the book to creating swag, bookmarks, banners, and more. Some may clear you for using the images in the book only and not for marketing materials. Be sure to add the permissions granted in the copyright section or even an illustration rights section as a type of appendix. It's always best to give credit where it's due on your copyright page at the very least.

Designing the Pages

Chapter books and middle grade books play a very important role in a reader's journey. They are the bridge between picture books and the adult books that will become the expectation for the rest of their lives. It seems quite foreboding, but it's the truth! It is here that a typesetter will have to span two worlds and be the first encounter in showing children what books look like, and even provide their first encounter with chapters. Unlike the young adult and adult variants, these books tend to have larger font, images sprinkled inside, often black-and-white interior, and still have the occasional fun font to push keywords. Be mindful to mimic the layout of a normal book while adding in fun elements that break the monotony to keep the layout engaging. A great example of this is *The Ituria Chronicles* by J.B. Moonstar or *Fortunately, the Milk* by Neil Gaiman.

Full Spread Layout

The image or text (not both) stretches across 2 pages, a left and right page, to show as one large landscape image or two pages of textual content. In a lot of cases the text may only be present on one page and not the other, but other layouts might have several spots all around the image to show the story unfolding in a sequence or multi-action spread. It's not uncommon to see images in a chapter book spreading across a spread or having elements interacting on occasion. Unlike a picture book where most spreads are designed together, a chapter book will do this sparingly and mimic a traditional book with header, footer, and body text a majority of the time.

Rule of Thirds Spread Layout

Across a two-page span, an image, graph, or pull quote will cover one complete page and a portion of the adjacent page to leave room on a far left or right edge for font to place. In concept, the object is using two-thirds of the design area to draw the eye to the text or away from the text by doing so. The Rule of Thirds is often used in marketing, print design, or even in filming. It splits the viewing area into thirds from top to bottom and side to side. From this point, you break the content and subject matter up at the key sections to help draw the eye in a certain direction or pull it towards or away.

Split Design Image & Text Page Layout

Again, this is similar to the Image + Text layout seen in picture books and textbooks. On a single page, whether it's the right or left, the image and text split the space. Sometimes this is done in a 50/50 spit, or a two-thirds split, but often features a white space or colored space where the text will be. You are more likely to see 2-5 spreads in this style, with body text filling one page and a full page with an image on the other side with chapter books. The best course of action is look at similar titles for your audience and see how often each layout type is being applied.

Whitespace Page Layout

This page is often an indicator of a chapter starting or ending. Sometimes it can be a section or partition marker of some kind. It's notorious for having a lot of white space or empty, unused space on the page spread. What little content is there usually is textual to guide or inform the reader in preparation of something changing or a transition within the book. You see this a lot in textbooks and fiction books with right page only chapter starts. In chapter books and beyond, this will usually only happen on sections, chapter start, and chapter end pages and rarely anywhere else.

EXAMPLES OF MANUSCRIPTS

Chapter books are often given in textual only format or textual with image placement. That doesn't mean you can't have key areas of the story laid out in a storyboard or provide a lot of detailed instructions. Fair warning: often the expectation for image placement and text will not fall where the author imagines. It's vital to be flexible in the way you are designing and creatively solve these obstacles when you come across them.

Below is a list of different ways you may receive or set a manuscript up. The most common in the industry are the first two options: Textual Only and Text with Image Placement. From chapter books tot, these are the typical format you will receive the textual content for typesetting. As you venture into workbooks, picture books, comic books, and graphic novels, you will want to use story bounce, detailed format, storyboarding, or script styles to capture all the parts. Unlike text-based or heavy books, these require guidance and cues as to where images or text should be placed on a page to accurately tell the story intended. Each book type will lean more so on one kind of manuscript, and it's important to be aware of this as you prep your manuscript for typesetting. This can be a huge influence on how well key elements are designed, whether you intend to format your own book or hand your book to someone else.

TEXTUAL ONLY

This is the most common manuscript for mass market fiction work. No images are tied into it, and it's simply importing the manuscript into the software and applying the indicated styling where deemed appropriate. A typesetter's aim is to streamline the text to the best of their abilities as to not break a reader's immersion with weird visual discrepancies such as a slight tweak in line spacing (common in manuscripts where portions where dictated via speech-to-text and other written on a computer). You have to remember that we've been reading books with the same patterns and margins for centuries and keeping those expectations while being creative can be a hardline to walk for anyone designing a book.

> *The most common in the industry are the first two options: Textual Only and Text with Image Placement.*

For a textual-based manuscript, follow the Do's and Don'ts to prevent any unseen issues in the content. As for trim and font choices, it will fall back to the audience, genre, and type of book you are working on. You should be able to copy-paste content into a clean Word document or use InDesign's "File > Place" feature to import text and its associated styles. In the case of the latter, be sure to run Scripts to lock in these styles and save time from having to do manual changes by using the PrepText and other tools often found in opensource or pre-programmed into InDesign for use. Most manuscripts imported this way come as double-spaced in Times or similar font at 12 pt. If the manuscript has a variety of font faces, I recommend streamlining it to a single font face to prevent issues when formatting the book. Also, be aware many of these come with double spacing, which is intended for editorial purposes. Never keep this line spacing!

TEXT WITH IMAGE PLACEMENT

For this book type, this is going to be the more common type encountered with textbooks, workbooks, or image heavy content. Throughout the text, there should be indications for image placement and should be clearly marked, much like a subhead or citation. For visual aid, I always encourage highlighting these yellow and treat them as their own paragraph. It's also helpful to use a keyword like "IMAGE" and brackets to help make the image placement stand up, for example:

[[IMAGE01: This picture shows the difference between nightshade and chili pepper flowers]]

These one-liners should be placed between the paragraphs they should be near or on the same page as the text. The importance of this is so when creating an eBook, the typesetter can make sure it falls inline at the right point of the content. It can also make it easier to play with the page layout as they apply the design and text begins to autoflow from page to page with the changes.

Story Bounce

This simply is stating what goes where in the manuscript as it bounces through the story beats or pages. Be mindful of how much textual content you are providing on pages and identify which image to be used concisely. For example, a manuscript using this format might appear like this:

- Title page (right)
- Copyright (left) with Dedication
  - Image01 at the top, small
  - Dedicated to all the kids who seek an adventure of their own
  - Copyright 1999 Author J. Smith etc.
- Page 1 (right) Image02
  - "Wow, the world sure is big when I'm all alone," marveled John.
- Page 2 & 3 (spread) Image03
  - John lost his dog when they moved. His mommy decided it was time little John Wick got a new puppy. Today, they would visit the animal shelter!
- Page 4 (left) Image04 & Image05
  - Image04: John couldn't believe the amount of doggies who needed homes.
  - Image05: Barking and bouncing, each one was excited to see him.
- Page 5 (right) Image06
  - They came in so many shapes, sizes, and colors. None of them reminded him of his old doggy Daisy.

Note how there is no mistake where in the book these images and their text go as you 'flip through' the book. It's important to leave nothing out while keeping your instructions consistent and cohesive with same naming methods and delivery. This gives the typesetter a little room for choosing where content falls and to adjust content if needed based on images and text needed on each spread. You can even leave it up to the typesetter to decide which keywords they emphasize or encourage them to do so.

Detailed Format

This is for authors who have something more specific in mind for placement, including giving instructions as to where the textual content falls and may give a variety of more in-depth directions. For comparison, this would be the above example with additional bullets where a greater level of instructions addresses text locations, specialty font changes, and even image placement for a variety of page layout styles. In this example, words in bold are assumed to need font or artistic touch to emphasize the word's meaning and provide visual clues for early readers.

- Font Face: Palatin Kids
- Size 24 where possible
- Emphasize highlighted words artfully
- Title page (right)
- Copyright (left) with Dedication
  - Image01 at the top, small
  - Text in larger font, italics:
    - Dedicated to all the kids who seek an adventure of their own
  - Copyright 1999 Author J. Smith etc.
- Page 1 (right) Image02
  - Text on the bottom of page
    - "Wow, the **world** sure is **big** when I'm all **alone**," marveled John.
- Page 2 & 3 (spread) Image03
  - Text on top left
    - John lost his dog when they moved. His mommy decided it was time little **John Wick got a new puppy**.
  - Text on bottom right
  - Today, they would visit the **animal shelter**!
- Page 4 (left) Image04 & Image05
  - Top left Image04: John couldn't believe the amount of **doggies** who needed **homes**.

- ◦ Bottom right Image05: **Barking** and **bouncing**, each one was excited to see him.
- Page 5 (right) Image06
  - ◦ Text at top of page:
    - They came in so many **shapes, sizes**, and **colors**.
    - Text on bottom of page:
    - None of them reminded him of his old doggy **Daisy**.

STORYBOARDING

When it comes to picture books, I highly recommend this method or combining one of the above with this as a visual guide or blueprint. You can print, cut, and paste the elements to rough out the entire book's look and feel. This is a fantastic way to build a mockup of the book you intend to make and format for print and give concise expectations to a typesetter or experiment with what you had in mind for the final product. Before starting digitally, this allows you to troubleshoot issues that may need you to adjust text and illustrations prior to formatting the book. Most issues found this way are still relatively easy to fix by simply changing methods, book options, or changing fonts and images. Storyboarding can also be a great means to discover how many images you will need the illustrator to make as well as to where they need to be mindful of page edges and space for text to overlay. The following types of issues can be revealed at a glance by this method:

- ✎ Illustrations not allowing enough space for text to overlay
- ✎ Images that have the characters too close to the edge and will be cut when stretched to the bleed edge and cross the trim
- ✎ Images that have text as part of the image in need of adjusting to fit trim
- ✎ Trim size and orientation versus illustration size and orientation
- ✎ Amount of text for the page (too much is the common issue)
- ✎ Number of illustrations needed
- ✎ Amount of pages the story needs
- ✎ Story page flip and how that impacts the reader and story

CREATING A STORYBOARD

One of the best ways to help you plan out your picture book is to outline it in the form of a storyboard as seen in comics and animated films. Print images and clip out text and move things around or take a sketchbook out and doodle a rough version. Stick figures and shapes work are just fine! You will need to account for the layout and limitations of the printed version from the beginning, even if you are still revising the text. Everything in a picture book impacts how the final look of a page turns out, for better or worse.

GET CRAFTY!

Sometimes it helps to roll up your sleeves and do more than write it or click and drag on the computer. One of my favorite things to see is where a picture book author has printed, cut, and pasted content in a mock-up book. Something about this can be eye-opening to an author and content awareness and available space become alarmingly tangible. I recommend using a manila folder and cardstock pages to piece this impromptu scrapbook together. Whether you have a portrait or landscape layout, you should be able to mimic the look enough to be able to understand how images, trim size, margins, and text interact within the design. Using a square trim size? Not biggie! Just cut the folder down to size!

Others simple staple pages together and cut and paste printed elements onto the page. This can serve as an excellent guide as you format the book or for your typesetter to rely on. Being able to see the real-world demo of the end-product may simply be stick fingers and glue stick cut outs, but it provides a kinetic means of design that you only see in workbooks. Well, if crafts aren't your thing, here's some worksheets to aid you in designing your storyboard for your book! Don't think this is only good for children's books. This can make a world of difference in creating and formatting comics, graphic novels, workbooks, and image layouts in textbooks.

PROJECT TITLE: _____ GENRE: _____

STORYBOARD

PICTURE [_____]

ACTION [_____]

_____
_____
_____
_____
_____
_____

PICTURE [_____]

ACTION [_____]

_____
_____
_____
_____
_____
_____

PICTURE [_____]

ACTION [_____]

_____
_____
_____
_____
_____
_____

PICTURE [_____]

ACTION [_____]

_____
_____
_____
_____
_____
_____

STORYBOARD — PORTRAIT

Formatting the Book

Hooray! Now that we've talked and prepped this thing to no end, you should be ready to format this book with confidence. Why? Because it is so much easier to resolve problems at the manuscript and prepping stage than when you are formatting and making the book. Though, as said before, I am an avid user of word to InDesign, I will do my best throughout the book to provide information in an all-encompassing and design angle. If you were looking for software tutorial, this isn't the book for you. Getting detailed instructions on how to set parameters in Word, Scribd, and similar word processors isn't the aim.

Instead, we will be focusing on the typesetter-based elements and areas that will be par the course for any book you design. Dependent on the software you are using to design your book in could present its own issues and information may be labeled slightly different or found in different areas. In tandem with a software book, this book may provide some keywords in order to gain the affects you were aiming for in order for you to gain a greater value out of using said programs. In my years of looking for instructional manuals for book design, most of what I have learned was via videos, trial and error, typography college courses, and simply diving into the industry headlong with an open mind and understanding of the roots of publishing and its history. It probably also helped I delved in some game design, development, and programming, so I could troubleshoot creative solutions.

Without further ado, it's time to make this book using these step-by-step, or page-by-page instructions below. Feel free to adjust this to suit your own style and needs since there are various methods to achieve the results seen here. Again, the aim here is to simply the process while being able to make quality print books, enhance eBooks, and create a PDF that falls close as possible to being ADA compliant (Americans with Disabilities Act).

File Setup

The file or page size should match the trim size in width and height. Make sure the intended orientation matches what you intended, specifically landscape versus portrait. Depending on the program, you may have to set bleed settings to include a 0.125" bleed on all sides or for outer margins. For some Print-on-Demand vendors, they may want the inner margin to have no bleed since this is the side of the page that is glued to the spine of the book. You usually get to set up or define the overall margins as well.

Be mindful that with picture books you will be saving a flat PDF for eBook design and that you don't have to fret over threading text boxes together as seen with all other book types. It's more important to make sure images are bleeding off to the marked edges just pass the trim edge, that elements are layered and overlayed in the right order, and textual content is within the margins provided by the printer or Print-on-Demand requirements of 0.5" from trim size edge. Here are my recommended settings for this book type:

Chapter Books & Middle Grade

- Industry Standard Numbers:
  - 0.125" Bleed from trim edge
  - 0.5" Margin for content inward from trim edge
  - Large page counts will require a larger 0.625" or higher inner margin or gutter
  - Special binding may change the needs for inner margins

- Inner or inside margin: 0.625" for books under 300 pages and

- 0.75" to 0.8" for books pushing far into the 500+ range since where the pages' bind needs more space to avoid words falling into the crack of the book.

- Granted, this is a picture book, and you can sometimes get away with a 0.5" margin.

- Outer or outside margins (including top and bottom) should be 0.5" to 0.625"
  - Typically have main body pages with header and footer set and you can increase the top and bottom margins to 0.8-0.875" to give yourself space to place and space these from your body text.

- Chapter and Middle Grade Books:
  - Margins only apply to page numbers, textual content, and similar.
  - Images in a majority of cases bleed off the page or pull within margins in line with text.

Wondering where these numbers come from? Your vendors should have File Creation Guides via a PDF or webpage. No matter if you plan on using offset printing, KDP, IngramSparks, or a similar vendor, these parameters never change. This is the basic needs of a file going to print and will give the press some wiggle room. These parameters will change if you choose more elaborate binding and use certain presses. Always make sure you get these settings from the printer and design the book with these in place from the start.

USING LAYERS

Most of the layout software allows you to create layers such as InDesign (not any of the word processors though they do have header footer options). These come in handy in keeping content stacked or arranged in the right order. This includes making sure watermarks are below the body text layer and even keeping the header and footer elements on the top and not lost behind images and such. A bonus to using this feature is the ability to lock them and make sure you don't accidently change, move, or delete them unintentionally. With picture books, you often use images that take up the entire page and risk losing these elements completely. Recommended layers include the following listed in the order they should fall and usage:

- **Header and Footer Layer** – This will have your top layer text boxes that contain the header and footer which usually hold page numbers, title, author, and/or current chapter. You can control these with master pages. In a word processor, this is an option or specific setting that is influenced by section breaks to change how they look from section to section of the book's layout.

- **Default or Body Text Layer** – Here you will manage the primary text box in which the main content autoflows through threaded textboxes or pages.

- **Background Layer** – At the bottom of the list, there should be a background layer that is designed for images, spreads, and watermarks that need to fall under the textual content.

This doesn't mean you need to use all these layers, but it's highly recommended to give you more control when formatting. If the program you are using doesn't provide layers, check for features that define objects on the page as needing to be "Ordered" or "Arranged" with sub-options for "Bring to Front" or "Bring to Back," which mimic what layering does. This should aid you in making sure text and images overlap appropriately.

MASTER PAGES

These pages, or templates, are premade pages you can drag and drop into the layout to help speed things along and stay consistent. Know that this is more commonly found as a feature in layout software such as InDesign. Even with a freeform style book, there's a level of consistency with placement of elements such as header, footer, page numbers, watermarks, and other elements that you may not want to shift and wish to keep level throughout the book. In any book, you are going to be applying a few key layout pages. I recommend the following master pages or templates be made in advance to speed up the typeset process:

- **A blank page** with only the margin lines set. You may include a primary text box version for dedication or anchoring title page images into place. Works great for print-on-demand with that last page needing to be blank as well. These will also set your title pages and copyright page as well.

- **A body page** made of a blank page with only the header and footer with a main text box. I recommend putting the header and footer on a top layer that's locked. Predesign a left and right page,

often featuring the book title on left and author name on right. You may even design a running header or chapter header that auto updates depending on the software you are using. Adding glyphs and art to page numbers and headers can add a nice creative flair.

- **A chapter page** that can add art, designs, and spacing shifts to accommodate the style implied. I always make right and left page versions, so if I need to change from right page only chapters to continuous, it's ready to adapt accordingly.

- **A numbered blank page** can be useful for areas that may contain images, maps, tables, and similar content where you simply want page numbers only.

- **Section breaks** become vital for non-fiction books. Occasionally these hard pages or spreads have an image or color to help standout when certain passing of time, events, topics, and provide a sense of dividers for the reader. Prepping a page or spread for these can save time and provide consistency when applicable.

FONT CHOICES AND PREP

Font has the most weight in typesetting and interior book design. Your choices and attention to detail to the spacing, size, and types will have a significant impact for better or worse. There are a few things you can do to help yourself prep and streamline your design depending on if you are using styles in Microsoft Word or a combination of Paragraph and Character styles in Adobe InDesign. Prepping and setting up pre-saved files with master pages and these elements can save a lot of

hunting and frustrations, especially if you want to shift or change fonts later. If you intend to do typesetting full time or work heavily with fonts, I recommend investing into Font Management programs such as FontExplorer. This can make it easier to keep your growing library from bogging down your computer while making it easier to test out and organize fonts.

PARAGRAPH STYLES OR STYLES

These will make up most of the formatting application in textual content. They work in particular order and repeat as you start a new section or chapter. Making a style in advance can help you quickly adjust, fix, or change the entire typeset without hunting and pecking for certain content in the book. Instead, applying a style and changing the style can shift and fix the book as a whole.

- **Chapter Header –** Should be the largest font and be a font face that reflects genre. Content here

is often just numbers, "Chapter" text, or some section marker text.

- **Headline –** This is often a subtitle or section title that follows behind the Chapter Header, normally directly below it. It should be the second largest text and also have a legible but creative font that captures the genre.

- **Subhead –** Should be a slight larger than the body text but clear and bolder in some way. It's common for these to be the same font as body text and simply in all-caps or small caps.

✐ **Drop Cap –** Whether it's a single letter, word, or line, this is the first paragraph in a chapter or section. It's a way to artfully signal to a reader where to begin reading or add more to the chapter page that makes it stand out other than whitespace.

✐ **Body Text –** This will be the majority of your content. It should be a legible font comfortable for readers and remain the same throughout the entire book. It builds the font foundation for Drop Caps, Citations/Quotes, Subheads, Tables and more.

✐ **Citations/Quote –** This paragraph style should center or have an indent of 0.25" to 0.05" on the right and left sides. It's also common to add space before and after this paragraph style so the quote or citations pops. Often there is an italics character style applied.

✐ **Bullet Points –** Lists and bullets have similar indentation and spacing. Setting the preference or making a variety of these to create multi-tier systems in the varying styles can save a typesetter grief as well as the means to remembering how APA, MLA, and CMS are different from one another.

CHARACTER STYLES OR SUBFAMILY FONTS

Creating premade character style can help you gain more control on the style of the manuscript as a whole. It also helps build coding within certain programs for eBook creation and keeps these vital aspects from disappearing in the process.

✐ **Bold** – used to identify keywords, bring words to the front, and stand out louder. There is never a need to make a whole manuscript bold. Instead, choose a thicker or heavier font.

✐ *Italics* – this has many uses from quotes, to signaling key elements in content, and even to signal internal dialogue in stories.

✐ Underline – much like bold, this is used to make content stand out, signify a reference (depending on styles like APA), hyperlinks (or clickable content in text), or signal something of importance.

✐ Keyword – This comes in handy when wanting to stay consistent in font face and size changes in books where you need vocabulary words or key visuals to pop.

✐ SMALL CAPS – Common to see in reference works or to address religious names or keywords, this is easier to manage as a character style and carries over into eBook better.

OBJECT STYLES OR TABLE STYLES

These are special styles that influence objects, images, and tables. They make sure designs and placement match and can even streamline how items show up in an eBook. Not every software has the means to define these or set them up. As for InDesign, these can help guide image frames, table cells, and more so that you can save time when adding content into the layout and saving you the grief of cracking open object options to adjust every detail.

Page-by-Page

Using *Russ and the Hidden Voice* by J.B. Moonstar for a point of reference, let's break down a chapter book. You will see immediately as we travel through the pages how much this mimics the average fiction book but with artful images and flair to keep the readers engaged. Most chapter books have short chapters unlike their Young Adult and Adult fiction counterparts. Regardless, the aim here is to introduce young readers to chapter books and the normal layout while keeping them immersed in the text heavy content. They've come from a realm of predominately picture-based storytelling where the maximum word count was roughly 1,200 words to numbers ranging from 10,000 to 60,000 words on average. This is a huge jump! Remember that larger font and spacing can go a long way here for early readers.

The Checklist!

Here is a checklist that should help you make sure you finished prepping the manuscript and materials before starting the formatting. Often we don't think to ask or double check to include some of these things and it can be detrimental in the final stages leading up to printing the actual book. Whether you are formatting your own book or formatting someone else's, this checklist is to help you gather everything you need before you start.

- Trim Size
- Book Title
- Subtitle
- Author Name (or Pen Name)
- Publisher and/or Logo
- Copyright Page
  - Author name and copyright year
  - Name illustrator, designer, editor, etc.
  - Permissions for any materials used.
  - Public domain or scripture cited.
  - ISBN numbers (Paperback, Hardcover, eBook, Audiobook, etc.)
  - LCCN (Pending or number)
  - Published information and logo
  - The usual legal jargon to protect you, your work, and the publisher.
- Front Matter
  - Foreword: Yes or No
  - Dedication: Yes or No
    - Above Copyrights or Own Page
- Images are ready, clearly named, and all accounted for
  - 300 – 600 DPI
  - Correct size for trim + bleed
  - CMYK color mode
- Manuscript – Text only edition
  - Has image directions that match image names
- Back Matter
  - Author Bio
  - Image
    - Hyperlinks
    - Illustrator Bio
    - Image
    - Hyperlinks

BOOK TITLE: _____

SUBTITLE: _____

TYPESET CHECKLIST

☐ Manuscript text in a DOC, DOCX, RTF file

☐ All the images listed in Manuscript present:

☐ CMYK mode

☐ Between 300-600 DPI.

☐ Trim Size _____ width x _____ height

☐ Author Pen Name - FIRST_____LAST_____

☐ Dedication: Yes or No

☐ Author Bio: Yes or No

☐ Copyright

☐ Publisher information

☐ Additional mention such as artist, design, or typesetter? _____

☐ Scriptures cited from…. Any public domain original publication mentions? _____

☐ Permission granted from… Any materials that have permissions needing to be listed here?

☐ ISBNs for Paperback: _____ Hardcover_____

☐ Audiobook_____ eBook_____

☐ LCCN pending or listed?_____

☐ Front Matter (Acknowledgements, Foreword, Preface, etc.)

☐ Do they want a Table of Contents: Yes or No

☐ Do they have tables to import: Yes or No

☐ Do they want pull quotes: Yes or No

THE WARM-UP

As mentioned in the front half of this book, the preferred method for designing books is using InDesign due to the amount of control. No matter what software you are using, the parameters and keywords are all the same and much of the process can be even reflected into when you design using a word processor, such as Microsoft© Word.

- Page size needs to be set to the trim size of your book.

- Bleed settings can always be added via page setup or page layout options depending on the program.

- Make sure page margins are keeping 0.5" within the trim or page size.

- If you intend to have headers and footers, be sure margin for body text are larger (0.75" for example) on the top and bottom to give space for them to fall within that 0.5" requirement.

- Choose your fonts in advance or make a list of possibilities for:
    - Chapter
    - Headline or Chapter Title
    - Header/Footer
    - Body Text
    - Pull Quotes

- Decide on Chapter Art or Typeset design for:
    - Spacing
    - Having samples on hand
    - Write down parameters in advance
    - Choose glyph or ornamental font options
    - Prepared images in advance

- Don't forget your checklist! You'll need it for Copyright pages and specifics!

- For chapter and middle grade books:
    - A sense of direction via the manuscript or a storyboard.
    - All images and artwork needed, labeled, and saved in correct format.
    - Font choices have been decided including for keywords to emphasize.
    - Decide if header will be included or not.
    - Check for Front and Back matter needs. These should increase in this book type!

BOOK TITLE: _____

SUBTITLE: _____

WARM-UP CHECKLIST

☐ Trim size set to the page or book size

☐ Add Bleed Settings for 0.125 inches

☐ Set your margins to 0.5 inch from trim edge

☐ Top margin for header set for 0.75 inch

☐ Bottom margin for footer set for 0.75 inch

☐ Inner margin or mirrored margins set to 0.675 omch or higher for spine/glue/page count

☐ Chapter font:_____

☐ Headline font:_____

☐ Header/Footer font:_____

☐ Body Text font:_____

☐ Pull Quote font:_____

☐ Body Text Base Font Size: _____ Line Spacing: _____

☐ Chapter Art prepped and ready to go

☐ Images saved in teh right format and size in advance

☐ Manuscript prepped and image placement clearly marked or Storyboard ready

☐ Glyph and Ornaments picked out. Font: _____

☐ Printer settings and requirements handy for saving and meeting their needs

☐ Templates or Master pages set up for key pages and special pages

☐ Paragraph Styles setup in advance or styles redesigned to match selection

☐ Are you ready?

FRONT MATTER

This is the first few pages that typically consist of title pages, copyrights, and dedication pages. This is the beginning of a book and rarely changes much no matter the genre of the book. As we are aiming to introduce the new normal for young readers, you'll see the same elements in most books but done with some artistic value or larger fonts to draw the eyes.

HALF TITLE

The only text here should be the title font. This page should leave room for the author to sign. It is completely optional though and can be replaced by a full title page.

FULL TITLE

Half title can feature a text title only and the full title can be the front cover of the book itself. If you decide to do a text-based version, this should have series name, title, subtitle, author name, illustrator, and publisher name and/or logo. You can even combine the two elements and create something unique like seen below.

COPYRIGHT

This will always be a left page on the back of the full title page. It should contain the normal legal jargon, author, copyright, publisher information, credits to key members (editor, designer, cover, typeset, photographer, illustrator, etc.), LCCN, ISBN, and similar information.

RUSS AND THE
HIDDEN VOICE
THE ITURIA CHRONICLES

BOOK I

RUSS AND THE
HIDDEN VOICE
THE ITURIA CHRONICLES

J.B. MOONSTAR

4 Horsemen
Publications, Inc.

Chapter Books & Middle Grade
Dedication/Acknowledgment

Many books have a dedication or even acknowledgments. This should go right after the copyright page.

Note to Readers

Common in various book genres, it's not uncommon to see notes to the reader or even a word from the author. This is to serve as an intimate moment between reader and author.

Dedication

To Peter, Wil, Armaan and Noor – thank you so much for your support and encouragement, it is very much appreciated! Thank you for believing in me, and in Ituria!

v

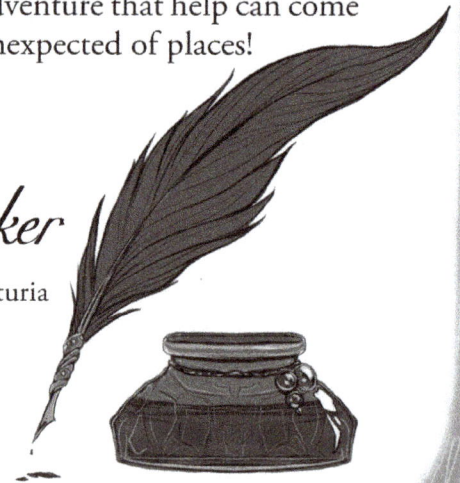

Dear Reader,

I have been asked by Ituria to document the interactions between his realm and the human world. This story takes place many years ago when a boy named Russ first visited Ituria's Island. A mysterious illness had attacked the plants, endangering the inhabitants of the Island. We needed a human knowledgeable about the flora on Earth, to help us save the plants and the Island itself. I learned on this adventure that help can come from the most unexpected of places!

Sincerely,

Knocker

First Guard to Ituria

vii

TABLE OF CONTENTS

Now we are dealing with chapters! This means it's time to dabble in making a Table of Contents. Always leave a blank right page for this and save its creation for last. Most layout software can auto-populate the Table of Contents, and you can adjust the paragraph and character styling from there. Within InDesign, if it adds weird or hit and miss font formatting, revisit your chapter headers and clear overrides. Some manuscripts just import dirty and don't always apply the styles and remove unwanted programming. It can even cause hit and miss bolded text in eBook Table of Contents!

TABLE OF CONTENTS

CONTENT

This is where the core of the content will be located. These are the pages with headers and footers, and the majority containing full pages of text. Be sure to set your margins so that none of the text falls into the 0.5" margin from the trim edge to prevent the printer from rejecting your book files later on.

INTRODUCTION OR FIRST CHAPTER PAGE

This is where you get to use that master page or drop the many fancy styles you took the time to prep! If you did pre-save those Chapter Header, Headline, Subhead, Drop-cap and other styles, you may want to do so as you design this first chapter. It'll make the rest of the book a breeze and make sure everything snaps and looks the same throughout the book. Work smarter! Not harder!

Chapter One

THE MOONLIGHT PATH

"The moon is full," whispered Knocker. "We can do it."

"But should we?" Ituria whispered back. "Is it worth the risk? Is *he* worth the risk?"

Knocker nodded. "I've been watching him. He's different than the others who enter the forest, only taking what he *needs*."

Watching from the shadows, the moon cast enough light to see two men creep up on a teenage boy as he slept on the riverbank. The boy was tall in stature, wearing only a pair of cut-off shorts, and there were a few rabbits in traps near him. Without warning, the men quickly grabbed him, blindfolded him, then tied his arms and legs with rope. Caught by surprise, the boy couldn't escape his bonds.

After securing the boy, the men argued between themselves for a minute as he lay on the ground struggling to free himself. Suddenly, they picked him up and threw him in the river. Try as he might, the boy could not keep his head above water and was sinking slowly to the bottom. Grabbing the trapped rabbits, the men ran off, not bothering to look back as the

1

BLEED VERSUS TEXT MARGINS

Make sure the bleed goes past the trim line or paper's edge to the end of the to the bleed line. If the signature or paper shifts in print slightly, it will cause a white line on the outer edges. Many designers place a white margin or offset the inner margins on spreads. This is dependent on the page spread, number of pages, and type of binding. For beginners you may want to default to treating this as a bleed edge. In picture books, you can push images off the page and across pages in creative ways, but when it comes to text placement, you must have it within 0.5" inch from the trim edge or paper edge. This is so if the signatures or pages shift that your textual content will never be at risk of being cutoff.

BODY TEXT SPREADS

Here you will get to double down on your header and footer design. Make sure things are updating if you decided to be fancy with auto-updating running headers. If not, the book title on the left and author to the right will always work with page numbers on the bottom. Don't be afraid to center the page numbers if you aren't sure if you are dropping content on the right and left pages. In software like InDesign, it shows you the way the book will be printed whereas Word you have to pay close attention or try adding a blank first page to offset it (But don't forget to delete it back out when you're done!).

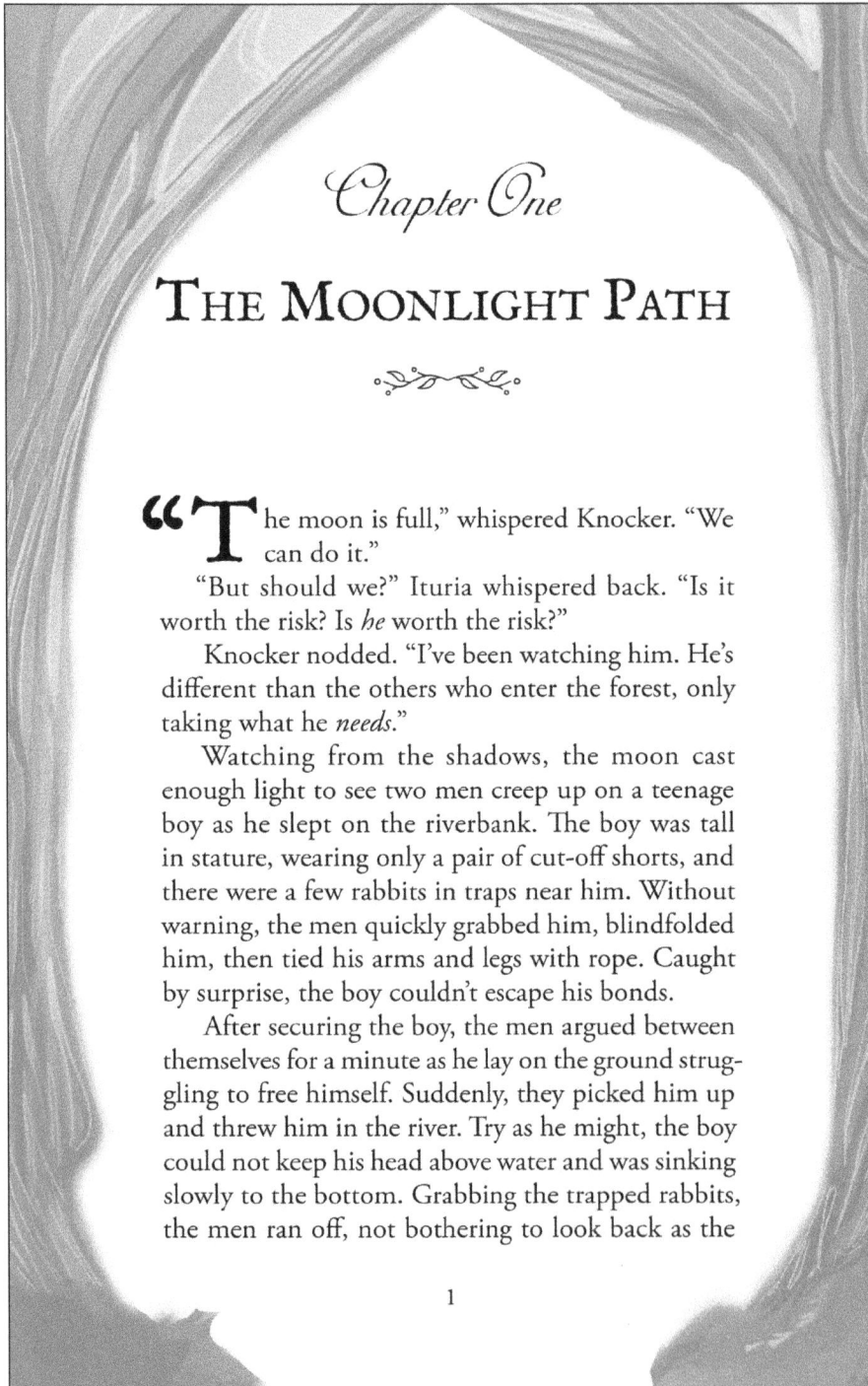

END OF CHAPTER

You have a few choices for the end of a chapter. Simply leave it blank with whitespace that naturally unfolds or design some extra art or flair. Always make sure the text flow to the top of the page. Often layout software defaults to justify on page and will stretch and spread lines across the page making it look weird.

Russ and the Hidden Voice

termites are responsible for making sure all cracks in the rocks and caverns are sealed . . ."

"Wait a second," interrupted Russ, "Do you mean to tell me you have trained termites to patch holes? How is that possible?"

"Russ," Knocker answered, "While on earth, mankind tends to think it is the only intelligent life on the planet and can kill or imprison all other lifeforms; however, that is not the truth. Each bird, animal, insect, and even fungus can be a positive contributor to the ecosystem. Man's failure to recognize that every creature on earth has value and is due respect is one of the reasons why Ituria started these islands."

"Let me go back to the beginning, as it is important you know why Ituria builds all these islands under the moon's surface. Let's stop for a few minutes and I'll explain."

Knocker and Russ sat down for a quick break, with Brigitte between them.

"Ituria started these islands as what he refers to as his 'Starfish Projects'. Several thousand years ago, he was so angry with humans for treating animals, trees, as well as other humans, so shamefully, that he wanted to do something to help those with no protection from the slaughter. But what could he do?"

Brigitte added her part to the story, "He talked to Melampus one day, right?"

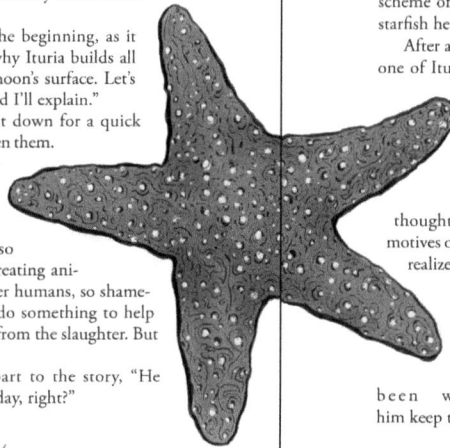

24

The Starfish Project

"Yes, Brigitte," Knocker agreed. "Ituria talked to Melampus. They were walking along the beach after a storm, and Melampus would repeatedly stop and pick-up starfish that had washed up on the beach, throwing them back into the sea. Ituria asked him why he was doing that, it was such a small amount he saved, and there was no way he could save all the starfish that had been washed up, it would be impossible."

Pausing for a moment, the emotion in Knocker's voice was evident. "This is where this story gets me every time. Melampus said that while in the grand scheme of things it may not be much, but for the starfish he does save, it means everything."

After another pause, Knocker continued, "I was one of Ituria's starfish if you look it that way. My mother was killed by humans when I was a very young dragon, and rather than leave me to die, he rescued me and took me to the moon to live with him. I owe my life to him."

As Knocker paused, lost in his own thoughts for a moment, Russ reflected on the motives of Ituria to keep these islands running, and realized it was a noble purpose indeed.

"Ituria apologized he was not in time to save my mother, and he pledged he would take care of me as long as I was with him, giving me a safe place to live where the hateful men would not find me. I have been with him for over 400 years now, helping him keep these fragile islands in balance."

25

Russ and the Hidden Voice

"How are you feeling?" said another voice. Ru recognized this voice —it was the one who ha rescued him from the water but not released fro his rope and blindfold. This voice had said son thing about rescuing him and broken rules that ha to be fixed.

Trying to get some context of what was going o Russ turned his head to the direction of the voic "Where am I? Who are you?" His last memory was heavy ropes, dragging him to the bottom of the riv as he struggled to breathe when he felt someone – something – grab him and pull him out of the water; "something" because the hands that had rescued him were not human hands. What else it could be, possibly the rescuer wore leather gloves?

"How much do you remember about last night?" said the first voice.

"Not much," Russ replied. "I had done some hunting earlier in the day, then rested with my catch before heading home. Some men, I think two men, grabbed me while I was napping, blindfolded me, tied me up, and threw me into the river. I remember someone pulling me from the river, and hearing talk about having to fix time or something, and we had to leave before the men returned. I am thankful to you for rescuing me, but I am at a loss as to who you are and where you came from. And by the way, where am I?"

"You're on Ituria's Island, and I'm Knocker," replied Knocker, adding with apparent pride. "I am First Guard to Ituria, the ruler of this Island."

6

---

immediate action was required to pull you from the river, and we brought you here."

Another pause, and Ituria's voice got serious. "Interfering with your forest is not something we take lightly, as anything that changes your time-line must be fixed before you can return to your home. In your case, we had no choice. If we had not intervened, you would have drowned. But," Ituria said, "before we remove your bindings, please be aware things aren't what you would expect. Hopefully, you realize we're here to help you. Don't feel threatened by us."

Russ could hear Ituria pacing before him as he spoke, rocks being scattered and sounds of shoes walking on stone, even if he could not see him. Ituria was pacing back and forth as he was explaining the situation. "If we wanted to harm you, we could have let you drown. Do you understand?"

Ituria stop moving; he must be standing right in front of him. Russ was silent, what could be next? He reasoned these two had rescued him, so they

7

Spies From Beneath

"What should we do?" asked Brigitte. "I can cover the stones with dirt if that would help, or would it alert her that we know about them?"

"Let's leave everything as it is and talk with Ituria. We know where this spot is now," Knocker replied. "Covering up the stones would let her know that we know she is watching us."

"We must be quick though," Knocker whispered. "Russ, pick up Brigitte and climb on my back; I am much faster than you and time is of the essence. We do not know if she can also hear us, and if she can, Granger might be in danger also."

Russ nodded, gently picked up Brigitte and, with a little difficulty, climbed onto Knocker's massive back, settling in on one side of the large spikes on his back, and holding with his free hand to Knocker's neck. "Hold on!" called Knocker as he flapped his giant wings and took off, flying between the treetops and the cavern ceiling, making a direct pathway to Ituria's home.

---

talk with Ituria," he said. "He may know of Granger and of a grave." On full alert now, although he could not hear the voice, the mention of Ituria made him realize this was no longer purely a quest to save Nya's trees, there might be another danger involved, and one threatening Ituria. "Ask how she can see us."

Russ nodded and did so. The reply confirmed their suspicion about the stones. "A rock was cracked, and small life flows in – light and moisture brought her daughter to life. The daughter is free. The mother watches from within. She reaches out through the crack. Help me, find me, free me."

34

Back Matter

Here you will be serving a few crucial roles or bits of information that had no place in the front or core content. For starters, this section is intended to introduce the reader to last thoughts, notes, information, resources, the author and/or illustrator, how to stay in touch, and any means to continue to connect and discover books via the author or publisher, sometimes both. It's a vital resource and a marketing tool in every book as long as the genre and audience make good use of it.

Story Ends

In children's books, sometimes there's a special "The End" page. It differs in every book whether this might be a spread or single page. Some even go as far as having special graphics for this page or moment while others keep it as part of that last bit of story. There is no wrong way to do this! It's completely ok not to have an official "THE END" or "TO BE CONTINUED" marker at the end of these books.

Note from Author

Note From The Author

Although this is a fantasy fiction adventure, the Earth's moon is a wonderful and mysterious place. Many of my concepts for Ituria's Island are based on real moon facts and research. Here are just a few examples:

There is something that has been observed on the moon for at least a thousand years called "Transient Lunar Phenomena" (TLP). These TLP include flashing lights or unusual gaseous colorations, brightening and even darkening spots. There is a record of 2,254 events going back to the sixth century, and at least one third of these were seen on the Aristarchus Plateau region. In Ituria's world, Aristarchus is the home of Guardian, who uses moon beams to transport Ituria and various animals to the moon and back, and that is why there are so many flashes (or TLP) at this specific location on the moon.

Also, while your first thought might be that you can't live in the caverns on the moon, scientists have been thinking about it for years! Many researchers are currently exploring the possibility of creating the first moon bases in caverns under the moon's surface. These caverns were created by lava flow many years

98

It's always a great idea to take a moment to discuss the lesson or follow up thoughts on the story you have told. With a younger audience, this is a great way to show that the events and themes presented to them have an impact in their world too. A note from the author also adds another layer of interaction with author and reader and can make a difference in a child's experience.

Bios for Author and/or Illustrator

It's common to see back pages that hold the biographies for the author and illustrator. This can be on the same page or on a spread across from one another. On occasion they start on their own right page, but this can jump your page count and color printing is pricey, so be mindful and flexible when including this.

Resources & Discussion Questions

Some books include some teacher and parent resources. This can be book club questions, fun activity pages, an information page leading to additional resources, or covering the topic in earnest. If you have a large amount of resources, you may want to create a companion piece such as a coloring book or activity book that can be purchased alongside the story. Other authors will provide these as exclusive PDFs offered when you sign up to their newsletter and often make great lead magnets for marketing or exclusive swag at special events.

Print-on-Demand page

If you are choosing to publish using Print-on-Demand, don't forget there will be a blank last even page in the back. This is where the printer will include a barcode that contains all the information as to where the book came from and more. Offset printed books don't have this feature at all.

Offset Printing—End Leaves

If you are planning to offset print the book, you may have to create additional files for end leaves. I highly recommend asking for templates from your specific printer since these are done slightly differently at times depending on the book binder equipment and process, they use to connect these to the cover and textual aspects of the book. If you are using Print-on-Demand, you bypassed the option to have these, or some do add solid white onto hard covers.

About the Author

J.B. moved to Florida in her early teens and has lived there ever since, enjoying the mild weather and abundance of wildlife. She even spent several seasons raising orphan squirrels. She graduated from the University of Central Florida and has spent her working career in the legal profession. Her novels are inspired by her family and nature, as well as her need to escape from the real world once in a while.

www.facebook.com/J.B.Moonstar

Instagram
@J.B.Moonstar

Twitter
@jb_moonstar

jbmoonstar.author@gmail.com

101

SAVING THE FILES

Now that you have completed the book, be sure you save the files appropriately. This means for both your work files and the final product for the printer. Be sure to always ask clients and printers what file format and needs are required. For the sake of all things, we will focus on the most common and most versatile versions. If you used InDesign, you can go to File > Package and the software will do its best to grab font files, images, and more into a folder. For those who are using other means, here's a breakdown of the work folder and what to save:

- FOLDER NAMED AFTER BOOK
  - Work File (InDesign, Word, etc.)
  - PDF (2001-xa format aka Press Quality with Bleed recommended)
  - EPUB (Optional, reflowable a must)
  - ORIGINAL folder
    - Holds original text file and any related materials

- FONT folder
  - Copies of font files used (truetype, openface, etc.)

- IMAGE folder
  - Any image used should be placed in here in case you need it or edit or replace later.

As for prepping files for upload to a vendor, the two main types will be PDF and EPUB (reflowable). No matter if you are self-publishing or using a service, these two are the current staple in the industry and have the ability to upload to a variety of distributors and vendors with very little issue.

- PDF Format

- This is used for print design applications, paperback, Print-on-Demand, and similar.
  - For printing, PDF-X/a: 2001 Format is the most accepted.
  - For web pdf, use web preferred file setting, but remember this file loses values needed for printing for a book.
  - Make sure Bleed Settings are applied or this could cause the file to kick back or be denied.

- EPUB Format
  - Always use reflowable.
  - Write in as much File Info and Metadata information as possible.
  - If attaching a cover image, it should be at least 1600x2400 pixels, 150 dpi, RGB color mode to avoid being kicked back from online vendors.
  - Most accepted eBook type currently with enhanced ability access.

BOOK TITLE: _____

SUBTITLE: _____

SAVING CHECKLIST

- ☐ A copy of the Manuscript or text file in a DOC, DOCX, RTF file that you used

- ☐ All the images in a LINKS or IMAGES folder

- ☐ Folder named after book to house all other files and folders

- ☐ Work files in folder (Recommend having a main one and back-up, i.e. *.indd and *idml)

- ☐ PDF version (2001-xa format for print-ready or print quality)

- ☐ EPUB (Reflowable) - optional

- ☐ Folder for fonts called FONT with copies of the files for future (they can go obsolete later)

- ☐ Did you save in the correct color profile (CMYK, RGB, 240% CMYK, etc)?

- ☐ Did you run ADA Compliance check in Adobe for ADA PDF needs? (optional)

- ☐ Do you need to convert EPUB to MOBI? (Consider using Calibre or similar converters)

- ☐ Has someone reviewed the file for issues besides you?

- ☐ Are the Header and Footers showing the correct text?

- ☐ Is your Table of Contents correct and numbered or not missing a chapter?

- ☐ Do your images bleed to the BLEED edge pass the TRIM edge?

- ☐ Double check that all your text is 0.5" from TRIM edge including Header and Footer

- ☐ Have you printed test pages on a local computer?

- ☐ Does your file meet the needs of your printer (Print-on-Demand AND Offset printers)

- ☐ Viewing for Web and Emails PDF - Did you save a "Reduced Size" PDF version?

- ☐ Has your customer signed off and reviewd the document before uploading to vendors?

BOOK TITLE: _____

SUBTITLE: _____

SAVING CHECKLIST

☐ A copy of the Manuscript or text file in a DOC, DOCX, RTF file that you used

☐ All the images in a LINKS or IMAGES folder

☐ Folder named after book to house all other files and folders

☐ Work files in folder (Recommend having a main one and back-up, i.e. *.indd and *idml)

☐ PDF version (2001-xa format for print-ready or print quality)

☐ EPUB (Reflowable) - optional

☐ Folder for fonts called FONT with copies of the files for future (they can go obsolete later)

☐ Did you save in the correct color profile (CMYK, RGB, 240% CMYK, etc)?

☐ Did you run ADA Compliance check in Adobe for ADA PDF needs? (optional)

☐ Do you need to convert EPUB to MOBI? (Consider using Calibre or similar converters)

☐ Has someone reviewed the file for issues besides you?

☐ Are the Header and Footers showing the correct text?

☐ Is your Table of Contents correct and numbered or not missing a chapter?

☐ Do your images bleed to the BLEED edge pass the TRIM edge?

☐ Double check that all your text is 0.5" from TRIM edge including Header and Footer

☐ Have you printed test pages on a local computer?

☐ Does your file meet the needs of your printer (Print-on-Demand AND Offset printers)

☐ Viewing for Web and Emails PDF - Did you save a "Reduced Size" PDF version?

☐ Has your customer signed off and reviewd the document before uploading to vendors?

Fiction, Young Adult, Memoirs, & Literary Books

When writing a novel,
that's pretty much entirely what life turns into:
'House burned down.
Car stolen.
Cat exploded.
Did 1,500 easy words, so all-in-all, it was a pretty good day.'

Neil Gaiman

Preparing the Manuscript

We've reached the book type that abandons images completely and focuses solely on textual content. It is vital that the manuscript in these genres come to the typesetter as clean as possible to save hours of work as well as miscommunication. For the starters, the use of alignment, bulleted points, and similar formatting elements should be consistent as to not mistaken the material as something else. A common issue is creative use to signify text messages or computer prompts being done in more than one way, and as a result, formatted drastically different by the typesetter. Remember they aren't proofreading your work, but simply using the consistency in your own formatting and style of writing as a jumping board of how to snap your work into the expectations of the readers and industry alike. Make sure hard returns are used properly, no unwanted manual line breaks, and other obstacles that can derail your efforts at the start of the process.

What Genre of Book?

More so than ever, genre is going to be calling the shots here regarding design and reader expectations. Font choice will need to match and set the ambience the book is about. Fancy chapter pages, drop-caps, informative headers, and fanciful footers are all huge parts in the design and layout of this type of book. Information and communication become a huge priority, as well as being mindful of word count and page count. Books typically in this section are black and white on crème paper or even groundwood.

For example, romance books tend to be smaller in trim size and have lots of calligraphy or script style font faces; science fiction and non-fiction books have a larger trim size and typically have sans-serif fonts for even body text; horror genre tends to have serif fonts with chapter fonts that are creepy or artful in some way to reflect the gore or horror aspect within the story. You will notice chapter art will shift as well and the style seen can be elaborate or text only depending on the preference of the designer and author.

Choosing a Trim Size

Books in this genre and type tend to be always portrait and 6.14 in x 9.21 inches to as small as 4 in by 6 inches. This goes for hardcover and paperback, no matter if the book is offset printed or Print-on-Demand. Be mindful that not all trim sizes are available in both hardcover and paperback. Do the research with your chosen printer to decide if you wish them to be the same size. Below is only a few of the sizes common in the industry for these books and available with printers. It can't be expressed enough to go to a bookstore and see what the genre of your book tends to favor. For example, 6 in x 9 in books are seen more often for collections and young adult novels whereas 5 in x 8 in are common for the standard speculative genre novel. Always aim to be aware of the reader's expectations and exposures so you can use them to your advantage to sell a book inside and out.

- 6.14 x 9.21 (Great for Hardcover)
- 6 x 9* (Paperback & Hardcover options)
- 5.5 x 8.5
- 5.25 x 8 (Paperback only)
- 5 x 8*
- 5 X 7*
- 4.25 x 6.87* (Common Mass Market)
- 4 x 7

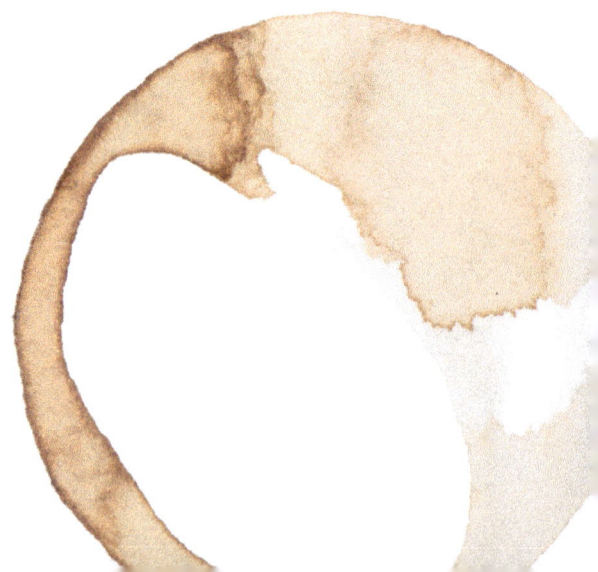

FONT EXPECTATIONS

Consistency is key, and limiting to one core font for the majority of the book based on your body font is best. Chapter header, headlines, subheads, header font, and footer fonts can all be reflective of the book's genre and artful. The focus has now shifted to using the page space as efficiently as possible. A few ways to combat high word count books besides increasing the trim size would be lowering the leading, pushing limitations to 10- to 11-point fonts, using a more efficient font face (Calibri is excellent for a "tight" typeset), limiting chapter page decorations and spacing, and always opting for a continuous chapter layout. Again, most of the selection is heavily based on the genre, and as we've recommended often, don't be afraid to look at comparable titles or titles in that same genre and audience to see what font and styles the readership is used to seeing. That doesn't mean to copy, but you see how you can add to the design in a way that helps your book standout on the bookshelf the moment a reader opens the book.

MAXIMUM WORD AND PAGE COUNTS

A typical novel can fall between 50,000 to 250,000 words on average. (A huge leap compared to middle grade and chapter books!). From a 150,000- to 250,000-word count, you are usually dealing with an epic fantasy, hard science fiction, or similar speculative fiction work. In cases like these, you must consider some abnormal solutions for typesetting, which include 10- to 11-point font size, Calibri or similar "dense and naturally well-spaced" font faces, lighter paper to allow more pages to be added into perfect bound, and so forth. That being said, many seasoned typesetters do their best to keep book under 300 pages since breaking this mile marker can raise the production cost of a book a lot, whether its offset or Print-on-Demand. At 500 pages, a perfect bound book tends to breakdown; although, this binding has improved quite a bit over the last decade. Even then, perfect bound, or glued binding, have a max page count that can range 900-1200 depending on paper weight. You never want to get close to this for a few reasons. First, this eats up space in the inner margin and takes away for the page layout to keep text from falling into the crack or spine of the book. The other reason is the chances of the glue letting go of the pages while reading increases drastically. Genre weighs heavily here as well as the type of content you're writing. Here's a chart on expected word counts found in *The Author's Accountability Planner* by 4 Horsemen Publications, Inc.:

MATERIALS AND PRINT OPTIONS

Saving on print cost comes easier for this selection of books. It doesn't mean you can't have images or artful design, but be mindful of the options you are choosing. The most common is black and white printing on cream (off-white, textured) or groundwood paper (very thin, seen in grocery story prints). If you are entertaining the idea of going with a color interior, be mindful of the cost increase that will carry over to the final retail cost. If you only have a few images, it's recommended to grayscale for print edition and use the color photos for eBook edition since color and black and white is decided via the reading device (and doesn't impact price of eBook).

Fancy chapter pages, drop-caps, informative headers, and fanciful footers are all huge parts in the design

---

You can always check out publisher compensation calculators (i.e. the one on Ingram's Lightning Source website) to see what royalties remain after its sold through a third-party vendor (i.e. Amazon, Barnes & Noble, Kobo, etc.). Default wholesale is normally 55% but many small presses drop this to 40% and larger publishers will drop further as low as 28%. For competitive pricing for retail, we recommend 40% or lower; however, be warned, the lower this discount, the less likely that bookstores and retailers will purchase large amounts of books to have in stock. Granted, much of this falls back to options dealing with Print-on-Demand and not every provider will give you the option to adjust this price.

I Want to Be a Writer

Take a look at all the projects and stories you want to complete for this coming year and predict your word count for them. It's okay to fall over or under—and you may massage these as the year progresses, but throw something out there to get started. Here's a rough scope of word counts to aid you in estimation:

TYPES	GENRE
Flash Fiction	Blog Posts
1,000 word or less	200-1,200
Short Story	Romance
1,200-10,000	50,000-70,000
Novelette	Paranormal
10,000-30,000	70,000-90,000
Novella	Fantasy
30,000-45,000	90,000-120,000
Novel	Crime
50,000-85,000	90,000-100,000
Epic Novel	Mystery/Thriller/Suspense
90,000-150,000	70,000-80,000
Textbook	Memoir
50,000-250,000	30,000-70,000
Young Adult	Science Fiction
50,000-80,000	90,000-125,000
Middle Grade	Horror
25,000-40,000	70,000-100,000
Chapter Books	Historical
10,000-20,000	80,000-120,000
Picture Books	Erotica
300-700	7,000-50,000

ILLUSTRATIONS, ILLUSTRATORS, & GRAPHIC DESIGNERS

If you know your trim size and orientation, then you're now ready to decide on how you want to create your illustrations. Some authors illustrate their books themselves, but that's not an option for others. You have a few options in this matter, and it's highly dependent on the type of book you're making such as a picture book, middle grade book, or textbook. If you are planning to hire someone to help you create and format your book, consider seeking out a graphic designer or illustrator who is knowledgeable in typesetting or at least picture book layouts. They will be able to incorporate and go through more steps with you as your guide. If you do this yourself, be sure to take your time to read the content in the Picture Book section for information specifically for making one and how to best prepare before starting.

Every book type has its own tweaks to the system or may have areas that are a must for one and not the others. If you intend to gather illustrations to give to a typesetter or format yourself, seek out an illustrator who draws in a style you enjoy and within the price range you need. They will not only need to be aware of the trim size and orientation for a picture book, but they need to include room for a 0.25" to 0.5" cutaway bleed so your core image doesn't get chopped when printed. For illustrations added to a section of a single page, you just simply need an image slightly bigger than intended use for best quality when it prints.

It's rare for this type of book to have images or illustrations. These should be reserved for younger audiences or non-fiction work in general.

If your illustrator is using a physical median (watercolor, markers, acrylics, etc.) over digital painting, make sure you pass on information for file type, resolution (DPI), color mode, and so on. The more information you provide, the easier it is for them to give you the correct variant of scans. If they aren't able to provide you with scans, I recommend hiring an art photographer. If your median is light colored or watercolors, you should consider digitally enhancing the coloration, performing a black/white balance, and checking the levels of said image. In the end, do not expect those colors to match or look the same as the original as there is a loss of detail, texture, and shift in colors that is impossible to recreate by the time it prints in the book.

No matter the book, there is a standard need for file type and settings here when you aim to use images in your book.

- These files should be in CMYK color mode
- Saved at 300-600 DPI (resolution)
- Be in these file types: JPEG, PNG, or TIFF

You can also utilize PDF and export out to image or place as PDF but be mindful most software will be converting all these into a more manageable JPEG format. Sticking with JPEG and saving editable originals can be very effective in keeping overall file size for the PDF and eBook formats down to acceptable levels. This often comes into play with vendors with files size maximums, such as Barnes & Noble requiring eBooks to be 20 MB or below.

To keep print cost as low as possible, always favor black and white deisgn and print options!

What if you can't find an illustrator or have funding restrictions? There's another possibility! Prepare to go on a deep search and rethink your initial book design. Stock photo sites are a wonderful resource for those who can't afford the illustrators or struggling to find one. This includes ShutterStock, DepositPhoto, iStockPhoto, Adobe Stock, and many more sites have a variety of artists who submit sheets and multiple images of characters for all audiences. A fitting example of this is the character you see throughout Writer's Bane! The more active an artist is on these sites, the better chance for the collection to grow and pull from. Some give you a means to reach out to them as well! You can always reach out to them and see if they will also commission pieces.

Basics of Digitally Enhancing Illustrations

Thanks to the digital age, many artists or illustrators have taken to producing art via software. This has made it a better means to reproduce images in a higher brilliance and sharper hues. That doesn't mean hand drawn artwork and watercolors can't join this high-tech advantage. Traditional art can be scanned or photographed to be pulled into the digital realm and in some cases, adjusted. This doesn't come without its share of pros and cons. One being the most common is the lack of capturing texture, hues, or even soft pencil strokes that all-too-often get washed out by the scanner or camera's light. If your art is too big to scan, an art photographer should be able to use a black/white balance card and even adjust and check it.

Once an image has been placed in digitally, you or a design have the freedom to adjust the image as needed. This can be moving elements, changing hues, brightening the overall saturation, and even resetting black and white tones to make richer levels so the image prints sharper. If you can apply a lot of these easy tricks to an image and balance the CMYK spectrum to a richer level, it will make a huge difference when printed. Not every image or color will be able to translate well; for example, blues and purples are often a struggle to lock in without shifting when ink is laid to paper.

Warning About Watercolors

Out of all the medians your illustrations can be made from, this one comes with a loss of detail and color just from scanning or photographing it. From there, it sways again depending on the options you choose. If you are ok with digitizing and drastically shifting your watercolors for print and not looking to match the original artwork, you will feel this impact the least. As for those looking to match it and capture the watercolor pieces as they are, you won't get this result. First, the act of scanning or taking a photo removes the texturing that watercolors often have, as well removing some of the sharpness and overlapping details. From there, I recommend offset printing with gloss or semi-gloss paper at about 100+lb. paper with alcohol-based printing for closest match to original work. If you decide to move forward with Print-on-Demand, be warned that you will continue to lose vibrancy and details due to the fact only matte paper is available and most are water-based ink printing and may cause saturation issues. This becomes most noticeable with a picture-book printer in Print-on-Demand.

Black and White Balance

If you are using Photoshop, Fire Alpaca, or some other photo editing software, you should be able to do this. Many of the photography editing software may be able to assist with this technique as well as the others to follow. Whichever software you use, there should be tutorials out there to assist you best as far as this book goes, the aim is to explain what it's meant to do and hint as to why you might want to apply this to your own formatting and images. As for this one, it helps establish true black and true white on the image and adjusts the image color range accordingly. Often when we scan an image, the black has a shine to it and might come off as a dark gray or even brown. This gives you a chance to "reset" the expectations and identify where these are on the image if you have both visible.

Levels in Spectrum

Images come with levels that spread a variety of hues and channels. Often black and white being on opposite ends, they come with slight dips beyond the peak of these colors that can take away from the overall sharpness of the image spectrum. Cutting out or knocking them to the peaks or using auto levels features can bring an image to pop more visually.

Hue & Saturation

Hue and saturations levels or using filters that shift these can do a wide range for an image. If the colors seem to have washed out, you might be able to recover faded colors using this feature. Also scanned or photographed images may have washed out and either you can darken the hue values or even adjust contrast and brightness settings to recover the look of the original artwork. Sometimes this setting allows a moment for you to change the hue or coloration of the art and make decisions you normally would have

missed out on. Using a masked layer stacked with this can even allow you to change a color on a single item in the image, but that's best for a tutorial as it delves into photo editing and is beyond this book's conversation focused on typesetting.

DPI, IMAGE SIZE, AND RESOLUTION ADJUSTMENTS

The resolution of an image is very important! The first aspect to this is the size. You don't need your image to be 44 inches by 21 inches if your book is only 11 inches by 8.5 inches. If you are bleeding images off the edge, the image needs to only be 11.25 inches by 8.75 inches at the very least to give some room for image placement that allows bleed and trim. It's always smart to have the image slightly bigger, but too large and it may cause the program or computer to crash (especially those on personal or home systems). It also makes saving backups or throwing it on a cloud storage much more feasible.

Once the size is within a reasonable range (exact with bleed or slightly larger in the same orientation or ratio), you need to make sure the resolution is set between 300-600 DPI. Anything under 300 is at risk to pixelate or be blurry. Know that most images saved from internet are usually only 72-96 DPI, so make sure what you are saving is the full image and not a smaller web version or down-sampled variant. Images that are over 600 DPI are at risk of the printer shrinking and may result in unwanted quality or results. It's always best to avoid these sorts of situations and keep the control and final product in your hands.

CMYK VERSUS RGB

Print and physical books are printed using CMYK colorations. This uses a set amount of cyan, magenta, yellow, and black layered on the page. Depending on the printer this can be applied with alcohol or water-based inks and vary in brightness (often influenced by the paper chosen). Water based inks are limited to 240% CMYK saturation level with paperweights at 70lbs or less as seen in Print-on-Demand applications.

IMAGE NAMING

Be sure to be consistent or concise with how you are naming your images. You can do this in a number of ways which includes consecutively (image01, image20, image03…), by location (Chapter01, Chapter02_SUBHEAD, Chapter02_Figure1.1), or labelled by what they are (Flowers01, RosesAndBees, AuntMayAndHerPig…). You should always avoid using

symbols and spaces since these may cause issues in final formats. Depending on your software and how you export for eBook format, having images with names that include open spaces, dollar signs ($), hashtags (#), and similar often will cause them not to load or fail when uploaded to a vendor. I highly recommend using only alphabet and numbers with underscore if need be. In programming we do this as well and often default to camelCase (LittleTimmysWagon, IHateThisPictureTheMost, ImageNameLikeThis…) as the safest means to prevent programming errors.

IMAGE FILE TYPES

Images come in a variety of types and the best ones to use for publishing are JPEG and TIFF formats. You can use a PNG, which preserves the transparency unlike JPEG or even a PDF file. You should keep these between 300-600 DPI and at least a little larger than the intended size to make sure you have room to trim the image if needed. TIFF is considered the best format and has been used in the printing and graphic design world as the superior option. Most Print-on-Demand printers want the files saved in PDF2001XA format, and this converts images to JPEG. Same thing happens when exporting to EPUB; the images are often converted to JPEG or PNG depending on what you are using. Thus, it is recommended to save in JPEG for several reasons, including the fact it's a smaller size, translates into eBook without issues, and prevents any issues when converting to final PDF format changes to the images.

PERMISSIONS & USAGE RIGHTS

Images and artwork can fall under public domain rights, but if they don't, you will need to purchase usage rights or get permission. If you pulled your images from a service like ShutterStock or similar stock photo site, they usually have different levels you can purchase for usage rights. This is the safest means for images and artwork. If you intend to hire an illustrator, be sure to cover the usage and contract with them how books are sold and their images will be used from the book to creating swag, bookmarks, banners, and more. Some may clear you for using the images in the book only and not for marketing materials. Be sure to add the permissions granted in the copyright section or even an illustration rights section as a type of appendix. It's always best to give credit where it's due on your copyright page at the very least.

DESIGNING THE PAGES

When it comes to this type, most of the designing happens on the chapter start pages and front/back matter of the book. This may pertain to blank pages or where maps are added to aid content as the material calls for it. The key here is making font choices that will make the content as legible as possible. Font Families that have a variety of sub-family variants and character styles can help create a consistent and clean layout. Beware of content with heavy italics and the body text font you choose, not every italic style is easily readable or will meet the look you want the content to hold. This is a common means for fiction writers to show internal dialogue or character's thoughts. That doesn't mean you can't have different font faces for chapter, headline, subheads, and similar aspects, but stay consistent using styles or paragraph styles. If you decide to change the look later, it's always a nice aspect to adjust the style and see all instances change without having to "re-typeset" those aspects.

Chapter starts can contain artwork, images, or glyphs that stay within the textual margins or bleed off the page. It depends how you want to include these, if anchored or in-line with text they will pull into the eBook, so be sure to check the EPUB export and settings for these images in Object Export Options in InDesign. If you place images as a page background or on the master page, don't be alarmed not to see them in the eBook. This is normal and to be expected. Also, it's completely ok to have only text and healthy portions of whitespace if this is your preference for what a book interior should look like. It's up to you!

FULL SPREAD LAYOUT

The image or text (not both) stretches across 2 pages, a left and right page, to show as one large landscape image or two pages of textual content. In a lot of cases the text may only be present on one page and not the other, but other layouts might have several spots all around the image to show the story unfolding in a sequence or multi-action spread.

RULE OF THIRDS SPREAD LAYOUT

Across a two-page span, an image, graph, or pull quote will cover one complete page and a portion of the adjacent page to leave room on a far left or right edge for font to place. In concept, the object is using two-thirds of the design area to draw the eye to the text or away from the text by doing so. The Rule of Thirds is often used in marketing, print design, or even in filming. It splits the viewing area into thirds from top to bottom and side to side. From this point, you break the content and subject matter up at the key sections to help draw the eye in a certain direction or pull it towards or away.

SPLIT DESIGN IMAGE & TEXT PAGE LAYOUT

Again, this is similar to the Image + Text layout seen in picture books and textbooks. On a single page, whether it's the right or left, the image and text split the space. Sometimes this is done in a 50/50 spit, or a two-thirds split, but often features a white space or colored space where the text will be.

WHITESPACE PAGE LAYOUT

This page is often an indicator of a chapter starting or ending. Sometimes it can be a section or partition marker of some kind. It's notorious for having a lot of white space or empty, unused space on the page spread. What little content is there usually is textual to guide or inform the reader in preparation of something changing or a transition within the book. You see this a lot in textbooks and fiction books with right page only chapter starts.

EXAMPLES OF MANUSCRIPTS

Below is a list of different ways you may receive or set a manuscript up. The most common in the industry are the first two options: Textual Only and Text with Image Placement. From chapter books to textbooks, these are the typical format you will receive the textual content for typesetting. As you venture into workbooks, picture books, comic books, and graphic novels, you will want to use story bounce, detailed format, storyboarding, or script styles to capture all the parts. Unlike text-based or heavy books, these require guidance and cues as to where images or text should be placed on a page to accurately tell the story intended. Each book type will lean more so on one kind of manuscript, and it's important to be aware of this as you prep your manuscript for typesetting. This can be a huge influence on how well key elements are designed, whether you intend to format your own book or hand your book to someone else.

TEXTUAL ONLY

This is the most common manuscript for mass market fiction work. No images are tied into it, and it's simply importing the manuscript into the software and applying the indicated styling where deemed appropriate. A typesetter's aim is to streamline the text to the best of their abilities as to not break a reader's immersion with weird visual discrepancies such as a slight tweak in line spacing (common in manuscripts where portions where dictated via speech-to-text and other written on a computer). You have to remember that we've been reading books with the same patterns and margins for centuries and keeping those expectations while being creative can be a hardline to walk for anyone designing a book.

For a textual-based manuscript, follow the Do's and Don'ts to prevent any unseen issues in the content. As for trim and font choices, it will fall back to the audience, genre, and type of book you are working on. You should be able to copy-paste content into a clean Word document or use InDesign's "File > Place" feature to import text and its associated styles. In the case of the latter, be sure to run Scripts to lock in these styles and save time from having to do manual changes by using the PrepText and other tools often found in opensource or pre-programmed into InDesign for use. Most manuscripts imported this way come as double-spaced in Times or similar font at 12 pt. If the manuscript has a variety of font faces, I recommend streamlining it to a single font face to prevent issues when formatting the book. Also, be aware many of these come with double spacing, which is intended for editorial purposes. Never keep this line spacing!

TEXT WITH IMAGE PLACEMENT

For this book type, this is going to be the more common type encountered with textbooks, workbooks, or image heavy content. Throughout the text, there should be indications for image placement and should be clearly marked, much like a subhead or citation. For visual aid, I always encourage highlighting these yellow and treat them as their own paragraph. It's also helpful to use a keyword like "IMAGE" and brackets to help make the image placement stand up, for example:

[[IMAGE01: This picture shows the difference between nightshade and chili pepper flowers]]

These one-liners should be placed between the paragraphs they should be near or on the same page as the text. The importance of this is so when creating an eBook, the typesetter can make sure it falls inline at the right point of the content. It can also make it easier to play with the page layout as they apply the design and text begins to autoflow from page to page with the changes.

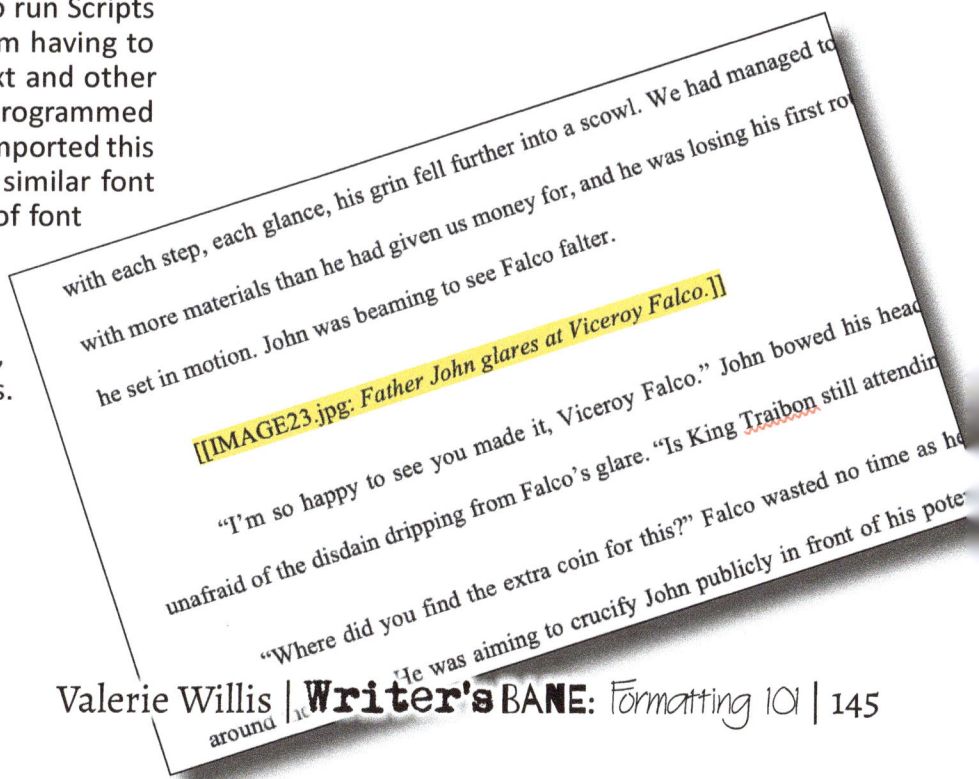

with each step, each glance, his grin fell further into a scowl. We had managed to with more materials than he had given us money for, and he was losing his first ro he set in motion. John was beaming to see Falco falter.

[[IMAGE23.jpg: *Father John glares at Viceroy Falco.*]]

"I'm so happy to see you made it, Viceroy Falco." John bowed his head unafraid of the disdain dripping from Falco's glare. "Is King Traibon still attendin

"Where did you find the extra coin for this?" Falco wasted no time as he was aiming to crucify John publicly in front of his pote around

Formatting the Book

Hooray! Now that we've talked and prepped this thing to no end, you should be ready to format this book with confidence. Why? Because it is so much easier to resolve problems at the manuscript and prepping stage than when you are formatting and making the book. Though, as said before, I am an avid user of word to InDesign, I will do my best throughout the book to provide information in an all-encompassing and design angle. If you were looking for software tutorial, this isn't the book for you. Getting detailed instructions on how to set parameters in Word, Scribd, and similar word processors isn't the aim.

Instead, we will be focusing on the typesetter-based elements and areas that will be par the course for any book you design. Dependent on the software you are using to design your book in could present its own issues and information may be labeled slightly different or found in different areas. In tandem with a software book, this book may provide some keywords in order to gain the affects you were aiming for in order for you to gain a greater value out of using said programs. In my years of looking for instructional manuals for book design, most of what I have learned was via videos, trial and error, typography college courses, and simply diving into the industry headlong with an open mind and understanding of the roots of publishing and its history. It probably also helped I delved in some game design, development, and programming, so I could troubleshoot creative solutions.

Without further ado, it's time to make this book using these step-by-step, or page-by-page instructions below. Feel free to adjust this to suit your own style and needs since there are various methods to achieve the results seen here. Again, the aim here is to simply the process while being able to make quality print books, enhance eBooks, and create a PDF that falls close as possible to being ADA compliant (Americans with Disabilities Act).

File Setup

The file or page size should match the trim size in width and height. Make sure the intended orientation matches what you intended, specifically landscape versus portrait. Depending on the program, you may have to set bleed settings to include a 0.125" bleed on all sides or for outer margins. For some Print-on-Demand vendors, they may want the inner margin to have no bleed since this is the side of the page that is glued to the spine of the book. You usually get to set up or define the overall margins as well.

Be mindful that with picture books you will be saving a flat PDF for eBook design and that you don't have to fret over threading text boxes together as seen with all other book types. It's more important to make sure images are bleeding off to the marked edges just pass the trim edge, that elements are layered and overlayed in the right order, and textual content is within the margins provided by the printer or Print-on-Demand requirements of 0.5" from trim size edge. Here are my recommended settings for this book type:

- Industry Standard Numbers:
  - 0.125" Bleed from trim edge
  - 0.5" Margin for content inward from trim edge
  - Large page counts will require a larger 0.625" or higher inner margin or gutter
  - Special binding may change the needs for inner margins

- Inner or inside margin: 0.625" for books under 300 pages and

- 0.75" to 0.8" for books pushing far into the 500+ range since where the pages' bind needs more space to avoid words falling into the crack of the book.
  - Granted, this is a picture book, and you can sometimes get away with a 0.5" margin.

- Outer or outside margins (including top and bottom) should be 0.5" to 0.625"
  - Typically have main body pages with header and footer set and you can increase the top and bottom margins to 0.8-0.875" to give yourself space to place and space these from your body text.

Wondering where these numbers come from? Your vendors should have File Creation Guides via a PDF or webpage. No matter if you plan on using offset printing, KDP, IngramSparks, or a similar vendor, these parameters never change. This is the basic needs of a file going to print and will give the press some wiggle room. These parameters will change if you choose more elaborate binding and use certain presses. Always make sure you get these settings from the printer and design the book with these in place from the start.

USING LAYERS

Most of the layout software allows you to create layers such as InDesign (not any of the word processors though they do have header footer options). These come in handy in keeping content stacked or arranged in the right order. This includes making sure watermarks are below the body text layer and even keeping the header and footer elements on the top and not lost behind images and such. A bonus to using this feature is the ability to lock them and make sure you don't accidently change, move, or delete them unintentionally. With picture books, you often use images that take up the entire page and risk losing these elements completely. Recommended layers include the following listed in the order they should fall and usage:

- **Header and Footer Layer** – This will have your top layer text boxes that contain the header and footer which usually hold page numbers, title, author, and/or current chapter. You can control these with master pages. In a word processor, this is an option or specific setting that is influenced by section breaks to change how they look from section to section of the book's layout.

- **Default or Body Text Layer** – Here you will manage the primary text box in which the main content autoflows through threaded textboxes or pages.

- **Background Layer** – At the bottom of the list should be a background layer that is designed for images, spreads, and watermarks that need to fall under the textual content.

- This doesn't mean you need to use all these layers, but it's highly recommended to give you more control when formatting. If the program you are using doesn't provide layers, check for features that define objects on the page as needing to be "Ordered" or "Arranged" with sub-options for "Bring to Front" or "Bring to Back" which mimic what layering does. This should aid you in making sure text and images overlap appropriately.

MASTER PAGES

These pages, or templates, are premade pages you can drag and drop into the layout to help speed things along and stay consistent. Know that this is more commonly found as a feature in layout software such as InDesign. Even with a freeform style book, there's a level of consistency with placement of elements such as header, footer, page numbers, watermarks, and other elements that you may not want to shift and wish to keep level throughout the book. In any book, you are going to be applying a few key layout pages. I recommend the following master pages or templates be made in advance to speed up the typeset process:

- **A blank page** with only the margin lines set. You may include a primary text box version for dedication or anchoring title page images into place. Works great for print-on-demand with that last page needing to be blank as well. These will also set your title pages and copyright page as well.

- **A body page** made of a blank page with only the header and footer with a main text box. I recommend putting the header and footer on a top layer that's locked. Predesign a left and right page, often featuring the book title on left and author name on right. You may even design a running header or chapter header that auto updates depending on the software you are using. Adding glyphs and art to page numbers and headers can add a nice creative flair.

- **A chapter page** that can add art, designs, and spacing shifts to accommodate the style implied. I always make right and left page versions, so if I need to change from right page only chapters to continuous, it's ready to adapt accordingly.

- **A numbered blank page** can be useful for areas that may contain images, maps, tables, and similar content where you simply want page numbers only.

- **Worksheets or Special Pages** should be designed or a foundation premade or decided on before getting too far into the design. Prepping these pages in advance can help in your efforts and provide a sense of how much space they truly need in order to interact with the content as your design the book.

- **A two-column body page or variants** can provide a means to design smart and save on page count where you can. Also, two-column pages can provide

easier means to place images as often seen in textbooks, reference books, and workbooks alike.

- **Section breaks** become vital for non-fiction books. Occasionally these hard pages or spreads have an image or color to help standout when certain passing of time, events, topics, and provide a sense of dividers for the reader. Prepping a page or spread for these can save time and provide consistency when applicable.

FONT CHOICES AND PREP

Font has the most weight in typesetting and interior book design. Your choices and attention to detail to the spacing, size, and types will have a significant impact for better or worse. There are a few things you can do to help yourself prep and streamline your design depending on if you are using styles in Microsoft Word or a combination of Paragraph and Character styles in Adobe InDesign. Prepping and setting up pre-saved files with master pages and these elements can save a lot of hunting and frustrations, especially if you want to shift or change fonts later. If you intend to do typesetting full time or work heavily with fonts, I recommend investing into Font Management programs such as FontExplorer. This can make it easier to keep your growing library from bogging down your computer while making it easier to test out and organize fonts.

PARAGRAPH STYLES OR STYLES

These will make up most of the formatting application in textual content. They work in particular order and repeat as you start a new section or chapter. Making a style in advance can help you quickly adjust, fix, or change the entire typeset without hunting and pecking for certain content in the book. Instead, applying a style and changing the style can shift and fix the book as a whole.

- **Chapter Header** – Should be the largest font and be a font face that reflects genre. Content here is often just numbers, "Chapter" text, or some section marker text.

- **Headline** – This is often a subtitle or section title that follows behind the Chapter Header, normally directly below it. It should be the second largest text and also have a legible but creative font that captures the genre.

- **Subhead** – Should be a slight larger than the body text but clear and bolder in some way. It's common for these to be the same font as body text and simply in all-caps or small caps.

- **Drop Cap** – Whether it's a single letter, word, or line, this is the first paragraph in a chapter or section. It's a way to artfully signal to a reader where to begin reading or add more to the chapter page that makes it stand out other than whitespace.

- **Body Text** – This will be the majority of your content. It should be a legible font comfortable for readers and remain the same throughout the entire book. It builds the font foundation for Drop Caps, Citations/Quotes, Subheads, Tables and more.

- **Citations/Quote** – This paragraph style should center or have an indent of 0.25" to 0.05" on the right and left sides. It's also common to add space before and after this paragraph style so the quote or citations pops. Often there is an italics character style applied.

- **Bullet Points** – Lists and bullets have similar indentation and spacing. Setting the preference or making a variety of these to create multi-tier systems in the varying styles can save a typesetter grief as well as the means to remembering how APA, MLA, and CMS are different from one another.

CHARACTER STYLES OR SUBFAMILY FONTS

Creating premade character style can help you gain more control on the style of the manuscript as a whole. It also helps build coding within certain programs for eBook creation and keeps these vital aspects from disappearing in the process.

- **Bold** – used to identify keywords, bring words to the front, and stand out louder. There is never a need to make a whole manuscript bold. Instead, choose a thicker or heavier font.

- Italics – this has many uses from quotes, to signaling key elements in content, and even to signal internal dialogue in stories.

- Underline – much like bold, this is used to make content stand out, signify a reference (depending on styles like APA), hyperlinks (or clickable content in text), or signal something of importance.

- Keyword – This comes in handy when wanting to stay consistent in font face and size changes in books where you need vocabulary words or key visuals to pop.

- SMALL CAPS – Common to see in reference works or to address religious names or keywords, this is easier to manage as a character style and carries over into eBook better.

OBJECT STYLES OR TABLE STYLES

These are special styles that influence objects, images, and tables. They make sure designs and placement match and can even streamline how items show up in an eBook. Not every software has the means to define these or set them up. As for InDesign, these can help guide image frames, table cells, and more so that you can save time when adding content into the layout and saving you the grief of cracking open object options to adjust every detail.

Page-by-Page

Out of all the typesets you will create, this should be the easiest and by-far fastest to typeset. A well-experienced typesetter can design a text only, 100,000-word count book in about 2 to 6 hours depending on the number of chapters, overall design, and if the piece needs careful attention to subheads, bullets, and citations. For first-time typesetters, take your time to develop ways to tweak your template to speed up the process up for the current book and future books. Taking the time to prep the manuscript, reviewing the checklist, creating styles in advance, and similar can make this a less daunting process and save time later. You should be able to assign styles for every part of the book and make font changes across the entire piece later when you decide to make changes or try other font faces, sizes, and adjust spacing. It's vital every component is assigned since this carries over to the eBook and can ensure choices carry over into electronic format. Always have information on margins and file guides from the intended distributor and/or printer as to avoid issues later in the process.

The Checklist!

Here is a checklist that should help you make sure you finished prepping the manuscript and materials before starting the formatting. Often we don't think to ask or double check to include some of these things and it can be detrimental in the final stages leading up to printing the actual book. Whether you are formatting your own book or formatting someone else's, this checklist is to help you gather everything you need before you start.

- Trim Size
- Book Title
- Subtitle
- Author Name (or Pen Name)
- Publisher and/or Logo
- Copyright Page
  - Author name and copyright year
  - Name illustrator, designer, editor, etc.
  - Permissions for any materials used.
  - Public domain or scripture cited.
  - ISBN numbers (Paperback, Hardcover, eBook, Audiobook, etc.)
  - LCCN (Pending or number)
  - Published information and logo
  - The usual legal jargon to protect you, your work, and the publisher.
- Front Matter
  - Foreword: Yes or No
  - Dedication: Yes or No
    - Above Copyrights or Own Page
- Images are ready, clearly named, and all accounted for
  - 300 – 600 DPI
  - Correct size for trim + bleed
  - CMYK color mode
- Manuscript – Text only edition
  - Has image directions that match image names
- Back Matter
  - Author Bio
  - Image
    - Hyperlinks
    - Illustrator Bio
    - Image
    - Hyperlinks

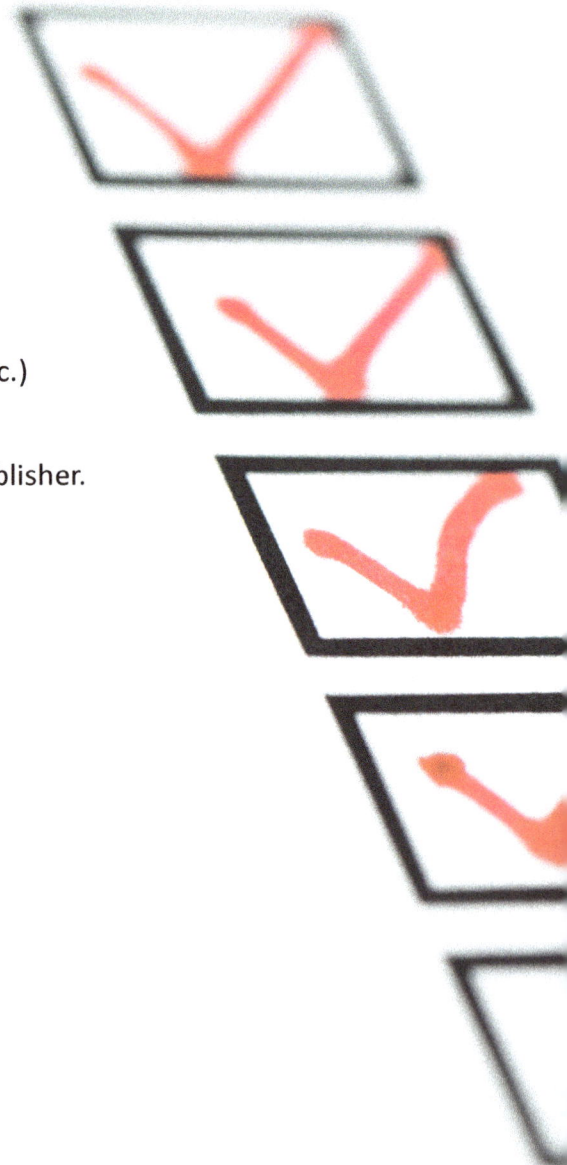

BOOK TITLE: _____

SUBTITLE: _____

TYPESET CHECKLIST

- [ ] Manuscript text in a DOC, DOCX, RTF file

- [ ] All the images listed in Manuscript present:

- [ ] CMYK mode

- [ ] Between 300-600 DPI.

- [ ] Trim Size _____ width x _____ height

- [ ] Author Pen Name - FIRST_____LAST_____

- [ ] Dedication: Yes or No

- [ ] Author Bio: Yes or No

- [ ] Copyright

- [ ] Publisher information

- [ ] Additional mention such as artist, design, or typesetter? _____

- [ ] Scriptures cited from…. Any public domain original publication mentions? _____

- [ ] Permission granted from… Any materials that have permissions needing to be listed here?

- [ ] ISBNs for Paperback: _____ Hardcover_____

- [ ] Audiobook_____ eBook_____

- [ ] LCCN pending or listed?_____

- [ ] Front Matter (Acknowledgements, Foreword, Preface, etc.)

- [ ] Do they want a Table of Contents: Yes or No

- [ ] Do they have tables to import: Yes or No

- [ ] Do they want pull quotes: Yes or No

THE WARM-UP

As mentioned in the front half of this book, the preferred method for designing books is using InDesign due to the amount of control. No matter what software you are using, the parameters and keywords are all the same and much of the process can be even reflected into when you design using a word processor such as Microsoft© Word.

- Page size needs to be set to the trim size of your book.

- Bleed settings can always be added via page setup or page layout options depending on the program.

- Make sure page margins are keeping 0.5" within the trim or page size.

- If you intend to have headers and footers, be sure margin for body text are larger (0.75" for example) on the top and bottom to give space for them to fall within that 0.5" requirement.

- Choose your fonts in advance or make a list of possibilities for:
  - Chapter
  - Headline or Chapter Title
  - Header/Footer
  - Body Text
  - Pull Quotes

- Decide on Chapter Art or Typeset design
  - Spacing
  - Having samples on hand
  - Write down parameters in advance
  - Choose glyph or ornamental font options
  - Prepared images in advance

- Don't forget your checklist! You'll need it for Copyright pages and specifics!

BOOK TITLE: _____

SUBTITLE: _____

WARM-UP CHECKLIST

☐ Trim size set to the page or book size

☐ Add Bleed Settings for 0.125 inches

☐ Set your margins to 0.5 inch from trim edge

☐ Top margin for header set for 0.75 inch

☐ Bottom margin for footer set for 0.75 inch

☐ Inner margin or mirrored margins set to 0.675 omch or higher for spine/glue/page count

☐ Chapter font:_____

☐ Headline font:_____

☐ Header/Footer font:_____

☐ Body Text font:_____

☐ Pull Quote font:_____

☐ Body Text Base Font Size: _____ Line Spacing: _____

☐ Chapter Art prepped and ready to go

☐ Images saved in teh right format and size in advance

☐ Manuscript prepped and image placement clearly marked or Storyboard ready

☐ Glyph and Ornaments picked out. Font: _____

☐ Printer settings and requirements handy for saving and meeting their needs

☐ Templates or Master pages set up for key pages and special pages

☐ Paragraph Styles setup in advance or styles redesigned to match selection

☐ Are you ready?

FRONT MATTER

This is the first few pages that typically consist of title pages, copyrights, and dedication pages. This is the beginning of a book and rarely changes much no matter the genre of the book. As we are aiming to introduce the new normal for young readers, you'll see the same elements in most books but done with some artistic value or larger fonts to draw the eyes.

ENDORSEMENTS/DEAR READER

Sometimes in romance or non-fiction genres, we will first open to a page full of blurbs, reviews, endorsements, and a statement to the reader. If it's not placed here, it sometimes shows up near the dedication or shortly after the Table of Contents.

HALF TITLE

The only text here should be the title font. This page should leave room for the author to sign. It is completely optional though and can be replaced by a full title page.

FULL TITLE

Half title can feature a text title only and the full title can be the front cover of the book itself. If you decide to do a text-based version, this should have series name, title, subtitle, author name, illustrator, and publisher name and/or logo. You can even combine the two elements and create something unique like seen below.

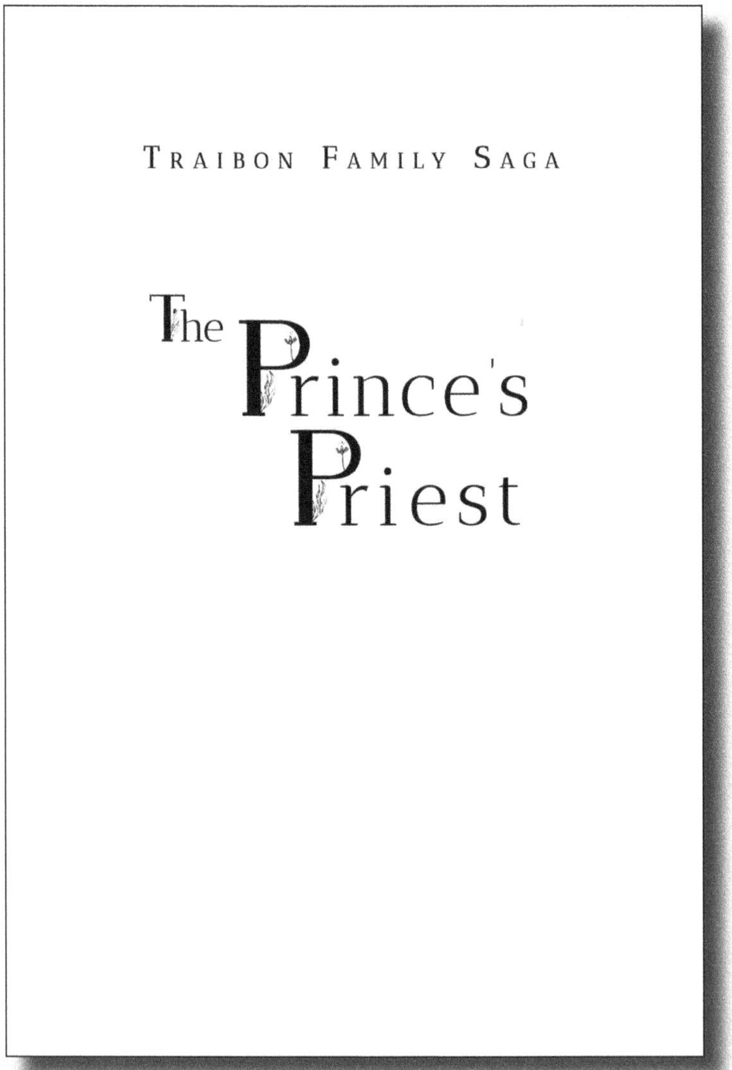

TRAIBON FAMILY SAGA

The Prince's Priest

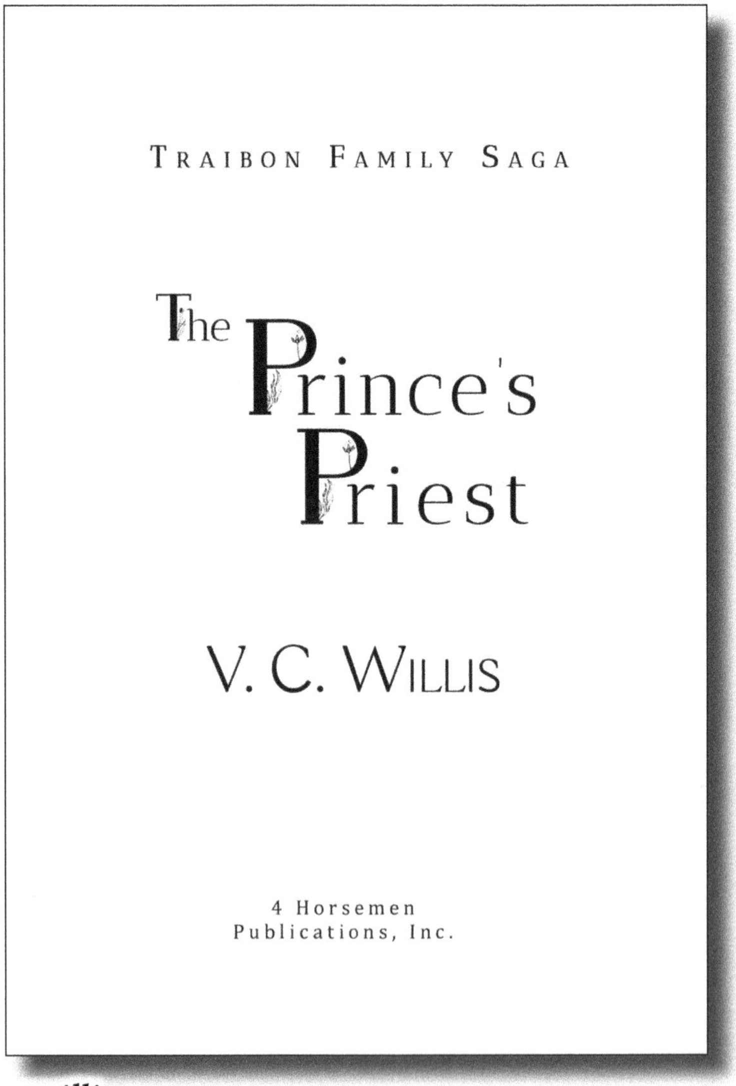

TRAIBON FAMILY SAGA

The Prince's Priest

V. C. WILLIS

4 Horsemen
Publications, Inc.

Fiction, Young Adult, Memoirs, & Literary Books

COPYRIGHT

This will always be a left page on the back of the full title page. It should contain the normal legal jargon, author, copyright, publisher information, credits to key members (editor, designer, cover, typeset, photographer, illustrator, etc.), LCCN, ISBN, and similar information.

DEDICATION/ACKNOWLEDGMENT

Many books have a dedication or even acknowledgments. This should go right after the copyright page.

NOTE TO READERS

Common in various book genres, it's not uncommon to see notes to the reader or even a word from the author. This is to serve as an intimate moment between reader and author.

Table of Contents

Depending on the author and audience, this is hit or miss whether the book will have a Table of Contents in the printed book. As for the EPUB or eBook version, it's required so as long as there is a Heading 1 or Chapter style established. The technology has a means of creating one for that purpose. Personally, I love having chapters as a reader and tend to carry this over into my designs (for those times I lose my bookmark I've been able to find or mark progress here!). Again, it's vital to program styles to produce Table of Contents that format fast and with ease to the setting you like. Most programs, including Word and InDesign, have a Table of Contents option or prompt that makes this painless and depends on the same system as an eBook by pulling from the styles assigned.

Table of Contents

vi

Preface, Prologue, Character Listing, Maps, or Similar Content

This is additional information that you want the reader to have as they venture through your book. This can fall after the Table of Contents for the most part and all work to inform and prepare the reader for the core content to follow shortly after. Much of this will use the same page layout as a chapter start in most cases.

Daemon, Daimon, or Demon

Pronunciation /ˈdiːmən/

1. a divinity, spirit, or supernatural being considered part god and part human.

2. An inner, attendant, or guardian spirit; inspiring force.

3. Ancient Greek and Latin for "godlike", "power", "fate"

v

CONTENT

This is where the core of the content will be located. These are the pages with headers, footers, and majority containing full pages of text. Be sure to set your margins so that none of the text falls into the 0.5" margin from the trim edge to prevent the printer from rejecting your book files later on.

INTRODUCTION OR FIRST CHAPTER PAGE

This is where you get to use that master page or drop the many fancy styles you took the time to prep! If you did pre-save those Chapter Header, Headline, Subhead, Drop-cap and other styles, you may want to do so as you design this first chapter. It'll make the rest of the book a breeze and make sure everything snaps and looks the same throughout the book. Work smarter! Not harder!

BLEED VERSUS TEXT MARGINS

Make sure the bleed goes past the trim line or paper's edge to the end of the to the bleed line. If the signature or paper shifts in print slightly it will cause a white line on the outer edges. Many designers place a white margin or offset the inner margins on spreads. This is dependent on the page spread, number of pages, and type of binding. For beginners you may want to default to treating this as a bleed edge. In picture books, you can push images off the page and across pages in creative ways, but when it comes to text placement, you must have it within 0.5" inch from the trim edge or paper edge. This is so if the signatures or pages shift that your textual content will never be at risk of being cutoff.

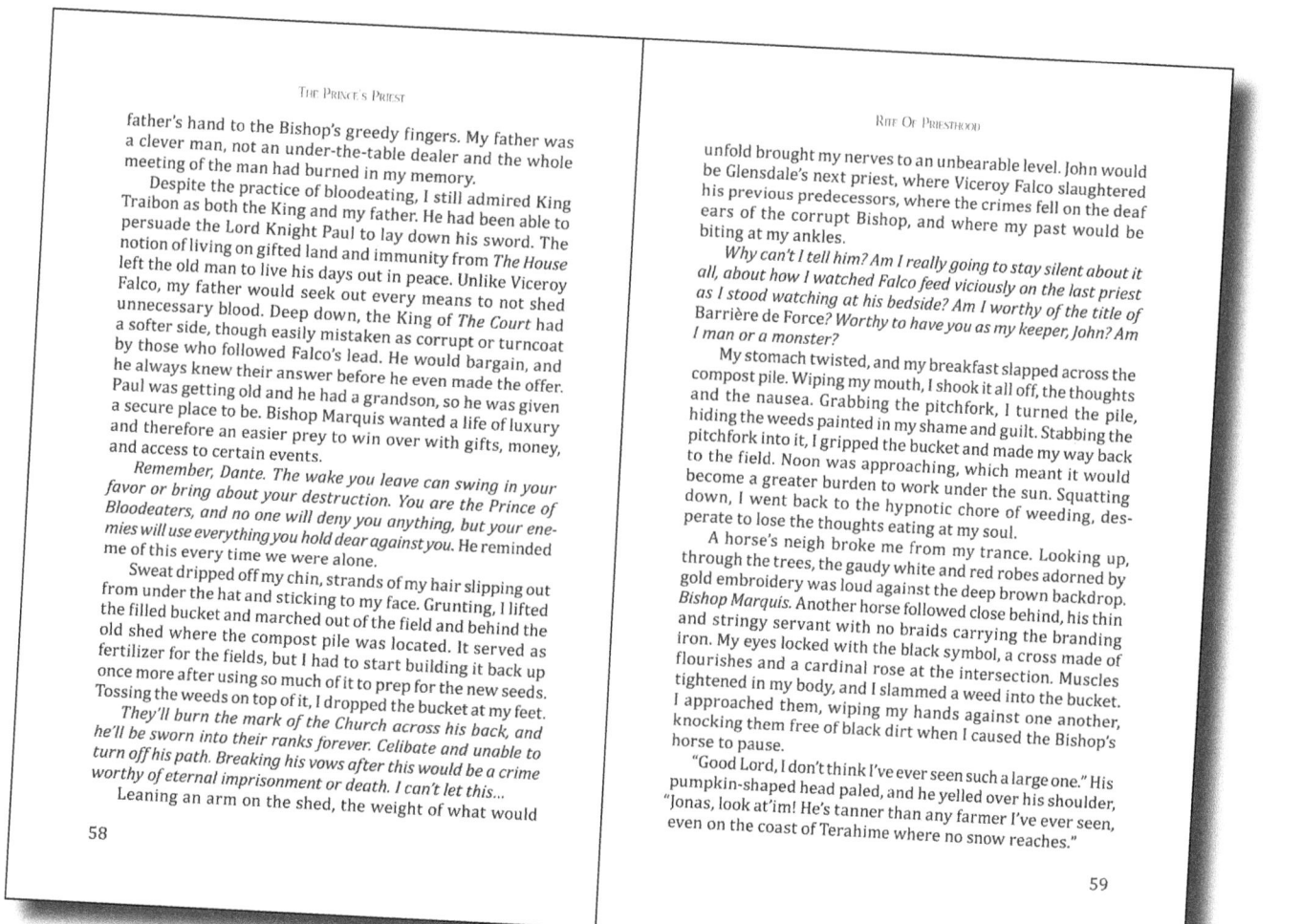

CHAPTER 7

The Time Apart

I began cooking the stew I had learned from the old man, watching John over my shoulder. He had been reading a book since we returned, the silence between us back. Stolen glances made both of us aware of how curious and intrigued we were to see how much we had changed in the time apart. Somewhere in the black night, a nightingale sang loud and true, drowning out the pops and crackling of the hearth's fire. John slammed the book shut, and I flinched. We locked eyes, and he gave me a smirk as he rose to his feet.

"So no one touched my room when I left?" John walked over, pushing the door open and walking in, then he placed his belongings on his bed.

"No." My voice came out softer than I had intended.

"There isn't dust. The bed stuffing is fresh." His forehead creased, more lines than I remembered across his brow. "You've been keeping everything in shape this whole time? Alone?"

"Yes." I kept my eyes on the stew, grabbing a knife and carrot.

49

---

father's hand to the Bishop's greedy fingers. My father was a clever man, not an under-the-table dealer and the whole meeting of the man had burned in my memory.

Despite the practice of bloodeating, I still admired King Traibon as both the King and my father. He had been able to persuade the Lord Knight Paul to lay down his sword. The notion of living on gifted land and immunity from *The House* left the old man to live his days out in peace. Unlike Viceroy Falco, my father would seek out every means to not shed unnecessary blood. Deep down, the King of *The Court* had a softer side, though easily mistaken as corrupt or turncoat by those who followed Falco's lead. He would bargain, and he always knew their answer before he even made the offer. Paul was getting old and he had a grandson, so he was given a secure place to be. Bishop Marquis wanted a life of luxury and therefore an easier prey to win over with gifts, money, and access to certain events.

Remember, Dante. The wake you leave can swing in your favor or bring about your destruction. You are the Prince of Bloodeaters, and no one will deny you anything, but your enemies will use everything you hold dear against you. He reminded me of this every time we were alone.

Sweat dripped off my chin, strands of my hair slipping out from under the hat and sticking to my face. Grunting, I lifted the filled bucket and marched out of the field and behind the old shed where the compost pile was located. It served as fertilizer for the fields, but I had to start building it back up once more after using so much of it to prep for the new seeds. Tossing the weeds on top of it, I dropped the bucket at my feet.

They'll burn the mark of the Church across his back, and he'll be sworn into their ranks forever. Celibate and unable to turn off his path. Breaking his vows after this would be a crime worthy of eternal imprisonment or death. I can't let this...

Leaning an arm on the shed, the weight of what would

58

---

unfold brought my nerves to an unbearable level. John would be Glensdale's next priest, where Viceroy Falco slaughtered his previous predecessors, where the crimes fell on the deaf ears of the corrupt Bishop, and where my past would be biting at my ankles.

Why can't I tell him? Am I really going to stay silent about it all, about how I watched Falco feed viciously on the last priest as I stood watching at his bedside? Am I worthy of the title of Barrière de Force? Worthy to have you as my keeper, John? Am I man or a monster?

My stomach twisted, and my breakfast slapped across the compost pile. Wiping my mouth, I shook it all off, the thoughts and the nausea. Grabbing the pitchfork, I turned the pile, hiding the weeds painted in my shame and guilt. Stabbing the pitchfork into it, I gripped the bucket and made my way back to the field. Noon was approaching, which meant it would become a greater burden to work under the sun. Squatting down, I went back to the hypnotic chore of weeding, desperate to lose the thoughts eating at my soul.

A horse's neigh broke me from my trance. Looking up, through the trees, the gaudy white and red robes adorned by gold embroidery was loud against the deep brown backdrop. *Bishop Marquis.* Another horse followed close behind, his thin and stringy servant with no braids carrying the branding iron. My eyes locked with the black symbol, a cross made of flourishes and a cardinal rose at the intersection. Muscles tightened in my body, and I slammed a weed into the bucket. I approached them, wiping my hands against one another, knocking them free of black dirt when I caused the Bishop's horse to pause.

"Good Lord, I don't think I've ever seen such a large one." His pumpkin-shaped head paled, and he yelled over his shoulder, "Jonas, look at'im! He's tanner than any farmer I've ever seen, even on the coast of Terahime where no snow reaches."

59

Body Text Spreads

Here you will get to double down on your header and footer design. Make sure things are updating if you decided to be fancy with auto-updating running headers. If not, the book title on the left and author to the right will always work with page numbers on the bottom. Don't be afraid to center the page numbers if you aren't sure if you are dropping content on the right and left pages. In software like InDesign, it shows you the way the book will be printed whereas Word you have to pay close attention or try adding a blank first page to offset it (But don't forget to delete it back out when you're done!).

End of Chapter

You have a few choices for the end of a chapter. Simply leave it blank with whitespace that naturally unfolds or design some extra art or flair. Always make sure the text flow to the top of the page. Often layout software defaults to justify on page and will stretch and spread lines across the page making it look weird.

THE PRINCE'S PRIEST

Nodding, I led the way through the forest in silence. The trees grew darker with every step, adding to the weight of John trailing so close behind me. Breaking into a small clearing, a big cherry tree took up the center. The air filled with the scent of its bloom; white flowers in long clumps bounced in the wind. I splashed my bucket at its base and flipped it upside down and took a seat, leaning on my knees. John mirrored my actions. Crickets chirped, announcing the night was creeping closer, and the air would soon cool. Taking in a deep inhale, I looked over at John. He was finishing a prayer, his closed eyes shedding a tear. A smile grew on his face, his eyebrows lifting.

What on earth is he thinking?

Opening his eyes, he turned to me, chuckling. "He hated cherries." He shook his head in amusement. "What possessed you to plant a cherry tree on his grave?"

I grinned, "It was payback for the scars."

We broke into laughter, the tension breaking as we headed back in time for night to take over.

Chapter 7

The Time Apart

I began cooking the stew I had learned from the old man, watching John over my shoulder. He had been reading a book since we returned, the silence between us back. Stolen glances made both of us aware of how curious and intrigued we were to see how much we had changed in the time apart. Somewhere in the black night, a nightingale sang loud and true, drowning out the pops and crackling of the hearth's fire. John slammed the book shut, and I flinched. We locked eyes, and he gave me a smirk as he rose to his feet.

"So no one touched my room when I left?" John walked over, pushing the door open and walking in, then he placed his belongings on his bed.

"No." My voice came out softer than I had intended.

"There isn't dust. The bed stuffing is fresh." His forehead creased, more lines than I remembered across his brow. "You've been keeping everything in shape this whole time? Alone?"

"Yes." I kept my eyes on the stew, grabbing a knife and carrot.

49

BACK MATTER

Here you will be serving a few crucial roles or bits of information that had no place in the front or core content. For starters, this section is intended to introduce the reader to last thoughts, notes, information, resources, the author and/or illustrator, how to stay in touch, and any means to continue to connect and discover books via the author or publisher, sometimes both. It's a vital resource and a marketing tool in every book as long as the genre and audience make good use of it.

EPILOGUE, CONCLUSION, AND SIMILAR CLOSING STATEMENTS

Depending on the genre and intent, many books end with one last thing before they transition into author information. Typically, in a fiction book, they may end with an epilogue that either shows a scene well in the future, sets the stage for the next book, or reflects on something unseen during the initial story that wouldn't have fit within the core content. In non-fiction books, they tend to have a conclusion or ending statement of some kind that closes up the topic covered and discussed throughout the book. It should always give the reader an idea what they should have taken away from the book after reading through it.

NOTE FROM AUTHOR

It's always a great idea to take a moment to discuss the lesson or follow up thoughts on the story you have told. This gives a moment for you to reflect and talk about things that would have spoiled the story if elaborated in a preface or revealed in the front matter. It can even show inspiration or reveal content that you didn't want the reader not to know entirely about. Not everything can be revealed in its full intent, and this gives an author time to share and have an intimate moment with their readers.

BIO FOR AUTHOR & LIST OF OTHER WORKS

It's common to see back pages that hold the biographies for the author. When it comes to this book type, it's strongly encouraged to have this in the book to help readers find your work online as well as connect and follow. This can be on the same page or on a spread across from one another. On occasion they start on their own right page. If you are working on a non-fiction book where the author is an expert in the topic, consider moving this to the front matter to show why this author is the best at discussing what the book it about. It's not uncommon on a non-fiction book to also see a smaller bio on the back cover along with the blurb to express the credibility of the content and the author writing on that particular topic.

ABOUT THE AUTHOR

V.C. Willis

Willis is an avid reader of male romances, whether its series like C.S. Pacat's Captive Prince Trilogy, a standalone novel such as The Song of Achilles by Madeline Miller or diving into the many mangas they've discovered published and independent artist and authors. With a passion for the characters, worlds, and plots in these fellow Fantasy Romances, V.C. Willis is still left thirsty for more and has taken up the pen to fill the gap in their own reading selection. Wither the debut novel, The Prince's Priest, a saga of two men who are broody in their own right and love each other, the aim is to introduce works with no other underlying motives. Enjoy sexual tension, raw romance, and amazing worlds. A touch of magic and paranormal should be expected as under other pen names this writer has earned their share of accolades and awards.

269

SAMPLE OF NEXT BOOK OR FIRST CHAPTER SAMPLE

Common in fiction books, typically romance and serials, is the sample of the next book in the series. This is to show the reader that there is a next book and use the first chapter or two to hook them. Technically this is a form of upselling to encourage follow-through buys. Granted, completed series and series spanning of over 3-6 books tend to see instant buys for the whole series more often than not.

RESOURCES & DISCUSSION QUESTIONS

Some books include some teacher and parent resources. This can be book club questions, fun activity pages, an information page leading to additional resources, or covering the topic in earnest. If you have a large amount of resources, you may want to create a companion piece such as a coloring book or activity book that can be purchased alongside the story. Other authors will provide these as exclusive PDFs offered when you sign up to their newsletter and often make great lead magnets for marketing or exclusive swag at special events. In some non-fiction pieces, they may include resources used or resource listings for the reader to use in order to contribute, learn more, or use as needed for support in context of the topics covered.

Appendix, Index, Glossary, and More

Within non-fiction books, it's not uncommon to see these elements added to the book. An appendix is referred to materials that require their own enclosed space best preserved at the back of the book. An index can be hit and miss, but it's highly recommended for cookbooks and similar topics to aid readers to find recipes that contain key ingredients. Most books are searchable via a PDF or the eBook, which defeats the concept of having an index. Be sure to build this last, and utilize the many tools built into programs to help speed this process up such as seen in Word and InDesign. At the end of this book, you will find a glossary. These are great where a vocabulary list is part of the lesson or book, such as this where many specialty terms and verbiage may take time to learn, or the reader may use the content out of order and not be familiar with the definition. On occasion non-fiction works will have end notes listed though much of the industry has leaned in favor of footnotes instead since this has proven better for eBooks and preferred by readers who don't want to lose their reading place within the book.

Call to Action

This is any page or content added in the back of the book to encourage readers to do something or take action. For example, where they can follow the author, sign up for the newsletter, leave a review reminder, or grab the next book or other book series. This sometimes can be an ad for relatable services too as seen in non-fiction books!

Other Works from the Publisher

An older practice, but one that still has an impact. It's a great way to mimic what a newsletter swap does online, but on a physical level. Harlequin and Avon romance books were famous for doing this in the 80's and 90's and lead to cross-promoted sales between their pool of authors and books series of similar genre and plots. Many of the small publishers are reviving this practice as they see readers reveal they discovered multiple books from their publications through the books themselves.

Print-on-Demand page

If you are choosing to publish using Print-on-Demand, don't forget there will be a blank last even page in the back. This is where the printer will include a barcode that contains all the information as to where the book came from and more. Offset printed books don't have this feature at all.

Offset Printing—End Leaves

If you are planning to offset print the book, you may have to create additional files for end leaves. I highly recommend asking for templates from your specific printer since these are done slightly differently at times depending on the book binder equipment and process, they use to connect these to the cover and textual aspects of the book. If you are using Print-on-Demand, you bypassed the option to have these, or some do add solid white onto hard covers.

MORE TO COME

Traibon Family Saga

The Prince's Priest

The Priest's Assassin

The Assassin's Saint

The Saint's Bloodeater

The Bloodeater's Lover

The Lover's King

The King's Priest

268

SAVING THE FILES

Now that you have completed the book, be sure you save the files appropriately. This means for both your work files and the final product for the printer. Be sure to always ask clients and printers what file format and needs are required. For the sake of all things, we will focus on the most common and most versatile versions. If you used InDesign, you can go to File > Package and the software will do its best to grab font files, images, and more into a folder. For those who are using other means, here's a breakdown of the work folder and what to save:

- ✎ FOLDER NAMED AFTER BOOK
  - 🖎 Work File (InDesign, Word, etc.)
  - 🖎 PDF (2001-xa format aka Press Quality with Bleed recommended)
  - 🖎 EPUB (Optional, reflowable a must)
  - 🖎 ORIGINAL folder
    - ➥ Holds original text file and any related materials
  - 🖎 FONT folder
    - ➥ Copies of font files used (truetype, openface, etc.)
  - 🖎 IMAGE folder
    - ➥ Any image used should be placed in here in case you need it or edit or replace later.

As for prepping files for upload to a vendor, the two main types will be PDF and EPUB (reflowable). No matter if you are self-publishing or using a service, these two are the current staple in the industry and have the ability to upload to a variety of distributors and vendors with very little issue.

- ✎ PDF Format

- ✎ This is used for print design applications, paperback, Print-on-Demand, and similar.
  - 🖎 For printing, PDF-X/a: 2001 Format is the most accepted.
  - 🖎 For web pdf, use web preferred file setting, but remember this file loses values needed for printing for a book.
  - 🖎 Make sure Bleed Settings are applied or this could cause the file to kick back or be denied.

- ✎ EPUB Format
  - 🖎 Always use reflowable.
  - 🖎 Write in as much File Info and Metadata information as possible.
  - 🖎 If attaching a cover image, it should be at least 1600x2400 pixels, 150 dpi, RGB color mode to avoid being kicked back from online vendors.
  - 🖎 Most accepted eBook type currently with enhanced ability access.

BOOK TITLE: _____

SUBTITLE: _____

SAVING CHECKLIST

- [ ] A copy of the Manuscript or text file in a DOC, DOCX, RTF file that you used

- [ ] All the images in a LINKS or IMAGES folder

- [ ] Folder named after book to house all other files and folders

- [ ] Work files in folder (Recommend having a main one and back-up, i.e. *.indd and *idml)

- [ ] PDF version (2001-xa format for print-ready or print quality)

- [ ] EPUB (Reflowable) - optional

- [ ] Folder for fonts called FONT with copies of the files for future (they can go obsolete later)

- [ ] Did you save in the correct color profile (CMYK, RGB, 240% CMYK, etc)?

- [ ] Did you run ADA Compliance check in Adobe for ADA PDF needs? (optional)

- [ ] Do you need to convert EPUB to MOBI? (Consider using Calibre or similar converters)

- [ ] Has someone reviewed the file for issues besides you?

- [ ] Are the Header and Footers showing the correct text?

- [ ] Is your Table of Contents correct and numbered or not missing a chapter?

- [ ] Do your images bleed to the BLEED edge pass the TRIM edge?

- [ ] Double check that all your text is 0.5" from TRIM edge including Header and Footer

- [ ] Have you printed test pages on a local computer?

- [ ] Does your file meet the needs of your printer (Print-on-Demand AND Offset printers)

- [ ] Viewing for Web and Emails PDF - Did you save a "Reduced Size" PDF version?

- [ ] Has your customer signed off and reviewd the document before uploading to vendors?

Non-Fiction: Self-Help, Reference, & Textbooks

Research is formalized curiosity.
It is poking and prying with a purpose.

Zora Neale Hurston

Preparing the Manuscript

A manuscript for this book type is normally text only with image placement. It is vital that the manuscript is consistent. Much of the non-fiction books that fall under self-help, reference, and textbooks (like this book!) have multiple tiered chapters of content that can get confusing when attempting to typeset. If the way the information is labeled uses inconsistent styles, or even if the way indents, character styles, and bullets are being used is never the same, it quickly can create a messy book or feel impossible to typeset. Out of all the books you create, this kind of book and workbooks will take the longest. Many academic-based designers and publishers often take a year or longer to design the first complete variant of the book. A skilled typesetter, a consistent manuscript with concise image placement, and a single point of contact to make decisions and identify trouble areas can shrink the time needed to create a book to as low as a few weeks or month.

> *When it comes to self-help books, they often straddle this realm as well as the previous book type of how a fiction book is designed. Always take in account how the manuscript is setup.*

It's vital to work close with the author or lead editorial representative when creating a book in this category since you can establish design elements and many aspects of the book from the start. Having a folder full of concisely named images that match the image placement can be a life saver at times. Also, it's encouraged to have storyboard or samples of styles and looks. As seen with other areas in this book, it can't be expressed enough how important it is to reference similar type of books and audience. Comparable titles and the reviews or feedback on them can provide a ton of insight on what to do and not to do when designing this book type.

When it comes to self-help books, they often straddle this realm as well as the previous book type of how a fiction book is designed. Always take in account how the manuscript is setup. If there are very few images included, I recommend referring to the previous chapter for the best outcome. On the other hand, if the manuscript has citations, multiple tiers, unique aspects, heavy image count, and so forth, use this section. As a point of reference, this entire book falls into the realm of what we are discussing, but for simplistic sake, I will be using a smaller self-help book in the screenshots and references called *Wonders & Miracles* by N.B. Johnson.

WHO IS YOUR AUDIENCE AND PURPOSE OF THE BOOK?

Your audience and intended purpose or use for the book is going to be calling the shots on both the design and how the reader's experience will unfold. Font choice will need to match and set the ambience the book is about. Fancy chapter pages, drop-caps, informative headers, and fanciful footers are all huge parts in the design and layout of this type of book. Information and communication become a huge priority as well as being mindful of word count and page count. Books typically in this section are black and white on crème paper or even groundwood. It's not uncommon to see sections in blocks, shaded areas, pull quotes, large captions, side notes, and similar among the normal typeset layout of the core content. Sometimes these books need special graphics created to capture the lesson as seen in textbooks, such as English and math textbooks. Depending on the needs and purpose of the book, there may be a need to design two books side-by-side, a teacher and student addition, to support the use of the content being taught.

When it comes to self-help books, they often straddle this realm as well as the previous book type of how a fiction book is designed. Always take in account how the manuscript is setup.

Front matter and back matter are going to be huge on a book of this kind covering resources, indexes, large-scale Table of Contents, large chapters within chapters, citations, credentials, illustrations, and beyond. Don't get discouraged; take advantage of the technology available. Table of Contents, list of illustrations, indexes, and similar aspects can be saved for last and auto-pulled based on styles used or even keywords. Be sure to research different ways to create these elements with the software you are using to typeset with before you start so you know how to mark content as you begin to design or possibly if you need to prep the manuscript in a way to aide in your efforts in doing so.

As you design, remember that this type of book requires some instructional design and may require creativity, slowing down a process, or ways to pull the reader's eyes so content is understood clearly and in the right order. If you're not familiar with instructional design, take a moment to dip into resources and research. A great activity to show the impact of slowing down and concisely guiding step-by-step would be to do the following:

- In 5-minutes, write down step by step how to make a peanut butter and jelly sandwich.

- Now, hand those instructions to someone and ask them to follow them EXACTLY as written.

Seems simple enough, but you'll realize quickly that there are key actions we assume everyone knows. For example, did you remind them to gather all the ingredients and utensils needed? Did you instruct them to open the jar and how to spread the peanut butter? Did you clarify when you put the two pieces together that the jelly and peanut butter should be on the inside facing one another? Did you follow through with how to eat it? There's a lot going on that we don't think about anymore because we know and have learned the task. You are now writing a book to teach something fresh and new, so skipping or assuming the reader knows the language, the items being discussed, and so forth can be detrimental. Glossing over the tiniest detail can spell disaster in terms of instructional design. When I first did this activity, I completely forgot to tell them to open the jar and which way to combine the sandwich! So messy!

Choosing a Trim Size

Now we are creating bigger books with huge spans of information. It's recommended to use larger trim sizes. Though there is more variety than what is listed, these are some core sizes that should be available in both hardcover and paperback options, no matter where you intend to print your book. Be mindful what the normal is for these. Often the hardcovers are Smyth sewn bound (offset printed) or Perfect bound (Print-on-Demand) with laminated covers in gloss. There's also a huge spike in paperback textbooks in hopes of saving in costs. Furthermore, there is the question of color interior versus black and white. For large textbooks, offset printing is best for color books that have a large image count such as seen in science and design textbooks where images and diagrams are vital. As for textual heavy work, like seen in English and math books, you most likely can use black and white options to save cost.

- 8.5 x 11
- 8 x 10
- 7 x 10
- 6.14 x 9.21
- 6 x 9

Font Expectations

Consistency is key, and limiting to one core font for the majority of the book based on your body font is best. Chapter header, headlines, subheads, header font, and footer fonts can all be reflective of the book's genre and artful. The focus has now shifted to using the page space as efficiently as possible. A few ways to combat high word count books besides increasing the trim size would be lowering the leading, pushing limitations to 10- to 11-point fonts, using a more efficient font face (Calibri is excellent for a "tight" typeset), limiting chapter page decorations and spacing, and always opting for a continuous chapter layout. Be careful going this route since most books here are meant for studying and researching from which means smaller font can cause the eyes to tire out sooner and make reading the content painful for readers and students.

Maximum Word and Page Counts

A typical book in this area can fall between 50,000 to 300,000 words on average. That being said, many seasoned typesetters do their best to keep book under 300 pages since breaking this mile marker can raise the production cost of a book a lot whether its offset or Print-on-Demand. Even then, many are perfect bound, or glued binding, and though the max page count can range 900-1200 depending on paper, you never want to get close to this for a few reasons. First, this eats up space in the inner margin and takes away for the page layout to keep text from falling into the crack or spine of the book. The other reason is the chances of the glue letting go of the pages while reading increases drastically. Thanks to the larger print options, this counters the increase of images and other elements and helps balance much of the need to make up for space to keep page count to a reasonable amount.

Materials and Print Options

Print costs can spiral fast when a textbook is involved. Many textbooks and hearty-sized reference books tend to peak over $50.00 USD very quickly due to the combination of high page count, color options, and hardcover design. Providing a paperback and hardcover option can help with this aspect, but even a 500-page paperback textbook at 8.5 in x 11 in trim size can have a retail price of $30.00 USD for black and white interior and $60.00 USD for a color edition with standard color and paperweight of only 70 lbs. (the lighter the paper, the cheaper the cost in most cases). In short, some of the most expensive books and longest design hours in typeset will come out of this type of book, and that is to be expected. Experimenting with print options in advance can go a long way to how you will design the book to fit the needs of the audience while keeping the retail pricing to a reasonable amount. An example of this would be the famous *Gardner's Art Through the Ages: A Global History 16th Edition* by Fred S. Kleiner. This book has high weighted, semi-gloss paper, colored interior, with 1,264 pages, and off-set printed costs $231.95 USD for the hardcover and $69.49 for eBook (as of Feb. 24, 2022 via Amazon).

ILLUSTRATIONS, ILLUSTRATORS, & GRAPHIC DESIGNERS

If you know your trim size and orientation, then you're now ready to decide on how you want to create your illustrations. Some authors illustrate their books themselves, but that's not an option for others. You have a few options in this matter, and it's highly dependent on the type of book you're making such as a picture book, middle grade book, or textbook. If you are planning to hire someone to help you create and format your book, consider seeking out a graphic designer or illustrator who is knowledgeable in typesetting or at least picture book layouts. They will be able to incorporate and go through more steps with you as your guide. If you do this yourself, be sure to take your time to read the content in the Picture Book section for information specifically for making one and how to best prepare before starting.

Saving a JPEG and editable originals to the side can be very effective in keeping overall file size down

Every book type has its own tweaks to the system or may have areas that are a must for one and not the others. If you intend to gather illustrations to give to a typesetter or format yourself, seek out an illustrator who draws in a style you enjoy and within the price range you need. They will not only need to be aware of the trim size and orientation for a picture book, but they need to include room for a 0.25" to 0.5" cutaway bleed so your core image doesn't get chopped when printed. For illustrations added to a section of a single page, you just simply need an image slightly bigger than intended use for best quality when it prints.

If your illustrator is using a physical median (watercolor, markers, acrylics, etc.) over digital painting, make sure you pass on information for file type, resolution (DPI), color mode, and so on. The more information you provide, the easier it is for them to give you the correct variant of scans. If they aren't able to provide you with scans, I recommend hiring an art photographer. If your median is light colored or watercolors, you should consider digitally enhancing the coloration, performing a black/white balance, and checking the levels of said image. In the end, do not expect those colors to match or look the same as the original as there is a loss of detail, texture, and shift in colors that is impossible to recreate by the time it prints in the book.

No matter the book, there is a standard need for file type and settings here when you aim to use images in your book.

- These files should be in CMYK color mode

- Saved at 300-600 DPI (resolution)

- Be in these file types: JPEG, PNG, or TIFF

You can also utilize PDF and export out to image or place as PDF but be mindful most software will be converting all these into a more manageable JPEG format. Sticking with JPEG and saving editable originals can be very effective in keeping overall file size for the PDF and eBook formats down to acceptable levels. This often comes into play with vendors with files size maximums, such as Barnes & Noble requiring eBooks to be 20 MB or below.

What if you can't find an illustrator or have funding restrictions? There's another possibility! Prepare to go on a deep search and rethink your initial book design. Stock photo sites are a wonderful resource for those who can't afford the illustrators or struggling to find one. This includes ShutterStock, DepositPhoto, iStockPhoto, Adobe Stock, and many more sites have a variety of artists who submit sheets and multiple images of characters for all audiences. A fitting example of this is the character you see throughout Writer's Bane! The more active an artist is on these sites, the better chance for the collection to grow and pull from. Some give you a means to reach out to them as well! You can always reach out to them and see if they will also commission pieces.

BASICS OF DIGITALLY ENHANCING ILLUSTRATIONS

Thanks to the digital age, many artists or illustrators have taken to producing art via software. This has made it a better means to reproduce images in a higher brilliance and sharper hues. That doesn't mean hand drawn artwork and watercolors can't join this high-tech advantage. Traditional art can be scanned or photographed to be pulled into the digital realm and in some cases, adjusted. This doesn't come without its share of pros and cons. One being the most common is the lack of capturing texture, hues, or even soft pencil strokes that all-too-often get washed out by the scanner or camera's light. If your art is too big to scan, an art photographer should be able to use a black/white balance card and even adjust and check it.

Once an image has been placed in digitally, you or a design have the freedom to adjust the image as needed. This can be moving elements, changing hues, brightening the overall saturation, and even resetting black and white tones to make richer levels so the image prints sharper. If you can apply a lot of these easy tricks to an image and balance the CMYK spectrum to a richer level, it will make a huge difference when printed. Not every image or color will be able to translate well; for example, blues and purples are often a struggle to lock in without shifting when ink is laid to paper.

WARNING ABOUT WATERCOLORS

Out of all the medians your illustrations can be made from, this one comes with a loss of detail and color just from scanning or photographing it. From there, it sways again depending on the options you choose. If you are ok with digitizing and drastically shifting your watercolors for print and not looking to match the original artwork, you will feel this impact the least. As for those looking to match it and capture the watercolor pieces as they are, you won't get this result. First, the act of scanning or taking a photo removes the texturing that watercolors often have, as well removing some of the sharpness and overlapping details. From there, I recommend offset printing with gloss or semi-gloss paper at about 100+lb. paper with alcohol-based printing for closest match to original work. If you decide to move forward with Print-on-Demand, be warned that you will continue to lose vibrancy and details due to the fact only matte paper is available and most are water-based ink printing and may cause saturation issues. This becomes most noticeable with a picture-book printer in Print-on-Demand.

BLACK AND WHITE BALANCE

If you are using Photoshop, Fire Alpaca, or some other photo editing software, you should be able to do this. Many of the photography editing software may be able to assist with this technique as well as the others to follow. Whichever software you use, there should be tutorials out there to assist you best as far as this book goes, the aim is to explain what it's meant to do and hint as to why you might want to apply this to your own formatting and images. As for this one, it helps establish true black and true white on the image and adjusts the image color range accordingly. Often when we scan an image, the black has a shine to it and might come off as a dark gray or even brown. This gives you a chance to "reset" the expectations and identify where these are on the image if you have both visible.

LEVELS IN SPECTRUM

Images come with levels that spread a variety of hues and channels. Often black and white being on opposite ends, they come with slight dips beyond the peak of these colors that can take away from the overall sharpness of the image spectrum. Cutting out or knocking them to the peaks or using auto levels features can bring an image to pop more visually.

HUE & SATURATION

Hue and saturations levels or using filters that shift these can do a wide range for an image. If the colors seem to have washed out, you might be able to recover faded colors using this feature. Also scanned or photographed images may have washed out and either you can darken the hue values or even adjust contrast and brightness settings to recover the look of the original artwork. Sometimes this setting allows a moment for you to change the hue or coloration of the art and make decisions you normally would have missed out on. Using a masked layer stacked with this can even allow you to change a color on a single item in the image, but that's best for a tutorial as it delves into photo editing and is beyond this book's conversation focused on typesetting.

DPI, Image Size, and Resolution Adjustments

The resolution of an image is very important! The first aspect to this is the size. You don't need your image to be 44 inches by 21 inches if your book is only 11 inches by 8.5 inches. If you are bleeding images off the edge, the image needs to only be 11.25 inches by 8.75 inches at the very least to give some room for image placement that allows bleed and trim. It's always smart to have the image slightly bigger, but too large and it may cause the program or computer to crash (especially those on personal or home systems). It also makes saving backups or throwing it on a cloud storage much more feasible.

Use offset printing with gloss or semi-gloss 100+lb. paper with alcohol-based ink for closest match to original work.

Once the size is within a reasonable range (exact with bleed or slightly larger in the same orientation or ratio), you need to make sure the resolution is set between 300-600 DPI. Anything under 300 is at risk to pixelate or be blurry. Know that most images saved from internet are usually only 72-96 DPI, so make sure what you are saving is the full image and not a smaller web version or down-sampled variant. Images that are over 600 DPI are at risk of the printer shrinking and may result in unwanted quality or results. It's always best to avoid these sorts of situations and keep the control and final product in your hands.

CMYK versus RGB

Print and physical books are printed using CMYK colorations. This uses a set amount of cyan, magenta, yellow, and black layered on the page. Depending on the printer this can be applied with alcohol or water-based inks and vary in brightness (often influenced by the paper chosen). Water based inks are limited to 240% CMYK saturation level with paperweights at 70lbs or less as seen in Print-on-Demand applications.

Image Naming

Be sure to be consistent or concise with how you are naming your images. You can do this in a number of ways which includes consecutively (image01, image20, image03...), by location (Chapter01, Chapter02_SUBHEAD, Chapter02_Figure1.1), or labelled by what they are (Flowers01, RosesAndBees, AuntMayAndHerPig...). You should always avoid using symbols and spaces since these may cause issues in final formats. Depending on your software and how you export for eBook format, having images with names that include open spaces, dollar signs ($), hashtags (#), and similar often will cause them not to load or fail when uploaded to a vendor. I highly recommend using only alphabet and numbers with underscore if need be. In programming we do this as well and often default to camelCase (LittleTimmysWagon, IHateThisPictureTheMost, ImageNameLikeThis...) as the safest means to prevent programming errors.

Image File Types

Images come in a variety of types and the best ones to use for publishing are JPEG and TIFF formats. You can use a PNG, which preserves the transparency unlike JPEG or even a PDF file. You should keep these between 300-600 DPI and at least a little larger than the intended size to make sure you have room to trim the image if needed. TIFF is considered the best format and has been used in the printing and graphic design world as the superior option. Most Print-on-Demand printers want the files saved in PDF2001XA format, and this converts images to JPEG. Same thing happens when exporting to EPUB; the images are often converted to JPEG or PNG depending on what you are using. Thus, it is recommended to save in JPEG for several reasons, including the fact it's a smaller size, translates into eBook without issues, and prevents any issues when converting to final PDF format changes to the images.

Permissions & Usage Rights

Images and artwork can fall under public domain rights, but if they don't, you will need to purchase usage rights or get permission. If you pulled your images from a service like ShutterStock or similar stock photo site, they usually have different levels you can purchase for usage rights. This is the safest means for images and artwork. If you intend to hire an illustrator, be sure to cover the usage and contract with them how books are sold and their images will be used from the book to creating swag, bookmarks, banners, and more. Some may clear you for using the images in the book only and not for marketing materials. Be sure to add the permissions granted in the copyright section or even an illustration rights section as a type of appendix. It's always best to give credit where it's due on your copyright page at the very least.

Designing the Pages

By far this will be the most difficult book to design. There's a lot of active troubleshooting and design work happening on every page which adds to the time needed to create a book. Not only are you dealing in most cases with an unusually large manuscript with massive content and style cues, but a lot of additional elements will have to be added, programmed for eBook, and often tables to address. You're going to get frustrated frequently, and it's important to take breaks often and circle back with fresh eyes when this happens or even gather feedback or compare similar designs and books. Prepare for moments where a solution may cause an issue later in the book and you may have to completely re-invent an aspect to be more versatile than originally attempted. If you are typesetting for someone other than yourself, it's important to show them designs of key pages and master pages before moving forward. What you envision may be opposite of what they wanted for their book, so always work in tandem and do not hesitate to present screenshots often to help guide the book in a way that means little backtracking for you and a more concrete typeset for the author or client.

Full Spread Layout

The image or text (not both) stretches across 2 pages, a left and right page, to show as one large landscape image or two pages of textual content. In a lot of cases the text may only be present on one page and not the other, but other layouts might have several spots all around the image to show the story unfolding in a sequence or multi-action spread. It's not uncommon to see images in a chapter books spreading across a spread or having elements interacting on occasion. Unlike a picture book where most spreads are designed together, a chapter book will do this sparingly and mimic a traditional book with header, footer, and body text a majority of the time.

Rule of Thirds Spread Layout

Across a two-page span, an image, graph, or pull quote will cover one complete page and a portion of the adjacent page to leave room on a far left or right edge for font to place. In concept, the object is using two-thirds of the design area to draw the eye to the text or away from the text by doing so. The Rule of Thirds is often used in marketing, print design, or even in filming. It splits the viewing area into thirds from top to bottom and side to side. From this point, you break the content and subject matter up at the key sections to help draw the eye in a certain direction or pull it towards or away.

Split Design Image & Text Page Layout

Again, this is similar to the Image + Text layout seen in picture books and textbooks. On a single page, whether it's the right or left, the image and text split the space. Sometimes this is done in a 50/50 spit, or a two-thirds split, but often features a white space or colored space where the text will be.

Whitespace Page Layout

This page is often an indicator of a chapter starting or ending. Sometimes it can be a section or partition marker of some kind. It's notorious for having a lot of white space or empty, unused space on the page spread. What little content is there usually is textual to guide or inform the reader in preparation of something changing or a transition within the book. You see this a lot in textbooks and fiction books with right page only chapter starts.

Two-Column Design

More commonly seen in back matter such as index, glossaries, and listings, or in large reference and textbooks, this mimics the above spreads with the added feature of two-columns. This can pull more text onto a page especially with a small gutter and margins teamed with single line spacing and 11- to 12-point font. If you are struggling with large page count, this could provide a means of dropping and managing it easier. It also allows for a more formula-based means to place images and captions, or even the occasional boxed content or pull quote. Not every page has to be in this style in a book, but it should be used consistently as to not throw the reader from the content presented on the page. Also, it's not uncommon that headings are set to span all columns or even opening paragraphs to content while the subhead information falls into two-column style. Play with the features and options, look at samples, and decide how to best apply these in a large book or workbook as needed. Recommended for large formats though, such as 7 x 10, 8 x 10, and 8.5 x 11.

DEVELOPING A PATTERN FOR FUNCTIONALITY

One of the most important things to know whether you are designing books or video games, is people are pattern-seeking apes. We love to see patterns, follow repetitive actions, and even see and find a means of creating these subconsciously when known are to be found. Pattern feeds consistency and that tends to create a sense of stability and control. When you are using workbooks and planners, it's often to provide a tool or means to establish or even change habits and patterns within a certain area of knowledge, skills, life, or similar topic. Hence, the functionality of the book becomes the primary focus when typesetting. It's going to be touch and go at times, frustrating, and will take several attempts to master a system and design that works for both the author and its intended audience. Let's break it down to some vital areas! This is vital for any book that will contain worksheets, instructional elements, and similar aspects like seen in planners.

Even in textbooks and reference books there is a pattern established for the delivery of content. A great example of this is the formatting seen in dictionaries and encyclopedias. At a glance, you can quickly tell which you have when flipping through the pages. You also know how to find what you are seeking thanks to the order being established via the alphabet, a common knowledge element!

PRODUCING THE ORDER

Slowing down and considering instructional design practices can go a long way here. The order and level of details given in directions is impacts by the intended use and audience. It's always best to overprovide than underprovide and leave them confused and lost. One can't simply get in car and start driving. You have to first unlock the car, sit in the driver seat, adjust the mirrors, start the engine, and put it in reverse to back out of the driveway before you can even start heading to where you're going. The order in which you create the content should do just that! First get them strapped in properly before starting the core content and purpose. In text heavy workbooks and textbooks, you see this in the form of chapters and subheads that may even use 1.1, 1.2, and other titling to step the reader through slower. There's no one way to achieve this.

REPEAT PAGES & DUPLICATION

It's ok and important to repeat or provide duplicates of key worksheets or areas where needed. Many get nervous about providing these. Be mindful of how you need them to use the book. If they should be able to make copies and just enter a few entries to try out during the lesson, then 3-5 duplicates should suffice. Some authors provide special PDFs for free that comprise of the worksheets only so readers can print the sheets. Repeated elements can help establish consistency and curb the need to reteach how to use areas of the book too! So keep in mind how they will be interacting and how to signal and direct at a glance can go a long way with how easy it is the use the materials provided. In textbooks you see this often to signal the start of examples or exercises to reflect what was taught in the lesson.

BUILDING A SENSE OF CONSISTENCY

As you design these elements for use, make sure to use font choices, layout, and backgrounds to signal and establish a sense of consistency. Flipping through a workbook, a reader should be able to tell where they will be writing versus reading a lesson at a glance. Even then, in a textbook this happens with key elements boxed and marked in the same manner over and over again throughout the book. If there are keywords or vocabulary needed to stand out, it's often in the same bold font whether it's chapter one or twenty. Don't be afraid to utilize practices commonly used to give your design a jumpstart of feeling familiar and stay consistent with the genre or book type standards used most often.

Examples of Manuscripts

Below is a list of different ways you may receive or set a manuscript up. The most common in the industry are the first two options: Textual Only and Text with Image Placement. From Chapter books to textbooks, these are the typical format you will receive the textual content for typesetting. As you venture into workbooks, picture books, comic books, and graphic novels, you will want to use story bounce, detailed format, storyboarding, or script styles to capture all the parts. Unlike text-based or heavy books, these require guidance and cues as to where images or text should be placed on a page to accurately tell the story intended. Each book type will lean more so on one kind of manuscript, and it's important to be aware of this as you prep your manuscript for typesetting. This can be a huge influence on how well key elements are designed, whether you intend to format your own book or hand your book to someone else.

When it comes to reference and textbook types, you will want a text only with image placement manuscript alongside any storyboarded sample of key visual aspects that needs to be designed. This is so that as you typeset, you can support the instructional design intended to deliver to the content to the reader or student. As we said before, these are some of the hardest books to design with a need for additional styles created, custom elements, and templated pages. A strong manuscript should be consistent in delivery of section formatting and/or markers along with image placement indicating where the image should fall closes to between paragraphs or even sentences. This should help make efforts less about guessing to focusing on tackling design issues that start to develop as you process so much content.

Textual Only

This is the most common manuscript for mass market fiction work. No images are tied into it, and it's simply importing the manuscript into the software and applying the indicated styling where deemed appropriate. A typesetter's aim is to streamline the text to the best of their abilities as to not break a reader's immersion with weird visual discrepancies, such as a slight tweak in line spacing (common in manuscripts where portions where dictated via speech-to-text and other written on a computer). You have to remember that we've been reading books with the same patterns and margins for centuries and keeping those expectations while being creative can be a hardline to walk for anyone designing a book.

For a textual-based manuscript, follow the Do's and Don'ts to prevent any unseen issues in the content. As for trim and font choices, it will fall back to the audience, genre, and type of book you are working on. You should be able to copy-paste content into a clean Word document or use InDesign's "File > Place" feature to import text and its associated styles. In the case of the latter, be sure to run Scripts to lock in these styles and save time from having to do manual changes by using the PrepText and other tools often found in opensource or pre-programmed into InDesign for use. Most manuscripts imported this way come as double-spaced in Times or similar font at 12 pt. If the manuscript has a variety of font faces, I recommend streamlining it to a single font face to prevent issues when formatting the book. Also, be aware many of these come with double spacing, which is intended for editorial purposes. Never keep this line spacing!

Text with Image Placement

For this book type, this is going to be the more common type encountered with textbooks, workbooks, or image heavy content. Throughout the text, there should be indications for image placement and should be clearly marked, much like a subhead or citation. For visual aid, I always encourage highlighting these yellow and treat them as their own paragraph. It's also helpful to use a keyword like "IMAGE" and brackets to help make the image placement stand up, for example:

[[IMAGE01: This picture shows the difference between nightshade and chili pepper flowers]]

These one-liners should be placed between the paragraphs they should be near or on the same page as the text. The importance of this is so when creating an eBook, the typesetter can make sure it falls inline at the right point of the content. It can also make it easier to play with the page layout as they apply the design and text begins to autoflow from page to page with the changes.

STORYBOARDING

I highly recommend combining one of the above with this as a visual guide or blueprint for key elements or areas. You can print, cut, and paste the elements to rough out the entire book's look and feel. This is a fantastic way to build a mockup of the book you intend to make and format for print and give concise expectations to a typesetter or experiment with what you had in mind for the final product. Before starting digitally, this allows you to troubleshoot issues that may need you to adjust text and illustrations prior to formatting the book. Most issues found this way are still relatively easy to fix by simply changing methods, book options, or changing fonts and images. Storyboarding can also be a great means to discover how many images you will need the illustrator to make as well as to where they need to be mindful of page edges and space for text to overlay. The following types of issues can be revealed at a glance by this method:

- Illustrations not allowing enough space for text to overlay
- Images that have the characters too close to the edge and will be cut when stretched to the bleed edge and cross the trim
- Images that have text as part of the image in need of adjusting to fit trim
- Trim size and orientation versus illustration size and orientation
- Amount of text for the page (too much is the common issue)
- Number of illustrations needed
- Amount of pages the story needs
- Story page flip and how that impacts the reader and story

CREATING A STORYBOARD

One of the best ways to help you plan out your book is to outline it in the form of a storyboard as seen in comics and animated films. Print images and clip out text and move things around or take a sketchbook out and doodle a rough version. Stick figures and shapes work are just fine! You will need to account for the layout and limitations of the printed version from the beginning, even if you are still revising the text.

Formatting the Book

Hooray! Now that we've talked and prepped this thing to no end, you should be ready to format this book with confidence. Why? Because it is so much easier to resolve problems at the manuscript and prepping stage than when you are formatting and making the book. Though, as said before, I am an avid user of word to InDesign, I will do my best throughout the book to provide information in an all-encompassing and design angle. If you were looking for software tutorial, this isn't the book for you. Getting detailed instructions on how to set parameters in Word, Scribd, and similar word processors isn't the aim.

Instead, we will be focusing on the typesetter-based elements and areas that will be par the course for any book you design. Dependent on the software you are using to design your book in could present its own issues and information may be labeled slightly different or found in different areas. In tandem with a software book, this book may provide some keywords in order to gain the affects you were aiming for in order for you to gain a greater value out of using said programs. In my years of looking for instructional manuals for book design, most of what I have learned was via videos, trial and error, typography college courses, and simply diving into the industry headlong with an open mind and understanding of the roots of publishing and its history. It probably also helped I delved in some game design, development, and programming, so I could troubleshoot creative solutions.

Without further ado, it's time to make this book using these step-by-step, or page-by-page instructions below. Feel free to adjust this to suit your own style and needs since there are various methods to achieve the results seen here. Again, the aim here is to simply the process while being able to make quality print books, enhance eBooks, and create a PDF that falls close as possible to being ADA compliant (Americans with Disabilities Act).

> *With textbooks, expect large word counts, several sections/chapters, and special formatted sections to teach and provide materials accordingly!*

Instructional Design

Though this book can't dive into the full spectrum of instructional design practices and methods, it is strongly recommended to seek put resources to assist when creating textbooks, workbooks, self-help, and similar books. The importance of how material is presented, the order in which it is given, and the amount of details in the directions can make a work of difference in how well someone can understand and master the content, or utilize the tools you've designed for them. Often I have felt this in programming software books where key steps or explanation of concepts are skipped and have found myself instantly lost and lacking a key step that was assumed I would know to use. It can be the difference in someone being frustrated and unable to continue versus mastering and singing the praises of a book. Remember we have to open the jars before making the sandwich and unlock the car and start the engine before taking that trip!

How to Use the Book

When it comes to books intended to be put to use, adding a section or discussing how to use the book can help prep a reader properly. It doesn't mean every reader will slow down and use it, but if they get stuck, they will search for guidance here. This should inform the readers what the intent of the book is, how they should be utilizing it, and how to best start using the tool you have created for them. If you are being diligent, the consistent markers and identifying aspects in the books should be shown and defined so they understand their intent and how to perceive them as they travel through the book.

EXAMPLES & SAMPLES

Giving samples and examples can make all the difference in understanding the content and lessons being taught. When providing worksheets, it's always a great idea to either review how to use them in the content or provide one filled out. In many math and English textbooks, you will find ample amounts of examples of problems and grammar being used incorrectly and correctly. The ability to see a math problem broken down into slower steps and done more than once in examples can make or break a student's ability to learn a new method or apply how to process a certain principal

WAYS TO GUIDE READERS

Play around with instructional design on a visual level. There are plenty of ways to guide readers through the content with using graphics and clever placement of materials. One of the more obvious means is the use of arrows placed on a page to point the eyes to read the content in the right way. Other means have included a character or boxing material in a consistent way to make it stand out in some way. Even then, laying out a page and its elements in a certain pattern for key moments can also clue the reader into knowing the difference between content, examples, and exercises at a glance without ever needing to read the text!

FILE SETUP

The file or page size should match the trim size in width and height. Make sure the intended orientation matches what you intended, specifically landscape versus portrait. Depending on the program, you may have to set bleed settings to include a 0.125" bleed on all sides or for outer margins. For some Print-on-Demand vendors, they may want the inner margin to have no bleed since this is the side of the page that is glued to the spine of the book. You usually get to set up or define the overall margins as well.

Be mindful that with picture books you will be saving a flat PDF for eBook design and that you don't have to fret over threading text boxes together as seen with all other book types. It's more important to make sure images are bleeding off to the marked edges just pass the trim edge, that elements are layered and overlayed in the right order, and textual content is within the margins provided by the printer or Print-on-Demand requirements of 0.5" from trim size edge. Here are my recommended settings for this book type:

- Industry Standard Numbers:
  - 0.125" Bleed from trim edge
  - 0.5" Margin for content inward from trim edge
  - Large page counts will require a larger 0.625" or higher inner margin or gutter
  - Special binding may change the needs for inner margins

- Inner or inside margin: 0.625" for books under 300 pages and

- 0.75" to 0.8" for books pushing far into the 500+ range since where the pages' bind needs more space to avoid words falling into the crack of the book.
  - Granted, this is a picture book, and you can sometimes get away with a 0.5" margin.

- Outer or outside margins (including top and bottom) should be 0.5" to 0.625"

- Typically have main body pages with header and footer set and you can increase the top and bottom margins to 0.8-0.875" to give yourself space to place and space these from your body text.

- For smaller self-help and non-fiction books:
  - Double check and mark special citations, pull quotes, elements, and similar.
  - Make decision on images versus print options, and with that, any the textual content that needs to shift to match it. For example, the 250-page book has two colored charts, but for costs efficiency its being printed in black and white, which means any reference to the colors on the chart needs to change to the letters marked instead.

- For textbooks and reference books:
  - Organize images and content by the chapter. This can help not overwhelm you when looking for key charts, images, and information. Consider naming the images in a way that shows location such as *Ch01_Intro_Horse.jpg* or *Ch24_MaximumWord_SillyPerson.jpg*
  - Decide early on if bleeding images or keeping within the margins. This can weigh heavily on the books overall look and feel.
  - Be patient. Prep additional pages and layouts before starting. Pre-designing key pages and worksheets can save you time when you start to work the content.

Wondering where these numbers come from? Your vendors should have File Creation Guides via a PDF or webpage. No matter if you plan on using offset printing, KDP, IngramSparks, or a similar vendor, these parameters never change. This is the basic needs of a file going to print and will give the press some wiggle room. These parameters will change if you choose more elaborate binding and use certain presses. Always make sure you get these settings from the printer and design the book with these in place from the start.

USING LAYERS

Most of the layout software allows you to create layers such as InDesign (not any of the word processors though they do have header footer options). These come in handy in keeping content stacked or arranged in the right order. This includes making sure watermarks are below the body text layer and even keeping the header and footer elements on the top and not lost behind images and such. A bonus to using this feature is the ability to lock them and make sure you don't accidently change, move, or delete them unintentionally. With picture books, you often use images that take up the entire page and risk losing these elements completely. Recommended layers include the following listed in the order they should fall and usage:

- **Header and Footer Layer** – This will have your top layer text boxes that contain the header and footer which usually hold page numbers, title, author, and/or current chapter. You can control these with master pages. In a word processor, this is an option or specific setting that is influenced by section breaks to change how they look from section to section of the book's layout.

- **Default or Body Text Layer** – Here you will manage the primary text box in which the main content autoflows through threaded textboxes or pages.

- **Background Layer** – At the bottom of the list, there should be a background layer that is designed for images, spreads, and watermarks that need to fall under the textual content.

This doesn't mean you need to use all these layers, but it's highly recommended to give you more control when formatting. If the program you are using doesn't provide layers, check for features that define objects on the page as needing to be "Ordered" or "Arranged" with sub-options for "Bring to Front" or "Bring to Back," which mimic what layering does. This should aid you in making sure text and images overlap appropriately.

MASTER PAGES

These pages, or templates, are premade pages you can drag and drop into the layout to help speed things along and stay consistent. Know that this is more commonly found as a feature in layout software such as InDesign. Even with a freeform style book, there's a level of consistency with placement of elements such as header, footer, page numbers, watermarks, and other elements that you may not want to shift and wish to keep level throughout the book. In any book,

you are going to be applying a few key layout pages. I recommend the following master pages or templates be made in advance to speed up the typeset process:

- **A blank page** with only the margin lines set. You may include a primary text box version for dedication or anchoring title page images into place. Works great for print-on-demand with that last page needing to be blank as well. These will also set your title pages and copyright page as well.

- **A body page** made of a blank page with only the header and footer with a main text box. I recommend putting the header and footer on a top layer that's locked. Predesign a left and right page, often featuring the book title on left and author name on right. You may even design a running header or chapter header that auto updates depending on the software you are using. Adding glyphs and art to page numbers and headers can add a nice creative flair.

- **A chapter page** that can add art, designs, and spacing shifts to accommodate the style implied. I always make right and left page versions, so if I need to change from right page only chapters to continuous, it's ready to adapt accordingly.

- **A numbered blank page** can be useful for areas that may contain images, maps, tables, and similar content where you simply want page numbers only.

- **Worksheets or Special Pages** should be designed or a foundation premade or decided on before getting too far into the design. Prepping these pages in advance can help in your efforts and provide a sense of how much space they truly need in order to interact with the content as your design the book.

- **A two-column body page or variants** can provide a means to design smart and save on page count where you can. Also, two-column pages can provide easier means to place images as often seen in textbooks, reference books, and workbooks alike.

- **Section breaks** become vital for non-fiction books. Occasionally these hard pages or spreads have an image or color to help standout when certain passing of time, events, topics, and provide a sense of dividers for the reader. Prepping a page or spread for these can save time and provide consistency when applicable.

FONT CHOICES AND PREP

Font has the most weight in typesetting and interior book design. Your choices and attention to detail to the spacing, size, and types will have a significant impact for better or worse. There are a few things you can do to help yourself prep and streamline your design depending on if you are using styles in Microsoft Word or a combination of Paragraph and Character styles in Adobe InDesign. Prepping and setting up pre-saved files with master pages and these elements can save a lot of hunting and frustrations, especially if you want to shift or change fonts later. If you intend to do typesetting full time or work heavily with fonts, I recommend investing into Font Management programs such as FontExplorer. This can make it easier to keep your growing library from bogging down your computer while making it easier to test out and organize fonts.

PARAGRAPH STYLES OR STYLES

These will make up most of the formatting application in textual content. They work in particular order and repeat as you start a new section or chapter. Making a style in advance can help you quickly adjust, fix, or change the entire typeset without hunting and pecking for certain content in the book. Instead, applying a style and changing the style can shift and fix the book as a whole.

- **Chapter Header** – Should be the largest font and be a font face that reflects genre. Content here is often just numbers, "Chapter" text, or some section marker text.

- **Headline** – This is often a subtitle or section title that follows behind the Chapter Header, normally directly below it. It should be the second largest text and also have a legible but creative font that captures the genre.

- **Subhead** – Should be a slight larger than the body text but clear and bolder in some way. It's common for these to be the same font as body text and simply in all-caps or small caps.

- **Drop Cap** – Whether it's a single letter, word, or line, this is the first paragraph in a chapter or section. It's a way to artfully signal to a reader where to begin reading or add more to the chapter page that makes it stand out other than whitespace.

- **Body Text** – This will be the majority of your content. It should be a legible font comfortable for readers and remain the same throughout the entire book. It builds the font foundation for Drop Caps, Citations/Quotes, Subheads, Tables and more.

- **Citations/Quote** – This paragraph style should center or have an indent of 0.25" to 0.05" on the right and left sides. It's also common to add space before and after this paragraph style so the quote or citations pops. Often there is an italics character style applied.

- **Bullet Points** – Lists and bullets have similar indentation and spacing. Setting the preference or making a variety of these to create multi-tier systems in the varying styles can save a typesetter grief as well as the means to remembering how APA, MLA, and CMS are different from one another.

CHARACTER STYLES OR SUBFAMILY FONTS

Creating premade character style can help you gain more control on the style of the manuscript as a whole. It also helps build coding within certain programs for eBook creation and keeps these vital aspects from disappearing in the process.

- **Bold** – used to identify keywords, bring words to the front, and stand out louder. There is never a need to make a whole manuscript bold. Instead, choose a thicker or heavier font.

- *Italics* – this has many uses from quotes, to signaling key elements in content, and even to signal internal dialogue in stories.

- Underline – much like bold, this is used to make content stand out, signify a reference (depending on styles like APA), hyperlinks (or clickable content in text), or signal something of importance.

OBJECT STYLES OR TABLE STYLES

These are special styles that influence objects, images, and tables. They make sure designs and placement match and can even streamline how items show up in an eBook. Not every software has the means to define these or set them up. As for InDesign, these can help guide image frames, table cells, and more so that you can save time when adding content into the layout and saving you the grief of cracking open object options to adjust every detail.

Page-by-Page

For the sake of comparison, we will be looking at two books: a reference book of *Bulfinch's Mythology* by Thomas Bulfinch as redesigned by Battle Goddess Productions and a self-help book called *Wonders & Miracles* by N.B. Johnson. This is to show the spanning difference between a smaller book that is barely stepping into this area versus a massive reference book. Many of us have at least one textbook in reach, and if that is not the case, consider this book as a very artsy version! There's no wrong way to create a textbook and they can at times be very creative in terms of page-to-page layout. Some feel as if no page is the same even when they soar over the 200-page mark or even grow to over 500 pages. Again, the focus here should always go back to relying on instructional design and visually engaging content that delivers the topics with consistency and accuracy for the sake of readers and students.

The Checklist!

Here is a checklist that should help you make sure you finished prepping the manuscript and materials before starting the formatting. Often we don't think to ask or double check to include some of these things and it can be detrimental in the final stages leading up to printing the actual book. Whether you are formatting your own book or formatting someone else's, this checklist is to help you gather everything you need before you start.

- Trim Size
- Book Title
- Subtitle
- Author Name (or Pen Name)
- Publisher and/or Logo
- Copyright Page
  - Author name and copyright year
  - Name illustrator, designer, editor, etc.
  - Permissions for any materials used.
  - Public domain or scripture cited.
  - ISBN numbers (Paperback, Hardcover, eBook, Audiobook, etc.)
  - LCCN (Pending or number)
  - Published information and logo
  - The usual legal jargon to protect you, your work, and the publisher.
- Front Matter
  - Foreword: Yes or No
  - Dedication: Yes or No
    - Above Copyrights or Own Page
- Images are ready, clearly named, and all accounted for
  - 300 – 600 DPI
  - Correct size for trim + bleed
  - CMYK color mode
- Manuscript – Text only edition
  - Has image directions that match image names
- Back Matter
  - Author Bio
  - Image
    - Hyperlinks
    - Illustrator Bio
    - Image
    - Hyperlinks

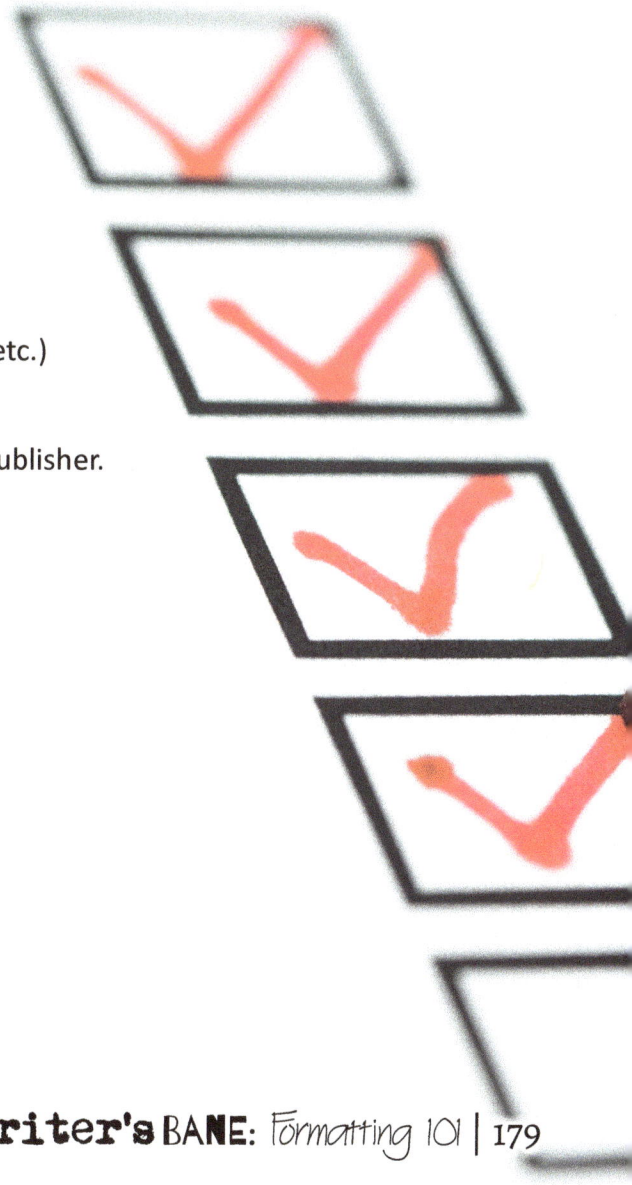

BOOK TITLE: _____

SUBTITLE: _____

TYPESET CHECKLIST

- [ ] Manuscript text in a DOC, DOCX, RTF file

- [ ] All the images listed in Manuscript present:

- [ ] CMYK mode

- [ ] Between 300-600 DPI.

- [ ] Trim Size _____ width x _____ height

- [ ] Author Pen Name - FIRST_____LAST_____

- [ ] Dedication: Yes or No

- [ ] Author Bio: Yes or No

- [ ] Copyright

- [ ] Publisher information

- [ ] Additional mention such as artist, design, or typesetter? _____

- [ ] Scriptures cited from.... Any public domain original publication mentions? _____

- [ ] Permission granted from... Any materials that have permissions needing to be listed here?

- [ ] ISBNs for Paperback: _____ Hardcover_____

- [ ] Audiobook_____ eBook_____

- [ ] LCCN pending or listed?_____

- [ ] Front Matter (Acknowledgements, Foreword, Preface, etc.)

- [ ] Do they want a Table of Contents: Yes or No

- [ ] Do they have tables to import: Yes or No

- [ ] Do they want pull quotes: Yes or No

THE WARM-UP

A s mentioned in the front half of this book, the preferred method for designing books is using InDesign due to the amount of control. No matter what software you are using, the parameters and keywords are all the same and much of the process can be even reflected into when you design using a word processor, such as Microsoft© Word.

- Page size needs to be set to the trim size of your book.

- Bleed settings can always be added via page setup or page layout options depending on the program.

- Make sure page margins are keeping 0.5" within the trim or page size.

- If you intend to have headers and footers, be sure margin for body text are larger (0.75" for example) on the top and bottom to give space for them to fall within that 0.5" requirement.

- Choose your fonts in advance or make a list of possibilities for:
  - Chapter
  - Headline or Chapter Title
  - Header/Footer
  - Body Text
  - Pull Quotes

- Decide on Chapter Art or Typeset design for:
  - Spacing
  - Having samples on hand
  - Write down parameters in advance
  - Choose glyph or ornamental font options
  - Prepared images in advance

- Don't forget your checklist! You'll need it for Copyright pages and specifics!

- For self-help, textbooks, and reference books:
  - Get a sense of direction via the manuscript or a storyboard.
  - Have all images and artwork needed, labeled, and saved in the correct format.
    - Remember that naming and dividing them out by chapter can help with image heavy and larger books!
  - Font choices have been decided including for keywords to emphasize.
  - Pre-design key elements, boxes, pull quotes, worksheets, and more.
  - Take breaks often! These are labor-intensive pieces, even for a seasoned typesetter.

BOOK TITLE: _____

SUBTITLE: _____

WARM-UP CHECKLIST

☐ Trim size set to the page or book size

☐ Add Bleed Settings for 0.125 inches

☐ Set your margins to 0.5 inch from trim edge

☐ Top margin for header set for 0.75 inch

☐ Bottom margin for footer set for 0.75 inch

☐ Inner margin or mirrored margins set to 0.675 omch or higher for spine/glue/page count

☐ Chapter font:_____

☐ Headline font:_____

☐ Header/Footer font:_____

☐ Body Text font:_____

☐ Pull Quote font:_____

☐ Body Text Base Font Size: _____ Line Spacing: _____

☐ Chapter Art prepped and ready to go

☐ Images saved in teh right format and size in advance

☐ Manuscript prepped and image placement clearly marked or Storyboard ready

☐ Glyph and Ornaments picked out. Font: _____

☐ Printer settings and requirements handy for saving and meeting their needs

☐ Templates or Master pages set up for key pages and special pages

☐ Paragraph Styles setup in advance or styles redesigned to match selection

☐ Are you ready?

FRONT MATTER

This is the first few pages that typically consist of title pages, copyrights, and dedication pages. This is the beginning of a book and rarely changes much no matter the genre of the book. As we are aiming to introduce the new normal for young readers, you'll see the same elements in most books but done with some artistic value or larger fonts to draw the eyes.

ENDORSEMENTS/DEAR READER

Sometimes in Romance of Non-fiction genres we will first open to a page full of blurbs, reviews, endorsements, and a statement to the reader. If it's not placed here, it sometimes shows up near the dedication or shortly after the Table of Contents.

HALF TITLE

The only text here should be the title font. This page should leave room for the author to sign. It is completely optional though and can be replaced by a full title page.

FULL TITLE

Half title can feature a text title only and the full title can be the front cover of the book itself. If you decide to do a text-based version, this should have series name, title, subtitle, author name, illustrator, and publisher name and/or logo. You can even combine the two elements and create something unique like seen below.

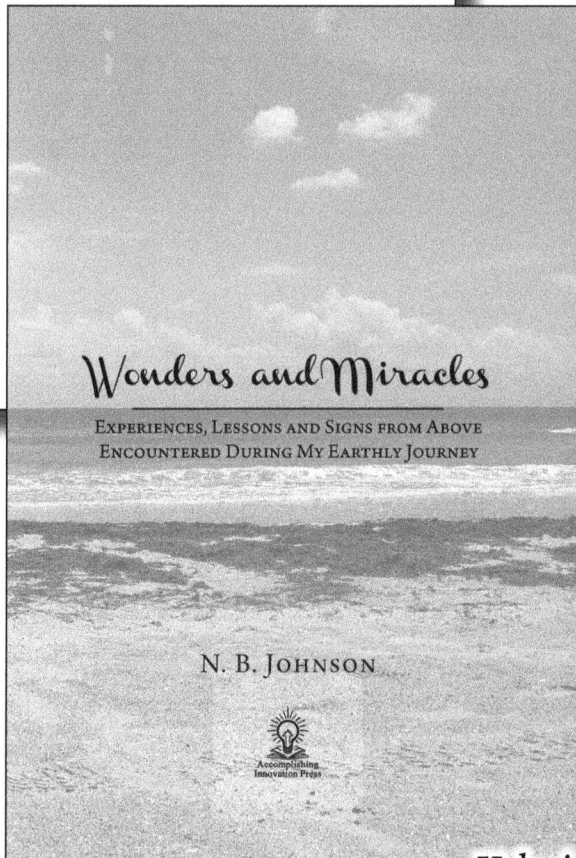

COPYRIGHT

This will always be a left page on the back of the full title page. It should contain the normal legal jargon, author, copyright, publisher information, credits to key members (editor, designer, cover, typeset, photographer, illustrator, etc.), LCCN, ISBN, and similar information.

DEDICATION/ACKNOWLEDGMENT

Many books have a dedication or even acknowledgments. This should go right after the copyright page.

NOTE TO READERS OR ABOUT THE BOOK

Common in various book genres, it's not uncommon to see notes to the reader or even a word from the author. This is to serve as an intimate moment between reader and author. For this book type and nonfiction in general, it's not uncommon to have an About the Book section or an Overview on the content or expectation of the topics it will cover.

Wonders & Miracles
Copyright © 2021 N.B. Johnson. All rights reserved.

Cover Designed by Deidre Johnson
Typesetting by Valerie Willis
Edited by Dr. Angela Campbell
Co-Edited by Deidre Johnson

All rights to the work within are reserved to the author and publisher. No part of this publication may be reproduced, stored in a retrieval system, or transmitted in any form or by any means, electronic, mechanical, photocopying, recording, scanning, or otherwise, except as permitted under Section 107 or 108 of the 1976 International Copyright Act, without prior written permission except in brief quotations embodied in critical articles and reviews. Please contact either the Publisher or Author to gain permission.

This book is meant as a reference guide. All characters, organizations, and events portrayed in this novel are either products of the author. All brands, quotes, and cited work respectfully belong to the original rights holders and bear no affiliation to the authors or publisher.

Library of Congress Control Number: 2022932803

Paperback ISBN-13: 978-1-64450-555-7
Audiobook ISBN-13: 978-1-64450-553-7
Ebook ISBN-13: 978-1-54450-554-0

Design and Layout, About the Book, Words from the Editor, Battle Goddess Production Name & Logos are Copyright ©2018-2021 Valerie Willis

Public Domain consists of Bulfinch's Mythology textual content and Artwork from Various Artists

Artwork from cover: FRONT "Ulrine in Flood" by Arthur Rackham, Border from Howard Pyle: SPINE: Flower border by Howard Pyle; BACK: "Mermaid" by Warwick Goble, Border by Howard Pyle;

Artwork from title page from top to bottom: 'Wagner's Ring Cycle" by Arthur Rackham, Photo of Thomas Bulfinch by Unknown Photographer, and Raven Logo by Valerie Willis.

Bulfinch's Mythology (Illustrated)
- Illustrations have been added
- Mild editing
- Reformatting of content
- Replacement of modern day spelling
- Suggested other spellings

Author: Thomas Bulfinch, 1796-1867
Initially Revised by: Rev. E. E. Hale
First published in 1859
Edited by: Valerie Willis
Cover Design: Valerie Willis
Interior Design: Valerie Willis
Interior Illustrations: Various Artists, Public Domain

4 Horsemen Publications, Inc.
1497 Main St. Suite 169
Dunedin, FL 34698
4horsemenpublications.com
info@4horsemenpublications.com

ACKNOWLEDGEMENTS

I'd like to thank my family. Their love, laughter and encouragement as observers and occasionally participants along my journey were greatly appreciated and accepted. Imagine living with, being married to, and a close relative of someone like me. There were many 'Aha' moments.

Thanks to Gloria Bekoe, an earthly mentor and guide, for her wisdom and encouragement. And to Harriet Leff, who literally found and coaxed me into using healing hands on people other than family. She also introduced me to a meditation retreat community that led to enhanced spiritual growth and development. I came into contact with several people at the retreat who literally changed my life. It was a blessing to receive the guidance of Orest Bedrij, a gifted author whose amazing aura is filled with light and love. William (*Bill*) Hungerford and Nancy Bragin exposed all attendees to a spiritually based method for raising consciousness levels.

Harvey Johnson, my Consultant, encouraged me to write about my experiences. He read my initial version and the revised ones, questioning and scribbling comments where he felt additional clarification was needed.

Finally, I'd like to offer sincere gratitude to my agent Deidre Johnson for her expertise. She took my quite inexperienced initial offering, and through editorial advising, patiently directed me into producing a manuscript worthy of being published.

Thank you to my editorial team: Deidre Johnson, Angela Campbell (*Ph.D.*) and Valerie Willis (a *gifted author*). Without their continuous persistence, guidance and patience this publication would not have been possible.

v

About This Book

Welcome to the Battle Goddess Edition of "Bulfinch's Mythology" by Thomas Bulfinch as revised by Rev. E. E. Hale. This is a cornerstone piece for anyone wanting to dive deeper into mythology of various kinds. Mr. Bulfinch does a wonderful job in making a collective account of stories for most of the entities he covers, including several excerpts from poets, historians, Milton, Homer, including his own brother, and many more. Traversing from Greek to Roman to Hindu to Celtic and beyond, this is a great book for any mythology lover. If this wasn't enticing enough, we added in the volumes of "King Arthur and His Knights" and even "Legends of Charlemagne" to give you an unforgettable resource and collection.

This book and its contents were created in the late 1800's and thus, the wording and spelling of many of the deities, places, and beyond are vastly different from their modern versions. In an attempt to bring this up to speed, while maintaining its original state, Battle Goddess Productions has replaced the spellings that may hinder someone's ability to discover more research on the stories and mythology found within. This includes the spelling of names, such as but not limited to, Corea – Korea, Thibet – Tibet, or in some cases we added the alternative spelling "Halcyone/Alcyone" in order not to lose the original grip it holds. Another change we did was break out the dialogue and excerpts so that they may stand out clearly and be easier read or found. Hope these extra efforts involving the textual content make this a more pleasant experience for discovering mythology.

The artwork found within is a collection of work from a mixture of artists from over a hundred years ago and older. A listing of artists can be found in the back matter so you may search for more of their work within our edition. Not all of the public domain images had the artist labelled, but we felt the "unknown" deserved to be shown off right along with the more well-known artists. The collective was known for illustrating fairy tales, mythology, or even prior versions of Bulfinch's own publications including Arthur Rackham, who is a personal favorite. Please note there will be two editions, a Black and White interior and a more pricey Colored version (due to added cost for coloration and paper). We wanted to make the paperback affordable, but also wanted to still provide the colored edition for those seeking something extraordinary.

If you have ever wondered where and how so many authors tie mythology into their work, then this may be the key you were looking for. Within this piece are many stories both familiar and lesser known. There will be information discovered in here that may shed light on modern retellings and inspired work like "American Gods" by Neil Gaiman to our very own "Cedric the Demonic Knight" by Valerie Willis.

By no means is this a complete collection of all things mythology, worldly, or monsters. Though, as a complete geek for mythology, it is a must-have as part of your at home collection. There are several other up to date sources, but there is a flavor you will not, cannot, find. If you wish to research these further, seek out other books such as J.A. Coleman's "Dictionary of Mythology," "The Encyclopedia of Celtic Mythology and Folklore" by Patricia Monaghan, "Norse Mythology A to Z" by Kathleen N. Daly and even Carol Rose's "Giants, Monsters, and Dragons" – all of these are found in our very own arsenal of go-to books for research.

i

Non-Fiction: Self-Help, Reference, & Textbooks

TABLE OF CONTENTS

Depending on the author and audience, this is hit or miss whether the book will have a Table of Contents in the printed book. As for the EPUB or eBook version, it's required so as long as there is a Heading 1 or Chapter style established, the technology has a means of creating one for that purpose. Personally, I love having chapters as a reader and tend to carry this over into my designs (for those times I lose my bookmark I've been able to find or mark progress here!). Again, it's vital to program styles to produce Table of Contents that format fast and with ease to the setting you like. Most programs, including Word and InDesign, have a Table of Contents option or prompt that makes this painless and depends on the same system as an eBook by pulling from the styles assigned.

Table of Contents

TABLE OF CONTENTS

PREFACE, PROLOGUE, CHARACTER LISTING, MAPS, OR SIMILAR CONTENT

This is additional information that you want the reader to have as they venture through your book. This can fall after the Table of Contents for the most part and all work to inform and prepare the reader for the core content to follow shortly after. Much of this will use the same page layout as a chapter start in most cases.

PREFACE

I've been asked many times about things and events encountered during this life's journey on Planet Earth. Family and friends encouraged me to put them into writing. They mentioned other relatives might have been involved in some of the same occurrences but were hesitant to voice them. So, here are some of my adventurous wonders and miracles. Included are also thoughts and beliefs, some born with and others acquired along the way.

All of the episodes in this book happened; however, I've changed names to protect the privacy of individuals involved.

Someone said we are spiritual beings having a physical experience on Planet Earth. I view this place as a school where we come to evolve. From my point of view, there are no right or wrong things, good or mistakes. There are only challenges and lessons to They offer an opportunity for us to evolve and consciousness. After reading, through the pros and

CONTENT

This is where the core of the content will be located. These are the pages with headers, footers, and majority containing full pages of text. Be sure to set your margins so that none of the text falls into the 0.5" margin from the trim edge to prevent the printer from rejecting your book files later on.

SECTION BREAK PAGE OR SPREAD

For this type of book, creating special division pages or markers is vital to understanding when topics or focuses are shifting. It provides a means to even have introductions or overviews and conclusions to unfold within a section several times in a book. This Is something that's important for the audience and content being reviewed.

INTRODUCTION OR FIRST CHAPTER PAGE

This is where you get to use that master page or drop the many fancy styles you took the time to prep! If you did pre-save those Chapter Header, Headline, Subhead, Drop-cap and other styles, you may want to do so as you design this first chapter. It'll make the rest of the book a breeze and make sure everything snaps and looks the same throughout the book. Work smarter! Not harder!

HOW TO USE THIS BOOK

If this book has a specific purpose, or function, or is intended to be a tool, its highly recommended to provide a sense of direction with adding a section like this, especially if a majority of the book will need to be filled out by the reader. Having a front section they can refer back to for detailed instructions, examples, or guidance can go a long way for a book's success, even in a textbook and reference book!

BLEED VERSUS TEXT MARGINS

Make sure the bleed goes past the trim line or paper's edge to the end of the to the bleed line. If the signature or paper shifts in print slightly, it will cause a white line on the outer edges. Many designers place a white margin or offset the inner margins on spreads. This is dependent on the page spread, number of pages, and type of binding. For beginners you may want to default

to treating this as a bleed edge. In picture books, you can push images off the page and across pages in creative ways, but when it comes to text placement, you must have it within 0.5" inch from the trim edge or paper edge. This is so if the signatures or pages shift that your textual content will never be at risk of being cutoff.

Body Text Spreads

Here you will get to double down on your header and footer design. Make sure things are updating if you decided to be fancy with auto-updating running headers. If not, the book title on the left and author to the right will always work with page numbers on the bottom. Don't be afraid to center the page numbers if you aren't sure if you are dropping content on the right and left pages. In software like InDesign, it shows you the way the book will be printed whereas Word you have to pay close attention or try adding a blank first page to offset it (But don't forget to delete it back out when you're done!).

WORKSHEETS AND PLANNER PAGES

These are pages that are primarily dependent on the reader filling in the blanks and following along with prompts. There should be blank areas or lines that provide space for them to interact with the book and content as intended. Usually in a textbook, this is rare since they expect you to take the exercises listed and use a sheet of paper to work through the problems often and revisit for practice later.

SPECIAL PAGES OR UNIQUE CONTENT

It's not uncommon for workbooks, textbooks, devotions, and planners to have elaborate special pages that provide visual guides or reference materials. Often these can be charts, diagrams, or illustrations intended for the readers to revisit as needed as they continue to use the book.

END OF CHAPTER

You have a few choices for the end of a chapter. Simply leave it blank with whitespace that naturally unfolds or design some extra art or flair. Always make sure the text flow to the top of the page. Often layout software defaults to justify on page and will stretch and spread lines across the page making it look weird.

Bulfinch's Mythology: Age of Fable

prompted the memory. They were nine in number, to each of whom was assigned the presidency over some particular department of literature, art, or science. Calliope was the muse of epic poetry, Clio of history, Euterpe of lyric poetry, Melpomene of tragedy, Terpsichore of choral dance and song, Erato of love-poetry, Polyhymnia of sacred poetry, Urania of astronomy, Thalia [Pronounced Tha-lei-a, with the emphasis on the second syllable] of comedy.

Spenser described the office of the Graces thus:

> "These three on men all gracious gifts bestow
> Which deck the body or adorn the mind,
> To make them lovely or well-favored show;
> As comely carriage, entertainment kind,
> Sweet semblance, friendly offices that bind,
> And all the compliments of courtesy;
> They teach us how to each degree and kind
> We should ourselves demean, to low, to high.
> To friends, to foes; which skill men call Civility."

The Fates were also three Clotho, Lachesis, and Atropos. Their office was to spin the thread of human destiny, and they were armed with shears, with which they cut it off when they pleased. They were the daughters of Themis (Law), who sits by Jove on his throne to give him counsel.

The Erinnyes, or Furies, were three goddesses who punished crimes by their secret stings. The heads of the Furies were wreathed with serpents, and their whole appearance was terrific and appalling. Their names were Alecto, Tisiphone, and Megaera. They were also called Eumenides.

Nemesis was also an avenging goddess. She represents the righteous anger of the gods, particularly towards the proud and insolent.

Pan [the name Pan means everything, and he is sometimes spoken of as the god of all nature] was the god of flocks and shepherds. His favorite residence, as the Greeks describe him, was in Arcadia.

The Satyrs were deities of the woods and fields. They were conceived to be covered with bristly hair, their heads decorated with short, sprouting horns, and their feet like goats' feet.

Momus was the god of laughter, and Plutus the god of wealth.

ROMAN DIVINITIES

The preceding are Grecian divinities, though received also by the Romans. Those which follow are peculiar to Roman mythology.

Saturn was an ancient Italian deity. The Roman poets tried to identify him with the Grecian god Kronos, and fabled that after his dethronement by Jupiter, he fled to Italy, where he reigned during what was called the Golden Age. In memory of his beneficent dominion, the feast of Saturnalia was held every year in the winter season. Then all public business was suspended, declarations of war and criminal executions were postponed, friends made presents to one another, and the slaves were indulged with great liberties. A feast was given them at which they sat at table, while their masters served them, to show the natural equality of men, and that all things belonged equally to all, in the reign of Saturn.

Faunus, or Fauna [there was also a goddess called Fauna, or], the grandson of Saturn, was worshipped as the god of fields and shepherds, and also as a prophetic god. His name in the plural, Fauns, expressed a class of gamesome deities, like the Satyrs of the Greeks.

Quirinus was a war god, said to be no other than Romulus the founder of Rome, exalted after his death to a place among the gods.

Bellona, a war goddess.

Terminus, the god of landmarks. His statue was a rude stone or post, set in the ground to mark the boundaries of fields.

Pales, the goddess presiding over cattle and pastures.

Pomona presided over fruit trees.

Flora, the goddess of flowers.

Lucina, the goddess of childbirth.

Vesta (the Hestia of the Greeks) was a deity presiding over the public and private hearth. A sacred fire, tended by six virgin priestesses called Vestals, flamed in her temple. As the safety of the city was held to be connected

---

Chapter 1: Roman Divinities

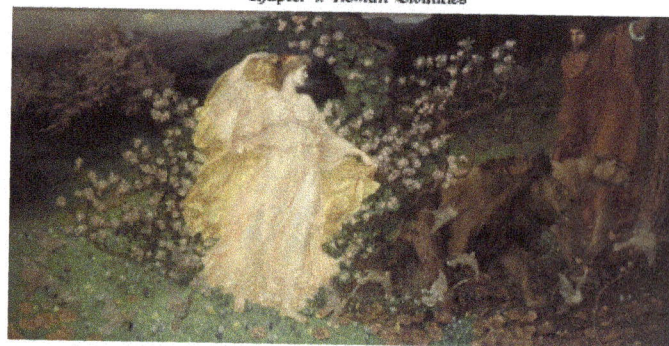

Figure 3: "Venus and Anchises" by William Blake Richmond

with its conservation, the neglect of the virgins, if they let it go out, was severely punished, and the fire was rekindled from the rays of the sun.

Liber is another Latin name of Bacchus; and Mulciber of Vulcan.

Janus was the porter of heaven. He opens the year, the first month being named after him. He is the guardian deity of gates, on which account he is commonly represented with two heads, because every door looks two ways. His temples at Rome were numerous. In war time the gates of the principal one were always open. In peace they were closed; but they were shut only once between the reign of Numa and that of Augustus.

The Penates were the gods who were supposed to attend to the welfare and prosperity of the family. Their name is derived from Penus, the pantry, which was sacred to them. Every master of a family was the priest to the Penates of his own house.

The Lares, or Lars, were also household gods, but differed from the Penates in being regarded as the deified spirits of mortals. The family Lars were held to be the souls of the ancestors, who watched over and protected their descendants. The words Lemur and Larva more nearly correspond to our word Ghost.

The Romans believed that every man had his Genius, and every woman her Juno; that is, a spirit who had given

them being, and was regarded as a protector through life. On birthdays men made offerings to their Genius, women to their Juno.

Macaulay thus alludes to some of the Roman gods:

> "Pomona loves the orchard,
> And Liber loves the vine,
> And Pales loves the straw-built shed
> Warm with the breath of kine;
> And Venus loves the whisper
> Of plighted youth and maid
> In April's ivory moonlight
> Beneath the Chestnut shade."
> "Prophecy of Capys."
> N.B.

It is to be observed that in proper names the final e and es are to be sounded. Thus, Cybele and Penates are words of three syllables. But Proserpine and Thebes have been so long used as English words, that they may be regarded as exceptions, to be pronounced as if English. Hecate is sometimes pronounced by the poets as a dissyllable. In the Index at the close of the volume, we shall mark the accented syllable, in all words which appear to require it.

18

19

BACK MATTER

Here you will be serving a few crucial roles or bits of information that had no place in the front or core content. For starters, this section is intended to introduce the reader to last thoughts, notes, information, resources, the author and/or illustrator, how to stay in touch, and any means to continue to connect and discover books via the author or publisher, sometimes both. It's a vital resource and a marketing tool in every book as long as the genre and audience make good use of it.

EPILOGUE, CONCLUSION, AND SIMILAR CLOSING STATEMENTS

Depending on the genre and intent, many books end with one last thing before they transition into author information. Typically, in a fiction book they may end with an epilogue that either shows a scene well in the future, sets the stage for the next book, or reflects on something unseen during the initially story that wouldn't have fit within the core content. In non-fiction books, they tend to have a conclusion or ending statement of some kind that closes up the topic covered and discussed throughout the book. It should always give the reader an idea what they should have taken away from the book after reading through it.

About the Author

REVEREND NELLIE JOHNSON, B.S., M.S.

EDUCATOR AND USUI REIKI MASTER TEACHER

I have always known my mother was exceptionally gifted. For the first time, she publicly shares moments of her surreal spiritual journey guided by angels and messengers of God. It's true that every human being has gifts but, not everyone recognizes their unique-ness. In becoming an author, she shares how she came to embrace her loving gifts and, to bridge two worlds in one lifetime along her remarkable sojourn to Oneness.

She taught me there is no judgement of others. That my own bright spots and pain points happen for a reason. That how you react guides your energy field as the co-creator of your circumstances.

What amazes her most is life's repeated patterns, and the ebb and flow with how it all unfolds.

Looking back, she appreciates that she always learned what she needed to know before she needed to know it. And, she always had what she needed when she needed it.

Her love, respect and appreciation for humanity and nature vibrate deeply through her writing. Drawing on more than thirty-five years as an educator, Non-denominational Minister, Usui Reiki Master, spirit

141

NOTE FROM AUTHOR

It's always a great idea to take a moment to discuss the lesson or follow up thoughts on the story you have told. This gives a moment for you to reflect and talk about things that would have spoiled the story if elaborated in a preface or revealed in the front matter. It can even show inspiration or reveal content that you didn't want the reader not to know entirely about. Not everything can be revealed in its full intent, and this gives an author time to share and have an intimate moment with their readers.

BIO FOR AUTHOR & LIST OF OTHER WORKS

It's common to see back pages that hold the biographies for the author. When it comes to this book type, it's strongly encouraged to have this in the book to help readers find your work online as well as connect and follow. This can be on the same page or on a spread across from one another. On occasion they start on their own right page. If you are working on a non-fiction book where the author is an expert in the topic, consider moving this to the front matter to show why this author is the best at discussing what the book it about. It's not uncommon on a non-fiction book to also see a smaller bio on the back cover along with the blurb to express the credibility of the content and the author writing on that particular topic.

SAMPLE OF NEXT BOOK OR FIRST CHAPTER SAMPLE

Common in fiction books, typically romance and serials, is the sample of the next book in the series. This is to show the reader that there is a next book and use the first chapter or two to hook them. Technically this is a form of upselling to encourage follow through buys. Granted, completed series and series spanning of over 3-6 books tend to see instant buys for the whole series more often then not.

Resources & Discussion Questions

Some books include some teacher and parent resources. This can be book club questions, fun activity pages, an information page leading to additional resources, or covering the topic in earnest. If you have a large amount of resources, you may want to create a companion piece such as a coloring book or activity book that can be purchased alongside the story. Other authors will provide these as exclusive PDFs offered when you sign up to their newsletter and often make great lead magnets for marketing, or exclusive swag at special events. In some non-fiction pieces, they may include resources used or resource listings for the reader to use in order to contribute, learn more, or use as needed for support in context of the topics covered.

APPENDIX, INDEX, GLOSSARY, AND MORE

Within non-fiction books, it's not uncommon to see these elements added to the book. Appendix are referred to materials that require their own enclosed space best preserved at the back of the book. Index are hit and miss, but highly recommended for cookbooks and similar topics to aid readers to find recipes that contain key ingredients. Most books are searchable via a PDF or the eBook which defeats the concept of having an Index. Be sure to build this last and utilize the many tools built into programs to help speed this process up such as seen in Word and InDesign. At the end of this book you will find a Glossary. These are great where a vocabulary list is part of the lesson or books such as this where many specialty terms and verbiage may take time to learn, or the reader may use the content out of order and not be familiar with the definition. On occasion non-fiction works will have End Notes listed though much of the industry has leaned in favor of Footnotes instead since this has proven better for eBooks and preferred by readers who don't want to loose where they are in their reading within the book.

CALL TO ACTION

This is any page or content added in the back of the book to encourage readers to do something or take action. For example, where they can follow the author, sign up for the newsletter, leave a review reminder, or grab the next book or other book series. This sometimes can be an ad for relatable services too as seen in non-fiction books!

OTHER WORKS FROM THE PUBLISHER

An older practice, but one that still has an impact. It's a great way to mimic what a newsletter swap does online, but on a physical level. Harlequin and Avon romance books were famous for doing this in the 80's and 90's and lead to cross-promoted sales between their pool of authors and books series of similar genre and plots. Many of the small publishers are reviving this practice as they see readers reveal they discovered multiple books from their publications through the books themselves.

PRINT-ON-DEMAND PAGE

If you are choosing to publish using Print-on-Demand, don't forget there will be a blank last even page in the back. This is where the printer will include a barcode that contains all the information as to where the book came from and more. Offset printed books don't have this feature at all.

OFFSET PRINTING—END LEAVES

If you are planning to offset print the book, you may have to create additional files for end leaves. I highly recommend asking for templates from your specific printer since these are done slightly differently at times depending on the book binder equipment and process, they use to connect these to the cover and textual aspects of the book. If you are using Print-on-Demand, you bypassed the option to have these, or some do add solid white onto hard covers.

Appendix A

CUTTING THE ETHERIC CORD

START:

- Find a quiet, peaceful, private place
- Light a candle
- Say a Prayer (*You can say the Our Father, 23rd Psalm, Hail Mary, or just words from your heart.*
- Take three deep breaths and go into a meditative or prayerful mode for several minutes to come to peace within.

HANDS:

- Place your hands in a prayer mode at heart level
- Bow your head and say:
- It is my intention to cut (*name of a person*) cord attachment to me at this time. I ask (*name*) to please forgive me for anything I may have done that caused unhappiness in any way. And I forgive you for anything you might have done to cause me unhappiness.
- I wish (*name*) whose Etheric Cord I am cutting love, peace and happiness. And I ask God to shower (*name*) with His blessings.

130

Non-Fiction: Self-Help, Reference, & Textbooks

Index of Figures

Glossary

ICOLUMKILL SEE Iona

IDA, Mount, a Trojan hill

IDAEUS, a Trojan herald

IDAS, son of Aphareus and Arena, and brother of Lynceus Idu?sa, wife of Bergi

IGERNE, wife of Gorlois, and mother, by Uther, of Arthur

ILIAD, epic poem of the Trojan War, by Homer

ILIONEUS, a son of Niobe

ILIUM SEE Troy

ILLYRIA, Adriatic countries north of Greece

IMOGEN, daughter of Pandrasus, wife of Trojan Brutus

INACHUS, son of Oceanus and Tethys, and father of Phoroneus and Io, also first king of Argos, and said to have given his name to the river Inachus

INCUBUS, an evil spirit, supposed to lie upon persons in their sleep

INDRA, Hindu god of heaven, thunder, lightning, storm and rain

INO, wife of Athamas, fleeing from whom with infant son she sprang into the sea and was changed to Leucothea

IO, changed to a heifer by Jupiter

IOBATES, King of Lycia

IOLAUS, servant of Hercules

IOLE, sister of Dryope

...NA, or Icolmkill, a small northern island near Scotland, where St Columba founded a missionary monastery (563 AD)

...NIA, coast of Asia Minor

...IGENIA, daughter of Agamemnon, offered as a sacrifice but ...rried away by Diana

..., died for love of Amaracus, 78

...YAS, friend of Hercules, killed by him

...oddess of the rainbow, messenger of Juno and Zeus

...IDE, Arthur's knight

...LLA, daughter of king of Galicia

...s of Osiris, described as the giver of death

...F THE BLESSED

..., first stop of Ulysses, returning from Trojan War

..., a son of Niobe, slain by Apollo

...riend of Rinaldo

...THE FAIR, beloved of Tristan

ISOUDE OF THE WHITE HANDS, married to Tristan

ISTHMIAN GAMES, See GAMES

ITHACA, home of Ulysses and Penelope

IULUS, son of Aeneas

IVO, Saracen king, befriending Rinaldo

IXION, once a sovereign of Thessaly, sentenced in Tartarus to be lashed with serpents to a wheel which a strong wind drove continually around

J

JANICULUM, Roman fortress on the Janiculus, a hill on the other side of the Tiber

JANUS, a deity from the earliest times held in high estimation by the Romans, temple of

JAPHET (Iapetus)

JASON, leader of the Argonauts, seeking the Golden Fleece

JOSEPH OF ARIMATHEA, who bore the Holy Grail to Europe

JOTUNHEIM, home of the giants in Northern mythology

JOVE (Zeus), chief god of Roman and Grecian mythology, See JUPITER

JOYOUS GARDE, residence of Sir Launcelot of the Lake

JUGGERNAUT, Hindu deity

JUNO, the particular guardian spirit of each woman (See Genius)

JUNO, wife of Jupiter, queen of the gods

JUPITER, JOVIS PATER, FATHER JOVE, JUPITER and JOVE used interchangeably, at Dodona, statue of the Olympian

JUPITER AMMON (See Ammon)

JUPITER CAPITOLINUS, temple of, preserving the Sibylline books

JUSTICE, See THEMIS

K

KADYRIATH, advises King Arthur

KAI, son of Kyner

KALKI, tenth avatar of Vishnu

KAY, Arthur's steward and a knight

KEDALION, guide of Orion

KERMAN, desert of

KICVA, daughter of Gwynn Gloy

Cutting The Etheric Cord

...issors in your hand and cut the cords using a scissor ...all around our body from head to toe. Say "I am ... (name) cord connection," while scissor snipping. ...nished, take three deep breaths and sit quietly for a ...f minutes.

...ur hands at heart level and say a Prayer ...t the candle.

...ur head and say Thank You ~ or ~ Namaste

SAVING THE FILES

Now that you have completed the book, be sure you save the files appropriately. This means for both your work files and the final product for the printer. Be sure to always ask clients and printers what file format and needs are required. For the sake of all things, we will focus on the most common and most versatile versions. If you used InDesign, you can go to File > Package and the software will do its best to grab font files, images, and more into a folder. For those who are using other means, here's a breakdown of the work folder and what to save:

- FOLDER NAMED AFTER BOOK
  - Work File (InDesign, Word, etc.)
  - PDF (2001-xa format aka Press Quality with Bleed recommended)
  - EPUB (Optional, reflowable a must)
  - ORIGINAL folder
    - Holds original text file and any related materials
  - FONT folder
    - Copies of font files used (truetype, openface, etc.)
  - IMAGE folder
    - Any image used should be placed in here in case you need it or edit or replace later.

As for prepping files for upload to a vendor, the two main types will be PDF and EPUB (reflowable). No matter if you are self-publishing or using a service, these two are the current staple in the industry and have the ability to upload to a variety of distributors and vendors with very little issue.

- PDF Format
  - This is used for print design applications, paperback, Print-on-Demand, and similar.
  - For printing, PDF-X/a: 2001 Format is the most accepted.
  - For web pdf, use web preferred file setting, but remember this file loses values needed for printing for a book.
  - Make sure Bleed Settings are applied or this could cause the file to kick back or be denied.

- EPUB Format
  - Always use reflowable.
  - Write in as much File Info and Metadata information as possible.
  - If attaching a cover image, it should be at least 1600x2400 pixels, 150 dpi, RGB color mode to avoid being kicked back from online vendors.
  - Most accepted eBook type currently with enhanced ability access.

BOOK TITLE: _____

SUBTITLE: _____

SAVING CHECKLIST

- ☐ A copy of the Manuscript or text file in a DOC, DOCX, RTF file that you used

- ☐ All the images in a LINKS or IMAGES folder

- ☐ Folder named after book to house all other files and folders

- ☐ Work files in folder (Recommend having a main one and back-up, i.e. *.indd and *idml)

- ☐ PDF version (2001-xa format for print-ready or print quality)

- ☐ EPUB (Reflowable) - optional

- ☐ Folder for fonts called FONT with copies of the files for future (they can go obsolete later)

- ☐ Did you save in the correct color profile (CMYK, RGB, 240% CMYK, etc)?

- ☐ Did you run ADA Compliance check in Adobe for ADA PDF needs? (optional)

- ☐ Do you need to convert EPUB to MOBI? (Consider using Calibre or similar converters)

- ☐ Has someone reviewed the file for issues besides you?

- ☐ Are the Header and Footers showing the correct text?

- ☐ Is your Table of Contents correct and numbered or not missing a chapter?

- ☐ Do your images bleed to the BLEED edge pass the TRIM edge?

- ☐ Double check that all your text is 0.5" from TRIM edge including Header and Footer

- ☐ Have you printed test pages on a local computer?

- ☐ Does your file meet the needs of your printer (Print-on-Demand AND Offset printers)

- ☐ Viewing for Web and Emails PDF - Did you save a "Reduced Size" PDF version?

- ☐ Has your customer signed off and reviewd the document before uploading to vendors?

BOOK TITLE: _____

SUBTITLE: _____

SAVING CHECKLIST

☐ A copy of the Manuscript or text file in a DOC, DOCX, RTF file that you used

☐ All the images in a LINKS or IMAGES folder

☐ Folder named after book to house all other files and folders

☐ Work files in folder (Recommend having a main one and back-up, i.e. *.indd and *idml)

☐ PDF version (2001-xa format for print-ready or print quality)

☐ EPUB (Reflowable) - optional

☐ Folder for fonts called FONT with copies of the files for future (they can go obsolete later)

☐ Did you save in the correct color profile (CMYK, RGB, 240% CMYK, etc)?

☐ Did you run ADA Compliance check in Adobe for ADA PDF needs? (optional)

☐ Do you need to convert EPUB to MOBI? (Consider using Calibre or similar converters)

☐ Has someone reviewed the file for issues besides you?

☐ Are the Header and Footers showing the correct text?

☐ Is your Table of Contents correct and numbered or not missing a chapter?

☐ Do your images bleed to the BLEED edge pass the TRIM edge?

☐ Double check that all your text is 0.5" from TRIM edge including Header and Footer

☐ Have you printed test pages on a local computer?

☐ Does your file meet the needs of your printer (Print-on-Demand AND Offset printers)

☐ Viewing for Web and Emails PDF - Did you save a "Reduced Size" PDF version?

☐ Has your customer signed off and reviewd the document before uploading to vendors?

Non-Fiction: Workbooks, Devotionals, & Planners

*In order to write the book you want to write,
in the end you have to become the person
you need to become to write that book.*

Junot Diaz

Preparing the Manuscript

If you thought textbooks were daunting, let's turn up the volume. When it comes to workbooks, devotionals, and planners, expect a lot of customizing from page to page. The most you can do is premade layouts that have key staples or elements that create a foundation. If you are using InDesign, one of my lifesaving aspects is the fact you can place guidelines onto the master pages and as you place them in, those guidelines drop in! Another visual element that may help when designing a book of this type is in the View settings of most software is the ability to turn on a Grid view. This can help you design with a sense of consistency or line up design elements.

Another method is designing worksheets and specialty elements as if they are images. Shutterstock is a great resource for premade templates, calendars, grids, and more that can save time and grief. Don't always assume you should be designing everything from scratch, so take a moment to really look for purchasable elements that can make this job easier or you can alter to fit your needs. The key here is to create some detailed format manuscript teamed with key storyboards to know how you want to organize and design the look. A great example of this book type is *The Author's Accountability Planner* by 4 Horsemen Publications.

What Functionality Does the Book Need?

These books are intended to be tools. They should be created with a sense of function and serve a purpose in the reader's or consumer's life in some capacity. The typeset takes on a very different focus. It's not as textual based as before, yet it requires much of the hands-on, pace-by-page attention that a textbook or picture book needs. The content and spreads are vital to draw the eye and instruct at a glance. Even then, there may be key care and functionalities on the same page or in their own sections. Most of these pieces will require storyboarding, sketches, or creating a base look to have as a background to tie the design together.

Unlike other books, thistype may require a large amount of custom pages and images to accomodate the purpose and function.

Even after designing a workbook or planner, it may require instructions and examples to increase the reader's understanding how to execute the design in a way to increase use and productivity. More so than ever, weigh the functionality against the written content that does exist. Is this an educational piece that has worksheets? Or is this a planner with opening content to help set a frame of mind and answer how to set goals using the templated pages that follow? Always understand why the book is created, and compare it with what your audience likes or uses currently.

Font choices will need to focus on crisp, concise, and consistency. Choosing a font face with a large variety of character styles will do best here.

Choosing a Trim Size

Trim size is normally in the larger selections, but many of these educational pieces have unique sizes and are mostly offset printed. If you do intend to do Print-on-Demand, refer to detail in the previous chapters regarding textbooks, reference books, and self-help for limitations and aspects. Regardless, these are again dependent on intended use and functionality. Planners are going to be in smaller trim sizes, so they can be carried in a bag or purse easily while books with worksheet are going to lean closer to large trim sizes to provide ample room to write and block out elements. Experiment and print storyboards, or sketched pages, out in different sizes and see which is best to support the usage of the book.

FONT EXPECTATIONS

There is usually very little in the way of textual content, but consistency will always be the first important aspect to anything you design that interacts with readers. We've taken a step back from maximizing a reader's ability to comfortably absorb massive amount of information in text to visual interactions. You can change up fonts for sections and play more, much like a picture book. It's more important to visual clue the user into when a section has changed or which way to use the areas they need to fill out or interact with.

MAXIMUM WORD AND PAGE COUNTS

Considering the artful intent and visual heavy guidance, these tend to be low in page count, hovering in the 100- to 200-page count with daily devotionals reaching 365 to 400 pages, dependent on the front and back matter needed. Again, this will be more dependent on the functionality of the book and the needs of the readers or consumers using this tool you are creating and preparing for them.

Remember: A 365 day devotional that starts fresh on each page is automatically a book over 365 pages.

MATERIALS AND PRINT OPTIONS

A lot of the books in this genre generally are colorful or at least contain graphic embellished backgrounds. Remember as you decide on offset or Print-on-Demand options, black and white will always be cheaper, and if there's no need to use color, leave it out to have a competitive retail price. Regardless, once you know the trim and final page count, you can shop around. Many workbooks and planners don't have eBooks or provide a purchasable PDF of some kind. Devotionals, on the other hand, can vary, so for large word count variants, I recommend diving into chapters for fiction and non-fiction books for the best information on this topic.

ILLUSTRATIONS, ILLUSTRATORS, & GRAPHIC DESIGNERS

If you know your trim size and orientation, then you're now ready to decide on how you want to create your illustrations. Some authors illustrate their books themselves, but that's not an option for others. You have a few options in this matter, and it's highly dependent on the type of book you're making such as a picture book, middle grade book, or textbook. If you are planning to hire someone to help you create and format your book, consider seeking out a graphic designer or illustrator who is knowledgeable in typesetting or at least picture book layouts. They will be able to incorporate and go through more steps with you as your guide. If you do this yourself, be sure to take your time to read the content in the Picture Book section for information specifically for making one and how to best prepare before starting.

Every book type has its own tweaks to the system or may have areas that are a must for one and not the others. If you intend to gather illustrations to give to a typesetter or format yourself, seek out an illustrator who draws in a style you enjoy and within the price range you need. They will not only need to be aware of the trim size and orientation for a picture book, but they need to include room for a 0.25" to 0.5" cutaway bleed so your core image doesn't get chopped when printed. For illustrations added to a section of a single page, you just simply need an image slightly bigger than intended use for best quality when it prints.

If your illustrator is using a physical median (watercolor, markers, acrylics, etc.) over digital painting, make sure you pass on information for file type, resolution (DPI), color mode, and so on. The more information you provide, the easier it is for them to give you the correct variant of scans. If they aren't able to provide you with scans, I recommend hiring an art photographer. If your median is light colored or watercolors, you should consider digitally enhancing the coloration, performing a black/white balance, and checking the levels of said image. In the end, do not expect those colors to match or look the same as the original as there is a loss of detail, texture, and shift in colors that is impossible to recreate by the time it prints in the book.

No matter the book, there is a standard need for file type and settings here when you aim to use images in your book.

- These files should be in CMYK color mode

- Saved at 300-600 DPI (resolution)

- Be in these file types: JPEG, PNG, or TIFF

You can also utilize PDF and export out to image or place as PDF but be mindful most software will be converting all these into a more manageable JPEG format. Sticking with JPEG and saving editable originals can be very effective in keeping overall file size for the PDF and eBook formats down to acceptable levels. This often comes into play with vendors with files size maximums, such as Barnes & Noble requiring eBooks to be 20 MB or below.

What if you can't find an illustrator or have funding restrictions? There's another possibility! Prepare to go on a deep search and rethink your initial book design. Stock photo sites are a wonderful resource for those who can't afford the illustrators or struggling to find one. This includes ShutterStock, DepositPhoto, iStockPhoto, Adobe Stock, and many more sites have a variety of artists who submit sheets and multiple images of characters for all audiences. A fitting example of this is the character you see throughout Writer's Bane! The more active an artist is on these sites, the better chance for the collection to grow and pull from. Some give you a means to reach out to them as well! You can always reach out to them and see if they will also commission pieces.

Basics of Digitally Enhancing Illustrations

Thanks to the digital age, many artists or illustrators have taken to producing art via software. This has made it a better means to reproduce images in a higher brilliance and sharper hues. That doesn't mean hand drawn artwork and watercolors can't join this high-tech advantage. Traditional art can be scanned or photographed to be pulled into the digital realm and in some cases, adjusted. This doesn't come without its share of pros and cons. One being the most common is the lack of capturing texture, hues, or even soft pencil strokes that all-too-often get washed out by the scanner or camera's light. If your art is too big to scan, an art photographer should be able to use a black/white balance card and even adjust and check it.

Once an image has been placed in digitally, you or a design have the freedom to adjust the image as needed. This can be moving elements, changing hues, brightening the overall saturation, and even resetting black and white tones to make richer levels so the image prints sharper. If you can apply a lot of these easy tricks to an image and balance the CMYK spectrum to a richer level, it will make a huge difference when printed. Not every image or color will be able to translate well; for example, blues and purples are often a struggle to lock in without shifting when ink is laid to paper.

Warning About Watercolors

Out of all the medians your illustrations can be made from, this one comes with a loss of detail and color just from scanning or photographing it. From there, it sways again depending on the options you choose. If you are ok with digitizing and drastically shifting your watercolors for print and not looking to match the original artwork, you will feel this impact the least. As for those looking to match it and capture the watercolor pieces as they are, you won't get this result. First, the act of scanning or taking a photo removes the texturing that watercolors often have, as well removing some of the sharpness and overlapping details. From there, I recommend offset printing with gloss or semi-gloss paper at about 100+lb. paper with alcohol-based printing for closest match to original work. If you decide to move forward with Print-on-Demand, be warned that you will continue to lose vibrancy and details due to the fact only matte paper is available and most are water-based ink printing and may cause saturation issues. This becomes most noticeable with a picture-book printer in Print-on-Demand.

Black and White Balance

If you are using Photoshop, Fire Alpaca, or some other photo editing software, you should be able to do this. Many of the photography editing software may be able to assist with this technique as well as the others to follow. Whichever software you use, there should be tutorials out there to assist you best as far as this book goes, the aim is to explain what it's meant to do and hint as to why you might want to apply this to your own formatting and images. As for this one, it helps establish true black and true white on the image and adjusts the image color range accordingly. Often when we scan an image, the black has a shine to it and might come off as a dark gray or even brown. This gives you a chance to "reset" the expectations and identify where these are on the image if you have both visible.

Levels in Spectrum

Images come with levels that spread a variety of hues and channels. Often black and white being on opposite ends, they come with slight dips beyond the peak of these colors that can take away from the overall sharpness of the image spectrum. Cutting out or knocking them to the peaks or using auto levels features can bring an image to pop more visually.

Hue & Saturation

Hue and saturations levels or using filters that shift these can do a wide range for an image. If the colors seem to have washed out, you might be able to recover faded colors using this feature. Also scanned or photographed images may have washed out and either you can darken the hue values or even adjust contrast and brightness settings to recover the look of the original artwork. Sometimes this setting allows a moment for you to change the hue or coloration of the art and make decisions you normally would have missed out on. Using a masked layer stacked with this can even allow you to change a color on a single item in the image, but that's best for a tutorial as it delves into photo editing and is beyond this book's conversation focused on typesetting.

DPI, IMAGE SIZE, AND RESOLUTION ADJUSTMENTS

The resolution of an image is very important! The first aspect to this is the size. You don't need your image to be 44 inches by 21 inches if your book is only 11 inches by 8.5 inches. If you are bleeding images off the edge, the image needs to only be 11.25 inches by 8.75 inches at the very least to give some room for image placement that allows bleed and trim. It's always smart to have the image slightly bigger, but too large and it may cause the program or computer to crash (especially those on personal or home systems). It also makes saving backups or throwing it on a cloud storage much more feasible.

---

*Make sure the resolution
is set between
300-600 DPI*

Once the size is within a reasonable range (exact with bleed or slightly larger in the same orientation or ratio), you need to make sure the resolution is set between 300-600 DPI. Anything under 300 is at risk to pixelate or be blurry. Know that most images saved from internet are usually only 72-96 DPI, so make sure what you are saving is the full image and not a smaller web version or down-sampled variant. Images that are over 600 DPI are at risk of the printer shrinking and may result in unwanted quality or results. It's always best to avoid these sorts of situations and keep the control and final product in your hands.

CMYK VERSUS RGB

Print and physical books are printed using CMYK colorations. This uses a set amount of cyan, magenta, yellow, and black layered on the page. Depending on the printer this can be applied with alcohol or water-based inks and vary in brightness (often influenced by the paper chosen). Water based inks are limited to 240% CMYK saturation level with paperweights at 70lbs or less as seen in Print-on-Demand applications.

IMAGE NAMING

Be sure to be consistent or concise with how you are naming your images. You can do this in a number of ways which includes consecutively (image01, image20, image03...), by location (Chapter01, Chapter02_SUBHEAD, Chapter02_Figure1.1), or labelled by what they are (Flowers01, RosesAndBees,

AuntMayAndHerPig...). You should always avoid using symbols and spaces since these may cause issues in final formats. Depending on your software and how you export for eBook format, having images with names that include open spaces, dollar signs ($), hashtags (#), and similar often will cause them not to load or fail when uploaded to a vendor. I highly recommend using only alphabet and numbers with underscore if need be. In programming we do this as well and often default to camelCase (LittleTimmysWagon, IHateThisPictureTheMost, ImageNameLikeThis...) as the safest means to prevent programming errors.

IMAGE FILE TYPES

Images come in a variety of types and the best ones to use for publishing are JPEG and TIFF formats. You can use a PNG, which preserves the transparency unlike JPEG or even a PDF file. You should keep these between 300-600 DPI and at least a little larger than the intended size to make sure you have room to trim the image if needed. TIFF is considered the best format and has been used in the printing and graphic design world as the superior option. Most Print-on-Demand printers want the files saved in PDF2001XA format, and this converts images to JPEG. Same thing happens when exporting to EPUB; the images are often converted to JPEG or PNG depending on what you are using. Thus, it is recommended to save in JPEG for several reasons, including the fact it's a smaller size, translates into eBook without issues, and prevents any issues when converting to final PDF format changes to the images.

PERMISSIONS & USAGE RIGHTS

Images and artwork can fall under public domain rights, but if they don't, you will need to purchase usage rights or get permission. If you pulled your images from a service like ShutterStock or similar stock photo site, they usually have different levels you can purchase for usage rights. This is the safest means for images and artwork. If you intend to hire an illustrator, be sure to cover the usage and contract with them how books are sold and their images will be used from the book to creating swag, bookmarks, banners, and more. Some may clear you for using the images in the book only and not for marketing materials. Be sure to add the permissions granted in the copyright section or even an illustration rights section as a type of appendix. It's always best to give credit where it's due on your copyright page at the very least.

DESIGNING THE PAGES

This will take a lot of custom work. Skills in PhotoShop or Illustrator, art design, and access to purchasing premade templates can go a long way with workbooks and planners. Here, more than ever, it's vital to design smarter and not overwork yourself. Have blank paper or sketchbooks handy to rough out ideas and concepts often. Once you've decided on a look or foundation for the key area, make as many master pages as you can to assist. The great thing about these is that later you can change the master page and update all the pages assigned to it at the same time if there is an issue. The layout goes from focusing on style of the text and its location, to providing instruction and space for the reader to add to the content being prompted from them. Mock-ups, feedback, and test copies can go a long way to a successful design here.

BOOK LAYOUTS

There are several ways to use images and textual content within a book. The most common is an image filling the entire page or spread with text added on a layer on top, a white space for caption, or even captions on the adjacent page per the spread. You see this more common in art books, wildlife books, or books with maps and similar graphics. Other designs have elements spread all over the page interacting with the text as often seen in textbooks with multiple columns or self-help books with pull quotes. Be sure to look at books your readers like and see how they are layering these elements. Does the font use up a lot of the page space? Are things layered or separated? How often does the placement of images change? Always keep up to date with the readership and competition.

When styling the pages, you have to be consistent since this is a means of relaying information based on the textual content. It cannot be said enough regarding formatting books on how important it is to walk the readers through the information with the chapter pages serving as mile markers of how far they've traveled through the book, story, or lesson. If you are sticking to industry expectations, be aware of how often images are interacting with the content in comparison to the expected age group.

Remember as you design your book that you can mix and match all the page and spread layouts to help tell your story visually with a combination of images and text. Picture books and workbooks both require a lot of designing to be completed in the forefront for best results (In short, work adjacent to illustrators, graphic designers, and storyboarding out sections or worksheets) unlike fiction and chapter books that are text only or have images sprinkled throughout. Prior to hiring an illustrator for your book, it's vital to know how many pages and layouts are in your book along with how many images are needed and where they will go within the layout. Creating a storyboard that you share with an illustrator or even a hired formatter can prevent many headaches on both ends and speed up the process.

PICTURE BOOK LAYOUTS

The most common picture book layout is an image filling the entire page or spread with text added on a layer above this. Sometimes in older books or self-published children's books you will have a spread split to a page with the image and a colored or white page featuring the text. Other designs have elements spread all over the page interacting with the text as often seen in Dr. Seuss books. When styling the pages of a picture book, you have to be consistent. It should walk the child and readers through the tale as if playing out a movie of sorts, the page flips timed in the right moment to make the child feel as if they are pushing the story forward. If you are sticking to industry expectations, you'll discover you have a very limited number of pages to tell the story visually. It

cannot be expressed enough that prior to hiring an illustrator, you need to create a storyboard or keen sense of direction in your manuscript. Picture books can prove a challenge for both sides, and the more communication exchanged with examples the better the outcome for all involved.

Image + Text Spread Layout

This is a dated and older layout style regarding the realm of picture books. It features the image on one page of the spread with the text of the story on the other. If you intend to compete aggressively on the market against other books, you may want to avoid using this layout. As for someone looking to tell a story to share with family and friends, this works perfectly well.

Image with Text Overlay Page Layout

The most common of the current layout choices for picture book designs is this one. In this layout, images cover all of the page (bleeding off the page), and the font is placed on top in a contrasting color, size, style, and/or faded background to pull it out of the image.

Multiple Image Page Layout

These pages usually have the most whitespace in all the picture book. Either a singular image or an array of single images with text emphasize the character or certain objects or even actions. This is a wonderful opportunity to recycle an image of a character from another scene and use it differently as seen in many mass market picture books such as *Mother Bruce.*

Full Spread Layout

The image or text (not both) stretches across 2 pages, a left and right page, to show as one large landscape image or two pages of textual content. In a lot of cases the text may only be present on one page and not the other, but other layouts might have several spots all around the image to show the story unfolding in a sequence or multi-action spread.

Rule of Thirds Spread Layout

Across a two-page span, an image, graph, or pull quote will cover one complete page and a portion of the adjacent page to leave room on a far left or right edge for font to place. In concept, the object is using two-thirds of the design area to draw the eye to the text or away from the text by doing so. The Rule of Thirds is often used in marketing, print design, or even in filming. It splits the viewing area into thirds from top to bottom and side to side. From this point, you break the content and subject matter up at the key sections to help draw the eye in a certain direction or pull it towards or away.

Split Design Image & Text Page Layout

Again, this is similar to the Image + Text layout seen in picture books and textbooks. On a single page, whether it's the right or left, the image and text split the space. Sometimes this is done in a 50/50 spit, or a two-thirds split, but often features a white space or colored space where the text will be. Again, this is an older means of designing a picture book, but it may be useful elsewhere.

Whitespace Page Layout

This page is often an indicator of a chapter starting or ending. Sometimes it can be a section or partition marker of some kind. It's notorious for having a lot of white space or empty, unused space on the page spread. What little content is there usually is textual to guide or inform the reader in preparation of something changing or a transition within the book. You see this a lot in textbooks and fiction books with right page only chapter starts.

Two-Column Design

More commonly seen in back matter such as index, glossaries, and listings, or in large reference and textbooks, this mimics the above spreads with the added feature of two-columns. This can pull more text onto a page especially with a small gutter and margins teamed with single lines pacing and 11- to 12-point font. If you are struggling with large page count, this could provide a means of dropping and managing it easier. It also allows for a more formula-based means to place images and captions, or even the occasional boxed content or pull quote. Not every page has to be in this style in a book, but it should be used consistently as to not throw the reader from the content presented on the page. Also, it's not uncommon that headings are set to span all columns or even opening paragraphs to content while the subhead information falls into two-column style. Play with the features and options, look at samples, and decide how to best apply these in a large book or workbook as needed. Recommended for large formats though, such as 7 x 10, 8 x 10, and 8.5 x 11.

Developing a Pattern for Functionality

One of the most important things to know whether you are designing books or video games, is people are pattern-seeking apes. We love to see patterns, follow repetitive actions, and even see and find a means of creating these subconsciously when known are to be found. Pattern feeds consistency and that tends to create a sense of stability and control. When you are using workbooks and planners, it's often to provide a tool or means to establish or even change habits and patterns within a certain area of knowledge, skills, life, or similar topic. Hence, the functionality of the book becomes the primary focus when typesetting. It's going to be touch and go at times, frustrating, and will take several attempts to master a system and design that works for both the author and its intended audience. Let's break it down to some vital areas! This is vital for any book that will contain worksheets, instructional elements, and similar aspects like seen in planners.

Even in textbooks and reference books there is a pattern established for the delivery of content. A great example of this is the formatting seen in dictionaries and encyclopedias. At a glance, you can quickly tell which you have when flipping through the pages. You also know how to find what you are seeking thanks to the order being established via the alphabet, a common knowledge element!

Producing the Order

Slowing down and considering instructional design practices can go a long way here. The order and level of details given in directions is impacts by the intended use and audience. It's always best to overprovide than underprovide and leave them confused and lost. One can't simply get in car and start driving. You have to first unlock the car, sit in the driver seat, adjust the mirrors, start the engine, and put it in reverse to back out of the driveway before you can even start heading to where you're going. The order in which you create the content should do just that! First get them strapped in properly before starting the core content and purpose. In text heavy workbooks and textbooks, you see this in the form of chapters and subheads that may even use 1.1, 1.2, and other titling to step the reader through slower. There's no one way to achieve this.

Repeat Pages & Duplication

It's ok and important to repeat or provide duplicates of key worksheets or areas where needed. Many get nervous about providing these. Be mindful of how you need them to use the book. If they should be able to make copies and just enter a few entries to try out during the lesson, then 3-5 duplicates should suffice. Some authors provide special PDFs for free that comprise of the worksheets only so readers can print the sheets. Repeated elements can help establish consistency and curb the need to reteach how to use areas of the book too! So keep in mind how they will be interacting and how to signal and direct at a glance can go a long way with how easy it is the use the materials provided. In textbooks you see this often to signal the start of examples or exercises to reflect what was taught in the lesson.

Building a Sense of Consistency

As you design these elements for use, make sure to use font choices, layout, and backgrounds to signal and establish a sense of consistency. Flipping through a workbook, a reader should be able to tell where they will be writing versus reading a lesson at a glance. Even then, in a textbook this happens with key elements boxed and marked in the same manner over and over again throughout the book. If there are keywords or vocabulary needed to stand out, it's often in the same bold font whether it's chapter one or twenty. Don't be afraid to utilize practices commonly used to give your design a jumpstart of feeling familiar and stay consistent with the genre or book type standards used most often.

Examples of Manuscripts

Unlike the other book types, this requires more art than formatting to be done. Due to this, it more likely to rely on a more Detail Formatted or Story Bounce styled manuscript. These are normally seen in picture books, but can serve for clear and concise creation of a planner or workbook that have very little written content. If they are more artful or variety in the over design as seen in artful prompt books, storyboarding may be the best course of action. Text heavy content would still fair best in a textual format with image placement aspects that might work more for flagging while key worksheets or materials should be showing up in the book to time instruction and tools at the right moment to have the most impact on the reader.

Textual Only

This is the most common manuscript for mass market fiction work. No images are tied into it, and it's simply importing the manuscript into the software and applying the indicated styling where deemed appropriate. A typesetter's aim is to streamline the text to the best of their abilities as to not break a reader's immersion with weird visual discrepancies, such as a slight tweak in line spacing (common in manuscripts where portions where dictated via speech-to-text and other written on a computer). You have to remember that we've been reading books with the same patterns and margins for centuries and keeping those expectations while being creative can be a hardline to walk for anyone designing a book.

For a textual-based manuscript, follow the Do's and Don'ts to prevent any unseen issues in the content. As for trim and font choices, it will fall back to the audience, genre, and type of book you are working on. You should be able to copy-paste content into a clean Word document or use InDesign's "File > Place" feature to import text and its associated styles. In the case of the latter, be sure to run Scripts to lock in these styles and save time from having to do manual changes by using the PrepText and other tools often found in opensource or pre-programmed into InDesign for use. Most manuscripts imported this way come as double-spaced in Times or similar font at 12 pt. If the manuscript has a variety of font faces, I recommend streamlining it to a single font face to prevent issues when formatting the book. Also, be aware many of these come with double spacing, which is intended for editorial purposes. Never keep this line spacing!

Text with Image Placement

For this book type, this is going to be the more common type encountered with textbooks, workbooks, or image heavy content. Throughout the text, there should be indications for image placement and should be clearly marked, much like a subhead or citation. For visual aid, I always encourage highlighting these yellow and treat them as their own paragraph. It's also helpful to use a keyword like "IMAGE" and brackets to help make the image placement stand up, for example:

[[IMAGE01: This picture shows the difference between nightshade and chili pepper flowers]]

These one-liners should be placed between the paragraphs they should be near or on the same page as the text. The importance of this is so when creating an eBook, the typesetter can make sure it falls inline at the right point of the content. It can also make it easier to play with the page layout as they apply the design and text begins to autoflow from page to page with the changes.

Story Bounce

This simply is stating what goes where in the manuscript as it bounces through the story beats or pages. Be mindful of how much textual content you are providing on pages and identify which image to be used concisely. For example, a manuscript using this format might appear like this:

- Title page (right)
- Copyright (left) with Dedication
  - Image01 at the top, small
  - Dedicated to all the kids who seek an adventure of their own
  - Copyright 1999 Author J. Smith etc.
- Page 1 (right) Image02
  - "Wow, the world sure is big when I'm all alone," marveled John.
- Page 2 & 3 (spread) Image03
  - John lost his dog when they moved. His mommy decided it was time little John Wick got a new puppy. Today, they would visit the animal shelter!
- Page 4 (left) Image04 & Image05
  - Image04: John couldn't believe the amount of doggies who needed homes.
  - Image05: Barking and bouncing, each one was excited to see him.
- Page 5 (right) Image06

- They came in so many shapes, sizes, and colors. None of them reminded him of his old doggy Daisy.

Note how there is no mistake where in the book these images and their text go as you 'flip through' the book. It's important to leave nothing out while keeping your instructions consistent and cohesive with same naming methods and delivery. This gives the typesetter a little room for choosing where content falls and to adjust content if needed based on images and text needed on each spread. You can even leave it up to the typesetter to decide which keywords they emphasize or encourage them to do so.

DETAILED FORMAT

This is for authors who have something more specific in mind for placement, including giving instructions as to where the textual content falls and may give a variety of more in-depth directions. For comparison, this would be the above example with additional bullets where a greater level of instructions addresses text locations, specialty font changes, and even image placement for a variety of page layout styles. In this example, words in bold are assumed to need font or artistic touch to emphasize the word's meaning and provide visual clues for early readers.

- Font Face: Palatin Kids
- Size 24 where possible
- Emphasize highlighted words artfully
- Title page (right)
- Copyright (left) with Dedication
  - Image01 at the top, small
  - Text in larger font, italics:
    - Dedicated to all the kids who seek an adventure of their own
  - Copyright 1999 Author J. Smith etc.
- Page 1 (right) Image02
  - Text on the bottom of page
    - "Wow, the **world** sure is **big** when I'm all **alone**," marveled John.
- Page 2 & 3 (spread) Image03
  - Text on top left
    - John lost his dog when they moved. His mommy decided it was time little **John Wick got a new puppy**.
    - Text on bottom right
    - Today, they would visit the **animal shelter**!
- Page 4 (left) Image04 & Image05
  - Top left Image04: John couldn't believe the amount of **doggies** who needed **homes**.

- Bottom right Image05: **Barking** and **bouncing**, each one was excited to see him.
- Page 5 (right) Image06
  - Text at top of page:
    - They came in so many **shapes, sizes**, and **colors**.
  - Text on bottom of page:
    - None of them reminded him of his old doggy **Daisy**.

STORYBOARDING

When it comes to picture books, I highly recommend this method or combining one of the above with this as a visual guide or blueprint. You can print, cut, and paste the elements to rough out the entire book's look and feel. This is a fantastic way to build a mockup of the book you intend to make and format for print and give concise expectations to a typesetter or experiment with what you had in mind for the final product. Before starting digitally, this allows you to troubleshoot issues that may need you to adjust text and illustrations prior to formatting the book. Most issues found this way are still relatively easy to fix by simply changing methods, book options, or changing fonts and images. Storyboarding can also be a great means to discover how many images you will need the illustrator to make as well as to where they need to be mindful of page edges and space for text to overlay. The following types of issues can be revealed at a glance by this method:

- Illustrations not allowing enough space for text to overlay
- Images that have the characters too close to the edge and will be cut when stretched to the bleed edge and cross the trim
- Images that have text as part of the image in need of adjusting to fit trim
- Trim size and orientation versus illustration size and orientation
- Amount of text for the page (too much is the common issue)
- Number of illustrations needed
- Amount of pages the story needs
- Story page flip and how that impacts the reader and story

Formatting the Book

Hooray! Now that we've talked and prepped this thing to no end, you should be ready to format this book with confidence. Why? Because it is so much easier to resolve problems at the manuscript and prepping stage than when you are formatting and making the book. Though, as said before, I am an avid user of word to InDesign, I will do my best throughout the book to provide information in an all-encompassing and design angle. If you were looking for software tutorial, this isn't the book for you. Getting detailed instructions on how to set parameters in Word, Scribd, and similar word processors isn't the aim.

Instead, we will be focusing on the typesetter-based elements and areas that will be par the course for any book you design. Dependent on the software you are using to design your book in could present its own issues and information may be labeled slightly different or found in different areas. In tandem with a software book, this book may provide some keywords in order to gain the affects you were aiming for in order for you to gain a greater value out of using said programs. In my years of looking for instructional manuals for book design, most of what I have learned was via videos, trial and error, typography college courses, and simply diving into the industry headlong with an open mind and understanding of the roots of publishing and its history. It probably also helped I delved in some game design, development, and programming, so I could troubleshoot creative solutions.

Without further ado, it's time to make this book using these step-by-step, or page-by-page instructions below. Feel free to adjust this to suit your own style and needs since there are various methods to achieve the results seen here. Again, the aim here is to simply the process while being able to make quality print books, enhance eBooks, and create a PDF that falls close as possible to being ADA compliant (Americans with Disabilities Act).

Instructional Design

Though this book can't dive into the full spectrum of instructional design practices and methods, it is strongly recommended to seek put resources to assist when creating textbooks, workbooks, self-help, and similar books. The importance of how material is presented, the order in which it is given, and the amount of details in the directions can make a work of difference in how well someone can understand and master the content, or utilize the tools you've designed for them. Often I have felt this in programming software books where key steps or explanation of concepts are skipped and have found myself instantly lost and lacking a key step that was assumed I would know to use. It can be the difference in someone being frustrated and unable to continue versus mastering and singing the praises of a book. Remember we have to open the jars before making the sandwich and unlock the car and start the engine before taking that trip!

How to Use the Book

When it comes to books intended to be put to use, adding a section or discussing how to use the book can help prep a reader properly. It doesn't mean every reader will slow down and use it, but if they get stuck, they will search for guidance here. This should inform the readers what the intent of the book is, how they should be utilizing it, and how to best start using the tool you have created for them. If you are being diligent, the consistent markers and identifying aspects in the books should be shown and defined so they understand their intent and how to perceive them as they travel through the book.

Examples & Samples

Giving samples and examples can make all the difference in understanding the content and lessons being taught. When providing worksheets, it's always a great idea to either review how to use them in the content or provide one filled out. In many math and English textbooks, you will find ample amounts of examples of problems and grammar being used incorrectly and correctly. The ability to see a math problem broken down into slower steps and done more than once in examples can make or break a student's ability to learn a new method or apply how to process a certain principal

Ways to Guide Readers

Play around with instructional design on a visual level. There are plenty of ways to guide readers through the content with using graphics and clever placement of materials. One of the more obvious means is the use of arrows placed on a page to point the eyes to read the content in the right way. Other means have included a character or boxing material in a consistent way to make it stand out in some way. Even then, laying out a page and its elements in a certain pattern for key moments can also clue the reader into knowing the difference between content, examples, and exercises at a glance without ever needing to read the text!

FILE SETUP

The file or page size should match the trim size in width and height. Make sure the intended orientation matches what you intended, specifically landscape versus portrait. Depending on the program, you may have to set bleed settings to include a 0.125" bleed on all sides or for outer margins. For some Print-on-Demand vendors, they may want the inner margin to have no bleed since this is the side of the page that is glued to the spine of the book. You usually get to set up or define the overall margins as well.

Be mindful that with picture books you will be saving a flat PDF for eBook design and that you don't have to fret over threading text boxes together as seen with all other book types. It's more important to make sure images are bleeding off to the marked edges just pass the trim edge, that elements are layered and overlayed in the right order, and textual content is withing the margins provided by the printer or Print-on-Demand requirements of 0.5" from trim size edge. Here are my recommended settings for this book type:

- Industry Standard Numbers:
  - 0.125" Bleed from trim edge
  - 0.5" Margin for content inward from trim edge
  - Large page counts will require a larger 0.625" or higher inner margin or gutter
  - Special binding may change the needs for inner margins

- Inner or inside margin: 0.625" for books under 300 pages and

- 0.75" to 0.8" for books pushing far into the 500+ range since where the pages' bind needs more space to avoid words falling into the crack of the book.
  - Granted, this is a picture book, and you can sometimes get away with a 0.5" margin.

- Outer or outside margins (including top and bottom) should be 0.5" to 0.625"
  - Typically have main body pages with header and footer set, and you can increase the top and bottom margins to 0.8-0.875" to give yourself space to place and space these from your body text.

Wondering where these numbers come from? Your vendors should have File Creation Guides via a PDF or webpage. No matter if you plan on using offset printing, KDP, IngramSparks, or a similar vendor, these parameters never change. This is the basic needs of a file going to print and will give the press some wiggle room. These parameters will change if you choose more elaborate binding and use certain presses. Always make sure you get these settings from the printer and design the book with these in place from the start.

USING LAYERS

Most of the layout software allows you to create layers such as InDesign (not any of the word processors though they do have header footer options). These come in handy in keeping content stacked or arranged in the right order. This includes making sure watermarks are below the body text layer and even keeping the header and footer elements on the top and not lost behind images and such. A bonus to using this feature is the ability to lock them and make sure you don't accidently change, move, or delete them unintentionally. With picture books, you often use images that take up the entire page and risk losing these elements completely. Recommended layers include the following listed in the order they should fall and usage:

- **Header and Footer Layer** – This will have your top layer text boxes that contain the header and footer which usually hold page numbers, title, author, and/or current chapter. You can control these with master pages. In a word processor, this is an option or specific setting that is influenced by section breaks to change how they look from section to section of the book's layout.

- **Default or Body Text Layer** – Here you will manage the primary text box in which the main content autoflows through threaded textboxes or pages.

- **Background Layer** – At the bottom of the list, there should be a background layer that is designed for images, spreads, and watermarks that need to fall under the textual content.

This doesn't mean you need to use all these layers, but it's highly recommended to give you more control when formatting. If the program you are using doesn't provide layers, check for features that define objects on the page as needing to be "Ordered" or "Arranged" with sub-options for "Bring to Front" or "Bring to Back," which mimic what layering does. This should aid you in making sure text and images overlap appropriately.

MASTER PAGES

These pages, or templates, are premade pages you can drag and drop into the layout to help speed things along and stay consistent. Know that this is more commonly found as a feature in layout software such as InDesign. Even with a freeform style book, there's a level of consistency with placement of elements such as header, footer, page numbers, watermarks, and other elements that you may not want to shift and wish to keep level throughout the book. In any book, you are going to be applying a few key layout pages. I recommend the following master pages or templates be made in advance to speed up the typeset process:

- **A blank page** with only the margin lines set. You may include a primary text box version for dedication or anchoring title page images into place. Works great for print-on-demand with that last page needing to be blank as well. These will also set your title pages and copyright page as well.

- **A body page** made of a blank page with only the header and footer with a main text box. I recommend putting the header and footer on a top

layer that's locked. Predesign a left and right page, often featuring the book title on left and author name on right. You may even design a running header or chapter header that auto updates depending on the software you are using. Adding glyphs and art to page numbers and headers can add a nice creative flair.

- **A chapter start page** that can add art, designs, and spacing shifts to accommodate the style implied. I always make right and left page versions, so if I need to change from right page only chapters to continuous, it's ready to adapt accordingly.

- **A numbered blank page** can be useful for areas that may contain images, maps, tables, and similar content where you simply want page numbers only.

- **Worksheets or Special Pages** should be designed or a foundation premade or decided on before getting too far into the design. Prepping these pages in advance can help in your efforts and provide a sense of how much space they truly need in order to interact with the content as your design the book.

- **A two-column body page or variants** can provide a means to design smart and save on page count where you can. Also, two-column pages can provide easier means to place images as often seen in textbooks, reference books, and workbooks alike.

- **Section breaks** become vital for non-fiction books. Occasionally these hard pages or spreads have an image or color to help standout when certain passing of time, events, topics, and provide a sense of dividers for the reader. Prepping a page or spread for these can save time and provide consistency when applicable.

FONT CHOICES AND PREP

Font has the most weight in typesetting and interior book design. Your choices and attention to detail to the spacing, size, and types will have a significant impact for better or worse. There are a few things you can do to help yourself prep and streamline your design depending on if you are using styles in Microsoft Word or a combination of Paragraph and Character styles in Adobe InDesign. Prepping and setting up pre-saved files with master pages and these elements can save a lot of hunting and frustrations, especially if you want to shift or change fonts later. If you intend to do typesetting full time or work heavily with fonts, I recommend investing into Font Management programs such as FontExplorer. This can make it easier to keep your growing library from bogging down your computer while making it easier to test out and organize fonts.

Paragraph Styles or Styles

These will make up most of the formatting application in textual content. They work in particular order and repeat as you start a new section or chapter. Making a style in advance can help you quickly adjust, fix, or change the entire typeset without hunting and pecking for certain content in the book. Instead, applying a style and changing the style can shift and fix the book as a whole.

- **Chapter Header –** Should be the largest font and be a font face that reflects genre. Content here is often just numbers, "Chapter" text, or some section marker text.

- **Headline –** This is often a subtitle or section title that follows behind the Chapter Header, normally directly below it. It should be the second largest text and also have a legible but creative font that captures the genre.

- **Subhead –** Should be a slight larger than the body text but clear and bolder in some way. It's common for these to be the same font as body text and simply in all-caps or small caps.

- **Drop Cap –** Whether it's a single letter, word, or line, this is the first paragraph in a chapter or section. It's a way to artfully signal to a reader where to begin reading or add more to the chapter page that makes it stand out other than whitespace.

- **Body Text –** This will be the majority of your content. It should be a legible font comfortable for readers and remain the same throughout the entire book. It builds the font foundation for Drop Caps, Citations/ Quotes, Subheads, Tables and more.

- **Citations/Quote –** This paragraph style should center or have an indent of 0.25" to 0.05" on the right and left sides. It's also common to add space before and after this paragraph style so the quote or citations pops. Often there is an italics character style applied.

- **Bullet Points –** Lists and bullets have similar indentation and spacing. Setting the preference or making a variety of these to create multi-tier systems in the varying styles can save a typesetter grief as well as the means to remembering how APA, MLA, and CMS are different from one another.

Character Styles or Subfamily fonts

Creating premade character style can help you gain more control on the style of the manuscript as a whole. It also helps build coding within certain programs for eBook creation and keeps these vital aspects from disappearing in the process.

- **Bold –** used to identify keywords, bring words to the front, and stand out louder. There is never a need to make a whole manuscript bold. Instead, choose a thicker or heavier font.

- *Italics –* this has many uses from quotes, to signaling key elements in content, and even to signal internal dialogue in stories.

- <u>Underline</u> – much like bold, this is used to make content stand out, signify a reference (depending on styles like APA), hyperlinks (or clickable content in text), or signal something of importance.

- Keyword – This comes in handy when wanting to stay consistent in font face and size changes in books where you need vocabulary words or key visuals to pop.

- Small Caps – Common to see in reference works or to address religious names or keywords, this is easier to manage as a character style and carries over into eBook better.

Object Styles or Table Styles

These are special styles that influence objects, images, and tables. They make sure designs and placement match and can even streamline how items show up in an eBook. Not every software has the means to define these or set them up. As for InDesign, these can help guide image frames, table cells, and more so that you can save time when adding content into the layout and saving you the grief of cracking open object options to adjust every detail.

Page-by-Page

Let's walk through making a workbook, or in this case, we'll be using *The Author's Accountability Planner* by 4 Horsemen Publications to show the key elements of a book like this. It's taken a lot of discussion and information to get to here, but as you take your time and refer back to key sections, you will find ways to improve and prepare. Be sure to take your time to prep your materials to avoid unwanted stress and troubleshooting for this stage. It can raise the hours this may take you to typeset, or format, exponentially no matter what your skill level may be. As an author doing your own formatting, these issues might be easier to solve on the fly, and if you intend on hiring someone or formatting for someone, this can bring production to a screeching halt until a decision or solution is made.

The Checklist!

Here is a checklist that should help you make sure you finished prepping the manuscript and materials before starting the formatting. Often we don't think to ask or double check to include some of these things and it can be detrimental in the final stages leading up to printing the actual book. Whether you are formatting your own book or formatting someone else's, this checklist is to help you gather everything you need before you start.

- Trim Size
- Book Title
- Subtitle
- Author Name (or Pen Name)
- Publisher and/or Logo
- Copyright Page
  - o Author name and copyright year
  - ◦ Name illustrator, designer, editor, etc.
  - ◦ Permissions for any materials used.
  - ◦ Public domain or scripture cited.
  - ◦ ISBN numbers (Paperback, Hardcover, eBook, Audiobook, etc.)
  - ◦ LCCN (Pending or number)
  - ◦ Published information and logo
  - ◦ The usual legal jargon to protect you, your work, and the publisher.
- Front Matter
  - ◦ Foreword: Yes or No
  - ◦ Dedication: Yes or No
    - ▪ Above Copyrights or Own Page
- Images are ready, clearly named, and all accounted for
  - ◦ 300 – 600 DPI
  - ◦ Correct size for trim + bleed
  - ◦ CMYK color mode
- Manuscript – Text only edition
  - ◦ Has image directions that match image names
- Back Matter
  - ◦ Author Bio
  - ◦ Image
    - ▪ Hyperlinks
    - ▪ Illustrator Bio
    - ▪ Image
    - ▪ Hyperlinks

TYPESET CHECKLIST

☐ Manuscript text in a DOC, DOCX, RTF file

☐ All the images listed in Manuscript present:

☐ CMYK mode

☐ Between 300-600 DPI.

☐ Trim Size _____ width x _____ height

☐ Author Pen Name - FIRST_____LAST_____

☐ Dedication: Yes or No

☐ Author Bio: Yes or No

☐ Copyright

☐ Publisher information

☐ Additional mention such as artist, design, or typesetter? _____

☐ Scriptures cited from.... Any public domain original publication mentions? _____

☐ Permission granted from... Any materials that have permissions needing to be listed here?

☐ ISBNs for Paperback: _____ Hardcover_____

☐ Audiobook_____ eBook_____

☐ LCCN pending or listed?_____

☐ Front Matter (Acknowledgements, Foreword, Preface, etc.)

☐ Do they want a Table of Contents: Yes or No

☐ Do they have tables to import: Yes or No

☐ Do they want pull quotes: Yes or No

THE WARM-UP

As mentioned in the front half of this book, the preferred method for designing books is using InDesign due to the amount of control. No matter what software you are using, the parameters and keywords are all the same and much of the process can be even reflected into when you design using a word processor, such as Microsoft© Word.

- Page size needs to be set to the trim size of your book.

- Bleed settings can always be added via page setup or page layout options depending on the program.

- Make sure page margins are keeping 0.5" within the trim or page size.

- If you intend to have headers and footers, be sure margin for body text are larger (0.75" for example) on the top and bottom to give space for them to fall within that 0.5" requirement.

- Choose your fonts in advance or make a list of possibilities for:
  - Chapter
  - Headline or Chapter Title
  - Header/Footer
  - Body Text
  - Pull Quotes

- Decide on Chapter Art or Typeset design for:
  - Spacing
  - Having samples on hand
  - Write down parameters in advance
  - Choose glyph or ornamental font options
  - Prepared images in advance

- Don't forget your checklist! You'll need it for Copyright pages and specifics!

- For workbooks and planners:
  - Get a sense of direction via the manuscript or a storyboard.
  - Have all images and artwork needed, labeled, and saved in the correct format.
  - Font choices have been decided including for keywords to emphasize.
  - Sketches and concept art can make things easier.
  - Pre-making foundation master pages to save time and prep for changes later.

BOOK TITLE: _____

SUBTITLE: _____

WARM-UP CHECKLIST

☐ Trim size set to the page or book size

☐ Add Bleed Settings for 0.125 inches

☐ Set your margins to 0.5 inch from trim edge

☐ Top margin for header set for 0.75 inch

☐ Bottom margin for footer set for 0.75 inch

☐ Inner margin or mirrored margins set to 0.675 omch or higher for spine/glue/page count

☐ Chapter font:_____

☐ Headline font:_____

☐ Header/Footer font:_____

☐ Body Text font:_____

☐ Pull Quote font:_____

☐ Body Text Base Font Size: _____ Line Spacing: _____

☐ Chapter Art prepped and ready to go

☐ Images saved in teh right format and size in advance

☐ Manuscript prepped and image placement clearly marked or Storyboard ready

☐ Glyph and Ornaments picked out. Font: _____

☐ Printer settings and requirements handy for saving and meeting their needs

☐ Templates or Master pages set up for key pages and special pages

☐ Paragraph Styles setup in advance or styles redesigned to match selection

☐ Are you ready?

FRONT MATTER

This is the first few pages that typically consist of title pages, copyrights, and dedication pages. This is the beginning of a book and rarely changes much no matter the genre of the book. One trend to note that is different in picture books is that it's common to see the dedication and copyright on the same page.

HALF TITLE

Not necessary for picture books and completely optional dependent on needs of book and formatting preferences. The first thing you want to prep is the front matter for the book. In this example, we are going for super basic and the most common story bounce that matches many of the mass market picture books to date. The only text here should be the title font. This page should leave room for the author to sign. It is completely optional though and can be replaced by a full title page.

THE **AUTHOR'S ACCOUNTABILITY** *Planner*

A Day-by-Day Guide for Writers

"Because Writing is Hard."

2022

FULL TITLE

Half title page versus full title page can be made simple in a picture book. Half title can feature a text title only and the full title can be the front cover of the book itself. If you decide to do a text-based version, this should have series name, title, subtitle, author name, illustrator, and publisher name and/or logo.

COPYRIGHT

Increasingly popular is the dedication above the copyright page. Typically, this will always be a left page on the back of the title page.

DEDICATION/ACKNOWLEDGMENT

Many chapter books have a dedication or even acknowledgments. This should go right after the copyright page.

TABLE OF CONTENTS

Now we are dealing with chapter! Which means it's time to dabble in making a Table of Contents. Always leave a blank right page for this and save its creation for last. Most layout software can auto-populate the Table of Contents and you can adjust the paragraph and character styling from there. Within InDesign if it adds weird or hit and miss font formatting, revisit your chapter headers, and clear overrides. Some manuscripts just import dirty and don't always apply the styles and remove unwanted programming. It can even cause hit and miss bolded text in eBook Table of Contents!

DEDICATION
To all the great writers working on achieving their dreams!

And those who joined the planner family in 2021!

CONTENT

Unlike other book types, picture books focus more on the image quality and placements. Another aspect is the fact there's no urgency or importance on threading the pages together. Instead, it comes down to making sure your images are falling on the correct pages and side of the spread, as well as making sure all your textual content is within the printer's requirements (Normally 0.5" from the trim edge). This is one of the rare occasions that you don't need to thread text boxes. You can move and put text boxes where needed, and most of the focus falls onto the images (make sure they are 300-600 dpi, CMYK!).

FIRST PAGE OR SPREAD

The book should be layered with images on bottom, story textboxes overlayed where needed, and header/footer on the top layer. Depending on the layout software, you might be able to apply drop shadow or add outer glows to help the text pop off the image or not blend into the image. Don't be afraid to change the text color as needed, change up font size, or create a variety of effects to emphasize what the word means. Slimy should have drippy lettering, fuzzy should be furry, and so on. Elements like these bring the story to life for readers who are learning what those words might mean.

BLEED VERSUS TEXT MARGINS

Make sure the bleed goes past the trim line or paper's edge to the end of the to the bleed line. If the signature or paper shifts in print slightly, it will cause a white line on the outer edges. Many designers place a white margin or offset the inner margins on spreads. This is dependent on the page spread, number of pages, and type of binding. For beginners you may want to default to treating this as a bleed edge. In picture books, you can push images off the page and across pages in creative ways, but when it comes to text placement, you must have it within 0.5" inch from the trim edge or paper edge. This is so if the signatures or pages shift that your textual content will never be at risk of being cutoff.

WEEK 1

NOVEMBER

DAILY ACCOMPLISHMENTS — TUESDAY 1

Word Count:_____ Marketing Hours:_____
Brainstorming Hours:_____ Research Hours:_____
Editing Hours:_____ Reading Hours:_____

DAILY ACCOMPLISHMENTS — WEDNESDAY 2

Word Count:_____ Marketing Hours:_____
Brainstorming Hours:_____ Research Hours:_____
Editing Hours:_____ Reading Hours:_____

DAILY ACCOMPLISHMENTS — THURSDAY 3

Word Count:_____ Marketing Hours:_____
Brainstorming Hours:_____ Research Hours:_____
Editing Hours:_____ Reading Hours:_____

DAILY ACCOMPLISHMENTS — FRIDAY 4

Word Count:_____ Marketing Hours:_____
Brainstorming Hours:_____ Research Hours:_____
Editing Hours:_____ Reading Hours:_____

DAILY ACCOMPLISHMENTS — SATURDAY 5

Word Count:_____ Marketing Hours:_____
Brainstorming Hours:_____ Research Hours:_____
Editing Hours:_____ Reading Hours:_____

DAILY ACCOMPLISHMENTS — SUNDAY 6

Word Count:_____ Marketing Hours:_____
Brainstorming Hours:_____ Research Hours:_____
Editing Hours:_____ Reading Hours:_____

DAILY ACCOMPLISHMENTS — MONDAY 7

Word Count:_____ Marketing Hours:_____
Brainstorming Hours:_____ Research Hours:_____
Editing Hours:_____ Reading Hours:_____

WEEKLY OVERVIEW

EXERCISE: Take 5-minutes to write something with the 2 words below:

Exuberant   **Mom**

Post your exercise on the 4HP Accountable Authors Group on Facebook!

What was your sprint time and top word count?
_____

List a new song you discovered this week:
_____

Favorite food or drink this week:
_____

How did you reward yourself?
_____

What project(s) did you work on?
_____

What are you reading?
_____

What went well this week?
_____

What could improve this week?
_____
_____
_____

TOTAL FOR THE WEEK

Word Count:_____ Marketing Hours:_____
Brainstorming Hours:_____ Research Hours:_____
Editing Hours:_____ Reading Hours:_____

Don't forget to color in your grid!

NOVEMBER

220   221

Story Flow and Other Pages

Be sure to change up the layout on occasion of placement of font and graphics to drive the story forwards and create a need to flip the page. Many formatters will adjust illustrations to white areas out or Photoshop content to allow more room for textual content. If you have the skills to do this, make sure the images blend well and appropriately. Many legacy pieces, or picture books meant for the author and family only, not to compete on a commercial level, have to fret over this less so. Always consider who the book is for and who you are aiming to compete with if at all. Picture books that complete on a commercial level have more red-tape and parameters to meet than that of a book being put together in a simpler straight-forward layout to share with family and friends.

THE AUTHOR'S ACCOUNTABILITY PLANNER

The Cheerleader

Focus on editing your work once this week. How's it coming along?

THE ARCHITECT

"Plot is people. Human emotions and desires founded on the realities of life, working at cross purposes, getting hotter and fiercer as they strike against each other until finally there's an explosion—that's Plot."
~ Leigh Brackett

222

THE MUSES

THE RESEARCHER

If you want your scene to come alive for the reader, try using all of your senses: smell, sound, touch, taste, and sight. When people gather, there's always that storyteller in the group. Listen carefully how often they make sounds, or talk about the feel and smells they encountered. Even in oral format, adding senses to storytelling immerses the reader faster and hooks them to listen.

THE TASKMASTER

Believe in yourself. Decide you are a great writer--and that's exactly what you will be.

223

NOVEMBER

Introduction or First Chapter Page

This is where you get to use that master page or drop the many fancy styles you took the time to prep! If you did pre-save those Chapter Header, Headline, Subhead, Drop-cap and other styles, you may want to do so as you design this first chapter. It'll make the rest of the book a breeze and make sure everything snaps and looks the same throughout the book. Work smarter! Not harder!

How to Use this Book

If this book has a specific purpose, or function, or is intended to be a tool, it's highly recommended to provide a sense of direction with adding a section like this, especially if a majority of the book will need to be filled out by the reader. Having a front section they can refer back to for detailed instructions, examples, or guidance can go a long way for a book's success, even in a textbook and reference book!

Non-Fiction: Workbooks, Devotionals, & Planners
BODY TEXT SPREADS

Here you will get to double down on your header and footer design. Make sure things are updating if you decided to be fancy with auto-updating running headers. If not, the book title on the left and author to the right will always work with page numbers on the bottom. Don't be afraid to center the page numbers if you aren't sure if you are dropping content on the right and left pages. In software like InDesign, it shows you the way the book will be printed whereas Word you have to pay close attention or try adding a blank first page to offset it (But don't forget to delete it back out when you're done!).

INTRODUCTION

"Guys, I need this in my life: An Author Accountability Guide."
The Researcher

"Yeah, we should do that!"   The Architect

"That's a great idea! Someone should do that!"
The Cheerleader

And so we became Someone.   The Taskmaster

Once upon a time, there were four Muses who decided to create a planner/ guide for writers. This magical book would be a new resource for those seeking to set goals, track progress (not just word count), and enjoy the Muse-inspired motivation to stick with it for an entire year. Thus, the Author's Accountability Planner was born.

We hope authors find this book useful through each stage of their writing journey. Writing and creating, whether full-time or part-time, require time and organization. This planner is designed to help track time, provide recommendations, and share what the Muses have discovered to be game changers on their own journeys.

Throughout the year, everyone faces the challenges of self-doubt, procrastination, and Life in General (Remember the 2020 pandemic jolting everyone around the ~~...~~
Muses are ~~...~~
We will ~~...~~

HOW TO USE THIS BOOK

The Muses have spent countless hours fine-tuning the functionality of this book (by deciding if it should record writing time or beyond that). In the end, the Muses decided to account for all of the time spent doing writer-type things (brainstorming, writing, researching, editing, marketing, etc.). Many books discuss word count, but so much more happens before, after, and during the process of laying a book on paper (both physically and digitally).

Finishing the story is the single most important and difficult part of being a writer. To succeed, writers need accountability, someone or something to keep them motivated week after week. The Muses are here to keep the adventure moving forward, fight writer's block, and offer strategies to achieve year-end goals. Life is unpredictable, offering a variety of momentum-destroying reasons. This book can help you fight through those tough times while maintaining high morale.

In the end, only YOU can write YOUR story. You're here now, ready to do this. Let's go!

THE LAYOUT

This book contains four parts: Introductory Material (you're here!), Goal Setting, Month-by-Month Tracking, and Year Review. Each month has three sections: Monthly Prep, Weekly Overviews, and Monthly Review.

---

eye-opening when you compare good and bad weeks. In the end, use these pages to fine-tune your writing schedule, optimizing your output for all your writing needs. Some of us perform better when pairing tasks with one another; other times we reach higher word counts after reading and researching. Use these numbers to maximize your potential and make goal setting more rewarding.

WORD COUNT

You know this one! Word count is a common measure among authors to track their progress.

BRAINSTORMING

Some of us are pantsers while others are plotters. At times, we combine strategies! Either way, we spend some time prepping a story, even if it's an hour at the cafe writing on a napkin.

EDITING

Most writers work on more than one project at a time. Divide your attention between writing one work while editing another. One story might be completely drafted but still needs revision and editing. This step should never be skipped—whether posting to a blog or pitching to agents or publishers. Check your work.

MARKETING

If you dream to be famous, build awareness, or publish books, it's important to keep your author platform active by engaging on social media, writing blogs, posting advertisements, sending out newsletters, hosting events, and more. Automate as much as possible, scheduling your posts in advance to give yourself more time to create content. Don't risk losing your reader's interest!

RESEARCH

Whether researching how to buy a horse or a new method for writing dialogue, count your time. You're working! As a writer no less! These hours count too. ting. Some projects might be more demanding than others, so log your time!

READING

As writers, we hear this advice often: Read what you're writing! It's true! Read widely and often—both in and out of your comfort zone. Pick up a classic or treat yourself with the newest release. Engage in the writing world in every way.

I WANT TO BE A WRITER

Take a look at all the projects and stories you want to complete for this coming year and predict your word count for them. It's okay to fall over or under— and you may massage these as the year progresses, but throw something out there to get started. Here's a rough scope of word counts to aid you in estimation:

TYPES	GENRE
Flash Fiction 1,000 word or less	Blog Posts 200-1,200
Short Story 1,200-10,000	Romance 50,000-70,000
Novelette 10,000-30,000	Paranormal 70,000-90,000
Novella 30,000-45,000	Fantasy 90,000-120,000
Novel 50,000-85,000	Crime 90,000-100,000
Epic Novel 90,000-150,000	Mystery/Thriller/Suspense 70,000-80,000
Textbook 50,000-250,000	Memoir 30,000-70,000
Young Adult 50,000-80,000	Science Fiction 90,000-125,000
Middle Grade 25,000-40,000	Horror 70,000-100,000
Chapter Books 10,000-20,000	Historical 80,000-120,000
Picture Books 300-700	Erotica 7,000-50,000

How many words will you write this year? _____

How many words did you complete last year?_____

How many projects will you complete?_____

Worksheets and Planner Pages

These are pages that are primarily dependent on the reader filling in the blanks and following along with prompts. There should be blank areas or lines that provide space for them to interact with the book and content as intended. Usually in a textbook this is rare since they expect you to take the exercises listed and use a sheet of paper to work through the problems often and revisit for practice later.

Special Pages or Unique Content

It's not uncommon for workbooks, textbooks, devotions, and planners to have elaborate special pages that provide visual guides or reference materials. Often these can be charts, diagrams, or illustrations intended for the readers to revisit as needed as they continue to use the book.

End of Chapter

You have a few choices for the end of a chapter. Simply leave it blank with whitespace that naturally unfolds or design some extra art or flair. Always make sure the text flow to the top of the page. Often layout software defaults to justify on page and will stretch and spread lines across the page making it look weird.

NOVEMBER

Week 2

TUESDAY 8

DAILY ACCOMPLISHMENTS
Word Count:
Brainstorming Hours:
Editing Hours:
Marketing Hours:
Research Hours:
Reading Hours:

WEDNESDAY 9

DAILY ACCOMPLISHMENTS
Word Count:
Brainstorming Hours:
Editing Hours:
Marketing Hours:
Research Hours:
Reading Hours:

THURSDAY 10

DAILY ACCOMPLISHMENTS
Word Count:
Brainstorming Hours:
Editing Hours:
Marketing Hours:
Research Hours:
Reading Hours:

FRIDAY 11

DAILY ACCOMPLISHMENTS
Word Count:
Brainstorming Hours:
Editing Hours:
Marketing Hours:
Research Hours:
Reading Hours:

SATURDAY 12

DAILY ACCOMPLISHMENTS
Word Count:
Brainstorming Hours:
Editing Hours:
Marketing Hours:
Research Hours:
Reading Hours:

SUNDAY 13

DAILY ACCOMPLISHMENTS
Word Count:
Brainstorming Hours:
Editing Hours:
Marketing Hours:
Research Hours:
Reading Hours:

MONDAY 14

DAILY ACCOMPLISHMENTS
Word Count:
Brainstorming Hours:
Editing Hours:
Marketing Hours:
Research Hours:
Reading Hours:

224

Weekly Overview

EXERCISE: Take 5 minutes to write something with the 2 words below:

Throne   **Maniacal**

Post your exercise on the 4HP Accountable Authors Group on Facebook!

What was your sprint time and top word count?

List a new song you discovered this week:

Favorite food or drink this week:

How did you reward yourself?

What project(s) did you work on?

What are you reading?

What went well this week?

What could improve this week?

TOTAL FOR THE WEEK

Word Count: Marketing Hours:
Brainstorming Hours: Research Hours:
Editing Hours: Reading Hours:

Don't forget to color in your grid!

225

NOVEMBER

Back Matter

This is where you'll get to provide information that pertains to the lesson, book, author, and similar. Here you can expect to find common elements that include author bios, resources, discussion questions, and where to find more books from both the author and publisher.

This can either end abruptly or provide a call of action or similar aspect that can help them conclude the activities and functionality of the book. Perhaps guidance or a self-reflection might come in handy here depending on the type and genre of book and audience this pertains to. Here are some varying aspects seen in a variety of books.

Epilogue, Conclusion, and Similar Closing Statements

Depending on the genre and intent, many books end with one last thing before they transition into author information. Typically, in a fiction book they may end with an epilogue that either shows a scene well in the future, sets the stage for the next book, or reflects on something unseen during the initially story that wouldn't have fit within the core content. In non-fiction books, they tend to have a conclusion or ending statement of some kind that closes up the topic covered and discussed throughout the book. It should always give the reader an idea what they should have taken away from the book after reading through it.

Note from Author

It's always a great idea to take a moment to discuss the lesson or follow up thoughts on the story you have told. This gives a moment for you to reflect and talk about things that would have spoiled the story if elaborated in a preface or revealed in the front matter. It can even show inspiration or reveal content that you didn't want the reader not to know entirely about. Not everything can be revealed in its full intent, and this gives an author time to share and have an intimate moment with their readers.

Bio for Author & List of Other Works

It's common to see back pages that hold the biographies for the author. When it comes to this book type, it's strongly encouraged to have this in the book to help readers find your work online as well as connect and follow. This can be on the same page or on a spread across from one another. On occasion they start on their own right page. If you are working on a non-fiction book where the author is an expert in the topic, consider moving this to the front matter to show why this author is the best at discussing what the book it about. It's not uncommon on a non-fiction book to also see a smaller bio on the back cover along with the blurb to express the credibility of the content and the author writing on that particular topic.

The year is Officially OVER!

Great job staying accountable!

Time for your Yearly Review!

Sample of Next Book or First Chapter Sample

Common in fiction books, typically romance and serials, is the sample of the next book in the series. This is to show the reader that there is a next book and use the first chapter or two to hook them. Technically this is a form of upselling to encourage follow through buys. Granted, completed series and series spanning of over 3-6 books tend to see instant buys for the whole series more often then not.

Resources & Discussion Questions

Some books include some teacher and parent resources. This can be book club questions, fun activity pages, an information page leading to additional resources, or covering the topic in earnest. If you have a large amount of resources, you may want to create a companion piece such as a coloring book or activity book that can be purchased alongside the story. Other authors will provide these as exclusive PDFs offered when you sign up to their newsletter and often make great lead magnets for marketing, or exclusive swag at special events. In some non-fiction pieces, they may include resources used or resource listings for the reader to use in order to contribute, learn more, or use as needed for support in context of the topics covered.

Appendix, Index, Glossary, and More

Within non-fiction books, it's not uncommon to see these elements added to the book. Appendix are referred to materials that require their own enclosed space best preserved at the back of the book. Index are hit and miss, but highly recommended for cookbooks and similar topics to aid readers to find recipes that contain key ingredients. Most books are searchable via a PDF or the eBook which defeats the concept of having an Index. Be sure to build this last and utilize the many tools built into programs to help speed this process up such as seen in Word and InDesign. At the end of this book you will find a Glossary. These are great where a vocabulary list is part of the lesson or books such as this where many specialty terms and verbiage may take time to learn, or the reader may use the content out of order and not be familiar with the definition. On occasion non-fiction works will have End Notes listed though much of the industry has leaned in favor of Footnotes instead since this has proven better for eBooks and preferred by readers who don't want to loose where they are in their reading within the book.

Call to Action

This is any page or content added in the back of the book to encourage readers to do something or take action. For example, where they can follow the author, sign up for the newsletter, leave a review reminder, or grab the next book or other book series. This sometimes can be an ad for relatable services too as seen in non-fiction books!

THE AUTHOR'S ACCOUNTABILITY PLANNER

MONTHLY ACTIVITY GRID

Writing
Brainstorming
Editing
Marketing
Research
Reading

JOURNAL

NOVEMBER

Word Count: _____ Divided by _____ days =

TOTAL FOR THE YEAR SO FAR

Word Coun

OTHER WORKS FROM THE PUBLISHER

An older practice, but one that still has an impact. It's a great way to mimic what a newsletter swap does online, but on a physical level. Harlequin and Avon romance books were famous for doing this in the 80's and 90's and lead to cross-promoted sales between their pool of authors and books series of similar genre and plots. Many of the small publishers are reviving this practice as they see readers reveal they discovered multiple books from their publications through the books themselves.

PRINT-ON-DEMAND PAGE

If you are choosing to publish using Print-on-Demand, don't forget there will be a blank last even page in the back. This is where the printer will include a barcode that contains all the information as to where the book came from and more. Offset printed books don't have this feature at all.

OFFSET PRINTING–END LEAVES

If you are planning to offset print the book, you may have to create additional files for end leaves. I highly recommend asking for templates from your specific printer since these are done slightly differently at times depending on the book binder equipment and process, they use to connect these to the cover and textual aspects of the book. If you are using Print-on-Demand, you bypassed the option to have these, or some do add solid white onto hard covers.

So I Failed...Now What?

You keep writing, that's what you do. Get back on the path and keep going. But it's probably a good time to reevaluate your goals. What is a more reasonable goal for you? Think about the reasons that caused you to fail this time. What can you do differently next time? What are some unanticipated issues you ran into this time? Why didn't you think they would be obstacles? What can you do to prevent more obstacles from knocking you off the writing path?

So I'm finished...Now What?

Yay!!! Cheer one more time for the level of amazingness that is you! Enjoy that sweet reward. You earned this. Relish the moment. Remember this feeling. (Maybe even write down how you feel right now, so you can remind Future You of what is possible.) Now, set the bar a little higher and push yourself to grow or attempt to hit the same goals twice in a row!

Keep that magic going. Keep doing what worked for you this time, and use it to write the next project. Create new rewards and punishments. Plan a new project. Get lost in another world that demands to be poured onto the page. Take note of what worked and what didn't. Like, literally write it down. Use those notes as a record of your writing journey. People change, and so does writing. Allow yourself to see the path you've been on (while looking forward to what comes next).

NEXT YEAR PREP

What projects do you want to complete next year?

_____

_____

_____

_____

_____

Make your Reading List for next year.

_____

_____

_____

_____

_____

_____

Stay accountable and grab the next edition!

SAVING THE FILES

Now that you have completed the book, be sure you save the files appropriately. This means for both your work files and the final product for the printer. Be sure to always ask clients and printers what file format and needs are required. For the sake of all things, we will focus on the most common and most versatile versions. If you used InDesign, you can go to File > Package and the software will do its best to grab font files, images, and more into a folder. For those who are using other means, here's a breakdown of the work folder and what to save:

- FOLDER NAMED AFTER BOOK
    - Work File (InDesign, Word, etc.)
    - PDF (2001-xa format aka Press Quality with Bleed recommended)
    - EPUB (Optional, reflowable a must)
    - ORIGINAL folder
        - Holds original text file and any related materials
    - FONT folder
        - Copies of font files used (truetype, openface, etc.)
    - IMAGE folder
        - Any image used should be placed in here in case you need it or edit or replace later.

As for prepping files for upload to a vendor, the two main types will be PDF and EPUB (reflowable). No matter if you are self-publishing or using a service, these two are the current staple in the industry and have the ability to upload to a variety of distributors and vendors with very little issue.

- PDF Format
    - This is used for print design applications, paperback, Print-on-Demand, and similar.
    - For printing, PDF-X/a: 2001 Format is the most accepted.
    - For web pdf, use web preferred file setting, but remember this file loses values needed for printing for a book.
    - Make sure Bleed Settings are applied or this could cause the file to kick back or be denied.

- EPUB Format
    - Always use reflowable.
    - Write in as much File Info and Metadata information as possible.
    - If attaching a cover image, it should be at least 1600x2400 pixels, 150 dpi, RGB color mode to avoid being kicked back from online vendors.
    - Most accepted eBook type currently with enhanced ability access.

SAVING CHECKLIST

- [ ] A copy of the Manuscript or text file in a DOC, DOCX, RTF file that you used

- [ ] All the images in a LINKS or IMAGES folder

- [ ] Folder named after book to house all other files and folders

- [ ] Work files in folder (Recommend having a main one and back-up, i.e. *.indd and *idml)

- [ ] PDF version (2001-xa format for print-ready or print quality)

- [ ] EPUB (Reflowable) - optional

- [ ] Folder for fonts called FONT with copies of the files for future (they can go obsolete later)

- [ ] Did you save in the correct color profile (CMYK, RGB, 240% CMYK, etc)?

- [ ] Did you run ADA Compliance check in Adobe for ADA PDF needs? (optional)

- [ ] Do you need to convert EPUB to MOBI? (Consider using Calibre or similar converters)

- [ ] Has someone reviewed the file for issues besides you?

- [ ] Are the Header and Footers showing the correct text?

- [ ] Is your Table of Contents correct and numbered or not missing a chapter?

- [ ] Do your images bleed to the BLEED edge pass the TRIM edge?

- [ ] Double check that all your text is 0.5" from TRIM edge including Header and Footer

- [ ] Have you printed test pages on a local computer?

- [ ] Does your file meet the needs of your printer (Print-on-Demand AND Offset printers)

- [ ] Viewing for Web and Emails PDF - Did you save a "Reduced Size" PDF version?

- [ ] Has your customer signed off and reviewd the document before uploading to vendors?

BOOK TITLE: _____

SUBTITLE: _____

SAVING CHECKLIST

☐ A copy of the Manuscript or text file in a DOC, DOCX, RTF file that you used

☐ All the images in a LINKS or IMAGES folder

☐ Folder named after book to house all other files and folders

☐ Work files in folder (Recommend having a main one and back-up, i.e. *.indd and *idml)

☐ PDF version (2001-xa format for print-ready or print quality)

☐ EPUB (Reflowable) - optional

☐ Folder for fonts called FONT with copies of the files for future (they can go obsolete later)

☐ Did you save in the correct color profile (CMYK, RGB, 240% CMYK, etc)?

☐ Did you run ADA Compliance check in Adobe for ADA PDF needs? (optional)

☐ Do you need to convert EPUB to MOBI? (Consider using Calibre or similar converters)

☐ Has someone reviewed the file for issues besides you?

☐ Are the Header and Footers showing the correct text?

☐ Is your Table of Contents correct and numbered or not missing a chapter?

☐ Do your images bleed to the BLEED edge pass the TRIM edge?

☐ Double check that all your text is 0.5" from TRIM edge including Header and Footer

☐ Have you printed test pages on a local computer?

☐ Does your file meet the needs of your printer (Print-on-Demand AND Offset printers)

☐ Viewing for Web and Emails PDF - Did you save a "Reduced Size" PDF version?

☐ Has your customer signed off and reviewd the document before uploading to vendors?

Comic Books &
Graphic Novels

Not all who wander are lost.

J.R.R. Tolkien

Preparing the Manuscript

Now we are crossing into a whole new type of book that no longer concerns itself with text unless you've been asked to place the text in the dialogue balloons. This is going to reflect a lot of the same concerns as picture books with the importance of making choices in advance including illustrations, trim size, print options, and more. Knowledge in script writing and graphic design will be beneficial when creating a book of this type, but it's not necessarily a make or break deal. In short, plan on producing a book with images only on the pages and next to no need to do the textual typesetting as seen in all the book types before.

Focus on page count, trim size to match, and high resolution images

What Makes This So Different?

Materials may simply consist of only images with only the need for a few pages with front and back matter, or more exactly, title and copyright page only if any at all. Regardless, you will want to make master pages that add a header and footer to provide title, author, and page numbers (especially in graphic novels). Make sure you understand and look at samples of what the final product should look like. Comic books tend to bleed off the page with low page count while a graph novel can be big as a fiction work. Be sure to check out book that go in deeper dives on the creation of a graphic novel before diving into how to typeset one such as *The Complete Idiot's Guide to Creating a Graphic Novel* by Nat Gertler and Steve Lieber.

Choosing a Trim Size

Unlike other book types, these become very standardized with simply a normal large size and one smaller variant as common ground. It's amazing to think that all comic books (a huge majority) fall under only four sizes listed below. It's vital more than ever to meet that expectations. Granted, that doesn't mean you can't experiment, but breaking the expectation may be more harmful than helpful in getting your book to be carried in a story later on.

Common Trim Sizes

- 6.625 x 10.187 (Standard Comic Book with bleed size)
- 5.83 x 8.27 (Graphic novels and manga type books)
- 5.5 x 8.5 (Smaller variant of comic book and sometimes graphic novels)
- 5 x 7 (smaller variant for graphic novels and manga)

Font Expectations

For the first time ever, you can use Comic Sans. Granted, that's if you are even using font at all as the typesetter. If you are filling in the dialogue balloons, using fonts that reflect the staple or expectation is a must. Comic Sans isn't the only choice, and I encourage exploring handwriting and architect-based font faces if you wish to find cleaner and a variant of this style. Using sans-serifs are always great for this book type, but depending on the topic and even the setting of the book. A futuristic book should have cyber inspired fonts while a medieval fantasy might find serif fonts more complementary. Use your judgment and experiment with test pages for best results!

Maximum Word and Page Counts

Page count becomes a very big deal in this genre and book type. Again, I can't express enough the importance of seeking out books on creating graphic novels and comic books to understand the industry standards and reader expectations. Below I've gathered the more common page count expectations and divided them into two groups to help you know where your book might fall among these. This book isn't intended to explain why and when; instead, it will provide a snapshot for those ready to pull together their book for designing and publishing.

- Comic books come in multiples of 4:
  - 8 (min for Saddle-Stitch)
  - 16
  - 24 (20 pages of plot plus ads and title pages)
  - 32 (roughly has 100 words per page)
  - 64
  - 92 (max for Saddle-Stitch binding)
  - 96
  - 188 (approx. 12,800-word count)

- Graphic Novel and Manga:
  - 60
  - 120 (Thick enough for titling and logo on spine)
  - 250 (Recommended max per book/volume)
  - 500
  - 576 (Higher page counts usually have black and white and lighter paper to offset cost)

Materials and Print Options

Note in the page count, there are notes about binding. For the first time in all the options, this is where the realm of binding options is split between saddle stitch and perfect bound. Most comic books are saddle stitched, most noted for the stapling of pages with no spine for text. As they get into larger variants or transition into graphic novels and manga, they start to be perfect bound. When choosing your printing options, be sure that they can provide the binding type your book needs. Not everyone provides saddle stitch. Another notable print option is the need for 70 lb. or higher paper with standard to premium color options. If you can, semi-gloss to gloss paper is common for high quality comics, but for those trying to limit costs or lower retail price, you may want to default to standard color, 50-70 lb. matte paper, or even consider a black and white style seen in large graphic novels and manga most often. This all falls back to identifying what kind of book you are creating!

ILLUSTRATIONS, ILLUSTRATORS, & GRAPHIC DESIGNERS

If you know your trim size and orientation, then you're now ready to decide on how you want to create your illustrations. Some authors illustrate their books themselves, but that's not an option for others. You have a few options in this matter, and it's highly dependent on the type of book you're making such as a picture book, middle grade book, or textbook. If you are planning to hire someone to help you create and format your book, consider seeking out a graphic designer or illustrator who is knowledgeable in typesetting or at least picture book layouts. They will be able to incorporate and go through more steps with you as your guide. If you do this yourself, be sure to take your time to read the content in the Picture Book section for information specifically for making one and how to best prepare before starting.

Every book type has its own tweaks to the system or may have areas that are a must for one and not the others. If you intend to gather illustrations to give to a typesetter or format yourself, seek out an illustrator who draws in a style you enjoy and within the price range you need. They will not only need to be aware of the trim size and orientation for a picture book, but they need to include room for a 0.25" to 0.5" cutaway bleed so your core image doesn't get chopped when printed. For illustrations added to a section of a single page, you just simply need an image slightly bigger than intended use for best quality when it prints.

If your illustrator is using a physical median (watercolor, markers, acrylics, etc.) over digital painting, make sure you pass on information for file type, resolution (DPI), color mode, and so on. The more information you provide, the easier it is for them to give you the correct variant of scans. If they aren't able to provide you with scans, I recommend hiring an art photographer. If your median is light colored or watercolors, you should consider digitally enhancing the coloration, performing a black/white balance, and checking the levels of said image. In the end, do not expect those colors to match or look the same as the original as there is a loss of detail, texture, and shift in colors that is impossible to recreate by the time it prints in the book.

No matter the book, there is a standard need for file type and settings here when you aim to use images in your book.

- These files should be in CMYK color mode
- Saved at 300-600 DPI (resolution)
- Be in these file types: JPEG, PNG, or TIFF

You can also utilize PDF and export out to image or place as PDF but be mindful most software will be converting all these into a more manageable JPEG format. Sticking with JPEG and saving editable originals can be very effective in keeping overall file size for the PDF and eBook formats down to acceptable levels. This often comes into play with vendors with files size maximums, such as Barnes & Noble requiring eBooks to be 20 MB or below.

What if you can't find an illustrator or have funding restrictions? There's another possibility! Prepare to go on a deep search and rethink your initial book design. Stock photo sites are a wonderful resource for those who can't afford the illustrators or struggling to find one. This includes ShutterStock, DepositPhoto, iStockPhoto, Adobe Stock, and many more sites have a variety of artists who submit sheets and multiple images of characters for all audiences. A fitting example of this is the character you see throughout Writer's Bane! The more active an artist is on these sites, the better chance for the collection to grow and pull from. Some give you a means to reach out to them as well! You can always reach out to them and see if they will also commission pieces.

BASICS OF DIGITALLY ENHANCING ILLUSTRATIONS

Thanks to the digital age, many artists or illustrators have taken to producing art via software. This has made it a better means to reproduce images in a higher brilliance and sharper hues. That doesn't mean hand drawn artwork and watercolors can't join this high-tech advantage. Traditional art can be scanned or photographed to be pulled into the digital realm and in some cases, adjusted. This doesn't come without its share of pros and cons. One being the most common is the lack of capturing texture, hues, or even soft pencil strokes that all-too-often get washed out by the scanner or camera's light. If your art is too big to scan, an art photographer should be able to use a black/white balance card and even adjust and check it.

Once an image has been placed in digitally, you or a design have the freedom to adjust the image as needed. This can be moving elements, changing hues, brightening the overall saturation, and even resetting black and white tones to make richer levels so the image prints sharper. If you can apply a lot of these easy tricks to an image and balance the CMYK spectrum to a richer level, it will make a huge difference when printed. Not every image or color will be able to translate well; for example, blues and purples are often a struggle to lock in without shifting when ink is laid to paper.

WARNING ABOUT WATERCOLORS

Out of all the medians your illustrations can be made from, this one comes with a loss of detail and color just from scanning or photographing it. From there, it sways again depending on the options you choose. If you are ok with digitizing and drastically shifting your watercolors for print and not looking to match the original artwork, you will feel this impact the least. As for those looking to match it and capture the watercolor pieces as they are, you won't get this result. First, the act of scanning or taking a photo removes the texturing that watercolors often have, as well removing some of the sharpness and overlapping details. From there, I recommend offset printing with gloss or semi-gloss paper at about 100+lb. paper with alcohol-based printing for closest match to original work. If you decide to move forward with Print-on-Demand, be warned that you will continue to lose vibrancy and details due to the fact only matte paper is available and most are water-based ink printing and may cause saturation issues. This becomes most noticeable with a picture-book printer in Print-on-Demand.

BLACK AND WHITE BALANCE

If you are using Photoshop, Fire Alpaca, or some other photo editing software, you should be able to do this. Many of the photography editing software may be able to assist with this technique as well as the others to follow. Whichever software you use, there should be tutorials out there to assist you best as far as this book goes, the aim is to explain what it's meant to do and hint as to why you might want to apply this to your own formatting and images. As for this one, it helps establish true black and true white on the image and adjusts the image color range accordingly. Often when we scan an image, the black has a shine to it and might come off as a dark gray or even brown. This gives you a chance to "reset" the expectations and identify where these are on the image if you have both visible.

It's important to decide in advance if this is a high page count black and white manga OR a low page count full color that might need to be offset printed.

LEVELS IN SPECTRUM

Images come with levels that spread a variety of hues and channels. Often black and white being on opposite ends, they come with slight dips beyond the peak of these colors that can take away from the overall sharpness of the image spectrum. Cutting out or knocking them to the peaks or using auto levels features can bring an image to pop more visually.

HUE & SATURATION

Hue and saturations levels or using filters that shift these can do a wide range for an image. If the colors seem to have washed out, you might be able to recover faded colors using this feature. Also scanned or photographed images may have washed out and either you can darken the hue values or even adjust contrast and brightness settings to recover the look of the original artwork. Sometimes this setting allows a moment for you to change the hue or coloration of the art and make decisions you normally would have missed out on. Using a masked layer stacked with this can even allow you to change a color on a single item in the image, but that's best for a tutorial as it delves into photo editing and is beyond this book's conversation focused on typesetting.

DPI, IMAGE SIZE, AND RESOLUTION ADJUSTMENTS

The resolution of an image is very important! The first aspect to this is the size. You don't need your image to be 44 inches by 21 inches if your book is only 11 inches by 8.5 inches. If you are bleeding images off the edge, the image needs to only be 11.25 inches by 8.75 inches at the very least to give some room for image placement that allows bleed and trim. It's always smart to have the image slightly bigger, but too large and it may cause the program or computer to crash (especially those on personal or home systems). It also makes saving backups or throwing it on a cloud storage much more feasible.

Image must be 300-600 DPI to print clear and free of blurring or pixelation!

Once the size is within a reasonable range (exact with bleed or slightly larger in the same orientation or ratio), you need to make sure the resolution is set between 300-600 DPI. Anything under 300 is at risk to pixelate or be blurry. Know that most images saved from internet are usually only 72-96 DPI, so make sure what you are saving is the full image and not a smaller web version or down-sampled variant. Images that are over 600 DPI are at risk of the printer shrinking and may result in unwanted quality or results. It's always best to avoid these sorts of situations and keep the control and final product in your hands.

CMYK, grayscale, or black and white color options are all great choices!

CMYK VERSUS RGB

Print and physical books are printed using CMYK colorations. This uses a set amount of cyan, magenta, yellow, and black layered on the page. Depending on the printer this can be applied with alcohol or water-based inks and vary in brightness (often influenced by the paper chosen). Water based inks are limited to 240% CMYK saturation level with paperweights at 70lbs or less as seen in Print-on-Demand applications.

IMAGE NAMING

Be sure to be consistent or concise with how you are naming your images. You can do this in a number of ways which includes consecutively (image01, image20, image03...), by location (Chapter01, Chapter02_SUBHEAD, Chapter02_Figure1.1), or labelled by what they are (Flowers01, RosesAndBees, AuntMayAndHerPig...). You should always avoid using symbols and spaces since these may cause issues in final formats. Depending on your software and how you export for eBook format, having images with names that include open spaces, dollar signs ($), hashtags (#), and similar often will cause them not to load or fail when uploaded to a vendor. I highly recommend using only alphabet and numbers with underscore if need be. In programming we do this as well and often default to camelCase (LittleTimmysWagon, IHateThisPictureTheMost, ImageNameLikeThis...) as the safest means to prevent programming errors.

IMAGE FILE TYPES

Images come in a variety of types and the best ones to use for publishing are JPEG and TIFF formats. You can use a PNG, which preserves the transparency unlike JPEG or even a PDF file. You should keep these between 300-600 DPI and at least a little larger than the intended size to make sure you have room to trim the image if needed. TIFF is considered the best format and has been used in the printing and graphic design world as the superior option. Most Print-on-Demand printers want the files saved in PDF2001XA format, and this converts images to JPEG. Same thing happens when exporting to EPUB; the images are often converted to JPEG or PNG depending on what you are using. Thus, it is recommended to save in JPEG for several reasons, including the fact it's a smaller size, translates into eBook without issues, and prevents any issues when converting to final PDF format changes to the images.

PERMISSIONS & USAGE RIGHTS

Images and artwork can fall under public domain rights, but if they don't, you will need to purchase usage rights or get permission. If you pulled your images from a service like ShutterStock or similar stock photo site, they usually have different levels you can purchase for usage rights. This is the safest means for images and artwork. If you intend to hire an illustrator, be sure to cover the usage and contract with them how books are sold and their images will be used from the book to creating swag, bookmarks, banners, and more. Some may clear you for using the images in the book only and not for marketing materials. Be sure to add the permissions granted in the copyright section or even an illustration rights section as a type of appendix. It's always best to give credit where it's due on your copyright page at the very least.

Designing the Pages

Much like with picture books, you are focusing on how the images are laid out on the pages, whether they will bleed or fall within a template or master page with a header and footer. This all comes down to identifying which type of book you are making. If you are tasked with placing images within a comic book layout, you will find Photoshop and similar software your best bet to create these and place.

Comic Book and Graphic Novel Layouts

This is where things get tricky. A lot of graphic design and art should be down in advance, but in the case you need to pull together the components, let's talk about what that might look like. You will need to use a layout and layers to aid you, and in some cases PhotoShop or similar programs might be your best option. This is so you can mask and layer the work as needed and save as an image out to import in for typeset for best results, especially if you intend on making an eBook version of the comic or graphic novel. Regardless, you will be creating custom line boxes and elements with the images provided with storyboards to assist how they should be put together. Luckily, there are plenty of premade templates, boxes, dialogue balloons and similar available as stock images and highly encouraged to use them as a jumping board. There are also manga or comic focus software that can also come in handy in these scenarios.

Evenly Divided Span

This is a comic that has 4-6 even squares on a page for the comic to exist. This is the most simplistic and easier to manage design-wise and most common seen as short one-shot scripts for web or social media originally and later printed once enough have been produced.

Classic Comic or Static Layout

Panels and diagonal and white spaced borders abound. These premade layouts can be grabbed up from stock photo or premade toolbox of templates to drag and drop as you see fit. These don't breakout beyond the intended margins, nothing bleeds off the page and always tend to have a page number at the least and sometimes headers.

Modern or Dynamic Layout

Now we are bleeding off the page in area of when emphasizing aspects of the story. In most modern comic books all the images usually do this or add characters taking up a third of a two-page layout to break the static or monotonous vibe of the former style. These work great for action-packed stories.

Full Spread Layout

The image or text (not both) stretches across 2 pages, a left and right page, to show as one large landscape image or two pages of textual content. In a lot of cases the text may only be present on one page and not the other, but other layouts might have several spots all around the image to show the story unfolding in a sequence or multi-action spread.

Rule of Thirds Spread Layout

Across a two-page span, an image, graph, or pull quote will cover one complete page and a portion of the adjacent page to leave room on a far left or right edge for font to place. In concept, the object is using two-thirds of the design area to draw the eye to the text or away from the text by doing so. The Rule of Thirds is often used in marketing, print design, or even in filming. It splits the viewing area into thirds from top to bottom and side to side. From this point, you break the content and subject matter up at the key sections to help draw the eye in a certain direction or pull it towards or away.

Split Design Image & Text Page Layout

Again, this is similar to the Image + Text layout seen in picture books and textbooks. On a single page, whether it's the right or left, the image and text split the space. Sometimes this is done in a 50/50 spit, or a two-thirds split, but often features a white space or colored space where the text will be. Again, this is an older means of designing a picture book, but it may be useful elsewhere.

Whitespace Page Layout

This page is often an indicator of a chapter starting or ending. Sometimes it can be a section or partition marker of some kind. It's notorious for having a lot of white space or empty, unused space on the page spread. What little content is there usually is a textual guide to inform the reader in preparation of something changing or a transition within the book. You see this a lot in textbooks and fiction books with right page only chapter starts.

EXAMPLES OF MANUSCRIPTS

Below is a list of different ways you may receive or set a manuscript up. The most common in the industry are the first two options: Textual Only and Text with Image Placement. From chapter books to textbooks, these are the typical format you will receive the textual content for typesetting. As you venture into workbooks, picture books, comic books, and graphic novels, you will want to use story bounce, detailed format, storyboarding, or script styles to capture all the parts. Unlike text-based or heavy books, these require guidance and cues as to where images or text should be placed on a page to accurately tell the story intended. Each book type will lean more so on one kind of manuscript, and it's important to be aware of this as you prep your manuscript for typesetting. This can be a huge influence on how well key elements are designed, whether you intend to format your own book or hand your book to someone else. The most common manuscript types you will be provided are going to be script and storyboarding. This is due to the need to provide more instruction or panel-by-panel guidance rather than providing text to format.

SCRIPT

Script writing is nothing like any other manuscript format you will encounter. This is mostly for video adaptation, plays, animation, comics, and graphic novels. In terms of typesetting, the most common scenario of receiving a manuscript written in this style will be for comics and graphic novels. This should tell you where images fall, and the textual content expected. Unlike the narrative and transitional paragraphs seen in normal textual content, this simplifies and divides the content into key elements. Settings, characters, scenes, camera angles, and dialogue are all broken out to be loud on the pages with special caps and indentations.

Be sure to meet or design side-by-side with your artist, author, and typesetter. Communication and storyboards can help pull the script together best so that the pages and visuals are in the right order per the author's intended visions. You can find free software to aid in script writing such as *Celtx.com* or books that can aid such as *Save the Cat! The Last Book on Screenwriting You'll Ever Need* by Blake Snyder. For comic books and graphic novels in specific, I recommend *The Art of Comic Book Writing* by Mark Kneece and *The Complete Idiot's Guide to Creating a Graphic Novel* by Nat Gertler and Steve Lieber.

STORY BOUNCE

This simply is stating what goes where in the manuscript as it bounces through the story beats or pages. Be mindful of how much textual content you are providing on pages and identify which image to be used concisely. For example, a manuscript using this format might appear like this:

- Title page (right)
- Copyright (left) with Dedication
- Image01 at the top, small
- Dedicated to all the kids who seek an adventure of their own
- Copyright 1999 Author J. Smith etc.
- Page 1 (right) Image02
- "Wow, the world sure is big when I'm all alone," marveled John.
- Page 2 & 3 (spread) Image03
- John lost his dog when they moved. His mommy decided it was time little John Wick got a new puppy. Today, they would visit the animal shelter!
- Page 4 (left) Image04 & Image05
- Image04: John couldn't believe the amount of doggies who needed homes.

```
TLE HERE BY AUTHOR NAME

.IOR OF INTERNET CAFE. JAMIE IS SITTING AT A TABLE WITH
OMPUTER, MINI-CAFETERIA AREA.

ly walks in and sits down. Jamie slides the hot tea he
ed for her closer to her.

                    BEVERLY
          Why are we meeting here again?

                    JAMIE
          Give me a minute.

's eyes start to glow steel green.

                    BEVERLY
          (whispering) Are you kidding me?
          That's illegal to do-

ises a hand to silence her, casually drinking his
e. She puffs her cheeks in frustration.

                    JAMIE
          What if I told you this is the second
          time I caught someone trying to hack
          YOUR system from here?

                    BEVERLY
          Wh-what?

                    JAMIE
          So, what is project Greenbacks anyhow?

                    BEVERLY
          And here I thought this was going to
          be a legitimate date...
```

- Image05: Barking and bouncing, each one was excited to see him.
- Page 5 (right) Image06
  - They came in so many shapes, sizes, and colors. None of them reminded him of his old doggy Daisy.

Note how there is no mistake where in the book these images and their text go as you 'flip through' the book. It's important to leave nothing out while keeping your instructions consistent and cohesive with same naming methods and delivery. This gives the typesetter a little room for choosing where content falls and to adjust content if needed based on images and text needed on each spread. You can even leave it up to the typesetter to decide which keywords they emphasize or encourage them to do so.

DETAILED FORMAT

This is for authors who have something more specific in mind for placement, including giving instructions as to where the textual content falls and may give a variety of more in-depth directions. For comparison, this would be the above example with additional bullets where a greater level of instructions addresses text locations, specialty font changes, and even image placement for a variety of page layout styles. In this example, words in bold are assumed to need font or artistic touch to emphasize the word's meaning and provide visual clues for early readers.

- Font Face: Palatin Kids
- Size 24 where possible
- Emphasize highlighted words artfully
- Title page (right)
- Copyright (left) with Dedication
  - Image01 at the top, small
  - Text in larger font, italics:
    - Dedicated to all the kids who seek an adventure of their own
  - Copyright 1999 Author J. Smith etc.
- Page 1 (right) Image02
  - Text on the bottom of page
    - "Wow, the **world** sure is **big** when I'm all **alone**," marveled John.
- Page 2 & 3 (spread) Image03
  - Text on top left
    - John lost his dog when they moved. His mommy decided it was time little **John Wick got a new puppy**.
    - Text on bottom right
    - Today, they would visit the **animal shelter**!
- Page 4 (left) Image04 & Image05

  - Top left Image04: John couldn't believe the amount of **doggies** who needed **homes**.
  - Bottom right Image05: **Barking** and **bouncing**, each one was excited to see him.
- Page 5 (right) Image06
  - Text at top of page:
    - They came in so many **shapes, sizes**, and **colors**.
    - Text on bottom of page:
    - None of them reminded him of his old doggy **Daisy**.

STORYBOARDING

When it comes to picture books, I highly recommend this method or combining one of the above with this as a visual guide or blueprint. You can print, cut, and paste the elements to rough out the entire book's look and feel. This is a fantastic way to build a mockup of the book you intend to make and format for print and give concise expectations to a typesetter or experiment with what you had in mind for the final product. Before starting digitally, this allows you to troubleshoot issues that may need you to adjust text and illustrations prior to formatting the book. Most issues found this way are still relatively easy to fix by simply changing methods, book options, or changing fonts and images. Storyboarding can also be a great means to discover how many images you will need the illustrator to make as well as to where they need to be mindful of page edges and space for text to overlay. The following types of issues can be revealed at a glance by this method:

- Illustrations not allowing enough space for text to overlay
- Images that have the characters too close to the edge and will be cut when stretched to the bleed edge and cross the trim
- Images that have text as part of the image in need of adjusting to fit trim
- Trim size and orientation versus illustration size and orientation
- Amount of text for the page (too much is the common issue)
- Number of illustrations needed
- Amount of pages the story needs
- Story page flip and how that impacts the reader and story

STORYBOARD

PICTURE [_____]   **ACTION** [_____]

_____
_____
_____
_____
_____
_____
_____

PICTURE [_____]   **ACTION** [_____]

_____
_____
_____
_____
_____
_____
_____
_____

PICTURE [_____]   **ACTION** [_____]

_____
_____
_____
_____
_____
_____
_____

PICTURE [_____]   **ACTION** [_____]

_____
_____
_____
_____
_____
_____
_____
_____

PROJECT TITLE: _____   GENRE: _____

STORYBOARD - LANDSCAPE

STORYBOARD - PORTRAIT

STORYBOARD — SQUARE

PROJECT TITLE: _____   GENRE: _____

COMIC STORYBOARD

COMIC STORYBOARD

PROJECT TITLE: _____ GENRE: _____

COMIC STORYBOARD

COMIC STORYBOARD

PROJECT TITLE: _____ GENRE: _____

COMIC STORYBOARD

COMIC STORYBOARD

FORMATTING THE BOOK

Hooray! Now that we've talked and prepped this thing to no end, you should be ready to format this book with confidence. Why? Because it is so much easier to resolve problems at the manuscript and prepping stage than when you are formatting and making the book. Though, as said before, I am an avid user of word to InDesign, I will do my best throughout the book to provide information in an all-encompassing and design angle. If you were looking for software tutorial, this isn't the book for you. Getting detailed instructions on how to set parameters in Word, Scribd, and similar word processors isn't the aim.

Instead, we will be focusing on the typesetter-based elements and areas that will be par the course for any book you design. Dependent on the software you are using to design your book in could present its own issues and information may be labeled slightly different or found in different areas. In tandem with a software book, this book may provide some keywords in order to gain the affects you were aiming for in order for you to gain a greater value out of using said programs. In my years of looking for instructional manuals for book design, most of what I have learned was via videos, trial and error, typography college courses, and simply diving into the industry headlong with an open mind and understanding of the roots of publishing and its history. It probably also helped I delved in some game design, development, and programming, so I could troubleshoot creative solutions.

Without further ado, it's time to make this book using these step-by-step, or page-by-page instructions below. Feel free to adjust this to suit your own style and needs since there are various methods to achieve the results seen here. Again, the aim here is to simply the process while being able to make quality print books, enhance eBooks, and create a PDF that falls close as possible to being ADA compliant (Americans with Disabilities Act).

FILE SETUP

The file or page size should match the trim size in width and height. Make sure the intended orientation matches what you intended, specifically landscape versus portrait. Depending on the program, you may have to set bleed settings to include a 0.125" bleed on all sides or for outer margins. For some Print-on-Demand vendors, they may want the inner margin to have no bleed since this is the side of the page that is glued to the spine of the book. You usually get to set up or define the overall margins as well.

Be mindful that with picture books you will be saving a flat PDF for eBook design and that you don't have to fret over threading text boxes together as seen with all other book types. It's more important to make sure images are bleeding off to the marked edges just pass the trim edge, that elements are layered and overlayed in the right order, and textual content is within the margins provided by the printer or Print-on-Demand requirements of 0.5" from trim size edge. Here are my recommended settings for this book type:

- Industry Standard Numbers:
  - 0.125" Bleed from trim edge
  - 0.5" Margin for content inward from trim edge
  - Large page counts will require a larger 0.625" or higher inner margin or gutter
  - Special binding may change the needs for inner margins

- Inner or inside margin: 0.625" for books under 300 pages and

- 0.75" to 0.8" for books pushing far into the 500+ range since where the pages' bind needs more space to avoid words falling into the crack of the book.
  - Granted, this is a picture book, and you can sometimes get away with a 0.5" margin.
  - Outer or outside margins (including top and bottom) should be 0.5" to 0.625"
    - Typically have main body pages with header and footer set and you can increase the top and bottom margins to 0.8-0.875" to give yourself space to place and space these from your body text.

- For Comic Books Graphic Novels:
  - Margins only apply to page numbers, textual content, and similar.

- Images in a majority of cases bleed off the page.
- 0.5" margin on all sides for an 18- to 34-page book is more than enough for Perfect Bound or Saddle Stitch books.
- 0.625"-0.75" inner margin will be needed for graphic novels pushing over 100+ pages and be perfect bound.

Wondering where these numbers come from? Your vendors should have File Creation Guides via a PDF or webpage. No matter if you plan on using offset printing, KDP, IngramSparks, or a similar vendor, these parameters never change. This is the basic needs of a file going to print and will give the press some wiggle room. These parameters will change if you choose more elaborate binding and use certain presses. Always make sure you get these settings from the printer and design the book with these in place from the start.

USING LAYERS

Most of the layout software allows you to create layers such as InDesign (not any of the word processors though they do have header footer options). These come in handy in keeping content stacked or arranged in the right order. This includes making sure watermarks are below the body text layer and even keeping the header and footer elements on the top and not lost behind images and such. A bonus to using this feature is the ability to lock them and make sure you don't accidently change, move, or delete them unintentionally. With picture books, you often use images that take up the entire page and risk losing these elements completely. Recommended layers include the following listed in the order they should fall and usage:

Fonts are going to mimic strong handwriting that's very legible. Architectural fonts may be a good alternative here!

- **Header and Footer Layer** – This will have your top layer text boxes that contain the header and footer which usually hold page numbers, title, author, and/or current chapter. You can control these with master pages. In a word processor, this is an option or specific setting that is influenced by section breaks to change how they look from section to section of the book's layout.

- **Default or Body Text Layer** – Here you will manage the primary text box in which the main content autoflows through threaded textboxes or pages.

- **Background Layer** – At the bottom of the list, there should be a background layer that is designed for images, spreads, and watermarks that need to fall under the textual content.

This doesn't mean you need to use all these layers, but it's highly recommended to give you more control when formatting. If the program you are using doesn't provide layers, check for features that define objects on the page as needing to be "Ordered" or "Arranged" with sub-options for "Bring to Front" or "Bring to Back," which mimic what layering does. This should aid you in making sure text and images overlap appropriately.

Master Pages

These pages, or templates, are premade pages you can drag and drop into the layout to help speed things along and stay consistent. Know that this is more commonly found as a feature in layout software such as InDesign. Even with a freeform style book, there's a level of consistency with placement of elements such as header, footer, page numbers, watermarks, and other elements that you may not want to shift and wish to keep level throughout the book. In any book, you are going to be applying a few key layout pages. I recommend the following master pages or templates be made in advance to speed up the typeset process:

- **A blank page** with only the margin lines set. You may include a primary text box version for dedication or anchoring title page images into place. Works great for print-on-demand with that last page needing to be blank as well. These will also set your title pages and copyright page as well.

- **A body page** made of a blank page with only the header and footer with a main text box. I recommend putting the header and footer on a top layer that's locked. Predesign a left and right page, often featuring the book title on left and author name on right. You may even design a running header or chapter header that auto updates depending on the software you are using. Adding glyphs and art to page numbers and headers can add a nice creative flair.

- **A chapter start page** that can add art, designs, and spacing shifts to accommodate the style implied. I always make right and left page versions, so if I need to change from right page only chapters to continuous, it's ready to adapt accordingly.

- **A numbered blank page** can be useful for areas that may contain images, maps, tables, and similar content where you simply want page numbers only.

- **Worksheets or Special Pages** should be designed or a foundation premade or decided on before getting too far into the design. Prepping these pages in advance can help in your efforts and provide a sense of how much space they truly need in order to interact with the content as your design the book.

- **A two-column body page or variants** can provide a means to design smart and save on page count where you can. Also, two-column pages can provide easier means to place images as often seen in textbooks, reference books, and workbooks alike.

- **Section breaks** become vital for non-fiction books. Occasionally these hard pages or spreads have an image or color to help standout when certain passing of time, events, topics, and provide a sense of dividers for the reader. Prepping a page or spread for these can save time and provide consistency when applicable.

Font Choices and Prep

Font has the most weight in typesetting and interior book design. Your choices and attention to detail to the spacing, size, and types will have a significant impact for better or worse. There are a few things you can do to help yourself prep and streamline your design depending on if you are using styles in Microsoft Word or a combination of Paragraph and Character styles in Adobe InDesign. Prepping and setting up pre-saved files with master pages and these elements can save a lot of hunting and frustrations, especially if you want to shift or change fonts later. If you intend to do typesetting full time or work heavily with fonts, I recommend investing into Font Management programs such as FontExplorer. This can make it easier to keep your growing library from bogging down your computer while making it easier to test out and organize fonts.

Paragraph Styles or Styles

These will make up most of the formatting application in textual content. They work in particular order and repeat as you start a new section or chapter. Making a style in advance can help you quickly adjust, fix, or change the entire typeset without hunting and pecking for certain content in the book. Instead, applying a style and changing the style can shift and fix the book as a whole.

- **Body Text –** This will be the majority of your content. It should be a legible font comfortable for readers and remain the same throughout the entire book. It builds the font foundation for Drop Caps, Citations/ Quotes, Subheads, Tables and more.

- **Dialogue Text –** Any time font is in a dialogue bubble, it should be in a handwritten or architect style font. The most infamous of these is Comic Sans. This should be a paragraph style or character style depending on the way you want to typeset the comic book or graphic novel. Regardless picking a consistent size, spacing, and similar can make it easier to read.

- **Boxed Text –** This is for text that is placed in a predesigned box or similar graphics that can sometimes be programmed into these. Keep it consistent if it's a sans-serif or serif font. This often should mimic similar size or spacing as the body or dialogue text depending on the type of book you are making.

Character Styles or Subfamily fonts

Creating premade character style can help you gain more control on the style of the manuscript as a whole. It also helps build coding within certain programs for eBook creation and keeps these vital aspects from disappearing in the process.

- **Bold** – used to identify keywords, bring words to the front, and stand out louder. There is never a need to make a whole manuscript bold. Instead, choose a thicker or heavier font.

- *Italics* – this has many uses from quotes, to signaling key elements in content, and even to signal internal dialogue in stories.

- <u>Underline</u> – much like bold, this is used to make content stand out, signify a reference (depending on styles like APA), hyperlinks (or clickable content in text), or signal something of importance.

- Keyword – This comes in handy when wanting to stay consistent in font face and size changes in books where you need vocabulary words or key visuals to pop.

- Small Caps – Common to see in reference works or to address religious names or keywords, this is easier to manage as a character style and carries over into eBook better.

- **Dialogue Text –** Any time font is in a dialogue bubble it should be in a handwritten or architect style font. The most infamous of these is Comic Sans.

Object Styles or Table Styles

These are special styles that influence objects, images, and tables. They make sure designs and placement match and can even streamline how items show up in an eBook. Not every software has the means to define these or set them up. As for InDesign, these can help guide image frames, table cells, and more so that you can save time when adding content into the layout and saving you the grief of cracking open object options to adjust every detail. This can make placing key images or comic pages easier with auto-snap or placement options as seen in InDesign. Always explore the software you intend to typeset in and the ways it can aid you in your work.

PAGE-BY-PAGE

It's taken a lot of discussion and information to get to here, but as you take your time and refer back to key sections, you will find ways to improve and prepare. Be sure to take your time to prep your materials to avoid unwanted stress and troubleshooting for this stage. It can raise the hours this may take you to typeset, or format, exponentially no matter what your skill level may be. As an author doing your own formatting, these issues might be easier to solve on the fly, and if you intend on hiring someone or formatting for someone, this can bring production to a screeching halt until a decision or solution is made.

THE CHECKLIST!

Here is a checklist that should help you make sure you finished prepping the manuscript and materials before starting the formatting. Often we don't think to ask or double check to include some of these things and it can be detrimental in the final stages leading up to printing the actual book. Whether you are formatting your own book or formatting someone else's, this checklist is to help you gather everything you need before you start.

- Trim Size
- Book Title
- Subtitle
- Author Name (or Pen Name)
- Publisher and/or Logo
- Copyright Page
  - Author name and copyright year
  - Name illustrator, designer, editor, etc.
  - Permissions for any materials used.
  - Public domain or scripture cited.
  - ISBN numbers (Paperback, Hardcover, eBook, Audiobook, etc.)
  - LCCN (Pending or number)
  - Published information and logo
  - The usual legal jargon to protect you, your work, and the publisher.
- Front Matter
  - Foreword: Yes or No
  - Dedication: Yes or No
    - Above Copyrights or Own Page
- Images are ready, clearly named, and all accounted for
  - 300 – 600 DPI
  - Correct size for trim + bleed
  - CMYK color mode
- Manuscript – Text only edition
  - Has image directions that match image names
- Back Matter
  - Author Bio
  - Image
    - Hyperlinks
    - Illustrator Bio
    - Image
    - Hyperlinks

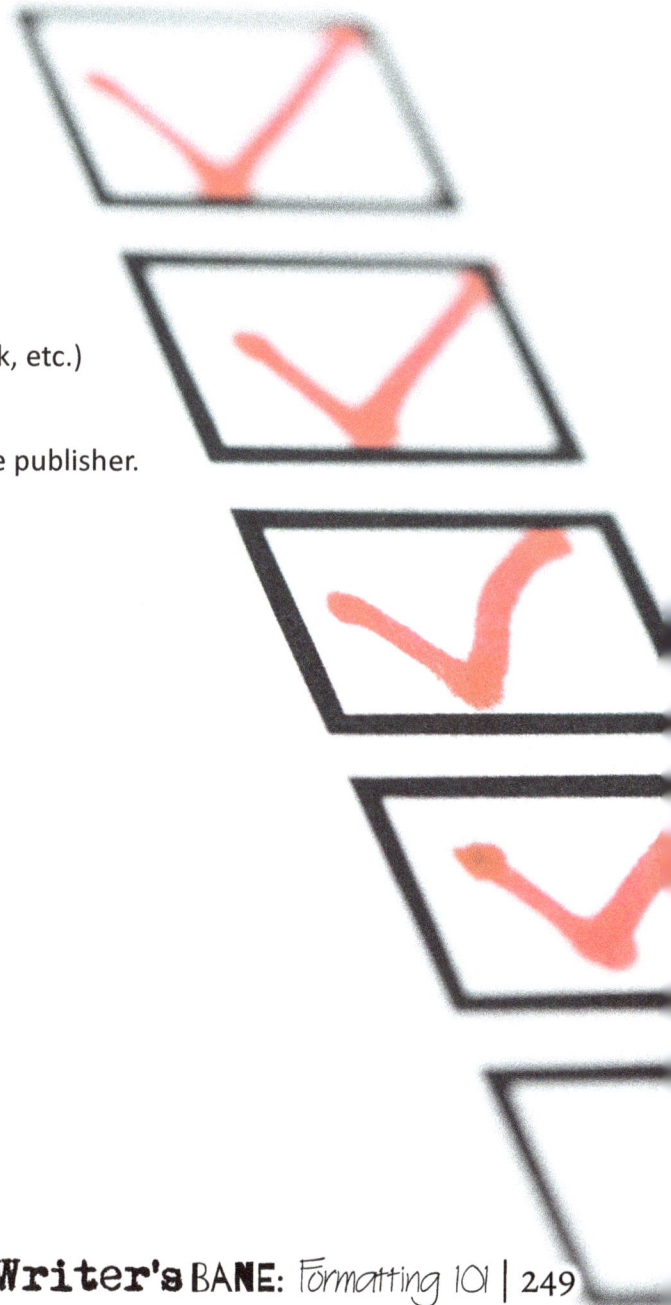

BOOK TITLE: _____

SUBTITLE: _____

TYPESET CHECKLIST

- [ ] Manuscript text in a DOC, DOCX, RTF file

- [ ] All the images listed in Manuscript present:

- [ ] CMYK mode

- [ ] Between 300-600 DPI.

- [ ] Trim Size _____ width x _____ height

- [ ] Author Pen Name - FIRST_____LAST_____

- [ ] Dedication: Yes or No

- [ ] Author Bio: Yes or No

- [ ] Copyright

- [ ] Publisher information

- [ ] Additional mention such as artist, design, or typesetter? _____

- [ ] Scriptures cited from…. Any public domain original publication mentions? _____

- [ ] Permission granted from… Any materials that have permissions needing to be listed here?

- [ ] ISBNs for Paperback: _____ Hardcover_____

- [ ] Audiobook_____ eBook_____

- [ ] LCCN pending or listed?_____

- [ ] Front Matter (Acknowledgements, Foreword, Preface, etc.)

- [ ] Do they want a Table of Contents: Yes or No

- [ ] Do they have tables to import: Yes or No

- [ ] Do they want pull quotes: Yes or No

THE WARM-UP

As mentioned in the front half of this book, the preferred method for designing books is using InDesign due to the amount of control. No matter what software you are using, the parameters and keywords are all the same and much of the process can be even reflected into when you design using a word processor, such as Microsoft© Word.

- Page size needs to be set to the trim size of your book.

- Bleed settings can always be added via page setup or page layout options depending on the program.

- Make sure page margins are keeping 0.5" within the trim or page size.

- If you intend to have headers and footers, be sure margin for body text are larger (0.75" for example) on the top and bottom to give space for them to fall within that 0.5" requirement.

- Choose your fonts in advance or make a list of possibilities for:

  - Chapter
  - Headline or Chapter Title
  - Header/Footer
  - Body Text
  - Pull Quotes

- Decide on Chapter Art or Typeset design for:

  - Spacing
  - Having samples on hand
  - Write down parameters in advance
  - Choose glyph or ornamental font options
  - Prepared images in advance

- Don't forget your checklist! You'll need it for Copyright pages and specifics!

- For comic books and graphic novels:

  - Have all images and artwork needed, labeled, and saved in the correct format.
  - Font choices have been decided including for keywords to emphasize.
  - Sketches and concept art can make things easier.
  - Pre-make foundation master pages to save time and prep for changes later.

BOOK TITLE: _____

SUBTITLE: _____

WARM-UP CHECKLIST

☐ Trim size set to the page or book size

☐ Add Bleed Settings for 0.125 inches

☐ Set your margins to 0.5 inch from trim edge

☐ Top margin for header set for 0.75 inch

☐ Bottom margin for footer set for 0.75 inch

☐ Inner margin or mirrored margins set to 0.675 omch or higher for spine/glue/page count

☐ Chapter font:_____

☐ Headline font:_____

☐ Header/Footer font:_____

☐ Body Text font:_____

☐ Pull Quote font:_____

☐ Body Text Base Font Size: _____ Line Spacing: _____

☐ Chapter Art prepped and ready to go

☐ Images saved in teh right format and size in advance

☐ Manuscript prepped and image placement clearly marked or Storyboard ready

☐ Glyph and Ornaments picked out. Font: _____

☐ Printer settings and requirements handy for saving and meeting their needs

☐ Templates or Master pages set up for key pages and special pages

☐ Paragraph Styles setup in advance or styles redesigned to match selection

☐ Are you ready?

Front Matter

This is the first few pages that typically consist of title pages, copyrights, and dedication pages. This is the beginning of a book and rarely changes much no matter the genre of the book. As we are aiming to introduce the new normal for young readers, you'll see the same elements in most books but done with some artistic value or larger fonts to draw the eyes.

Endorsements/Dear Reader

Sometimes in Romance of Non-fiction genres we will first open to a page full of blurbs, reviews, endorsements, and a statement to the reader. If it's not placed here, it sometimes shows up near the dedication or shortly after the Table of Contents. It's not uncommon to see similar pages in comic books and graphic novels too!

Full Title or Cover

Half title can feature a text title only and the full title can be the front cover of the book itself. If you decide to do a text-based version, this should have series name, title, subtitle, author name, illustrator, and publisher name and/or logo. You can even combine the two elements and create something unique like seen below. Sometimes this is skipped entirely, which puts all the pressure onto the cover!

Copyright

This will always be a left page on the back of the full title page. It should contain the normal legal jargon, author, copyright, publisher information, credits to key members (editor, designer, cover, typeset, photographer, illustrator, etc.), LCCN, ISBN, and similar information. Or even behind the cover!

Dedication/ Acknowledgment

Many books have a dedication or even acknowledgments. This should go right after the copyright page.

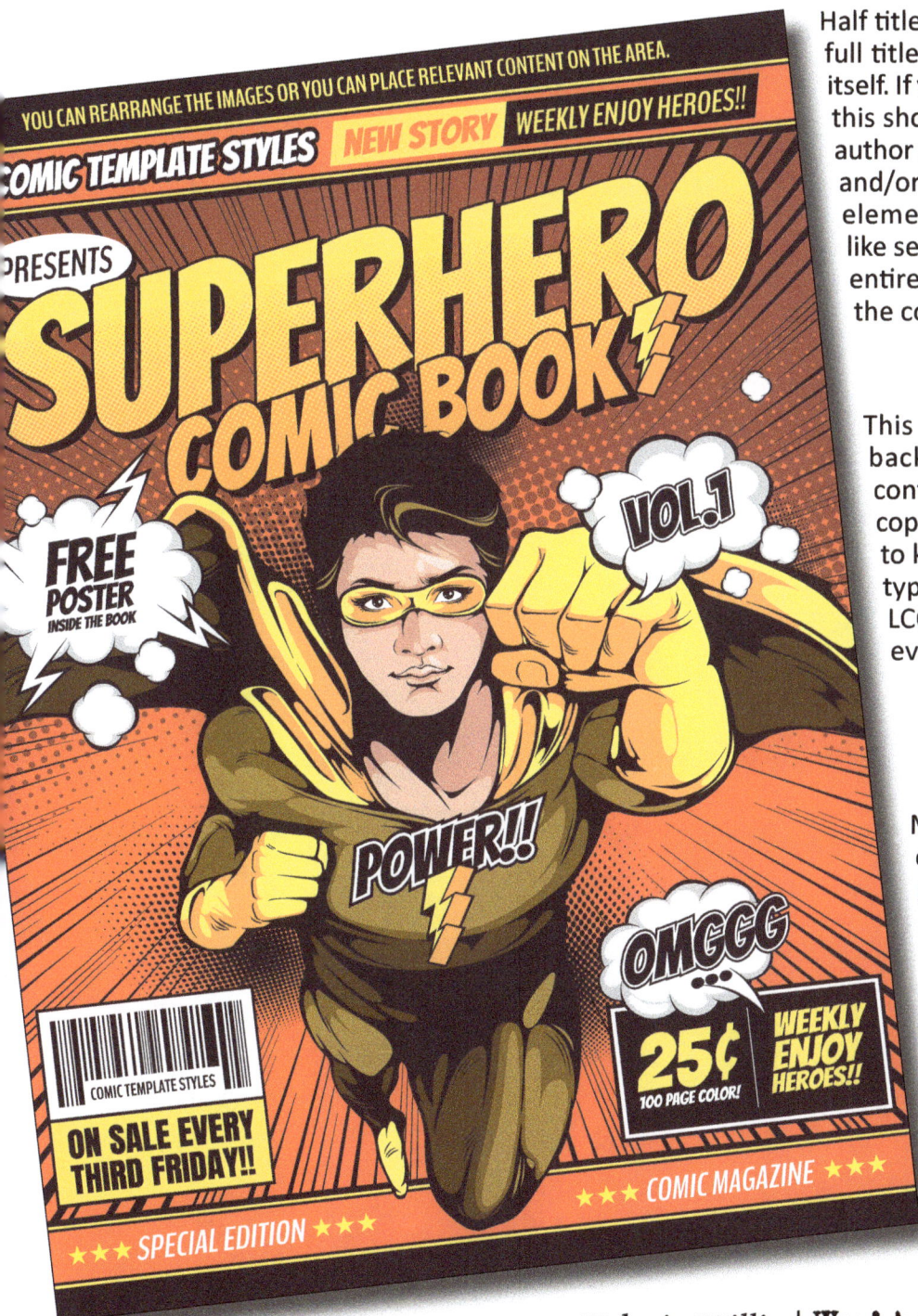

YOU CAN REARRANGE THE IMAGES OR YOU CAN PLACE RELEVANT CONTENT ON THE AREA.

COMIC TEMPLATE STYLES   NEW STORY   WEEKLY ENJOY HEROES!!

PRESENTS

SUPERHERO COMIC BOOK!

VOL.1

FREE POSTER INSIDE THE BOOK

POWER!!

OMGGG

25¢ 100 PAGE COLOR!

WEEKLY ENJOY HEROES!!

COMIC TEMPLATE STYLES

ON SALE EVERY THIRD FRIDAY!!

★★★ SPECIAL EDITION ★★★

★★★ COMIC MAGAZINE ★★★

CONTENT

This is where the core of the content will be located. These are the pages with headers, footers, and majority containing full pages of text. Be sure to set your margins so that none of the text falls into the 0.5" margin from the trim edge to prevent the printer from rejecting your book files later on.

BLEED VERSUS TEXT MARGINS

Make sure the bleed goes past the trim line or paper's edge to the end of the to the bleed line. If the signature or paper shifts in print slightly, it will cause a white line on the outer edges. Many designers place a white margin or offset the inner margins on spreads. This is dependent on the page spread, number of pages, and type of binding. For beginners you may want to default to treating this as a bleed edge. In picture books, you can push images off the page and across pages in creative ways, but when it comes to text placement, you must have it within 0.5" inch from the trim edge or paper edge. This is so if the signatures or pages shift that your textual content will never be at risk of being cutoff.

BODY TEXT SPREADS

Here you will get to double down on your header and footer design. Make sure things are updating if you decided to be fancy with auto-updating running headers. If not, the book title on the left and author to the right will always work with page numbers on the bottom. Don't be afraid to center the page numbers if you aren't sure if you are dropping content on the right and left pages. In software like InDesign, it shows you the way the book will be printed whereas Word you have to pay close attention or try adding a blank first page to offset it (But don't forget to delete it back out when you're done!).

BACK MATTER

Here you will be serving a few crucial roles or bits of information that had no place in the front or core content. For starters, this section is intended to introduce the reader to last thoughts, notes, information, resources, the author and/or illustrator, how to stay in touch, and any means to continue to connect and discover books via the author or publisher, sometimes both. It's a vital resource and a marketing tool in every book as long as the genre and audience make good use of it.

EPILOGUE, CONCLUSION, AND SIMILAR CLOSING STATEMENTS

Depending on the genre and intent, many books end with one last thing before they transition into author information. Typically, in a fiction book they may end with an epilogue that either shows a scene well in the future, sets the stage for the next book, or reflects on something unseen during the initially story that wouldn't have fit within the core content. In non-fiction books, they tend to have a conclusion or ending statement of some kind that closes up the topic covered and discussed throughout the book. It should always give the reader an idea what they should have taken away from the book after reading through it.

NOTE FROM AUTHOR

It's always a great idea to take a moment to discuss the lesson or follow up thoughts on the story you have told. This gives a moment for you to reflect and talk about things that would have spoiled the story if elaborated in a preface or revealed in the front matter. It can even show inspiration or reveal content that you didn't want the reader not to know entirely about. Not everything can be revealed in its full intent, and this gives an author time to share and have an intimate moment with their readers.

BIO FOR AUTHOR & LIST OF OTHER WORKS

It's common to see back pages that hold the biographies for the author. When it comes to this book type, it's strongly encouraged to have this in the book to help readers find your work online as well as connect and follow. This can be on the same page or on a spread across from one another. On occasion they start on their own right page. If you are working on a non-fiction book where the author is an expert in the topic, consider moving this to the front matter to show why this author is the best at discussing what the book it about. It's not uncommon on a non-fiction book to also see a smaller bio on the back cover along with the blurb to express the credibility of the content and the author writing on that particular topic.

CALL TO ACTION

This is any page or content added in the back of the book to encourage readers to do something or take action. For example, where they can follow the author, sign up for the newsletter, leave a review reminder, or grab the next book or other book series. This sometimes can be an ad for relatable services too as seen in non-fiction books!

OTHER WORKS FROM THE PUBLISHER

An older practice, but one that still has an impact. It's a great way to mimic what a newsletter swap does online, but on a physical level. Harlequin and Avon romance books were famous for doing this in the 80's and 90's and lead to cross-promoted sales between their pool of authors and books series of similar genre and plots. Many of the small publishers are reviving this practice as they see readers reveal they discovered multiple books from their publications through the books themselves.

PRINT-ON-DEMAND PAGE

If you are choosing to publish using Print-on-Demand, don't forget there will be a blank last even page in the back. This is where the printer will include a barcode that contains all the information as to where the book came from and more. Offset printed books don't have this feature at all.

OFFSET PRINTING—END LEAVES

If you are planning to offset print the book, you may have to create additional files for end leaves. I highly recommend asking for templates from your specific printer since these are done slightly differently at times depending on the book binder equipment and process, they use to connect these to the cover and textual aspects of the book. If you are using Print-on-Demand, you bypassed the option to have these, or some do add solid white onto hard covers.

SAVING THE FILES

Now that you have completed the book, be sure you save the files appropriately. This means for both your work files and the final product for the printer. Be sure to always ask clients and printers what file format and needs are required. For the sake of all things, we will focus on the most common and most versatile versions. If you used InDesign, you can go to File > Package and the software will do its best to grab font files, images, and more into a folder. For those who are using other means, here's a breakdown of the work folder and what to save:

- FOLDER NAMED AFTER BOOK
  - Work File (InDesign, Word, etc.)
  - PDF (2001-xa format aka Press Quality with Bleed recommended)
  - EPUB (Optional, reflowable a must)
  - ORIGINAL folder
    - Holds original text file and any related materials
  - FONT folder
    - Copies of font files used (truetype, openface, etc.)
  - IMAGE folder
    - Any image used should be placed in here in case you need it or edit or replace later.

As for prepping files for upload to a vendor, the two main types will be PDF and EPUB (reflowable). No matter if you are self-publishing or using a service, these two are the current staple in the industry and have the ability to upload to a variety of distributors and vendors with very little issue.

- PDF Format
  - This is used for print design applications, paperback, Print-on-Demand, and similar.
  - For printing, PDF-X/a: 2001 Format is the most accepted.
  - For web pdf, use web preferred file setting, but remember this file loses values needed for printing for a book.
  - Make sure Bleed Settings are applied or this could cause the file to kick back or be denied.

- EPUB Format
  - Always use reflowable.
  - Write in as much File Info and Metadata information as possible.
  - If attaching a cover image, it should be at least 1600x2400 pixels, 150 dpi, RGB color mode to avoid being kicked back from online vendors.
  - Most accepted eBook type currently with enhanced ability access.

BOOK TITLE: _____

SUBTITLE: _____

SAVING CHECKLIST

- [ ] A copy of the Manuscript or text file in a DOC, DOCX, RTF file that you used

- [ ] All the images in a LINKS or IMAGES folder

- [ ] Folder named after book to house all other files and folders

- [ ] Work files in folder (Recommend having a main one and back-up, i.e. *.indd and *idml)

- [ ] PDF version (2001-xa format for print-ready or print quality)

- [ ] EPUB (Reflowable) - optional

- [ ] Folder for fonts called FONT with copies of the files for future (they can go obsolete later)

- [ ] Did you save in the correct color profile (CMYK, RGB, 240% CMYK, etc)?

- [ ] Did you run ADA Compliance check in Adobe for ADA PDF needs? (optional)

- [ ] Do you need to convert EPUB to MOBI? (Consider using Calibre or similar converters)

- [ ] Has someone reviewed the file for issues besides you?

- [ ] Are the Header and Footers showing the correct text?

- [ ] Is your Table of Contents correct and numbered or not missing a chapter?

- [ ] Do your images bleed to the BLEED edge pass the TRIM edge?

- [ ] Double check that all your text is 0.5" from TRIM edge including Header and Footer

- [ ] Have you printed test pages on a local computer?

- [ ] Does your file meet the needs of your printer (Print-on-Demand AND Offset printers)

- [ ] Viewing for Web and Emails PDF - Did you save a "Reduced Size" PDF version?

- [ ] Has your customer signed off and reviewd the document before uploading to vendors?

BOOK TITLE: _____

SUBTITLE: _____

SAVING CHECKLIST

☐ A copy of the Manuscript or text file in a DOC, DOCX, RTF file that you used

☐ All the images in a LINKS or IMAGES folder

☐ Folder named after book to house all other files and folders

☐ Work files in folder (Recommend having a main one and back-up, i.e. *.indd and *idml)

☐ PDF version (2001-xa format for print-ready or print quality)

☐ EPUB (Reflowable) - optional

☐ Folder for fonts called FONT with copies of the files for future (they can go obsolete later)

☐ Did you save in the correct color profile (CMYK, RGB, 240% CMYK, etc)?

☐ Did you run ADA Compliance check in Adobe for ADA PDF needs? (optional)

☐ Do you need to convert EPUB to MOBI? (Consider using Calibre or similar converters)

☐ Has someone reviewed the file for issues besides you?

☐ Are the Header and Footers showing the correct text?

☐ Is your Table of Contents correct and numbered or not missing a chapter?

☐ Do your images bleed to the BLEED edge pass the TRIM edge?

☐ Double check that all your text is 0.5" from TRIM edge including Header and Footer

☐ Have you printed test pages on a local computer?

☐ Does your file meet the needs of your printer (Print-on-Demand AND Offset printers)

☐ Viewing for Web and Emails PDF - Did you save a "Reduced Size" PDF version?

☐ Has your customer signed off and reviewd the document before uploading to vendors?

Publishing Your Book

I just knew there were stories
I wanted to tell.

Octavia E. Butler

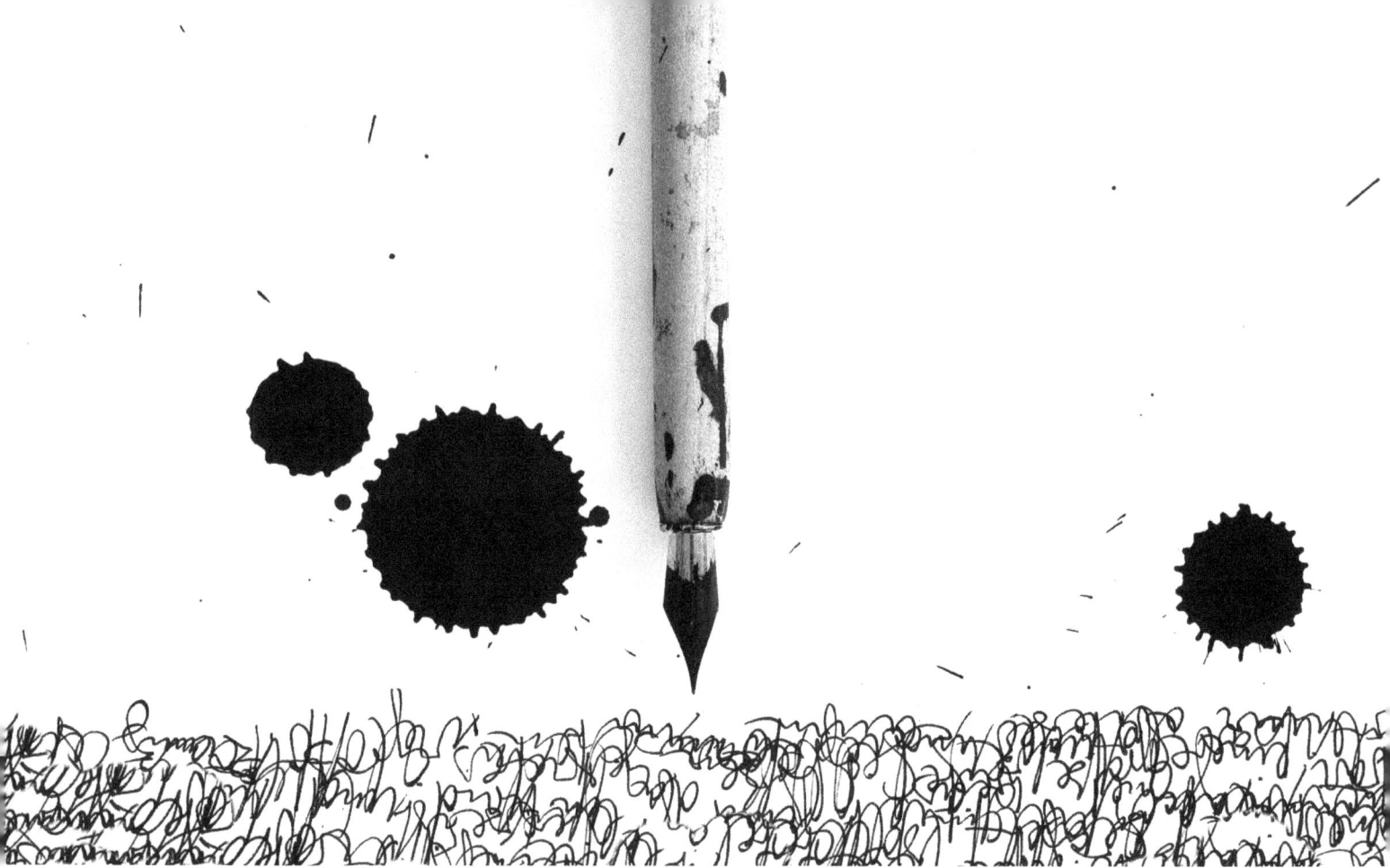

I'VE FORMATTED MY BOOK! NOW WHAT?

When it comes to saving and prepping those finished books, it's important that you are including more than the file itself. It's always a great idea to have all the images in a folder and all the text files copied into a folder as well. This is so you can always have the materials with you! If you are using InDesign, there is a FILE > PACKAGE feature that can do this for you. If you are using Word, double check that the options say you are embedding your fonts. There's a number of ways to make sure the materials (fonts, images, & similar) are preserved in case of changes or moving onto a new computer. In the end, you should also be saving a PDF version of the complete book, and in most cases an EPUB file as well. Granted, not every program lets you create a EPUB file, and you may have to use a third-party software like Calibre to make one from a Word file or Rich Text File.

SAVING FOR SUCCESS

Again, I can't express how important it is to double check and save again. Sometimes is a great idea to date this final version, so you know what the work file was and the one used to publish from. The cleaner the files, the easier it is to make changes or pass the files to someone else to alter and update at a later time. In the end, no matter what program you use, it's vital to always have your original images and a copy of text files included. I can't tell you how often I revisit a ten-year-old book and the font file is no longer in my list, but luckily, I saved a copy in the file to reinstall it with. Computers aren't perfect, and sometimes when we upgrade and change systems, we don't always realize we've lost something in the background like a font file we used for that one project a decade ago.

SAVING THE FILES VERSUS OPTIONS

Now that you have completed the book, be sure you save the files appropriately. This means for both your work files and the final product for the printer. Be sure to always ask clients and printers what file format and needs are required. For the sake of all things, we will focus on the most common and most versatile versions. If you used InDesign, you can go to File > Package and the software will do its best to grab font files, images, and more into a folder. For those who are using other means, here's a breakdown of the work folder and what to save:

- ✎ FOLDER NAMED AFTER BOOK
  - ✎ Work File (InDesign, Word, etc.)
  - ✎ PDF (2001-xa format aka Press Quality with Bleed recommended)
  - ✎ EPUB (Optional, reflowable a must)
  - ✎ ORIGINAL folder
    - ➥ Holds original text file and any related materials

- ✎ FONT folder
  - ➥ Copies of font files used (truetype, openface, etc.)
- ✎ IMAGE folder
  - ➥ Any image used should be placed in here in case you need it or edit or replace later.

As for prepping files for upload to a vendor, the two main types will be PDF and EPUB (reflowable). No matter if you are self-publishing or using a service, these two are the current staple in the industry and have the ability to upload to a variety of distributors and vendors with very little issue.

- ✎ PDF Format
  - ✎ This is used for print design applications, paperback, Print-on-Demand, and similar.
  - ✎ For printing, PDF-X/a: 2001 Format is the most accepted.
  - ✎ For web pdf, use web preferred file setting, but remember this file loses values needed for printing for a book.
  - ✎ Make sure Bleed Settings are applied or this could cause the file to kick back or be denied.

- ✎ EPUB Format
  - ✎ Always use reflowable.
  - ✎ Write in as much File Info and Metadata information as possible.
  - ✎ If attaching a cover image, it should be at least 1600x2400 pixels, 150 dpi, RGB color mode to avoid being kicked back from online vendors.
  - ✎ Most accepted eBook type currently with enhanced ability access.

MATERIALS AND PRINT OPTIONS

Saving on print cost comes easier for this selection of books. It doesn't mean you can't have images or artful design, but be mindful of the options you are choosing. The most common is black and white printing on cream (off-white, textured) or groundwood paper (very thin, seen in grocery story prints). If you are entertaining the idea of going with a color interior, be mindful of the cost increase that will carry over to the final retail cost. If you only have a few images, it's recommended to grayscale for print edition and use the color photos for eBook edition since color or black and white is decided via the reading device (and doesn't impact price of eBook).

PAGE COUNT

The number of pages is highly dependent on several variables that include genre, book types, industry and reader expectations, word count of content, overall design, functionality, and more. Depending on where this final page count falls, it can limit your options for binding, paper type, and color options. Regardless, from this point, understanding those influences and deciding on the best publishing avenue can open and close doors and decide what the production and retail pricing looks like.

PAPER TYPES

For the most part, the three core types tend to be groundwood (30-35 lb. thin, brown-tone), cream (50-70 lb., off-white, textured), and white (50-70 lb., smooth white). If you are making a photobook, picture book, or comic books, often use higher weighted paper (70-110 lb.) that is either semi-gloss or glossy. Know that the higher the weight, the thicker or denser the paper tends to be, which can handle higher color saturation. If you are using Print-on-Demand, this will limit the paper options back to only the core three, and you will need to save your files to stay below 240% CMYK saturation. The easiest way to tackle this is creating or downloading a color profile to add to your selection to automate this process. In essence, darker images are at a higher threat of peaking over this tipping point. If you want more paper selections, then consider off-set printing options.

COLOR OPTIONS

Black and white options will always be the cheapest price wise. The moment you make the decision to print in color, expect a huge jump in production cost immediately that rises exponentially alongside page counts. Many places offer different levels of color printing, sometimes as simple as standard versus premium. Always ask what the difference is between these. In most cases, this should be water-based ink versus alcohol-based, which is far superior. Also, it could mean the ability to print at higher saturation levels and many other bonuses. Most Print-on-Demand options will be using a water-based ink.

BINDING TYPES

If you aim for Print-on-Demand, your two most common choices with be saddle stitch (small page count, stapled binding) and perfect bound (glued signatures on cover). Moving into the realm of offset printing, you will discover a larger variety with Smyth sewn (signatures glued and sewn together and attached to a cover) as that is the most common for hardcover or larger books. This is a recommended type for special edition books, textbooks, and hardcover work. Though it's not an option for Print-on-Demand, know that hardcovers can also be created as a perfect bound book.

WHOLESALE DISCOUNT

You can always check out publisher compensation calculators (i.e. the one on Ingram's Lightning Source website) to see what royalties remain after its sold through a third-party vendor (i.e. Amazon, Barnes & Noble, Kobo, etc.). Default wholesale is normally 55% but many small presses drop this to 40% and larger publishers will drop further as low as 28%. For competitive pricing for retail, we recommend 40% or lower; however, be warned, the lower this discount, the less likely for bookstores and retailers will purchase large amounts of books to have in stock. Granted, much of this falls back to options dealing with Print-on-Demand and not every provider will give you the option to adjust this price.

RETAILERS AND DISTRIBUTORS

There are two sides to getting your book into the hands of readers. You can choose one, both, or a selection of retailers and distributors. A book distributor is an entity who delivers your book to readers and retailers (Target, Walmart, Amazon, etc.) directly on your behalf. As for a retailer, some provide their own means for you to create and sell your book directly through them, including Amazon and Barnes & Noble.

Prepping Your Files for Upload

In short, you always want to save your PDF files as a Press Ready type. The most common one among printers is the PDF/X-1a:2001 version. This is designed to pack all the information into the PDF, including embedding fonts, converting images to JPEG, and several other factors that make sure the book prints. It's always good to take a look at the PDF you've created for quality control purposes because occasional something will shift or a font isn't able to embed (double check its free for commercial use or you bought the rights to use).

Creating the PDF

Let's talk about Quality Control. There're a few things you will want to check and make sure before saving as a PDF and things to watch for after you save as a PDF. Here is a check list that can help you slow down and double check your work. Looking at a book you spent hours designing can make it easy to miss slight changes, and this will help you catch a lot of simple mistakes before the book goes to print. Granted, some of these line items may be only relevant for some software, so be careful and shift this list to your needs and software preference. Also keep in mind this should have items that reflect the printer's needs. For example, some printers require a bleed of 0.125 in. where others request 0.0 in. for inner margin.

As a fair warning, don't check and view your PDF via the web browser app or plugin. In my experience, I have seen some really weird issues such as orange font, missing images, a weird symbol replacing a letter, and more. Instead, always quality control the PDF within Adobe Acrobat so you see the full file as it was intended to be seen and accessed.

Adding Metadata

There are two places you can add metadata for a PDF file. The first involves the word processor or software you created the typeset with. Simply locate file information area and here you should be able to fill in creator info, publisher, description, and much more. The second place is File > Properties area in Adobe Reader, where you can find much of this information under several tabs and change them to the appropriate information. Don't forget to hit save to make those changes stick!

COMMON TROUBLESHOOTING FOR PDF

Below is a list of common issues that are flagged at upload or retailer levels and what they mean. If you took your time and read a lot of the preparation sections in this book, we discussed certain ways of working with files and materials to help prevent these. Each issue has more than one method for solving it, but depending on who and why they are flagging the file, there's a chance one solution is preferred over the rest. Be sure to take heed on the following common flags:

240% SATURATION LEVEL

- Adding a color profile that auto shifts to keep all images under this mark.
- Checking through software what the CMYK Saturation is on key color areas on the image and adjusting the images manually.
- Being aware of darker or hard coloration images that could be potential offenders of hitting over 240% CMYK mark.

CMYK MODE, NOT RGB

- Make sure all images are in Grayscale or CMYK mode for print purposes.
- Check the color profile when saving.
- Switch color mode/profile in software, change it accordingly, and resave.

LOW RESOLUTION IMAGE

- An image in the file is reading below 300 DPI per the placement and size it is in the document.
- Make sure all images you are using are 300-600 DPI or run a risk of them printing blurry or pixelated if forced through.
- Shrink the image to be closer to actual size.
- Remove any image under 300 DPI. Remember most web images are 72 or 96 DPI.
- Replace with a higher DPI version of the image.

TRANSPARENCIES!

- PNG file needs to be replaced with a JPEG or TIFF version.
- Run a remove transparencies Preflight using Adobe Acrobat.
- Add a white background to the image and fill in transparent areas.
- Remove image.

BEWARE OF THE COLOR BLUE

- One of the hardest colors to pinpoint!
- Looks too purple – try lowering the amount of red/magenta.
- Looks too teal – try lowering the amount of yellow.
- Test print and adjust from there. Always go with a shade lighter and remember this color tends to look darker when printed.
- Figuring out the exact CMYK code for the type of blue you want to print and ignore how it looks on screen.
- Assign a Pantone or Spot color. This is how big companies print logos in the same colors, no matter when and where it's printed.

FONTS CHANGING

- This is a sign your fonts aren't embedded.
- Try embedding fonts and making sure they are active/installed on your system.
- Run preflight in Adobe Acrobat to embed fonts.
- Check File > Properties for font list in Adobe Reader. See which one isn't embedding and replace with a different font and resave file.

BOOK TITLE: _____

SUBTITLE: _____

PDF CHECKLIST

- [] Book Title and Pen Name match

- [] All the images listed in Manuscript present:
  - [] CMYK mode
  - [] Between 300-600 DPI
  - [] Did you delete unused and unwanted RGB swatches in the Swatch panel?
  - [] Are all objects and images linked to the appropriate file?

- [] Trim Size _____ width x _____ height
  - [] Is document Bleed settings correct based on printer need (0.125" or 0")?
  - [] Are you saving PDF with Bleed option on?

- [] Copyright
  - [] Publisher information
  - [] Additional mention such as artist, design, or typesetter
  - [] Scriptures cited from.... Any public domain original publication mentions
  - [] Permission granted from... Any materials that have permissions need to be listed here
  - [] ISBNs for Paperback, Hardcover, Audiobook, or eBook
  - [] LCCN pending or listed?

- [] Dedication? Yes or No

- [] Front Matter (Acknowledgements, Foreword, Preface, etc.)

- [] Do the pages match in the Table of Contents? Yes or No

- [] Do the tables land on the page correctly? Yes or No

- [] Do the pull quotes land on the page correctly? Yes or No

- [] Double check the Header and Footer are reading and updating correctly.

- [] Are the Chapter pages consistent?

- [] Are the Drop-caps not overlapping with other content?

- [] Last page of a section and chapter all flow to top of page?

- [] Is this Print-on-Demand? If so, did you leave a blank even page at the end?

- [] Are images and objects anchored to text on the page for EPUB export?

CHECKING THE PDF

- [] Did all the fonts embed?

- [] Did it save in PDF/X-1a:2001 format?

- [] Does the PDF size match trim plus bleed amounts?

- [] Did all the images save and appear?

- [] Do you need to use Preflight to save as Grayscale for B&W printing?

- [] No watermarks or splash sheet.

- [] Even number of pages?

- [] If Print-on-Demand, is the last page blank?

CREATING THE EPUB

When saving out for EPUB file to use for your eBook uploads, you always want to save a EPUB (reflowable). For a long time, there was a great divide of EPUB (widely accepted with enhanced capabilities) and MOBI (Amazon's special format for Kindle). In 2021 Amazon abandoned its MOBI format and now only uses EPUB. Also, most vendors, distributors, and retailers only accept the reflowable version of the EPUB. These files use styles and inline text elements to know where content lands, flows, and divides. If you are using InDesign, you will discover that styles menus and properties have an EPUB/HTML section where custom programming and a checkbox allows it to tell the EPUB format to add digital page breaks. Always look into tips and tricks of EPUB programming for the software you are using. Another option to create an eBook is to use an open-source software called *Calibre* that has many tools and even the ability to edit the coding manually. It's up to you to decide which way you are best suited for and most comfortable in learning.

ADDING METADATA

There are three ways you can add metadata for a EPUB file. The first involves the word processor or software you created the typeset with. Simply locate the file information area; here you should be able to fill in creator info, publisher, description, and much more. The second place is dependent on the program you are using. For InDesign users and similar, when you Export out to save it as EPUB (reflowable), you should have another window with several sections. Take the time to fill out the information here to carry over to eBook devices. Lastly, you can take advantage of open-source software like *Calibre* and add or edit metadata using the features. You can even convert to other formats and change out the book cover!

- [] No watermarks or splash sheet.
- [] Even number of pages?
- [] If Print-on-Demand, is the last page blank?

COMMON TROUBLESHOOTING FOR EPUB

B elow is a list of common issues that are flagged at upload or retailer levels and what they mean. If you took your time and read a lot of the preparation sections in this book, we discussed certain ways of working with files and materials to help prevent these. Each issue has more than one method for solving it but depending on who and why they are flagging the file, there's a chance one solution is preferred over the rest. Be sure to take heed on the following common flags:

4 MILLION PIXELS

- An image some place is far too big to be digested by a digital device. Shrink all images (and cover file) to be no larger than a 6x9 ratio, 96-150 DPI, and saved in a JPEG format for best results for avoiding this issue.

- Use *Calibre's* Edit Book feature and run Tool > Compress Images feature.

CMYK vs RGB

- Make sure all images and cover are saved or converted into a RGB coloration format.

IMAGE NOT FOUND

- Check that the image does exist. If not, reattach it and save out again.

- Check the name of the image for symbols ($, %, ^, &, #, @, etc.) and remove them. Resave the EPUB file and try again. Many vetting systems remove these, and the EPUB no longer can find the file since names and EPUB programming don't match anymore.

- Image isn't showing in the content means you didn't anchor it or paste it in line with the text to pull into the eBook on creation of the EPUB file.

TABLE TOO BIG

- eBooks and eReaders can't process big tables. They have a maximum character count as well as a max row limit. Break it up!

- Convert the tables into images to avoid the issue completely!

EPUB FLOWS IN REVERSE

- This usually happens with books that might feature a foreign language someplace such as Arabic, Hebrew, Greek, and similar.

- Use *Calibre* and delete additional language codes listed in Metadata. (English should be the only one). Save the book and check from there.

- Manual code adjustment using *Calibre* or some other means. Open "content.opf" file and delete unwanted "<dc:language>" lines until only "en-US" remains. Save and load out again!

BOOK TITLE: _____

SUBTITLE: _____

EPUB Checklist

- [] Book Title and Pen Name match

- [] All the images listed in Manuscript present:
  - [] CMYK mode
  - [] Between 300-600 DPI
  - [] Did you delete unused and unwanted RGB swatches in the Swatch panel?
  - [] Are all objects and images linked to the appropriate file?

- [] Trim Size _____ width x _____ height
  - [] Is document Bleed settings correct based on printer need (0.125" or 0")?
  - [] Are you saving PDF with Bleed option on?

- [] Copyright
  - [] Publisher information
  - [] Additional mention such as artist, design, or typesetter
  - [] Scriptures cited from…. Any public domain original publication mentions
  - [] Permission granted from… Any materials that have permissions need to be listed here
  - [] ISBNs for Paperback, Hardcover, Audiobook, or eBook
  - [] LCCN pending or listed?

- [] Dedication? Yes or No

- [] Front Matter (Acknowledgements, Foreword, Preface, etc.)

- [] Do the pages match in the Table of Content? Yes or No

- [] Do the tables land on the page correctly? Yes or No

- [] Do the pull quotes land on the page correctly? Yes or No

- [] Double check the Header and Footer are reading and updating correctly.

- [] Are the Chapter pages consistent?

- [] Are the Drop-caps not overlapping with other content?

- [] Last page of a section and chapter all flow to top of page?

- [] Is this Print-on-Demand? If so, did you leave a blank even page at the end?

- [] Are images and objects anchored to text on the page for EPUB export?

CHECKING THE EPUB

- [] Did all the fonts embed?

- [] Did it save in PDF/X-1a:2001 format?

- [] Does the PDF size match trim plus bleed amounts?

- [] Did all the images save and appear?

- [] Do you need to use Preflight to save as Grayscale for B&W printing?

- [] No watermarks or splash sheet.

- [] Even number of pages?

- [] If Print-on-Demand, is the last page blank?

PRINT-ON-DEMAND

The current mainstream means for self-publishers, small presses, and even the top publishers to catch when they runout of limited print runs is using a Print-on-Demand supplier. Below I cover some well-known entities who make-up a majority for the current market in regards to uploading files for books printed for self-publishers to large publishers. These are listed in order of popularity and for this portion we are more focused on printed books, though I will cover what other options each of these can provide as I do so.

INGRAMSPARKS, LIGHTNING SOURCE, AND CORESOURCE+

Ingram is one of the biggest distributors for Print-on-Demand and digital options. CoreSource+ has over a 450+ channel reach that includes academia, libraries, big retailers (Amazon, Barnes & Noble, Walmart, and more), and 20+ audiobook venues (Audible, Apple, Storytel, Hoopla, and more). Self-publishers and small publishers often start with IngramSparks (simply sign up and you're good to go!), for more print options you must apply to gain access to Lightning Source. A step above that and you gain a paid contract to gain a digital reach on par with top publishers including large imprints and new publishers such as Avon, Harlequin, Macmillan, Simon and Schuster, HarperCollins, 4 Horsemen Publications, and Kensington.

Print options include paperbacks of varying sizes, laminate case hardcover, and even dust jacket options. As for their digital reach, they take in EPUB format and MP3 or WAV Audiobook formats and can distribute to many of the other distributors and retailers listed below with access to hard-to-reach channels. For example, to publish work through OverDrive, you must provide a minimum of 100+ titles per month. Many starting out or only publishing their own work can't meet this demand in order to get their books into libraries, so using Ingram or a similar distributor can help you achieve this. Another advantage is the level of control you have with a books metadata, pricing, and even wholesale discounts. This is the means in which I recommend for those reasons.

AMAZON, KDP, AND ACX

A pro-consumer market, Amazon makes up 50-60% of the digital market for eBook sales for almost a decade now. With growing trends and accessibility, they are losing their ground, but it's not uncommon for publishers and authors to only publish here (and in some cases, prefer not to publish here at all!). The KDP dashboard and account for publishing books on Kindle or Paperback has made several changes in the last few years since they absorbed CreateSpace. Now authors and small publishers can do both within the same location with worldwide access. Because many of the metadata and wholesale options are pulled away or simplified, launching a book via KDP can be less daunting than other areas though you give much control of pricing and other aspects over to Amazon to do with it as they see fit. You can get worldwide reach via Amazon and a limited number of third-party associations. What these are, it's not exactly clear but with Amazon giving KDP user exclusive access to control series landing pages, promotions, and similar exclusive deals it can be tempting for most to use this platform alongside many others.

BARNES & NOBLE AND NOOKPRESS

Publishing through Barnes & Noble requires you to use Nook Press. Again, this only published via their store's chains and the few partners they are connected. With direct nook and paperback sales, you do get a slightly bigger cut in royalties going direct. Unlike Amazon, they don't offer much in the ways of exclusive and also don't give the author and publisher access to fully control wholesale and similar aspects. They have their own category system that can prove hard to navigate for some though opens the door for some niche markets while completely missing more common ones.

LULU.COM

Back in the early years of self-publishing Print-on-Demand books, Lulu and CreateSpace were leading go-to distributors. After CreateSpace was swallowed up by Amazon, Lulu found itself still standing and reaching to provide better services to compete with the growing number of aggregators that made eBooks easier over print books. Now authors and publishers can print not only paperbacks and hardcovers, but also find options for photobooks, comics, magazines, yearbooks, and calendars. You will find much of the selection here a simplified selection compared to Ingram's options.

They also provide optional binding such as coil bound (similar to spiral bound notebooks), perfect bound (paperback and hardcover), and saddle stitch. Cost per book is competitive with Ingram and Amazon, and like Ingram, provide templates to aid in prepping files and covers for final product. You can sell your book directly via Lulu, bulk order, and/or open it up to the few channels they have with retailers including Amazon, Apple, Kobo, and similar. They are user friendly and provide a lot of resources that can help first time publishers.

OFF-SET PRINTING

Bigger publishers and those with access, contracts, or funding, tend to favor off-set printing. These printers and presses can produce books with a broader spectrum of materials and options. Some of the options only found here is Smyth-sewn bound hardcovers, board books, higher paperweights and brightness, slipcovers for books and book sets, leather options, faux leather, embossing, gold-leaf elements, and lower overall production cost. Though the amount needed upfront to bulk print, or do a limited print run, can be costly. After that, a means for warehousing and shipping the books will need to be arranged or established. There are places that provide this type of distribution but it's not uncommon for small publishers to handle this in-house. Certain retailers, such as Amazon, have a warehouse and shipped based foundation and there are ways to provide product to them to house and sell on their sites in the manner. It's completely up to you to provide product placement with retailers at this point or use a distributor with established contracts to act on your behalf to do so. Many offset print houses with the best pricing are located out of the Asian markets including China, India, and Korea. That doesn't mean printers out of the United States, Canada, and United Kingdom that can't provide similar services with competitive pricing. A lot of these printers provide other products and packaging such as Tarot cards and specialty products. Always research and review their previously produced products as a point of reference.

AGGREGATORS

An aggregator is a service that does a few things for the author. First, it's capable of converting your book into other formats as long as you provide the core filetype they request. Secondly, they will then broadcast your book to vendor sites. These sometimes require money to gain wider access or more services.

BOOKBABY

This is more in the realm of author services, but much like Draft2Digital, BookBaby provides a large selection of print and eBook packages. Some of these are more in line with offset printing, and others are for Print-on-Demand setups. They can do formatting, conversions, and more. I can't say I've used their service directly, but I love the blog and newsletters. They often have up-to-date industry practices and ready information, and that alone makes them a resource worthy of mentioning or making authors aware of.

DRAFT2DIGITAL

I have met many of their team in person at conferences and conventions. They are amazing and provide great customer service and support to their authors. If formatting proves a challenge, this company also provides services to format your book for you as well! Just like with SmashWords, they take a DOC or RTF of your manuscript and convert it into an eBook. From there, they will broadcast your book to vendors including Amazon, Barnes & Noble, Kobo, and more. Authors that I know personally who have used them have been very happy with their experience.

SMASHWORDS

A free eBook-based aggregator but be mindful on what is needed to get your book cleared for the Premium Catalog. This is the side of SmashWords that will allow your book to gain access to the bigger vendors including Kobo and Barnes & Noble. They often host sales, and you have wider control on book pricing than you will find anywhere else. They do take a cut, so be sure to read the fine print and make sure you're ok with the terms of using them as a means to broadcast the digital version of your books.

WHAT OTHER OPTIONS DO I HAVE?

You have gotten this far and might be feeling overwhelmed looking at the software and aggregators thinking, "What other options are out there?" And you're right! There are other options out there that you might have tried for or can't decide on. Even if you choose one of these paths, remember this book is meant not only to guide someone aiming to make their book themselves, but to also help the communicate with someone else that might be making the book for you. So, who would that be?

PUBLISHERS

Querying a publisher is one way to get a book out there. You might have already tried this option or previously decided not to go down this path. With this option, you don't get much of a say-so in the final results, but if you need to point out issues, this book should provide the vocabulary you need to get those corrections and adjustments done more accurately.

AUTHOR SERVICES & VANITY PRESSES

These are publishers you pay to make and publish your book. Traditional track or vanity presses not only need payment for the services to make your manuscript into a book, but you have to buy a certain number of copies before they will go any further. On the other end of this type is author services or digital printing services. Many aggregators also straddle this realm with package pricing for different facets of making a book with cover design, typeset or formatting, uploading fees, and even annual renewal costs to keep the book published.

Depending on the company and process, you might have a lot of input on the design and focus while others may be no different from a regular publisher and you don't have any input on the final result. I always advise caution when choosing a publisher in this realm since they aren't as accommodating as an aggregator or other options. There are far more predatory companies in this scope than any other part of the industry. Consumer beware!

SUBCONTRACTORS OR FREELANCERS

If typesetting your own book is overwhelming or too hard of a learning curve to meet the deadline you have set, then consider finding a professional formatter, typesetter, and/or graphic designer. Much like any other field, I recommend exploring their credentials as well as scope out their previous work. Consider your book a house being built, and you just put on your general contractor's hat. You will coordinate with all the other hats or roles from there, including editorial, cover design, typesetting, illustrator, marketer, and more.

This too can be an overwhelming undertaking and using this book to help create a more concrete communication between you and typesetter can make a world of difference in the final outcome. Make sure the professional you choose can show similar genre work and styles for what you are hoping to have within the pages of your book. Have they designed a picture book before? Do they know how to create and adjust an eBook? Are they familiar with upload file requirements and how to troubleshoot them? How much do they charge for revisions or corrections?

Asking questions and choosing someone who can double as a guide into the next stages can help tremendously for first time self-publishers. It is perfectly ok and even recommended to schedule a meeting and review what it is you are hoping the end result to look like as well as what they need from you to make that happen. Be sure to know to who and where you will be uploading your book, so you can get the files in the correct size and format from the start. Better yet, if you are making a picture book, be sure to have a three-way meeting to make sure everyone involved can communicate needs and address concerns, and you can make decisions sooner and not find yourself in a standstill and paying extra for changes that could have been avoided.

You can find freelancers and subcontractors in a variety of places. Some professionals have websites that list their services and you can reach out via email or contact forms. Others use websites like Fiverr and Upwork too.

Glossary & Terms

Get it down.
Take chances.
It may be bad,
but it's the only way
you can do anything good.

William Faulkner

Glossary & Terms

About the Author – A page with information about the author, such as a biography, a picture, book listing, and links to where to connect with them on social media or online.

Aggregator – A company or service that takes in one file type and processes it to be applicable to several more. Often distributes these conversions out to the associated vendors on behalf of the client, such as SmashWords and Draft2Digital.

Alignment or Page Alignment – Most books use justified page alignment, using top alignment for last page of a chapter to pull the content up, bottom alignment for the copyright page, and center alignment for dedication and similar content.

All Caps – Font is all capitalized and the same size. Example, TOM GOES TO VEGAS.

Anchor – This is the means in which an image in a file has been assigned an anchor or point of connection within the inline text. InDesign and Word both have a means of doing this. Be mindful anchored images move with the text and will show in an eBook. Unanchored images stay where they are placed on the page but will not show in an eBook.

APA style – American Psychological Association styling parameters.

Back Matter – Refers to content that follows after the main content. For example, *index, bibliography, end notes, about the author*, etc.

Back of a Page – Left page is the backside of the previous page.

Bibliography – A list of reference books and materials used to create the content or support the content with the book. Sometimes titled as references or sources.

Binding or Book Binding – In short, how are the pages connect to one another and the cover. The most common types are *perfect bound* and *Smyth-sewn*. There are others like *cross-stitch* and more, but they may require special stipulations on how to format.

Bleed or Bleed Edge – The area outside of a *trim edge* in which you design beyond in case during trimming or production of the book, it shifts slightly and will not create unwanted white edges.

Chapter Header – Often labelled as "chapter" or the

numbers in which it identifies the starting of a chapter. This can start on the *right page* or be *continuous*. Always start on fresh page overall.

Chapter Header Art – Refers to the art and images used to design the layout for this page or *spread* in particular.

Character – Any letter, digit, space, or symbol as a stand-alone as assigned to a key on the keyboard usually.

Character Count – The amount of digits, letters, and symbols. This sometimes includes spacing.

Character Spacing *see Kerning.*

Character Style – This refers to font styles that are subsets of a main *font face* such as bold, italic, wide, condensed, underline, etc.

CMS Style – Chicago Manual Style is the most widely referred to and used formatting guide for the Publishing Industry. That doesn't mean it's followed to the letter, but a majority of spacing, paragraph styles, and editorial decisions are going to come from this resource more often than not, especially in fiction work.

CMYK – For print, you should always save color files in CMYK or Cyan Magenta Yellow Black color mode. This reflects the different inks used to produce your book and may not match images that were done in *RGB* or digital color modes. For example, blue and purple are often notorious for shifting in printed format if you fail to calibrate your monitor, software, and/or printer correctly.

Continuous Chapters – Chapter that starts on either the left or right page. Always on a fresh page. A fantastic way to save *page count* and limit the number of empty *left pages*.

Copyright Page – Contains publication information including *publisher*, rights owner (author or *publisher* with year filed/published), legality statements, permissions, *public domains*, author, designer, editors, and similar content. Always falls on the page after the *full title page*.

Cream Paper – A paper type that is off white or cream in color, often textured, and a lighter *paperweight* for lowering print cost. Most common in fiction books.

Cropmarks – Depending on the press and style of book

Glossary & Terms

binding that needs *CMYK* and Targeted marks as to how to line up and print the pages. Often used in special children's books, picture books, and similar high-end offset printed products. Very rarely used in digital printing.

Cross-stitch – A style of book binding that has pages stitched together. This often requires overlapping left and right page content to accommodate for stitching and folding in the *signatures*. Only seen at specialty offset printers for traditional publishing.

CSS3 – Common style sheet system used in conjunction to program websites and eBooks alongside HTML5.

DOC or DOCX – The file type used by Microsoft Word that uses XML coding to maintain the look of the content written inside.

Downsample – This is the process of when a program lowers the DPI or Resolution of an image and runs a risk of pixelating or blurring the image.

DPI or PPI – Short for Dot Per Inch or Pixel Per Inch. In most cases, the resolution of your book's content should be 300 to 600 DPI for print while for digital format, or eBook, 150-300 DPI. Anything below the minimum is at risk of being blurry or pixelated. As for going over, the printer or press may manually shrink the images, so it's advised to keep them no larger than 600 DPI.

Drop Cap – This is the larger letter or ornamental *glyph* that starts with the first letter(s) in the first paragraph at the start of a chapter.

End Leaves or End Pages – Decorative cardstock glued on the back of the cover at and makes up the first and last page of most picture books or offset printed books. These can be patterned, custom art, or simply a solid color.

Endnotes – Small superscript letters, asterisks, or numbers that reference a section at the end of the book to cite the source for what is written there. Often vendors request to convert these to footnotes for eBook format.

EPUB – The most common file type for eBooks on the market. It supports embedded fonts, enhanced typesetting, and allows readers to change font face, size, and color as needed to make reading easier for them.

Face – *see Font.*

Font or Font Face – Refers to the type of font you are using such as Times, Arial, Garamond, etc.

Footnotes – Small superscript letters, asterisks, or numbers that reference a section at the bottom of the page to cite the source for what is written there or provide additional information to the reader. Amazon and many vendors prefer these in eBooks and in digital format at the end of the chapter.

Foundry or Foundries – These refer to the original creators of typeset tiles. Foundries would have blacksmith, metalworkers, or similar create and smelt metal tiles that contain each letter. The tiles would be slide into slots on a plate for printing. Companies who own fonts are often still referred to as foundries.

Front Matter – Sections that come before the main content of the book. This includes *dedication, preface, foreword, introduction*, etc.

Glyph – Decorative, font-based imagery often used in the *Chapter Header, Headline, Subhead, Page Break,* or *Line Break.*

Half Title Page – The very first page seen under the front cover. Traditionally only has the *title* of the book and leaves ample room for an author to sign or leave a message to readers. Optional, but recommended to keep.

Headline – Either the chapter title or title for a back/front matter section. This is the first level of Headers that can contain levels of subheads under it within the same chapter.

HTML, or HTML5 – This is a program language more commonly found in web design and website programming (and now eBook programming). HTML5 uses call commands that uses style sheets, JavaScript, and other coding to create something through a mixture of resources. These are often viewable on a wide variety of devices.

Hyperlink – The often blue or clickable text that will lead to an outside source via a URL on the internet or jump to another designated space within the book.

Imprint – A publishing company within the umbrella of a larger publisher. For example, HarperCollins is the publisher for imprints Avon Romance and Harlequin Enterprises.

INDD – A file type for InDesign work files.

Indent – This term implies spacing related between the margin and an entire paragraph, first line, or hanging lines.

Index – A means of referring pages for key search elements. With new technology, PDF searches and eBook search capabilities has replaced this and far more sufficient and save on page count.

Inline – When placing text or an image, "inline" within a document implies you are wanting to add it to where the cursor is blinking in an active text frame.

ISBN – A number assigned by Bowker for a book that registers to the publisher and contains book information including title, author, book format, retail price, trim size, and more.

Justification – The alignment of text within a paragraph. The common types are align left or justified for most books. Right alignment is usually used for citation captions whereas center alignment is reserved for dedication, book listings, quotes, and website listings.

Kerning – Character spacing between letters, digits, and other font characters.

Landscape – Horizontal orientation. Remember this: as you pan the landscape, it's wider than it is tall.

LCCN – The Library of Congress Control Number a book is registered and links all the

Leading – This is the line spacing between lines. Depending on the font face, this spacing can vary and commonly falls between single spacing (1.00) and 1.25 spacing. Double spacing should be reserved for manuscripts and editing. It helps leave room to pen in marks and corrections.

Left Page – Backside of a page.

Line Break – Either noted by a double return, though not recommended. In final typeset or product, it is often an asterisk, a glyph, and ornamental line art.

Line Spacing *see Leading.*

Macro – Programming feature that runs certain coding or repeats steps to adjust the manuscript in a special way. It is best not to use these when submitting a file to be formatted into a book. If your macro simply speeds up prebuilt in steps within the program, it should be ok. As for macros that have more advance custom programming that creates an index or pulls commands from a third-party plugin, it can break, unravel, or change what is imported for typesetting. Rule of thumb: *when in doubt, leave it out!*

Margins – This is the spacing from the page edge or trim edge to the textual content.

Master Page – A term used most often with InDesign that refers to premade templates of page or spread layouts that can be dragged and dropped. It's very similar to the premade layouts as seen in PowerPoint or Google Slides.

MLA Style – Modern Language Association styling parameters.

MOBI – Amazon produced file type for use on the Kindle. As of October 2020, they are switching to EPUB.

Offset Printer or Printing – This is a traditional means of printing. A large number of prints are produced and stored in warehouses or specific locations to be shipped to vendors. This often requires a lot of upfront costs but can save production cost per book. Many of the printers and presses with the best cost efficiency are more commonly located in the Asian markets, primarily China, India, and Korea.

Open source–Websites, forums, and individuals who provide tools or resources they've created for free to others for use in various programs or even coding.

Overlay – This is where you stack one element over another. For example, in picture books you will be overlaying text via a text frame over an image or blank page.

Page Break – Where content is broken and pushed to the next page. Often between chapters or major sections.

Page Count – The number of pages. It's vital to end on an even number for presses and publishers. This sometimes requires a blank even page as the last page due to *Print-on-Demand* needing a spot to print a barcode as to where the book printed from.

Pantone Color – Pantone colors come with specific codes so a printer/press can match a color exactly. This is commonly used for logos or making sure the content has the correct color no matter where the book is sent for printing and limiting the risk of color shifts between printing rounds.

Paper Brightness – Simply refers to the how bright or white toned the paper looks to the eye. Usually this is measured by the amount of light is reflects off!

Paperweight – The density of the actual paper. This is often signified by the pounds, 30, 50, and 70 being the most common. Be mindful the lower the weight, the more pages that can be bound in a book. The thicker the paper, the higher success in printing dark photos and images with higher saturation.

Paragraph Spacing – This is the spacing that comes before or after a paragraph. In most body text, this happens for content shift or in lieu of a first line indent. No indent with paragraph spacing after is the most common as well as a paragraph space after to imply a line break.

Paragraph Style – Defines the parameters and options of a paragraph type including indentations, spacing, character styles, font size, EPUB page breaks, and more.

PDF – The file type used by Adobe and many programs to embed images and fonts for digital consumption. It has the ability to preserve a design, so it does not alter when viewed in other software or systems. It's the most common filetype requested of Print-on-Demand and offset printers for final production and often default to 2001XA variant.

Perfect Bound – The most common book binding type for mass market and Print-on-Demand books. This is the art of gluing signatures to the cover and trimming the book to size afterwards.

Plugin – This is a special add-on or batch system that works as a kind of extension within an existing software. Some plugins are to smooth integration between operating systems and other software which often come from the company who designed it. Third-party plugins are designed by outside sources or non-affiliated parties and should be used with caution. These often cause issues when importing manuscripts into other software if they are meant to change layout automatically for the user.

Print Run – Using an offset printer, the run a large print order normally ranging in the 1,000 to 10,000 range. Once these books are sold, they book is either marked as sold out until a new print run or order is made with an offset printer, or the book switches to a Print-on-Demand method until more books are ordered.

Print-on-Demand – A digital publishing process that sends digital files (cover and interior) to the closest press or printer and deliver the finished book from that locations. Last page that has a barcode to notate date and publish location. A variety of self-published authors, publishers, and entities use this method to produce books they do not wish to use offset printing methods for. This does have a higher production cost per book but does not require as high of upfront costs nor any warehouse fees. Note this route has limitation as to the type of binding, paper options, a set template, and far fewer creative options for the final product due to the ideal this is to be accessible across a wide range of printers worldwide.

Printer or Press – The company or print house that has the machinery that can produce or print a book. These presses or printer locations receive files digitally and often use the parameters defined by a publisher to create books and ship them out to the appropriate vendor or customer. Depending on the press or printer, they may have multiple options for traditional publishing, including a variety of book binding, paper choices, cover finishes, and etc. These may increase your upfront cost to obtain.

Portrait – Vertical orientation. Remember this: as you look at a portrait of Mona Lisa or the statue of David, it is taller than it is wide.

Premium Color – Often used to refer to color printers who use laser printing or use alcohol-based inks that dry faster.

PSD – A file type for Photoshop work files.

Public Domain – A previously published or created content that is deemed free for public use. Please always check the copyrights of such materials. Depending on year of publication or death of author/artist can designate when a piece becomes free for public use. In the United States, a large amount falls into Public Domain at 70 years while in other countries it ranges as high as 100 years.

Publisher – This is often who the ISBN is registered to and the company in which has administrative rights, contract rights, and publishing rights to a book. This can be a sole proprietor or author,

Glossary & Terms

self-publish platform (KDP, amazon independent, IngramSparks, CreateSpace, etc.), imprint (Viking Press, Avon Romance, Harlequin, McGraw-Hill, etc.), or publishing house (Penguin Random House, HarperCollins, MacMillan).

Reflowable EPUB – This is the primary file type for eBooks used today. It has the ability to allow devices to change aspects of the digital book to meet the user's needs and wants. As the font, size, and spacing are changed it is designed to reflow or rearrange the content accordingly.

Resolution – Based on pixels, DPI, or PPI, this refers to how big or small the image is and the level of data it contains. The higher the pixel/DPI/PPI count, the more detailed the image will be and less likely to pixelate, break, become fuzzy, or print with issues. For printing, this resolution needs to be 300 to 600 DPI whereas the average images for internet fall between 72-96 DPI.

RGB – Red Green Blue refers to the color mode monitors and televisions use. It's common for image pulled from the internet are in this format at 72 *DPI*. Unfortunately, these parameters are not ok for print that requires *CMYK* at 300-600 DPI. As for eBooks, they recommend 150-300 DPI for images saved in RGB format.

Right Page – Front side of a page.

Right Sided or Right Page Chapters – Chapters that always start on the right side. Sometimes these feature spread design to fill in the blank back pages of previous chapters. This was traditional in older book design and has been replaced with Continuous for cost efficiency, especially for Print-on-Demand books.

RTF – Rich Text Format that is widely available on a large range of programs and software. This maintains character styles such as bold, italics, and underline. Saving to this format can flush out issues with XML coding that is carrying over when importing a manuscript into layout software.

Rule of Thirds – A terminology commonly studied in design and film where the canvas or stage is broken into thirds from top to bottom, and right to left. Using this breakdown, you can design content the will help make the viewer force their eyes into certain focus points or create pleasing composition for viewing.

Sans-Serif – A font that does not feature foot pieces, such as Arial, Helvetica, Calibri, Gill Sans, etc.

Section Header – Signifies the start of a new section in which contains chapters and subheads. This can be a stand-alone section as seen in section non-fiction books or mimic the style of a chapter start, depending on genre and purpose.

Self-Published – When an author or individual produces the book under their own name or imprint. This could be achieved in a number of ways whether they do all the production themselves or hire contractors for all or each component.

Serif – A more traditional font and more common in larger books and fiction that has foot pieces or serifs. For example, Times, Garamond, Baskerville, Georgia, etc.

Signature – Paper for books often come in prebound sets of pages via the printer. They are always an even number such as 16, 24, 48… and are stacked in such a way to piece together a book. Print-on-Demand is based on the most common signatures found in a majority of printers and presses.

Small Caps – Font is in capitalized format but contains a mixture of small and large versions. Example, TOM GOES TO VEGAS.

Smyth-sewn – This style of binding is super common for hardcover books. It's noticeable by the threading and can handle opening and closing of the book more so than in a perfect bound book. Often this is a recommended binding for offset printing.

Spread – Two-page layout. Contains a left and right page and flow into one another for a complete design. Most common in picture books and books with unique Chapter Header or Section Header designs.

Standard Color – Refers to inkjet printers that use water-based inks. Most at home printers use this type.

Styles – A way to define textual content. Also, the way Word labels its own paragraph styles. *Also see Paragraph Styles.*

Subhead – Headlines that fall under the main chapter or headline. There can be several levels and most common in textbooks, non-fiction, and workbooks.

Subscript – Tiny lower font seen most often in mathematics such as seen here: Xx_2

Superscript – A more common occurrence and used for footnotes, endnotes, and specialty scenarios such as Microsoft©, 9th, and Xx^2.

Tab – The key that makes an indent, though it is replaced during formatting since it can cause issues in the book design and eBook. Its function is for creating tables in programming and runs a risk of skewing XML coding.

Table – Sometimes noticeable when borders are applied, this is a section made of a set number of rows and columns. Textual content can flow around these elements and don't always carry over into eBook format cleanly. Some vendors limit the amount of characters that one can have such as Amazon/KDP with a max of 200,000.

Table Style – Defines the parameters and options for tables, cells, rows, columns, and headers. This includes borders, text style, spacing, coloration, and more.

Third-Party Plugin, *see Plugin.*

Title Page – Contains the *title, subtitle*, author, and *imprint* logo. Reflects all the textual content found on front cover.

Traditional Publisher – The definition varies depending on where you look in the industry. For the sake of our definition, we will use solely the overlapping components as a registered company (LLC, INC, etc.) who produces a variety of work for a large scope of authors, as a means of worldwide book distribution, and owns or copyrights to a selection of books as company assets. They often own and manage several contracts for work and/or authors and pay said parties an agreed amount in several forms whether that is allowances, royalties, and/or copies of the product. They often have multiple imprints, employee overhead, and hold contracts with a variety of vendors, agents, and other media groups.

Trim Edge – The edge of the page where the book will be cut in order to be the right trim size. Anything close to or outside of this edge is a risk of being cut off or not there at all.

Trim Size – This is the book's size given in width by height and often given in inches. It's vital to be aware of the order of the information given since

an 8.5 in. x 11 in. book is in portrait and a 11in. by 8.5 in. would be landscape orientation.

TXT – A file type for the most basic level of text files. These cannot save special formatting, such as bold, italics, or underline.

Typesetting – Interior book design. This is done digitally in most cases and rarely done in the original art, which was managed by foundries in past centuries. They often utilize programs, such as InDesign and QuarkXpress, to create books for both offset and Print-on-Demand. The person who has mastered this art is often referred to as a typesetter or graphic designer.

Watermark – When an image or text are ghosted on top of or behind content to add visual effect or mark an item for branding purposes. Often these can be added to final products to protect them from being stolen and disrupt copiers and digital image to text converters.

White paper – A bright, white paper often used in color printing or certain books. It is often smooth and comes in 50 or 70lb. paperweight.

Whitespace – A term that refers to spans of whitespace on a page. For example, it's normal to see whitespace on all four side of a page of text because that's what signifies the amount of margin applied.

XML Coding – The program language used to create eBooks, Microsoft Word files, and used in a number of software, such as InDesign and QuarkXpress. This uses a limited selection of HTML coding with CSS stylesheets to set the parameters for fonts, paragraphs, and image placement. It does not have the ability to overlap or layer materials and calls each element in a row. This coding allows eBook devices to change said parameters to make text and content easier for each individual reader to making the act of reading easier for their visual needs.

Worksheets

Just write every day of your life.
Read intensely.
Then see what happens.
Most of my friends who are put on that diet
have very pleasant careers.

Ray Bradbury

STORYBOARD

PICTURE [_____] **ACTION** [_____]

_____
_____
_____
_____
_____

PICTURE [_____] **ACTION** [_____]

_____
_____
_____
_____
_____

PICTURE [_____] **ACTION** [_____]

_____
_____
_____
_____
_____

PICTURE [_____] **ACTION** [_____]

_____
_____
_____
_____
_____

PROJECT TITLE: _____   GENRE: _____

STORYBOARD

PICTURE [_____]

ACTION [_____]

_____
_____
_____
_____
_____
_____
_____

PICTURE [_____]

ACTION [_____]

_____
_____
_____
_____
_____
_____
_____

PICTURE [_____]

ACTION [_____]

_____
_____
_____
_____
_____
_____
_____

PICTURE [_____]

ACTION [_____]

_____
_____
_____
_____
_____
_____
_____

STORYBOARD

PICTURE [_____]

ACTION [_____]

_____
_____
_____
_____
_____
_____
_____

PICTURE [_____]

ACTION [_____]

_____
_____
_____
_____
_____
_____
_____

PICTURE [_____]

ACTION [_____]

_____
_____
_____
_____
_____
_____
_____

PICTURE [_____]

ACTION [_____]

_____
_____
_____
_____
_____
_____
_____

STORYBOARD

PICTURE [_____]

ACTION [_____]

_____
_____
_____
_____
_____
_____

PICTURE [_____]

ACTION [_____]

_____
_____
_____
_____
_____
_____

PICTURE [_____]

ACTION [_____]

_____
_____
_____
_____
_____
_____

PICTURE [_____]

ACTION [_____]

_____
_____
_____
_____
_____
_____

STORYBOARD

PICTURE [_____]

ACTION [_____]

_____
_____
_____
_____
_____
_____

PICTURE [_____]

ACTION [_____]

_____
_____
_____
_____
_____
_____
_____

PICTURE [_____]

ACTION [_____]

_____
_____
_____
_____
_____
_____
_____

PICTURE [_____]

ACTION [_____]

_____
_____
_____
_____
_____
_____
_____

PROJECT TITLE: _____ GENRE: _____

STORYBOARD - PORTRAIT

STORYBOARD - PORTRAIT

STORYBOARD - PORTRAIT

STORYBOARD - PORTRAIT

STORYBOARD - PORTRAIT

STORYBOARD – PORTRAIT

PROJECT TITLE: _____ GENRE: _____

STORYBOARD - LANDSCAPE

STORYBOARD - LANDSCAPE

PROJECT TITLE: _____   GENRE: _____

STORYBOARD - LANDSCAPE

PROJECT TITLE: _____ GENRE: _____

STORYBOARD - LANDSCAPE

PROJECT TITLE: _____ GENRE: _____

STORYBOARD - LANDSCAPE

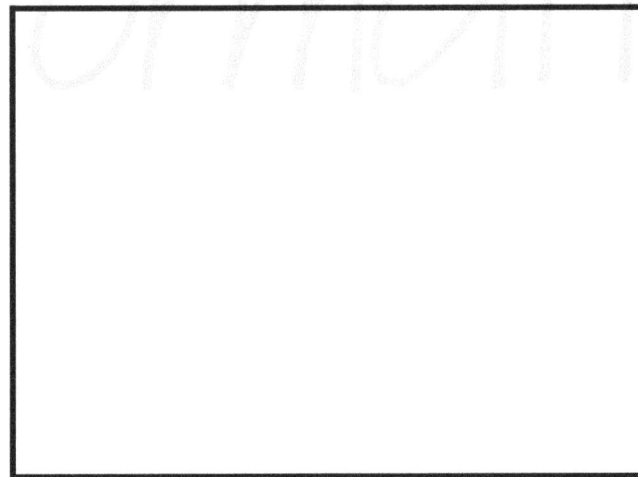

PROJECT TITLE: _____ GENRE: _____

STORYBOARD - LANDSCAPE

STORYBOARD - SQUARE

STORYBOARD - SQUARE

STORYBOARD - SQUARE

STORYBOARD - SQUARE

STORYBOARD - SQUARE

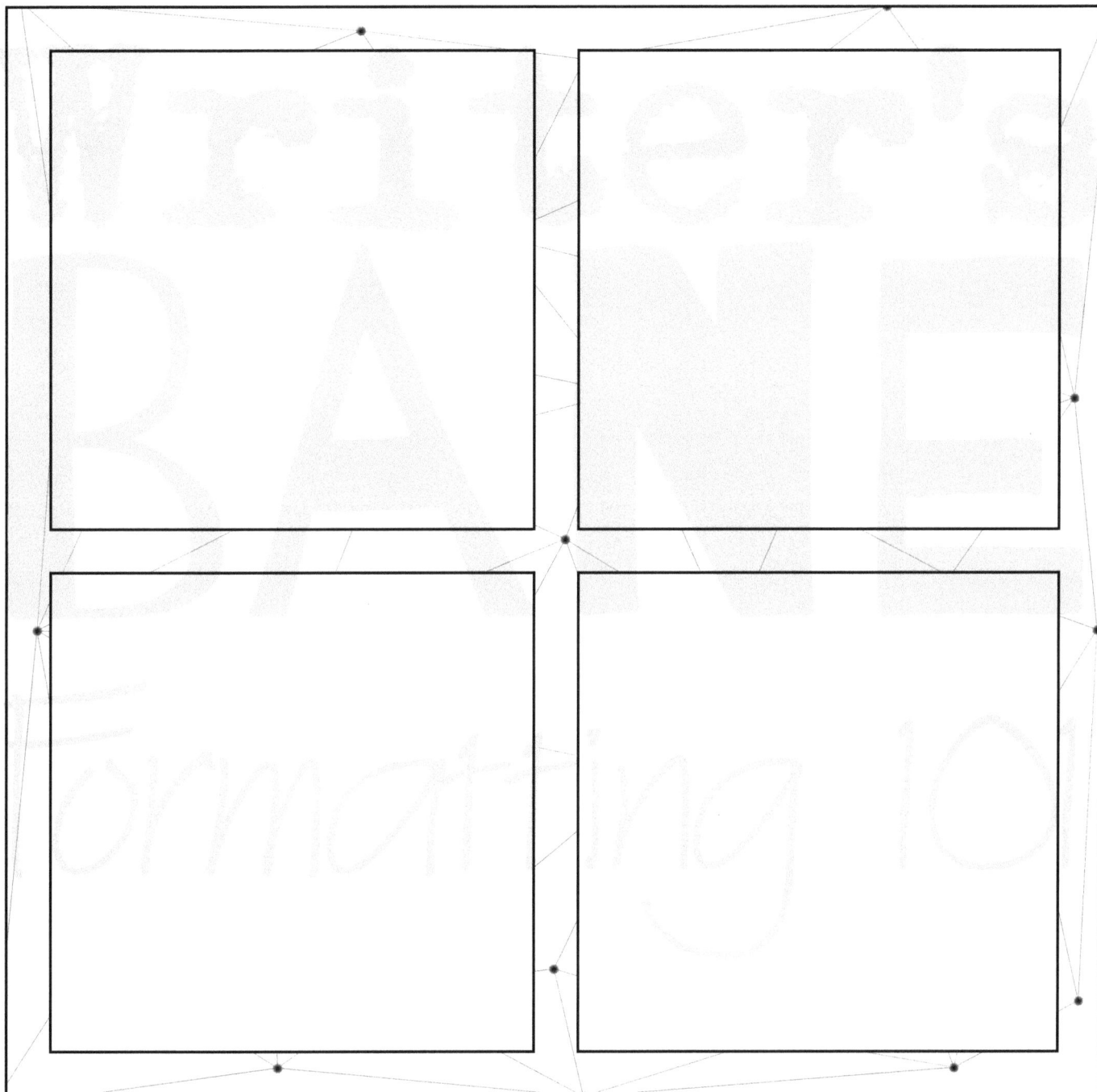

STORYBOARD - SQUARE

PROJECT TITLE: _____ GENRE: _____

COMIC STORYBOARD

COMIC STORYBOARD

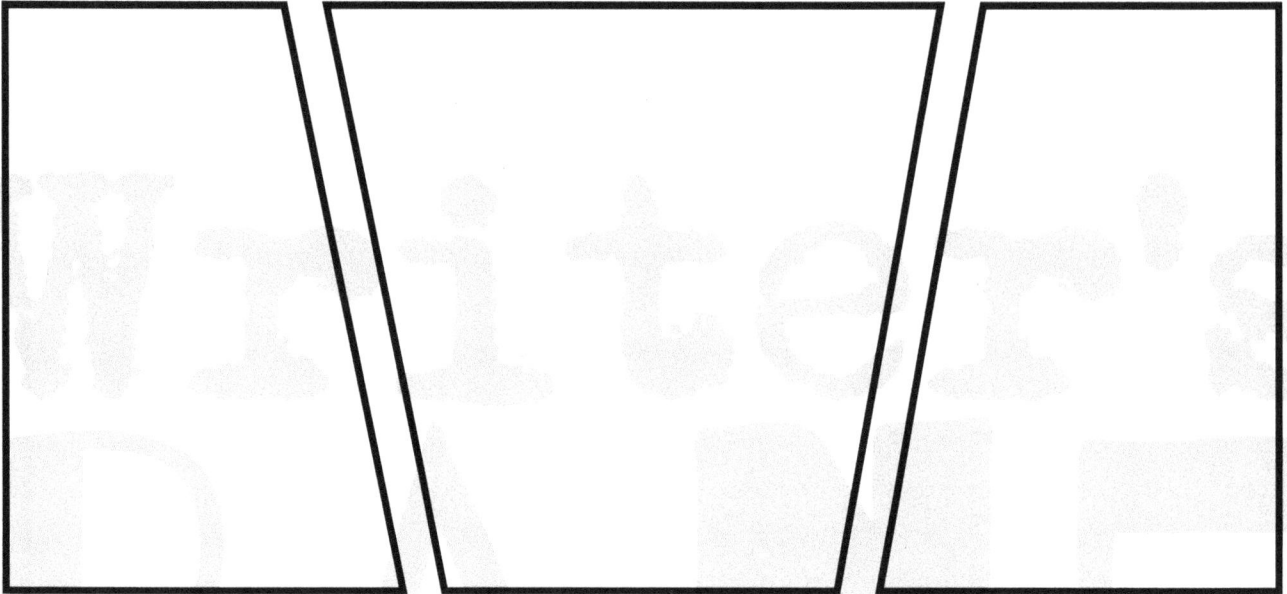

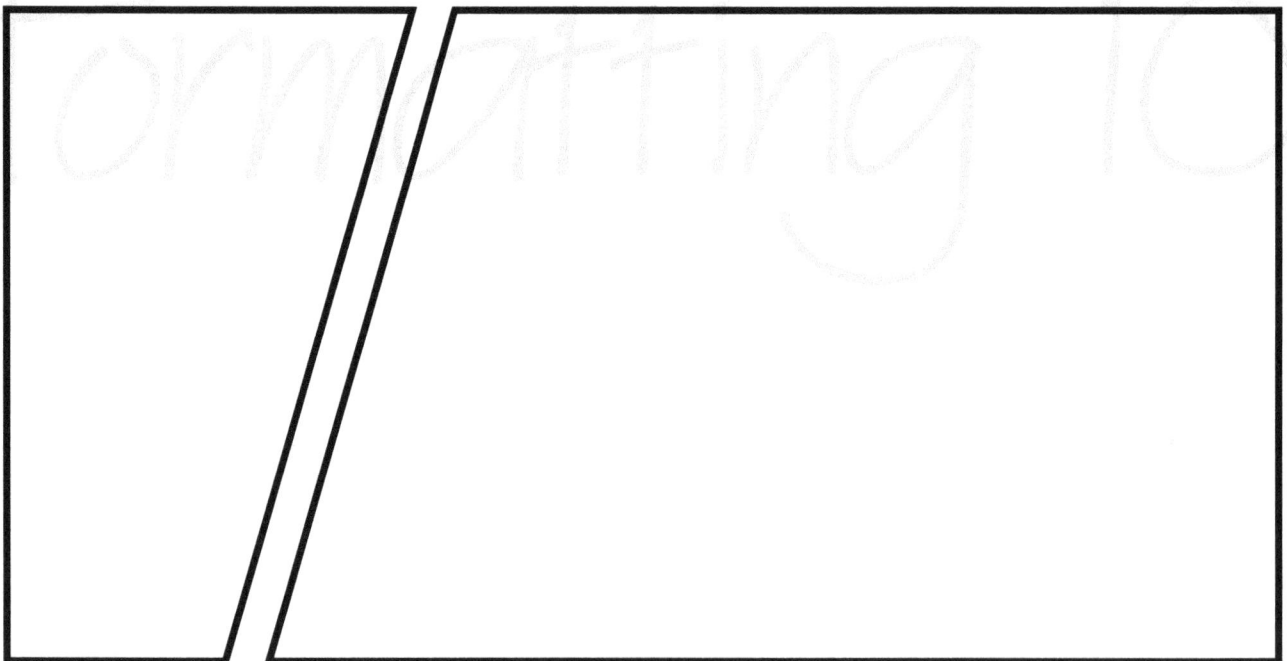

COMIC STORYBOARD

COMIC STORYBOARD

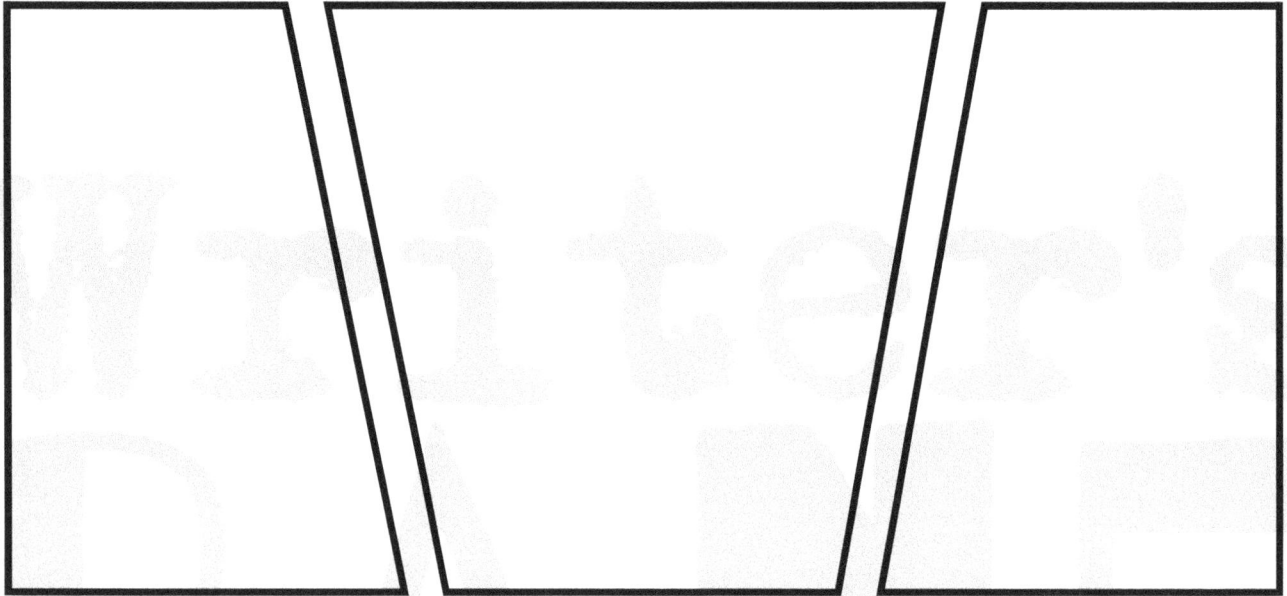

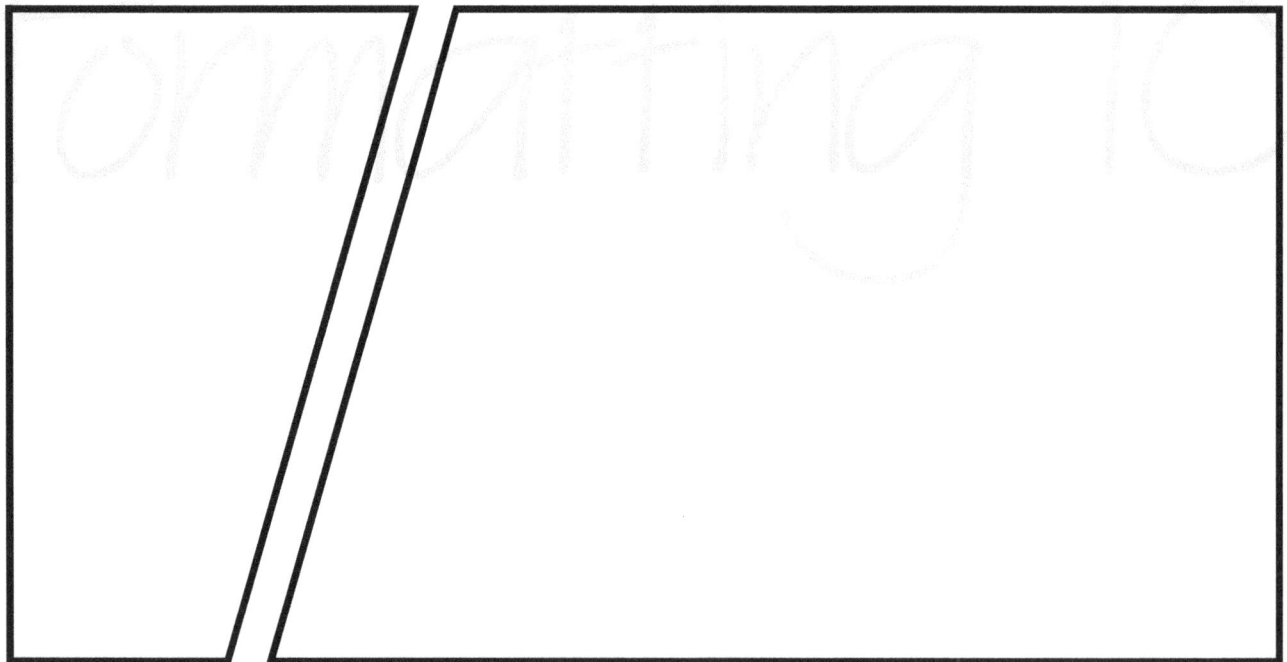

COMIC STORYBOARD

COMIC STORYBOARD

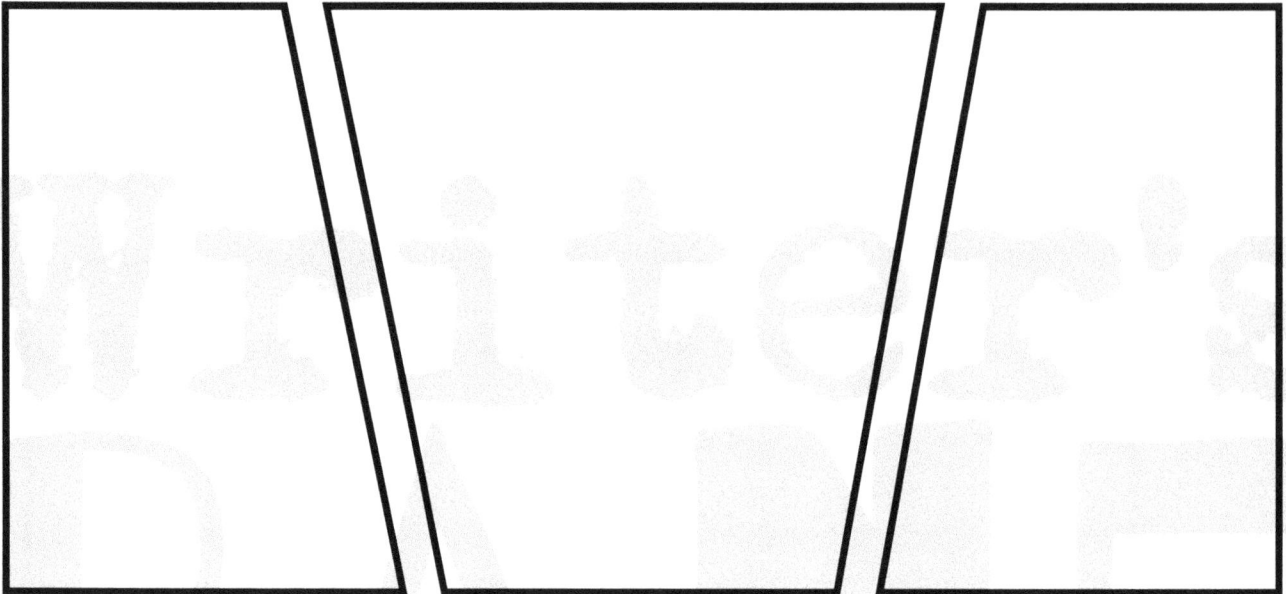

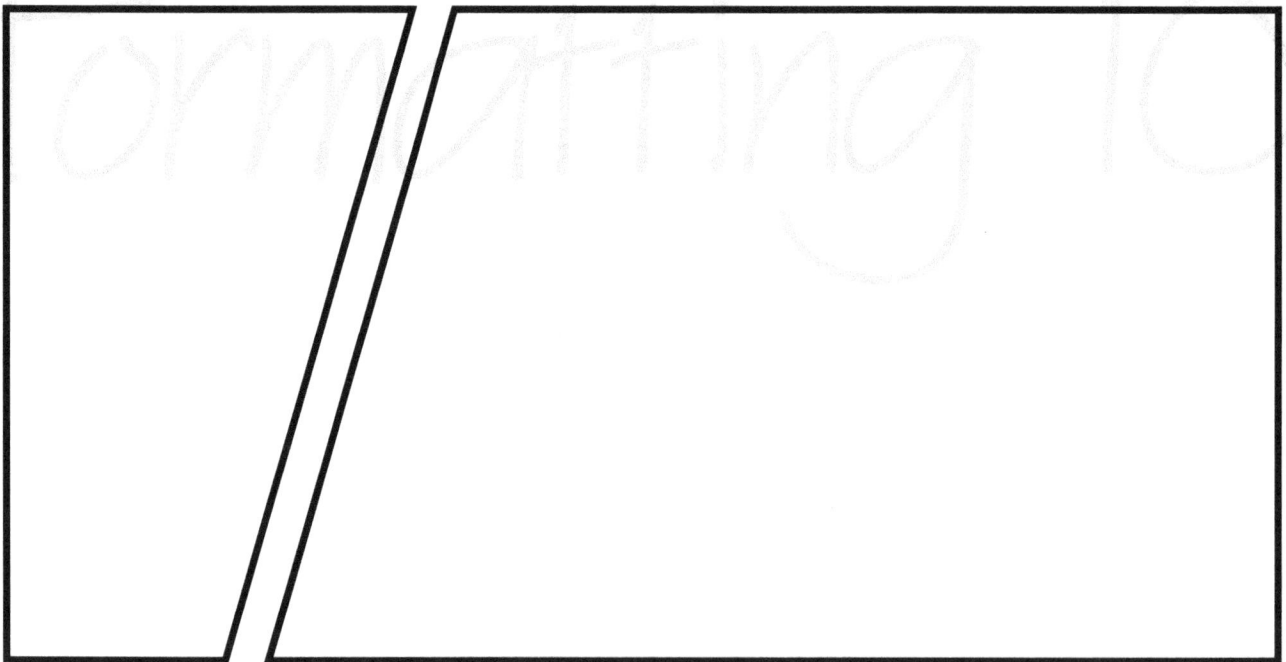

COMIC STORYBOARD

COMIC STORYBOARD

COMIC STORYBOARD

COMIC STORYBOARD

COMIC STORYBOARD

PROJECT TITLE: _____   GENRE: _____

COMIC STORYBOARD

PROJECT TITLE: _____ GENRE: _____

COMIC STORYBOARD

COMIC STORYBOARD

COMIC STORYBOARD

COMIC STORYBOARD

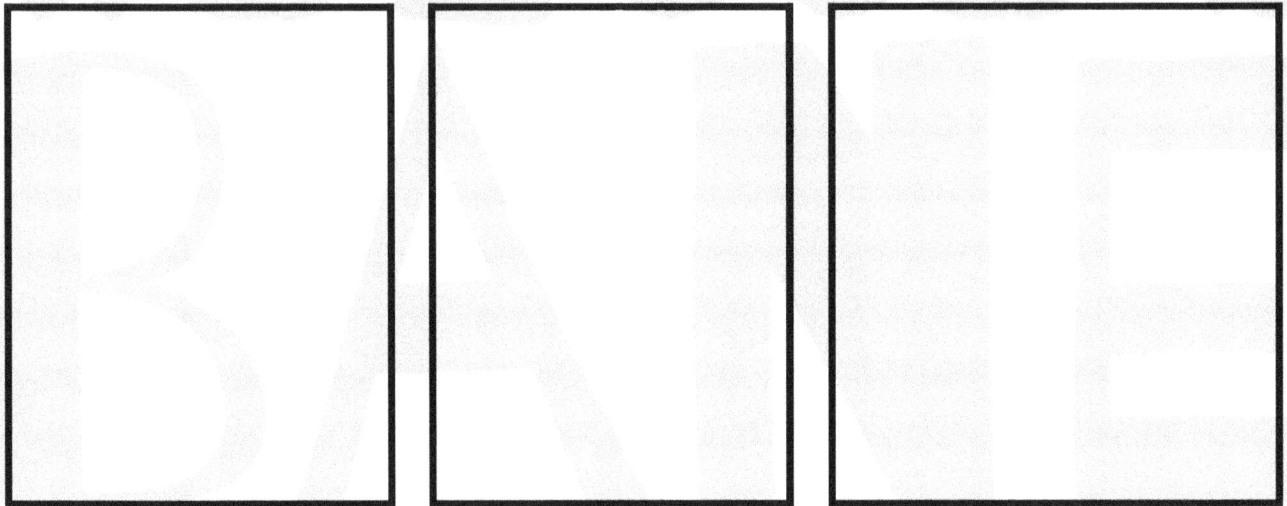

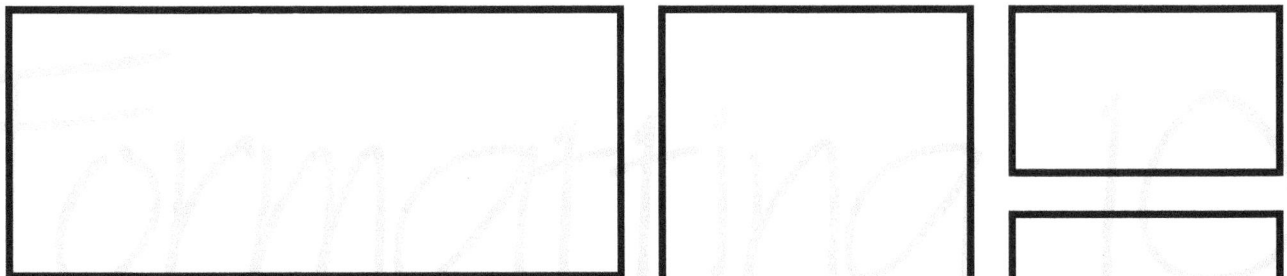

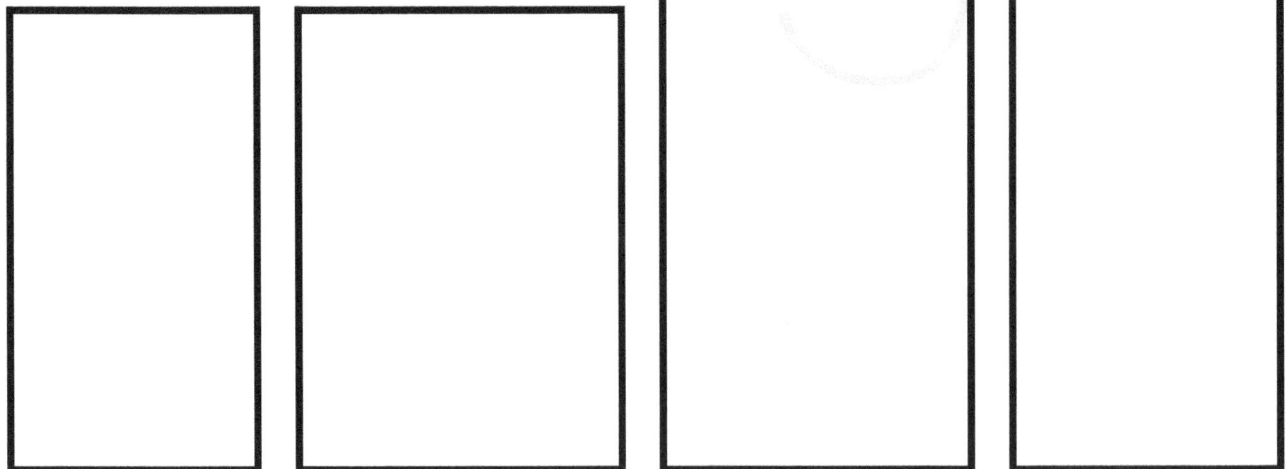

PROJECT TITLE: _____ GENRE: _____

COMIC STORYBOARD

PROJECT TITLE: _____   GENRE: _____

COMIC STORYBOARD

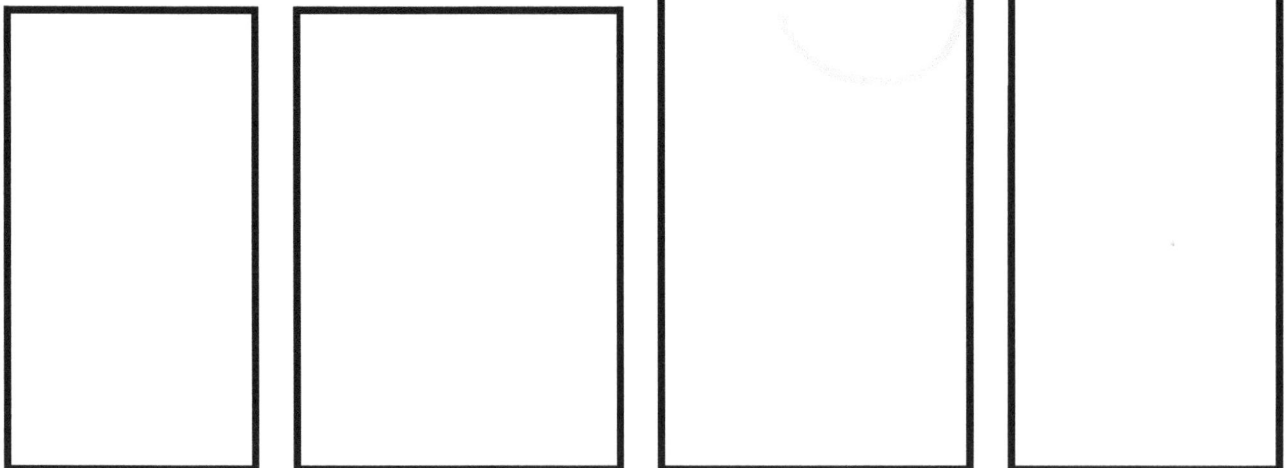

BOOK TITLE: _____

SUBTITLE: _____

TYPESET CHECKLIST

☐ Manuscript text in a DOC, DOCX, RTF file

☐ All the images listed in Manuscript present:

☐ CMYK mode

☐ Between 300-600 DPI.

☐ Trim Size _____ width x _____ height

☐ Author Pen Name - FIRST_____LAST_____

☐ Dedication: Yes or No

☐ Author Bio: Yes or No

☐ Copyright

☐ Publisher information

☐ Additional mention such as artist, design, or typesetter? _____

☐ Scriptures cited from…. Any public domain original publication mentions? _____

☐ Permission granted from… Any materials that have permissions needing to be listed here?

☐ ISBNs for Paperback: _____ Hardcover_____

☐ Audiobook_____ eBook_____

☐ LCCN pending or listed?_____

☐ Front Matter (Acknowledgements, Foreword, Preface, etc.)

☐ Do they want a Table of Contents: Yes or No

☐ Do they have tables to import: Yes or No

☐ Do they want pull quotes: Yes or No

BOOK TITLE: _____

SUBTITLE: _____

TYPESET CHECKLIST

☐ Manuscript text in a DOC, DOCX, RTF file

☐ All the images listed in Manuscript present:

☐ CMYK mode

☐ Between 300-600 DPI.

☐ Trim Size _____ width x _____ height

☐ Author Pen Name - FIRST_____LAST_____

☐ Dedication: Yes or No

☐ Author Bio: Yes or No

☐ Copyright

☐ Publisher information

☐ Additional mention such as artist, design, or typesetter? _____

☐ Scriptures cited from…. Any public domain original publication mentions? _____

☐ Permission granted from… Any materials that have permissions needing to be listed here?

☐ ISBNs for Paperback: _____ Hardcover_____

☐ Audiobook_____ eBook_____

☐ LCCN pending or listed?_____

☐ Front Matter (Acknowledgements, Foreword, Preface, etc.)

☐ Do they want a Table of Contents: Yes or No

☐ Do they have tables to import: Yes or No

☐ Do they want pull quotes: Yes or No

BOOK TITLE: _____

SUBTITLE: _____

TYPESET CHECKLIST

☐ Manuscript text in a DOC, DOCX, RTF file

☐ All the images listed in Manuscript present:

☐ CMYK mode

☐ Between 300-600 DPI.

☐ Trim Size _____ width x _____ height

☐ Author Pen Name - FIRST_____LAST_____

☐ Dedication: Yes or No

☐ Author Bio: Yes or No

☐ Copyright

☐ Publisher information

☐ Additional mention such as artist, design, or typesetter? _____

☐ Scriptures cited from…. Any public domain original publication mentions? _____

☐ Permission granted from… Any materials that have permissions needing to be listed here?

☐ ISBNs for Paperback: _____ Hardcover_____

☐ Audiobook_____ eBook_____

☐ LCCN pending or listed?_____

☐ Front Matter (Acknowledgements, Foreword, Preface, etc.)

☐ Do they want a Table of Contents: Yes or No

☐ Do they have tables to import: Yes or No

☐ Do they want pull quotes: Yes or No

BOOK TITLE: _____

SUBTITLE: _____

TYPESET CHECKLIST

☐ Manuscript text in a DOC, DOCX, RTF file

☐ All the images listed in Manuscript present:

☐ CMYK mode

☐ Between 300-600 DPI.

☐ Trim Size _____ width x _____ height

☐ Author Pen Name - FIRST_____LAST_____

☐ Dedication: Yes or No

☐ Author Bio: Yes or No

☐ Copyright

☐ Publisher information

☐ Additional mention such as artist, design, or typesetter? _____

☐ Scriptures cited from…. Any public domain original publication mentions? _____

☐ Permission granted from… Any materials that have permissions needing to be listed here?

☐ ISBNs for Paperback: _____ Hardcover_____

☐ Audiobook_____ eBook_____

☐ LCCN pending or listed?_____

☐ Front Matter (Acknowledgements, Foreword, Preface, etc.)

☐ Do they want a Table of Contents: Yes or No

☐ Do they have tables to import: Yes or No

☐ Do they want pull quotes: Yes or No

BOOK TITLE: _____

SUBTITLE: _____

TYPESET CHECKLIST

- [ ] Manuscript text in a DOC, DOCX, RTF file

- [ ] All the images listed in Manuscript present:

- [ ] CMYK mode

- [ ] Between 300-600 DPI.

- [ ] Trim Size _____ width x _____ height

- [ ] Author Pen Name - FIRST_____LAST_____

- [ ] Dedication: Yes or No

- [ ] Author Bio: Yes or No

- [ ] Copyright

- [ ] Publisher information

- [ ] Additional mention such as artist, design, or typesetter? _____

- [ ] Scriptures cited from.... Any public domain original publication mentions? _____

- [ ] Permission granted from... Any materials that have permissions needing to be listed here?

- [ ] ISBNs for Paperback: _____ Hardcover_____

- [ ] Audiobook_____ eBook_____

- [ ] LCCN pending or listed?_____

- [ ] Front Matter (Acknowledgements, Foreword, Preface, etc.)

- [ ] Do they want a Table of Contents: Yes or No

- [ ] Do they have tables to import: Yes or No

- [ ] Do they want pull quotes: Yes or No

BOOK TITLE: _____

SUBTITLE: _____

TYPESET CHECKLIST

☐ Manuscript text in a DOC, DOCX, RTF file

☐ All the images listed in Manuscript present:

☐ CMYK mode

☐ Between 300-600 DPI.

☐ Trim Size _____ width x _____ height

☐ Author Pen Name - FIRST_____ LAST_____

☐ Dedication: Yes or No

☐ Author Bio: Yes or No

☐ Copyright

☐ Publisher information

☐ Additional mention such as artist, design, or typesetter? _____

☐ Scriptures cited from.... Any public domain original publication mentions? _____

☐ Permission granted from... Any materials that have permissions needing to be listed here?

☐ ISBNs for Paperback: _____ Hardcover_____

☐ Audiobook_____ eBook_____

☐ LCCN pending or listed?_____

☐ Front Matter (Acknowledgements, Foreword, Preface, etc.)

☐ Do they want a Table of Contents: Yes or No

☐ Do they have tables to import: Yes or No

☐ Do they want pull quotes: Yes or No

BOOK TITLE: _____

SUBTITLE: _____

WARM-UP CHECKLIST

☐ Trim size set to the page or book size

☐ Add Bleed Settings for 0.125 inches

☐ Set your margins to 0.5 inch from trim edge

☐ Top margin for header set for 0.75 inch

☐ Bottom margin for footer set for 0.75 inch

☐ Inner margin or mirrored margins set to 0.675 omch or higher for spine/glue/page count

☐ Chapter font:_____

☐ Headline font:_____

☐ Header/Footer font:_____

☐ Body Text font:_____

☐ Pull Quote font:_____

☐ Body Text Base Font Size: _____ Line Spacing: _____

☐ Chapter Art prepped and ready to go

☐ Images saved in teh right format and size in advance

☐ Manuscript prepped and image placement clearly marked or Storyboard ready

☐ Glyph and Ornaments picked out. Font: _____

☐ Printer settings and requirements handy for saving and meeting their needs

☐ Templates or Master pages set up for key pages and special pages

☐ Paragraph Styles setup in advance or styles redesigned to match selection

☐ Are you ready?

BOOK TITLE: _____

SUBTITLE: _____

WARM-UP CHECKLIST

☐ Trim size set to the page or book size

☐ Add Bleed Settings for 0.125 inches

☐ Set your margins to 0.5 inch from trim edge

☐ Top margin for header set for 0.75 inch

☐ Bottom margin for footer set for 0.75 inch

☐ Inner margin or mirrored margins set to 0.675 omch or higher for spine/glue/page count

☐ Chapter font:_____

☐ Headline font:_____

☐ Header/Footer font:_____

☐ Body Text font:_____

☐ Pull Quote font:_____

☐ Body Text Base Font Size: _____ Line Spacing: _____

☐ Chapter Art prepped and ready to go

☐ Images saved in teh right format and size in advance

☐ Manuscript prepped and image placement clearly marked or Storyboard ready

☐ Glyph and Ornaments picked out. Font: _____

☐ Printer settings and requirements handy for saving and meeting their needs

☐ Templates or Master pages set up for key pages and special pages

☐ Paragraph Styles setup in advance or styles redesigned to match selection

☐ Are you ready?

BOOK TITLE: _____

SUBTITLE: _____

WARM-UP CHECKLIST

☐ Trim size set to the page or book size

☐ Add Bleed Settings for 0.125 inches

☐ Set your margins to 0.5 inch from trim edge

☐ Top margin for header set for 0.75 inch

☐ Bottom margin for footer set for 0.75 inch

☐ Inner margin or mirrored margins set to 0.675 omch or higher for spine/glue/page count

☐ Chapter font:_____

☐ Headline font:_____

☐ Header/Footer font:_____

☐ Body Text font:_____

☐ Pull Quote font:_____

☐ Body Text Base Font Size: _____ Line Spacing: _____

☐ Chapter Art prepped and ready to go

☐ Images saved in teh right format and size in advance

☐ Manuscript prepped and image placement clearly marked or Storyboard ready

☐ Glyph and Ornaments picked out. Font: _____

☐ Printer settings and requirements handy for saving and meeting their needs

☐ Templates or Master pages set up for key pages and special pages

☐ Paragraph Styles setup in advance or styles redesigned to match selection

☐ Are you ready?

BOOK TITLE: _____

SUBTITLE: _____

WARM-UP CHECKLIST

☐ Trim size set to the page or book size

☐ Add Bleed Settings for 0.125 inches

☐ Set your margins to 0.5 inch from trim edge

☐ Top margin for header set for 0.75 inch

☐ Bottom margin for footer set for 0.75 inch

☐ Inner margin or mirrored margins set to 0.675 omch or higher for spine/glue/page count

☐ Chapter font:_____

☐ Headline font:_____

☐ Header/Footer font:_____

☐ Body Text font:_____

☐ Pull Quote font:_____

☐ Body Text Base Font Size: _____ Line Spacing: _____

☐ Chapter Art prepped and ready to go

☐ Images saved in teh right format and size in advance

☐ Manuscript prepped and image placement clearly marked or Storyboard ready

☐ Glyph and Ornaments picked out. Font: _____

☐ Printer settings and requirements handy for saving and meeting their needs

☐ Templates or Master pages set up for key pages and special pages

☐ Paragraph Styles setup in advance or styles redesigned to match selection

☐ Are you ready?

BOOK TITLE: _____

SUBTITLE: _____

WARM-UP CHECKLIST

☐ Trim size set to the page or book size

☐ Add Bleed Settings for 0.125 inches

☐ Set your margins to 0.5 inch from trim edge

☐ Top margin for header set for 0.75 inch

☐ Bottom margin for footer set for 0.75 inch

☐ Inner margin or mirrored margins set to 0.675 omch or higher for spine/glue/page count

☐ Chapter font:_____

☐ Headline font:_____

☐ Header/Footer font:_____

☐ Body Text font:_____

☐ Pull Quote font:_____

☐ Body Text Base Font Size: _____ Line Spacing: _____

☐ Chapter Art prepped and ready to go

☐ Images saved in teh right format and size in advance

☐ Manuscript prepped and image placement clearly marked or Storyboard ready

☐ Glyph and Ornaments picked out. Font: _____

☐ Printer settings and requirements handy for saving and meeting their needs

☐ Templates or Master pages set up for key pages and special pages

☐ Paragraph Styles setup in advance or styles redesigned to match selection

☐ Are you ready?

BOOK TITLE: _____

SUBTITLE: _____

WARM-UP CHECKLIST

☐ Trim size set to the page or book size

☐ Add Bleed Settings for 0.125 inches

☐ Set your margins to 0.5 inch from trim edge

☐ Top margin for header set for 0.75 inch

☐ Bottom margin for footer set for 0.75 inch

☐ Inner margin or mirrored margins set to 0.675 omch or higher for spine/glue/page count

☐ Chapter font:_____

☐ Headline font:_____

☐ Header/Footer font:_____

☐ Body Text font:_____

☐ Pull Quote font:_____

☐ Body Text Base Font Size: _____ Line Spacing: _____

☐ Chapter Art prepped and ready to go

☐ Images saved in teh right format and size in advance

☐ Manuscript prepped and image placement clearly marked or Storyboard ready

☐ Glyph and Ornaments picked out. Font: _____

☐ Printer settings and requirements handy for saving and meeting their needs

☐ Templates or Master pages set up for key pages and special pages

☐ Paragraph Styles setup in advance or styles redesigned to match selection

☐ Are you ready?

BOOK TITLE: _____

SUBTITLE: _____

SAVING CHECKLIST

- ☐ A copy of the Manuscript or text file in a DOC, DOCX, RTF file that you used

- ☐ All the images in a LINKS or IMAGES folder

- ☐ Folder named after book to house all other files and folders

- ☐ Work files in folder (Recommend having a main one and back-up, i.e. *.indd and *idml)

- ☐ PDF version (2001-xa format for print-ready or print quality)

- ☐ EPUB (Reflowable) - optional

- ☐ Folder for fonts called FONT with copies of the files for future (they can go obsolete later)

- ☐ Did you save in the correct color profile (CMYK, RGB, 240% CMYK, etc)?

- ☐ Did you run ADA Compliance check in Adobe for ADA PDF needs? (optional)

- ☐ Do you need to convert EPUB to MOBI? (Consider using Calibre or similar converters)

- ☐ Has someone reviewed the file for issues besides you?

- ☐ Are the Header and Footers showing the correct text?

- ☐ Is your Table of Contents correct and numbered or not missing a chapter?

- ☐ Do your images bleed to the BLEED edge pass the TRIM edge?

- ☐ Double check that all your text is 0.5" from TRIM edge including Header and Footer

- ☐ Have you printed test pages on a local computer?

- ☐ Does your file meet the needs of your printer (Print-on-Demand AND Offset printers)

- ☐ Viewing for Web and Emails PDF - Did you save a "Reduced Size" PDF version?

- ☐ Has your customer signed off and reviewd the document before uploading to vendors?

BOOK TITLE: _____

SUBTITLE: _____

SAVING CHECKLIST

☐ A copy of the Manuscript or text file in a DOC, DOCX, RTF file that you used

☐ All the images in a LINKS or IMAGES folder

☐ Folder named after book to house all other files and folders

☐ Work files in folder (Recommend having a main one and back-up, i.e. *.indd and *idml)

☐ PDF version (2001-xa format for print-ready or print quality)

☐ EPUB (Reflowable) - optional

☐ Folder for fonts called FONT with copies of the files for future (they can go obsolete later)

☐ Did you save in the correct color profile (CMYK, RGB, 240% CMYK, etc)?

☐ Did you run ADA Compliance check in Adobe for ADA PDF needs? (optional)

☐ Do you need to convert EPUB to MOBI? (Consider using Calibre or similar converters)

☐ Has someone reviewed the file for issues besides you?

☐ Are the Header and Footers showing the correct text?

☐ Is your Table of Contents correct and numbered or not missing a chapter?

☐ Do your images bleed to the BLEED edge pass the TRIM edge?

☐ Double check that all your text is 0.5" from TRIM edge including Header and Footer

☐ Have you printed test pages on a local computer?

☐ Does your file meet the needs of your printer (Print-on-Demand AND Offset printers)

☐ Viewing for Web and Emails PDF - Did you save a "Reduced Size" PDF version?

☐ Has your customer signed off and reviewd the document before uploading to vendors?

BOOK TITLE: _____

SUBTITLE: _____

SAVING CHECKLIST

- [ ] A copy of the Manuscript or text file in a DOC, DOCX, RTF file that you used

- [ ] All the images in a LINKS or IMAGES folder

- [ ] Folder named after book to house all other files and folders

- [ ] Work files in folder (Recommend having a main one and back-up, i.e. *.indd and *idml)

- [ ] PDF version (2001-xa format for print-ready or print quality)

- [ ] EPUB (Reflowable) - optional

- [ ] Folder for fonts called FONT with copies of the files for future (they can go obsolete later)

- [ ] Did you save in the correct color profile (CMYK, RGB, 240% CMYK, etc)?

- [ ] Did you run ADA Compliance check in Adobe for ADA PDF needs? (optional)

- [ ] Do you need to convert EPUB to MOBI? (Consider using Calibre or similar converters)

- [ ] Has someone reviewed the file for issues besides you?

- [ ] Are the Header and Footers showing the correct text?

- [ ] Is your Table of Contents correct and numbered or not missing a chapter?

- [ ] Do your images bleed to the BLEED edge pass the TRIM edge?

- [ ] Double check that all your text is 0.5" from TRIM edge including Header and Footer

- [ ] Have you printed test pages on a local computer?

- [ ] Does your file meet the needs of your printer (Print-on-Demand AND Offset printers)

- [ ] Viewing for Web and Emails PDF - Did you save a "Reduced Size" PDF version?

- [ ] Has your customer signed off and reviewd the document before uploading to vendors?

BOOK TITLE: _____

SUBTITLE: _____

SAVING CHECKLIST

☐ A copy of the Manuscript or text file in a DOC, DOCX, RTF file that you used

☐ All the images in a LINKS or IMAGES folder

☐ Folder named after book to house all other files and folders

☐ Work files in folder (Recommend having a main one and back-up, i.e. *.indd and *idml)

☐ PDF version (2001-xa format for print-ready or print quality)

☐ EPUB (Reflowable) - optional

☐ Folder for fonts called FONT with copies of the files for future (they can go obsolete later)

☐ Did you save in the correct color profile (CMYK, RGB, 240% CMYK, etc)?

☐ Did you run ADA Compliance check in Adobe for ADA PDF needs? (optional)

☐ Do you need to convert EPUB to MOBI? (Consider using Calibre or similar converters)

☐ Has someone reviewed the file for issues besides you?

☐ Are the Header and Footers showing the correct text?

☐ Is your Table of Contents correct and numbered or not missing a chapter?

☐ Do your images bleed to the BLEED edge pass the TRIM edge?

☐ Double check that all your text is 0.5" from TRIM edge including Header and Footer

☐ Have you printed test pages on a local computer?

☐ Does your file meet the needs of your printer (Print-on-Demand AND Offset printers)

☐ Viewing for Web and Emails PDF - Did you save a "Reduced Size" PDF version?

☐ Has your customer signed off and reviewd the document before uploading to vendors?

BOOK TITLE: _____

SUBTITLE: _____

SAVING CHECKLIST

☐ A copy of the Manuscript or text file in a DOC, DOCX, RTF file that you used

☐ All the images in a LINKS or IMAGES folder

☐ Folder named after book to house all other files and folders

☐ Work files in folder (Recommend having a main one and back-up, i.e. *.indd and *idml)

☐ PDF version (2001-xa format for print-ready or print quality)

☐ EPUB (Reflowable) - optional

☐ Folder for fonts called FONT with copies of the files for future (they can go obsolete later)

☐ Did you save in the correct color profile (CMYK, RGB, 240% CMYK, etc)?

☐ Did you run ADA Compliance check in Adobe for ADA PDF needs? (optional)

☐ Do you need to convert EPUB to MOBI? (Consider using Calibre or similar converters)

☐ Has someone reviewed the file for issues besides you?

☐ Are the Header and Footers showing the correct text?

☐ Is your Table of Contents correct and numbered or not missing a chapter?

☐ Do your images bleed to the BLEED edge pass the TRIM edge?

☐ Double check that all your text is 0.5" from TRIM edge including Header and Footer

☐ Have you printed test pages on a local computer?

☐ Does your file meet the needs of your printer (Print-on-Demand AND Offset printers)

☐ Viewing for Web and Emails PDF - Did you save a "Reduced Size" PDF version?

☐ Has your customer signed off and reviewd the document before uploading to vendors?

BOOK TITLE: _____

SUBTITLE: _____

SAVING CHECKLIST

☐ A copy of the Manuscript or text file in a DOC, DOCX, RTF file that you used

☐ All the images in a LINKS or IMAGES folder

☐ Folder named after book to house all other files and folders

☐ Work files in folder (Recommend having a main one and back-up, i.e. *.indd and *idml)

☐ PDF version (2001-xa format for print-ready or print quality)

☐ EPUB (Reflowable) - optional

☐ Folder for fonts called FONT with copies of the files for future (they can go obsolete later)

☐ Did you save in the correct color profile (CMYK, RGB, 240% CMYK, etc)?

☐ Did you run ADA Compliance check in Adobe for ADA PDF needs? (optional)

☐ Do you need to convert EPUB to MOBI? (Consider using Calibre or similar converters)

☐ Has someone reviewed the file for issues besides you?

☐ Are the Header and Footers showing the correct text?

☐ Is your Table of Contents correct and numbered or not missing a chapter?

☐ Do your images bleed to the BLEED edge pass the TRIM edge?

☐ Double check that all your text is 0.5" from TRIM edge including Header and Footer

☐ Have you printed test pages on a local computer?

☐ Does your file meet the needs of your printer (Print-on-Demand AND Offset printers)

☐ Viewing for Web and Emails PDF - Did you save a "Reduced Size" PDF version?

☐ Has your customer signed off and reviewd the document before uploading to vendors?

BOOK TITLE: _____

SUBTITLE: _____

PDF CHECKLIST

- ✏ [] Book Title and Pen Name match

- ✏ [] All the images listed in Manuscript present:
  - ✎ [] CMYK mode
  - ✎ [] Between 300-600 DPI
  - ✎ [] Did you delete unused and unwanted RGB swatches in the Swatch panel?
  - ✎ [] Are all objects and images linked to the appropriate file?

- ✏ [] Trim Size _____ width x _____ height
  - ✎ [] Is document Bleed settings correct based on printer need (0.125" or 0")?
  - ✎ [] Are you saving PDF with Bleed option on?

- ✏ [] Copyright
  - ✎ [] Publisher information
  - ✎ [] Additional mention such as artist, design, or typesetter
  - ✎ [] Scriptures cited from…. Any public domain original publication mentions
  - ✎ [] Permission granted from… Any materials that have permissions need to be listed here
  - ✎ [] ISBNs for Paperback, Hardcover, Audiobook, or eBook
  - ✎ [] LCCN pending or listed?

- ✏ [] Dedication? Yes or No

- ✏ [] Front Matter (Acknowledgements, Foreword, Preface, etc.)

- ✏ [] Do the pages match in the Table of Contents? Yes or No

- ✏ [] Do the tables land on the page correctly? Yes or No

- ✏ [] Do the pull quotes land on the page correctly? Yes or No

- ✏ [] Double check the Header and Footer are reading and updating correctly.

- ✏ [] Are the Chapter pages consistent?

- ✏ [] Are the Drop-caps not overlapping with other content?

- ✏ [] Last page of a section and chapter all flow to top of page?

- ✏ [] Is this Print-on-Demand? If so, did you leave a blank even page at the end?

- ✏ [] Are images and objects anchored to text on the page for EPUB export?

CHECKING THE PDF

- ✏ [] Did all the fonts embed?
- ✏ [] Did it save in PDF/X-1a:2001 format?
- ✏ [] Does the PDF size match trim plus bleed amounts?
- ✏ [] Did all the images save and appear?

- ✏ [] Do you need to use Preflight to save as Grayscale for B&W printing?
- ✏ [] No watermarks or splash sheet.
- ✏ [] Even number of pages?
- ✏ [] If Print-on-Demand, is the last page blank?

BOOK TITLE: _____

SUBTITLE: _____

PDF Checklist

- [] Book Title and Pen Name match
- [] All the images listed in Manuscript present:
    - [] CMYK mode
    - [] Between 300-600 DPI
    - [] Did you delete unused and unwanted RGB swatches in the Swatch panel?
    - [] Are all objects and images linked to the appropriate file?
- [] Trim Size _____ width x _____ height
    - [] Is document Bleed settings correct based on printer need (0.125" or 0")?
    - [] Are you saving PDF with Bleed option on?
- [] Copyright
    - [] Publisher information
    - [] Additional mention such as artist, design, or typesetter
    - [] Scriptures cited from…. Any public domain original publication mentions
    - [] Permission granted from… Any materials that have permissions need to be listed here
    - [] ISBNs for Paperback, Hardcover, Audiobook, or eBook
    - [] LCCN pending or listed?
- [] Dedication? Yes or No
- [] Front Matter (Acknowledgements, Foreword, Preface, etc.)
- [] Do the pages match in the Table of Contents? Yes or No
- [] Do the tables land on the page correctly? Yes or No
- [] Do the pull quotes land on the page correctly? Yes or No
- [] Double check the Header and Footer are reading and updating correctly.
- [] Are the Chapter pages consistent?
- [] Are the Drop-caps not overlapping with other content?
- [] Last page of a section and chapter all flow to top of page?
- [] Is this Print-on-Demand? If so, did you leave a blank even page at the end?
- [] Are images and objects anchored to text on the page for EPUB export?

Checking the PDF

- [] Did all the fonts embed?
- [] Did it save in PDF/X-1a:2001 format?
- [] Does the PDF size match trim plus bleed amounts?
- [] Did all the images save and appear?
- [] Do you need to use Preflight to save as Grayscale for B&W printing?
- [] No watermarks or splash sheet.
- [] Even number of pages?
- [] If Print-on-Demand, is the last page blank?

BOOK TITLE: _____

SUBTITLE: _____

PDF CHECKLIST

- ✏ [] Book Title and Pen Name match

- ✏ [] All the images listed in Manuscript present:
  - ✎ [] CMYK mode
  - ✎ [] Between 300-600 DPI
  - ✎ [] Did you delete unused and unwanted RGB swatches in the Swatch panel?
  - ✎ [] Are all objects and images linked to the appropriate file?

- ✏ [] Trim Size _____ width x _____ height
  - ✎ [] Is document Bleed settings correct based on printer need (0.125" or 0")?
  - ✎ [] Are you saving PDF with Bleed option on?

- ✏ [] Copyright
  - ✎ [] Publisher information
  - ✎ [] Additional mention such as artist, design, or typesetter
  - ✎ [] Scriptures cited from…. Any public domain original publication mentions
  - ✎ [] Permission granted from… Any materials that have permissions need to be listed here
  - ✎ [] ISBNs for Paperback, Hardcover, Audiobook, or eBook
  - ✎ [] LCCN pending or listed?

- ✏ [] Dedication? Yes or No

- ✏ [] Front Matter (Acknowledgements, Foreword, Preface, etc.)

- ✏ [] Do the pages match in the Table of Contents? Yes or No

- ✏ [] Do the tables land on the page correctly? Yes or No

- ✏ [] Do the pull quotes land on the page correctly? Yes or No

- ✏ [] Double check the Header and Footer are reading and updating correctly.

- ✏ [] Are the Chapter pages consistent?

- ✏ [] Are the Drop-caps not overlapping with other content?

- ✏ [] Last page of a section and chapter all flow to top of page?

- ✏ [] Is this Print-on-Demand? If so, did you leave a blank even page at the end?

- ✏ [] Are images and objects anchored to text on the page for EPUB export?

CHECKING THE PDF

- ✏ [] Did all the fonts embed?
- ✏ [] Did it save in PDF/X-1a:2001 format?
- ✏ [] Does the PDF size match trim plus bleed amounts?
- ✏ [] Did all the images save and appear?

- ✏ [] Do you need to use Preflight to save as Grayscale for B&W printing?
- ✏ [] No watermarks or splash sheet.
- ✏ [] Even number of pages?
- ✏ [] If Print-on-Demand, is the last page blank?

BOOK TITLE: _____

SUBTITLE: _____

PDF Checklist

- [] Book Title and Pen Name match

- [] All the images listed in Manuscript present:
  - [] CMYK mode
  - [] Between 300-600 DPI
  - [] Did you delete unused and unwanted RGB swatches in the Swatch panel?
  - [] Are all objects and images linked to the appropriate file?

- [] Trim Size _____ width x _____ height
  - [] Is document Bleed settings correct based on printer need (0.125" or 0")?
  - [] Are you saving PDF with Bleed option on?

- [] Copyright
  - [] Publisher information
  - [] Additional mention such as artist, design, or typesetter
  - [] Scriptures cited from.... Any public domain original publication mentions
  - [] Permission granted from... Any materials that have permissions need to be listed here
  - [] ISBNs for Paperback, Hardcover, Audiobook, or eBook
  - [] LCCN pending or listed?

- [] Dedication? Yes or No

- [] Front Matter (Acknowledgements, Foreword, Preface, etc.)

- [] Do the pages match in the Table of Contents? Yes or No

- [] Do the tables land on the page correctly? Yes or No

- [] Do the pull quotes land on the page correctly? Yes or No

- [] Double check the Header and Footer are reading and updating correctly.

- [] Are the Chapter pages consistent?

- [] Are the Drop-caps not overlapping with other content?

- [] Last page of a section and chapter all flow to top of page?

- [] Is this Print-on-Demand? If so, did you leave a blank even page at the end?

- [] Are images and objects anchored to text on the page for EPUB export?

CHECKING THE PDF

- [] Did all the fonts embed?

- [] Did it save in PDF/X-1a:2001 format?

- [] Does the PDF size match trim plus bleed amounts?

- [] Did all the images save and appear?

- [] Do you need to use Preflight to save as Grayscale for B&W printing?

- [] No watermarks or splash sheet.

- [] Even number of pages?

- [] If Print-on-Demand, is the last page blank?

BOOK TITLE: _____

SUBTITLE: _____

PDF Checklist

- ✐ [] Book Title and Pen Name match

- ✐ [] All the images listed in Manuscript present:
    - ✎ [] CMYK mode
    - ✎ [] Between 300-600 DPI
    - ✎ [] Did you delete unused and unwanted RGB swatches in the Swatch panel?
    - ✎ [] Are all objects and images linked to the appropriate file?

- ✐ [] Trim Size _____ width x _____ height
    - ✎ [] Is document Bleed settings correct based on printer need (0.125" or 0")?
    - ✎ [] Are you saving PDF with Bleed option on?

- ✐ [] Copyright
    - ✎ [] Publisher information
    - ✎ [] Additional mention such as artist, design, or typesetter
    - ✎ [] Scriptures cited from…. Any public domain original publication mentions
    - ✎ [] Permission granted from… Any materials that have permissions need to be listed here
    - ✎ [] ISBNs for Paperback, Hardcover, Audiobook, or eBook
    - ✎ [] LCCN pending or listed?

- ✐ [] Dedication? Yes or No

- ✐ [] Front Matter (Acknowledgements, Foreword, Preface, etc.)

- ✐ [] Do the pages match in the Table of Contents? Yes or No

- ✐ [] Do the tables land on the page correctly? Yes or No

- ✐ [] Do the pull quotes land on the page correctly? Yes or No

- ✐ [] Double check the Header and Footer are reading and updating correctly.

- ✐ [] Are the Chapter pages consistent?

- ✐ [] Are the Drop-caps not overlapping with other content?

- ✐ [] Last page of a section and chapter all flow to top of page?

- ✐ [] Is this Print-on-Demand? If so, did you leave a blank even page at the end?

- ✐ [] Are images and objects anchored to text on the page for EPUB export?

CHECKING THE PDF

- ✐ [] Did all the fonts embed?

- ✐ [] Did it save in PDF/X-1a:2001 format?

- ✐ [] Does the PDF size match trim plus bleed amounts?

- ✐ [] Did all the images save and appear?

- ✐ [] Do you need to use Preflight to save as Grayscale for B&W printing?

- ✐ [] No watermarks or splash sheet.

- ✐ [] Even number of pages?

- ✐ [] If Print-on-Demand, is the last page blank?

BOOK TITLE: _____

SUBTITLE: _____

PDF CHECKLIST

- [] Book Title and Pen Name match

- [] All the images listed in Manuscript present:
    - [] CMYK mode
    - [] Between 300-600 DPI
    - [] Did you delete unused and unwanted RGB swatches in the Swatch panel?
    - [] Are all objects and images linked to the appropriate file?

- [] Trim Size _____ width x _____ height
    - [] Is document Bleed settings correct based on printer need (0.125" or 0")?
    - [] Are you saving PDF with Bleed option on?

- [] Copyright
    - [] Publisher information
    - [] Additional mention such as artist, design, or typesetter
    - [] Scriptures cited from…. Any public domain original publication mentions
    - [] Permission granted from… Any materials that have permissions need to be listed here
    - [] ISBNs for Paperback, Hardcover, Audiobook, or eBook
    - [] LCCN pending or listed?

- [] Dedication? Yes or No

- [] Front Matter (Acknowledgements, Foreword, Preface, etc.)

- [] Do the pages match in the Table of Contents? Yes or No

- [] Do the tables land on the page correctly? Yes or No

- [] Do the pull quotes land on the page correctly? Yes or No

- [] Double check the Header and Footer are reading and updating correctly.

- [] Are the Chapter pages consistent?

- [] Are the Drop-caps not overlapping with other content?

- [] Last page of a section and chapter all flow to top of page?

- [] Is this Print-on-Demand? If so, did you leave a blank even page at the end?

- [] Are images and objects anchored to text on the page for EPUB export?

CHECKING THE PDF

- [] Did all the fonts embed?

- [] Did it save in PDF/X-1a:2001 format?

- [] Does the PDF size match trim plus bleed amounts?

- [] Did all the images save and appear?

- [] Do you need to use Preflight to save as Grayscale for B&W printing?

- [] No watermarks or splash sheet.

- [] Even number of pages?

- [] If Print-on-Demand, is the last page blank?

BOOK TITLE: _____

SUBTITLE: _____

EPUB CHECKLIST

- [] Book Title and Pen Name match

- [] All the images listed in Manuscript present:
  - [] CMYK mode
  - [] Between 300-600 DPI
  - [] Did you delete unused and unwanted RGB swatches in the Swatch panel?
  - [] Are all objects and images linked to the appropriate file?

- [] Trim Size _____ width x _____ height
  - [] Is document Bleed settings correct based on printer need (0.125" or 0")?
  - [] Are you saving PDF with Bleed option on?

- [] Copyright
  - [] Publisher information
  - [] Additional mention such as artist, design, or typesetter
  - [] Scriptures cited from.... Any public domain original publication mentions
  - [] Permission granted from... Any materials that have permissions need to be listed here
  - [] ISBNs for Paperback, Hardcover, Audiobook, or eBook
  - [] LCCN pending or listed?

- [] Dedication? Yes or No

- [] Front Matter (Acknowledgements, Foreword, Preface, etc.)

- [] Do the pages match in the Table of Content? Yes or No

- [] Do the tables land on the page correctly? Yes or No

- [] Do the pull quotes land on the page correctly? Yes or No

- [] Double check the Header and Footer are reading and updating correctly.

- [] Are the Chapter pages consistent?

- [] Are the Drop-caps not overlapping with other content?

- [] Last page of a section and chapter all flow to top of page?

- [] Is this Print-on-Demand? If so, did you leave a blank even page at the end?

- [] Are images and objects anchored to text on the page for EPUB export?

CHECKING THE EPUB

- [] Did all the fonts embed?

- [] Did it save in PDF/X-1a:2001 format?

- [] Does the PDF size match trim plus bleed amounts?

- [] Did all the images save and appear?

- [] Do you need to use Preflight to save as Grayscale for B&W printing?

- [] No watermarks or splash sheet.

- [] Even number of pages?

- [] If Print-on-Demand, is the last page blank?

BOOK TITLE: _____

SUBTITLE: _____

EPUB Checklist

- ✒ [] Book Title and Pen Name match

- ✒ [] All the images listed in Manuscript present:
  - ✎ [] CMYK mode
  - ✎ [] Between 300-600 DPI
  - ✎ [] Did you delete unused and unwanted RGB swatches in the Swatch panel?
  - ✎ [] Are all objects and images linked to the appropriate file?

- ✒ [] Trim Size _____ width x _____ height
  - ✎ [] Is document Bleed settings correct based on printer need (0.125" or 0")?
  - ✎ [] Are you saving PDF with Bleed option on?

- ✒ [] Copyright
  - ✎ [] Publisher information
  - ✎ [] Additional mention such as artist, design, or typesetter
  - ✎ [] Scriptures cited from.... Any public domain original publication mentions
  - ✎ [] Permission granted from... Any materials that have permissions need to be listed here
  - ✎ [] ISBNs for Paperback, Hardcover, Audiobook, or eBook
  - ✎ [] LCCN pending or listed?

- ✒ [] Dedication? Yes or No

- ✒ [] Front Matter (Acknowledgements, Foreword, Preface, etc.)

- ✒ [] Do the pages match in the Table of Content? Yes or No

- ✒ [] Do the tables land on the page correctly? Yes or No

- ✒ [] Do the pull quotes land on the page correctly? Yes or No

- ✒ [] Double check the Header and Footer are reading and updating correctly.

- ✒ [] Are the Chapter pages consistent?

- ✒ [] Are the Drop-caps not overlapping with other content?

- ✒ [] Last page of a section and chapter all flow to top of page?

- ✒ [] Is this Print-on-Demand? If so, did you leave a blank even page at the end?

- ✒ [] Are images and objects anchored to text on the page for EPUB export?

CHECKING THE EPUB

- ✒ [] Did all the fonts embed?

- ✒ [] Did it save in PDF/X-1a:2001 format?

- ✒ [] Does the PDF size match trim plus bleed amounts?

- ✒ [] Did all the images save and appear?

- ✒ [] Do you need to use Preflight to save as Grayscale for B&W printing?

- ✒ [] No watermarks or splash sheet.

- ✒ [] Even number of pages?

- ✒ [] If Print-on-Demand, is the last page blank?

BOOK TITLE: _____

SUBTITLE: _____

EPUB Checklist

- ✎ [] Book Title and Pen Name match
- ✎ [] All the images listed in Manuscript present:
  - ✎ [] CMYK mode
  - ✎ [] Between 300-600 DPI
  - ✎ [] Did you delete unused and unwanted RGB swatches in the Swatch panel?
  - ✎ [] Are all objects and images linked to the appropriate file?

- ✎ [] Trim Size _____ width x _____ height
  - ✎ [] Is document Bleed settings correct based on printer need (0.125" or 0")?
  - ✎ [] Are you saving PDF with Bleed option on?

- ✎ [] Copyright
  - ✎ [] Publisher information
  - ✎ [] Additional mention such as artist, design, or typesetter
  - ✎ [] Scriptures cited from…. Any public domain original publication mentions
  - ✎ [] Permission granted from… Any materials that have permissions need to be listed here
  - ✎ [] ISBNs for Paperback, Hardcover, Audiobook, or eBook
  - ✎ [] LCCN pending or listed?

- ✎ [] Dedication? Yes or No
- ✎ [] Front Matter (Acknowledgements, Foreword, Preface, etc.)
- ✎ [] Do the pages match in the Table of Content? Yes or No
- ✎ [] Do the tables land on the page correctly? Yes or No
- ✎ [] Do the pull quotes land on the page correctly? Yes or No
- ✎ [] Double check the Header and Footer are reading and updating correctly.
- ✎ [] Are the Chapter pages consistent?
- ✎ [] Are the Drop-caps not overlapping with other content?
- ✎ [] Last page of a section and chapter all flow to top of page?
- ✎ [] Is this Print-on-Demand? If so, did you leave a blank even page at the end?
- ✎ [] Are images and objects anchored to text on the page for EPUB export?

Checking the EPUB

- ✎ [] Did all the fonts embed?
- ✎ [] Did it save in PDF/X-1a:2001 format?
- ✎ [] Does the PDF size match trim plus bleed amounts?
- ✎ [] Did all the images save and appear?
- ✎ [] Do you need to use Preflight to save as Grayscale for B&W printing?
- ✎ [] No watermarks or splash sheet.
- ✎ [] Even number of pages?
- ✎ [] If Print-on-Demand, is the last page blank?

BOOK TITLE: _____

SUBTITLE: _____

EPUB CHECKLIST

✏ [] Book Title and Pen Name match

✏ [] All the images listed in Manuscript present:
- ✎ [] CMYK mode
- ✎ [] Between 300-600 DPI
- ✎ [] Did you delete unused and unwanted RGB swatches in the Swatch panel?
- ✎ [] Are all objects and images linked to the appropriate file?

✏ [] Trim Size _____ width x _____ height
- ✎ [] Is document Bleed settings correct based on printer need (0.125" or 0")?
- ✎ [] Are you saving PDF with Bleed option on?

✏ [] Copyright
- ✎ [] Publisher information
- ✎ [] Additional mention such as artist, design, or typesetter
- ✎ [] Scriptures cited from…. Any public domain original publication mentions
- ✎ [] Permission granted from… Any materials that have permissions need to be listed here
- ✎ [] ISBNs for Paperback, Hardcover, Audiobook, or eBook
- ✎ [] LCCN pending or listed?

✏ [] Dedication? Yes or No

✏ [] Front Matter (Acknowledgements, Foreword, Preface, etc.)

✏ [] Do the pages match in the Table of Content? Yes or No

✏ [] Do the tables land on the page correctly? Yes or No

✏ [] Do the pull quotes land on the page correctly? Yes or No

✏ [] Double check the Header and Footer are reading and updating correctly.

✏ [] Are the Chapter pages consistent?

✏ [] Are the Drop-caps not overlapping with other content?

✏ [] Last page of a section and chapter all flow to top of page?

✏ [] Is this Print-on-Demand? If so, did you leave a blank even page at the end?

✏ [] Are images and objects anchored to text on the page for EPUB export?

CHECKING THE EPUB

✏ [] Did all the fonts embed?

✏ [] Did it save in PDF/X-1a:2001 format?

✏ [] Does the PDF size match trim plus bleed amounts?

✏ [] Did all the images save and appear?

✏ [] Do you need to use Preflight to save as Grayscale for B&W printing?

✏ [] No watermarks or splash sheet.

✏ [] Even number of pages?

✏ [] If Print-on-Demand, is the last page blank?

BOOK TITLE: _____

SUBTITLE: _____

EPUB Checklist

✎ [] Book Title and Pen Name match

✎ [] All the images listed in Manuscript present:
- ✎ [] CMYK mode
- ✎ [] Between 300-600 DPI
- ✎ [] Did you delete unused and unwanted RGB swatches in the Swatch panel?
- ✎ [] Are all objects and images linked to the appropriate file?

✎ [] Trim Size _____ width x _____ height
- ✎ [] Is document Bleed settings correct based on printer need (0.125" or 0")?
- ✎ [] Are you saving PDF with Bleed option on?

✎ [] Copyright
- ✎ [] Publisher information
- ✎ [] Additional mention such as artist, design, or typesetter
- ✎ [] Scriptures cited from…. Any public domain original publication mentions
- ✎ [] Permission granted from… Any materials that have permissions need to be listed here
- ✎ [] ISBNs for Paperback, Hardcover, Audiobook, or eBook
- ✎ [] LCCN pending or listed?

✎ [] Dedication? Yes or No

✎ [] Front Matter (Acknowledgements, Foreword, Preface, etc.)

✎ [] Do the pages match in the Table of Content? Yes or No

✎ [] Do the tables land on the page correctly? Yes or No

✎ [] Do the pull quotes land on the page correctly? Yes or No

✎ [] Double check the Header and Footer are reading and updating correctly.

✎ [] Are the Chapter pages consistent?

✎ [] Are the Drop-caps not overlapping with other content?

✎ [] Last page of a section and chapter all flow to top of page?

✎ [] Is this Print-on-Demand? If so, did you leave a blank even page at the end?

✎ [] Are images and objects anchored to text on the page for EPUB export?

Checking the EPUB

✎ [] Did all the fonts embed?

✎ [] Did it save in PDF/X-1a:2001 format?

✎ [] Does the PDF size match trim plus bleed amounts?

✎ [] Did all the images save and appear?

✎ [] Do you need to use Preflight to save as Grayscale for B&W printing?

✎ [] No watermarks or splash sheet.

✎ [] Even number of pages?

✎ [] If Print-on-Demand, is the last page blank?

BOOK TITLE: _____

SUBTITLE: _____

EPUB CHECKLIST

✏ [] Book Title and Pen Name match

✏ [] All the images listed in Manuscript present:
- ✎ [] CMYK mode
- ✎ [] Between 300-600 DPI
- ✎ [] Did you delete unused and unwanted RGB swatches in the Swatch panel?
- ✎ [] Are all objects and images linked to the appropriate file?

✏ [] Trim Size _____ width x _____ height
- ✎ [] Is document Bleed settings correct based on printer need (0.125" or 0")?
- ✎ [] Are you saving PDF with Bleed option on?

✏ [] Copyright
- ✎ [] Publisher information
- ✎ [] Additional mention such as artist, design, or typesetter
- ✎ [] Scriptures cited from.... Any public domain original publication mentions
- ✎ [] Permission granted from... Any materials that have permissions need to be listed here
- ✎ [] ISBNs for Paperback, Hardcover, Audiobook, or eBook
- ✎ [] LCCN pending or listed?

✏ [] Dedication? Yes or No

✏ [] Front Matter (Acknowledgements, Foreword, Preface, etc.)

✏ [] Do the pages match in the Table of Content? Yes or No

✏ [] Do the tables land on the page correctly? Yes or No

✏ [] Do the pull quotes land on the page correctly? Yes or No

✏ [] Double check the Header and Footer are reading and updating correctly.

✏ [] Are the Chapter pages consistent?

✏ [] Are the Drop-caps not overlapping with other content?

✏ [] Last page of a section and chapter all flow to top of page?

✏ [] Is this Print-on-Demand? If so, did you leave a blank even page at the end?

✏ [] Are images and objects anchored to text on the page for EPUB export?

CHECKING THE EPUB

✏ [] Did all the fonts embed?

✏ [] Did it save in PDF/X-1a:2001 format?

✏ [] Does the PDF size match trim plus bleed amounts?

✏ [] Did all the images save and appear?

✏ [] Do you need to use Preflight to save as Grayscale for B&W printing?

✏ [] No watermarks or splash sheet.

✏ [] Even number of pages?

✏ [] If Print-on-Demand, is the last page blank?

www.ingramcontent.com/pod-product-compliance
Lightning Source LLC
Chambersburg PA
CBHW040259100426
42811CB00011B/1315